The Kurds and the Politics of Turkey

The Kurds and the Politics of Turkey

Agency, Territory and Religion

Deniz Çifçi

I.B. TAURIS
LONDON • NEW YORK • OXFORD • NEW DELHI • SYDNEY

I.B. TAURIS
Bloomsbury Publishing Plc
50 Bedford Square, London, WC1B 3DP, UK
1385 Broadway, New York, NY 10018, USA
29 Earlsfort Terrace, Dublin 2, Ireland

BLOOMSBURY, I.B. TAURIS and the I.B. Tauris logo are
trademarks of Bloomsbury Publishing Plc

First published in Great Britain 2019
Paperback edition first published 2021

Copyright © Deniz Çifçi, 2019

Deniz Çifçi has asserted his right under the Copyright,
Designs and Patents Act, 1988, to be identified as Author of this work.

For legal purposes the Acknowledgements on p. xii constitute
an extension of this copyright page.

Cover design by Terry Woodley
Cover image: Syrian Kurds in demonstration against the military operation
by the Turkish army against the Kurdish YPG forces in Syria's Afrin, February 2, 2018.
(© SAFIN HAMED/AFP/Getty Images)

All rights reserved. No part of this publication may be reproduced or
transmitted in any form or by any means, electronic or mechanical,
including photocopying, recording, or any information storage or retrieval
system, without prior permission in writing from the publishers.

Bloomsbury Publishing Plc does not have any control over, or responsibility for,
any third-party websites referred to or in this book. All internet addresses given
in this book were correct at the time of going to press. The author and publisher
regret any inconvenience caused if addresses have changed or sites have
ceased to exist, but can accept no responsibility for any such changes.

A catalogue record for this book is available from the British Library.

A catalog record for this book is available from the Library of Congress.

ISBN: HB: 978-1-7845-3995-5
PB: 978-0-7556-4278-6
ePDF: 978-1-7883-1638-5
eBook: 978-1-7883-1637-8

Typeset by Integra Software Services Pvt. Ltd.

To find out more about our authors and books visit
www.bloomsbury.com and sign up for our newsletters.

To the Yezidi Kurds ....

Contents

List of Illustrations	viii
List of Abbreviations	ix
Acknowledgements	xii
Preface	xiii
Introduction	1
1 Defining the Political Models the Kurds Demand	9
2 Kurdish Identity	37
3 History of Variation in the Kurds' Political Demands: 1920–80	57
4 Demand for Democratic Autonomy	71
5 Demand for the Cultural Rights Only Model	111
6 Demand for Federalism	139
7 Demand for a Nation State	175
8 Theoretical Analysis of the Research Findings	191
Conclusion	213
Appendix 1	226
Notes	234
Bibliography	251
Index	293

Illustrations

Figures

I.1 The political models demanded by the Kurds — 2
4.1 Immigration of Kurds: Share of the immigrated population in the population of the first ten western provinces — 94
5.1 The geographical distribution of Alevis across Turkey — 122
6.1 Socio-Economic Development Index (2011) — 165

Tables

I.1 A classification of the Kurds' political demands and the groups' (along with some affiliated and independent organizations') struggle for these models — 4
2.1 List of interviewees — 226

Abbreviations

AKP	Justice and Development Party
Azadî Initiative	The Kurdistan Islamic Initiative for Rights, Justice and Freedom
BDP	Peace and Democracy Party
CHP	Republican People's Party
CUP	Committee of Union and Progress
DDKD	Revolutionary Democratic Culture Association
DDKO	Revolutionist Eastern Cultural Societies
DBP	Democratic Regions Party
DEP	Democracy Party
DEHAP	Democratic People's Party
DHF	Democratic Rights Federations
DTK	Democratic Society Congress
DTP	Democratic Society Party
DOKH	Democratic and Free Women Movement
DP	Democrat Party
EMEP	Labour Party
FP	Virtue Party
HADEP	People's Democracy Party
Hak-Par	Rights and Freedoms Party
HDP	People's Democratic Party
HEP	People's Labor Party

Hüda-Par	Free Cause Party
IBV	Ismail Beşikçi Foundation
ISIS	Islamic State of Iraq and Sham
İşçi-Köylü/ Kizil Bayrak	Workers and Peasants Group
KADEP	Participatory Democracy Party
KCK	Kurdistan Communities Union
KDP	Kurdistan Democratic Party
KDPT	Democratic Party of Turkey's Kurdistan
KİP	Workers' Party of Kurdistan
KRG	Kurdistan Regional government
KKH	Kurdistan Communist Movement
Kom-Kar	The Union of Associations from Kurdistan
KNMC	Society for the Spread of Kurdish Education
KTHC	Kurdish Student Society of Hope
KTTC	Kurdish Party of Cooperation and Progress
KTC	Society for the Rise of Kurdistan
KSH	Kurdistan Socialist Movement
KUK	National Salvation Party of Kurdistan
MASIAD	Marmara Industrialists Businessmen Associations
Med-Zehra	Med-Zehra Religious Community
MHP	Nationalist Movement Party
ÖSP	Freedom and Socialism Party
PAK	Kurdistan Freedom Party
PKK	Kurdistan Workers' Party
PSK	Kurdistan Socialist Party

PYD	Democratic Union Party
RP	Welfare Party
SHP	Social Democratic People's Party
TDRA	Turkey's Directorate of Religious Affairs
TİP	Workers Party of Turkey
TKDP	Kurdistan Democratic Party of Turkey
T-KDP	Turkey's Kurdistan Democratic Party
TKSP	The Socialist Party of Turkish Kurdistan
TÜMSİAD	All Industrialist's and Businessman's Association
WMC	Wise Man Committee

Acknowledgements

This study is based on my PhD dissertation in political science and international relations. The work took me more than five years to complete because of the extent of the fieldwork that was conducted. Wanting to carry out extensive fieldwork, a significant number of interviews were conducted with many groups, some of which were proven to be very difficult to reach – like the armed groups such as the PKK and Hezbollah. As a result of this, I spent more than two years for completing fieldwork in Turkey, Iraq and the UK.

Before presenting the study, I would like to take a moment to express my deepest gratitude to my supervisor, Dr Ebru Altınoğlu, for her patience, editing, reading and valuable comments. The constructive criticisms that she provided; her great expertise in methodology; and her sensitiveness, perfectionism and objectivity were invaluable contributions to my research and influenced my approach to academia.

I must also give a special thanks to Ferya Taş-Çifçi, not only for her academic support but also for her genuine, natural and truthful companionship. Her patience was invaluable during the most stressful moments of this monograph. Without her support and encouragement, this work would not have been completed in London. Thank you so much for not giving up, and for believing in this research. Last but not least, I would like to thank Arîn Aryen Çifçi for bringing happiness and meaning to my life. Without her, I would not be in London and complete this manuscript.

I would also like to thank the BDP/HDP, DBP, Hak-Par, Kadep, Hüda-Par, PAK, T-KDP, DDKD, ÖSP, Kom-Kar, IBV, Zehra Community, Azadî Initiative, Kurdish Alevi organizations and those that cannot be named, plus their representatives.

Preface

It was in the early 1990s that I was first acquainted with the Kurdish issue. It was a time when the PKK was becoming increasingly active, and took control of a number of towns and villages in Kurdish areas, including my village. Around the same time, between 1991 and 1993, the PKK was establishing (de-facto) alternative authority on a more socialist ground in many areas in the Kurdish region, as well as my home village.

Despite the Turkish state security forces' intervention and impediment, the PKK would have expanded exponentially during this time. During that time the PKK was able to establish militia forces, public relations, a tax committee alongside women organizations (and many other committees in many villages); appoint judges; and create a headman. The PKK intended to show its power, and dedication to providing equality, justice and freedom. By doing so, its ultimate aim was to convince people that a Kurdish state would soon be established. The PKK's socialist system, ideology and idea of revolutionary war and struggle resonated with many people, especially amongst the youth in many areas, as well as in my village.

However, not all Kurds were supportive of PKK's system; some people challenged the PKK's ideology and the establishment of a Kurdish state. This resistance further intensified when the PKK applied a policy of recruiting some youths by force and without the consent of families, thereby putting pressure on families to comply. Consequently, although in my home and other villages many youths joined the PKK of their own free will, some were taken by force and without their consent. Naturally, this policy caused significant tension between Kurdish families and the PKK, and also amongst Kurdish families (between those who supported and did not support the PKK). Such tensions led to divisions amongst Kurdish communities, which were further heightened when some Kurdish families began to cooperate with the state.

The PKK's policy did not prove to be very successful, as many youths who joined the PKK, especially those who were recruited by force, escaped from the group. And, with regard to the youths who chose to join the PKK voluntarily, many of them lost their lives fighting against the Turkish state security forces. As a result, most of those who participated in the struggle either left the group or lost their lives within the PKK's ranks. Many of those people happened to be my close friends at school, having shared the same accommodation and even my room during my years at secondary school in the city.

By mid-1993, the state's security forces had aggressively responded to the activities of the PKK and begun to take back complete control of the areas where the PKK was powerful, as well as my home village. Yet this was not without consequences: many people were given severe collective punishments, including killings, arrests, torture and forced migration. Subsequent to the state's control and the PKK's withdrawal, my village, for example, was divided into three main camps: those that had sympathy for the PKK and the idea of a Kurdish state; those that challenged this and cooperated with the state; and those who supported the national rights of Kurds but challenged the PKK's strategy and method of struggle. The events that occurred in my village are a somewhat accurate representation of what happened in the Kurdish region in general.

During this period, I was under the age of 13 (in 1992), and therefore was not recruited by the PKK, but in order to continue my education, I had to leave the village. Leaving the village in that state, I was riddled with questions in my mind, especially, *what do the Kurds want and why don't they unite and gather to resist the state's rather severe oppression?* With the formation of various Kurdish groups, and the ever-intensifying tension and conflict amongst the Kurdish groups and with the state, such questions became of further importance to me. Therefore, the division amongst the Kurds and the vast variations in their political demands motivated me to examine these issues in this monograph.

Introduction

Since the formation of modern Turkey, the Kurds have been in tension with the state and have experienced the state's severe military and political oppression to various degrees. The Kurds have reacted to the Turkish state's denial of and pressure on Kurdish identity through several rebellions and democratic platforms, especially after the 1970s. The Kurds' struggle against the Turkish state has on the one hand resulted in severe damage to their social, political and economic structure, alongside severe demographic changes. Yet on the other hand their struggle has intensely contributed to the construction of Kurdish ethno-national consciousness in various forms and to different degrees. Particularly through the PKK's armed struggle, the Kurds have experienced a lengthy and ongoing nationalization process. However, despite the varying degrees of nationalization and national consciousness raising, the Kurdish population has been unable to propose a common political agenda and political model.

The Kurds have pointed to a wide spectrum of political models they deem to be the solution to the Kurdish question (see Figure I.1). Currently, the political demands conveyed by the Kurds can be classified into four main categories: democratic autonomy, the granting of cultural rights only, ethnic federalism and national self-determination (the creation of a Kurdish nation state). With consideration to the relevant literature, these models can also be classified into further three categories, or branches. The first branch, cultural rights, is regarded as a non-ethnic and non-territorial political model, allowing minorities to have a limited amount of power over their internal affairs (McGarry and Moore 2005, 68). The second branch, ethnic federalism and national self-determination, is ethnic territorial political model which offers power to minorities over their internal affairs via various means – through ethnic federalism, such as education, the provision of local security, parliamentary control, access to economic resources and taxation (Safran 2000, 12). The third branch refers to democratic autonomy, which can be classified as a non-ethnic, territorial, political model. Democratic autonomy relies on the idea of a non-ethnic administrative autonomy, based on a system of regional autonomy similar to the one conducted in Germany (Kapmaz 2010, 316).

Despite the variance in political demands, support for democratic autonomy is by far in the majority. A nationwide opinion survey conducted (by SAMER) in the eleven mostly Kurd-inhabited districts revealed that 41.2 per cent of Kurds call for a democratic autonomy, 19.3 per cent call for independence, 11.7 per cent call for federalism and 9.3 per cent want an administrative autonomy, to solve the Kurdish issue. Meanwhile, 9.1 per cent challenge granting Kurds a constitutional status (see Figure I.1) (SAMER 2012, 27–28).

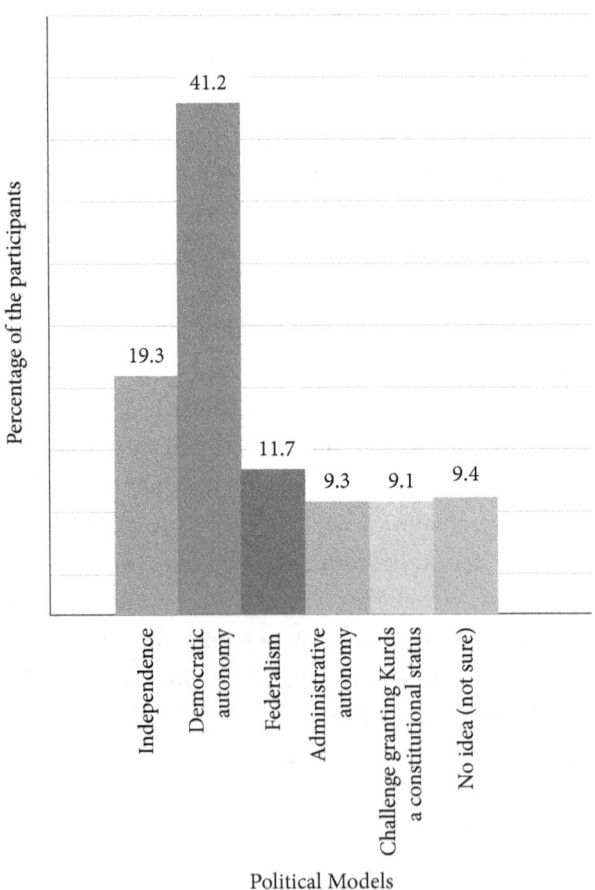

Figure I.1 The political models demanded by the Kurds. Source: (SAMER 2012).

The political variation amongst the Kurds, namely the non-ethnic and non-territorial, non-ethnic territorial and ethnic territorial political demands, allows us to consider the relevant questions: *What are the fundamental factors that lead to the differentiation among the Kurds in relation to their political demands since the PKK's formation? More specifically, why do some of the Kurds in Turkey have ethnic territorial political demands, while others oppose it?* Therefore, the basic problem of research is to describe and study the groups that seek to acknowledge only the Kurds' cultural rights, democratic autonomy, federalism and independence, and to explain the fundamental factors that lead to differentiation among the Kurds in relation to their political demands.

Classification of the groups through demanded political models

This monograph, within the context of the framework provided, aims to explore the variations that have emerged among the Kurds in relation to their demand for the models on an organizational and elite level, respectively. To clarify, organizations refer to non-governmental organizations (NGOs), social groups and political parties (along with some affiliated organizations) (see Table I.1). Recently, a considerable number of the Kurds have gathered in the BDP/HDP and DBP, those Kurds who have sympathy with the PKK, or the groups gathered under the umbrella of the KCK (which is an over-arching organization for legal and outlawed Kurdish organizations), and EMEP vocally express their demand for democratic autonomy. On the other hand, a considerable number of Kurds who have political connections with the AKP and CHP disagree with the territorial and ethnic political models and instead request that Kurds be granted their basic cultural rights, within the existing political framework.[1] In contrast, some Kurds see neither of these two models as a solution, and instead demand the installation of ethnic federalism and the creation of a Kurdish nation state.[2] In this regard, the Kurds have connections with the Med-Zehra and Zehra religious groups, Hüda-Par,[3] Hezbollah, Hak-Par, Kadep, T-KDP, ÖSP and PSK call for federalism. While the Kurds are involved with the Azadî Initiative, PAK, Kizil Bayrak, KKH, IBV and DHF all recognize the Kurds' national self-determination rights. Along with the mentioned main groups, some of these groups' affiliated organizations are also considered (see Table I.1).

Table I.1 A classification of the Kurds' political demands and the groups' (along with some affiliated and independent organizations') struggle for these models.

		Non-Ethnic Territorial	Non-Ethnic Non-Territorial	Ethnic Territorial	
		Democratic Autonomy	Cultural Rights	Ethnic Federalism	Nation State
Organizations: Political Parties, Social, Cultural, Religious and Economic Groups	Main Groups	BDP	AKP	Med-Zehra, Zehra Communities	Azadi Initiative
		HDP	CHP	Hüda-Par	PAK
		DBP		Hezbollah	KKH
		KCK		Hak-Par	DHF
		PKK		ÖSP	Kizil Bayrak
		EMEP		PSK	
				Kadep	
				T-KDP	
	Affiliated and Independent organizations support the same political model	DÖKH	London Alevi Centre	DDKD	IBV
		Peace Assembly	British Alevi Federation	Mustazaf-Der	
		Yüzleşme	Wise Man Committee	Nubihar	
		Zaza-Der	MASIAD	Tev-Kurd	
		Roj Women	TUMSIAD		
		London Kurdish Community	Martyrs Family Associations		
		Kurdish Institute	Glasgow Alevi Federation		

Methodology

Explaining the causes for diversity among the Kurds' political demands, the study is designed around a single-case comparative study (within case variation and comparison) by following an inductive approach. A single-case comparison-based research strategy allows us to 'look at a large number of intervening variables and inductively observe any unexpected aspects of the operation of a particular causal mechanism' (George and Bennet 2005, 21). Therefore, this facilitates the possibility of examining many variables that could potentially cause fragmentation in the Kurds' political demands. From this regard, the monograph uses the *multi-causality* (conjectural-joint causality) methodology to generate hypotheses for theories relating to the Kurds' political demands, by exhibiting an in-depth exploration and explanations of the facts. In line with the research design and method provided, the monograph follows the *explanatory* research strategy (Yin 2002) to develop and explain hypotheses (instead of theory testing).

Case selection

This study concerns itself with a macro-level analysis, dealing with groups, processes and structures at the group level (Landman 2003, 18). To explore the variance in the Kurds' current political demands at a group level, three types of groups are included in the analysis: primary political parties; NGOs; and socio-cultural, economic and political groups. When selecting the organizations for research, two primary conditions were considered: first, they must indicate support for one of the political models; and secondly, they must be of Kurdish origin, or be supported by a considerable number of the Kurds with representative power. In providing these conditions, religious communities and armed movements such as the PKK and Hezbollah and the organizations that have an intellectual influence on determination of the Kurdish political demands such as IBV were also studied. Specific criteria were also established when considering interviewees. The primary principles considered in selecting the interviewees were as follows: being of Kurdish origin, advocating one of the political models, supporting the political group that defends the Kurds' political model(s), holding a representative position and having knowledge of the Kurdish political models discussed in this research. In addition to the criteria, the mentioned organizations' official outlets, such as webpages and written and visual media, were deliberated on and observed before selecting the organizations and the interviewees.

Data collection

The monograph is based on a qualitative method. The research data, to a great extent, relies on the fieldwork, being in-depth interviews conducted with the representatives and activists of the groups considered. The interviewees included parties and organization leaders, provincial and town heads of political parties, directors, mayors, members of parliament and the directors of some groups and NGOs with representative power. In addition to the interviews, the groups' official publications, leaders or members' books, articles and speeches were also utilized as primary sources. The observation techniques used in the research consist of semi-structured and unstructured in-depth elite interviews and focus group discussions.

Extensive fieldwork was organized and conducted; 112 participants were interviewed. Most of the interviewees allowed me to record the conversations and use their real names, organizations and positions. However, because of strict security concerns, some of the interviewees prohibited the recording of the conversations, and only taking of notes was allowed. Moreover, in some cases only some parts of the interview were allowed to be recorded. Again, because of security concerns and the sensitivity concerning their positioning in their organizations, some interviewees did not permit the use of their real name. In order to ensure confidentiality and anonymity, pseudonyms were used for these cases, while other interviewees used their real name and surnames.[4]

The interviews were held in three countries: Turkey, Iraq and the UK. The majority of the interviews were conducted in the cities of İstanbul, Diyarbakır, Batman, Bingöl and Tunceli, where the Kurds have different political stances and socio-cultural pluralisms. Most of the interviews in Turkey were done in person, but because of the security restrictions as well as some technical conditions, some interviews were made via telephone, e-mail, Facebook or Skype. Those who were interviewed by these methods were based in the cities of Şırnak, Hakkari, Iğdır, Van, Gaziantep and Çanakkale. The interviews in Iraq were held in the city of Erbil. In the UK they were conducted in the city of London. Interviewees were granted the preference of what language they wished to conduct the interview in; therefore, questions were asked in the Kurdish, Turkish or English language.

Outline of the book

This book is structurally divided into two main parts; the first part consists of a general introduction and three chapters. These chapters are intended to clarify the research question and methodology, the research's main concepts and the case study, alongside the contextual historical background. The second part of monograph concerns itself with the research analysis, separated into five main chapters. In the light of the data established by the fieldwork, this part of the book explains the causal mechanisms behind the variation within the Kurds' recent political demands.

The introduction addresses the main research question and explains the problem of the research. It then moves on to highlighting the main political demands of the Kurds and the specific groups that raise these demands. The methodology section addresses the research's case type and case selection while also clarifying the data collection methods. The first chapter of the research defines the political demands of the Kurds. It provides a discussion on nation state, autonomy, federalism, democratic autonomy and cultural rights. The second chapter defines the case of the research – the Kurds – paying attention to their ethno-national and religious identity. In this regard, the chapter identifies the main components of Kurdish ethnic identity, particularly territory and language and the construction of Kurdish ethnic and national identity. The relationship between religion and Kurdish identity is also examined in this context. The third chapter concerns itself with the political context and historical background of the variation in the Kurds' political demands. The historical background of these demands is evaluated within the period 1923–80. More significantly, this chapter provides detailed information on the relationship between the Kurds and the state, Kurdish rebellions, the relationships among the Kurdish population and their main organizations within the context of their varying political demands.

Moving on to part two of the study (analysis part), the following five chapters constitute the analysis section. The first four chapters (Chapters 4 to 7) release the empirical findings of the research. Each chapter is separated into two further parts. The first outlines the development of a particular political demand within the framework of its respective defender organizations using the secondary sources. Furthermore, the profile of the adherents of each of these models is also elucidated through the organizations they are involved in. The second part of each chapter explores the causes underlying the adherents' political stance together with an explanation as to why the supporters refuse alternative political models, using primary sources obtained in the fieldwork.

Looking at the chapters concerning the analysis more closely, Chapter 4 examines the Kurds' call for the democratic autonomy model. More specifically, the first part of this chapter defines the relevant political actors (groups) who currently support the political model of democratic autonomy – namely, the PKK and the pro-Kurdish political party BDP/HDP and DBP. The second part analyses the underlying factors behind the demand for democratic autonomy and rejection of other political models – specifically, cultural rights, federalism and nation state models.

Chapter 5 scrutinizes the Kurds' demand for cultural rights. Again, the first part seeks to clarify the political groups in support of this, namely the AKP and CHP. It becomes apparent that they acknowledge this demand as the solution to the Kurdish question, by recognizing Kurds' cultural rights (at the individual level) in relation to their political claims. The second part elucidates the motives that led to the demand to establish Kurdish cultural rights over other political models.

Chapter 6 investigates the Kurds' political demand for federalism. Part one identifies the Kurdish groups who support federalism, those being the Med-Zehra and Zehra communities, Hüda-Par, Hezbollah Hak-Par, Kadep, T-KDP and ÖSP. More significantly, comparisons are made between their ideology, social structure and relations with the state and each other, and, most importantly, the ideological and historical connections with previous Kurdish organizations. This is followed in the second part of the chapter by an analysis of the main motives which influenced these groups to propose federalism as a political model over other political models.

Chapter 7 explores the Kurds' claim for national self-determination and/or independence. The first part briefly identifies the groups in support of this demand, namely Azadî, PAK, KKH, IBV, DHF and Kizil Bayrak. The second part focuses on the causes that contribute to the demand for the formation of a Kurdish nation state and rejection of other political models.

Chapter 8 provides a theoretical discussion on the empirical findings of the research. Each political demand, specifically democratic autonomy, cultural rights, federalism and nation state, is discussed through relevant literature.

1

Defining the Political Models the Kurds Demand

The type of political model Kurds demand varies both from within and according to their diverse principles. Those political models are categorized as non-ethnic territorial models of democratic autonomy, non-ethnic and non-territorial cultural rights, and as ethnic territorial models of ethnic federalism and the formation of a Kurdish state. Looking at the surrounding neighbourhood of the Middle East, some states evidence a non-democratic and religious structure. This highlights the significant question of which type of state the Kurds seek to establish, especially considering the fact that some religious Kurds support the creation of a Kurdish state. Despite coming from diverse social, economic and ideological backgrounds, the Kurds who argue for a nation state wish to see the Kurdish question answered through the establishment of a state comparable to the European model of a modern[1] state or nation state.[2]

This question regarding what type of political model the Kurds seek, however, became far more important in the case of autonomy, since there are various types of autonomy. Despite agreeing on the fundamental principles of autonomy, models of autonomy all differ slightly. Such differences become more apparent when we compare federalism to democratic autonomy. While federalism's exponents associate territoriality with a particular ethnicity, that is the Kurds, democratic autonomy avoids limiting its application of the political model to the Kurdish ethnicity and the Kurdish region. Instead of ethnicity, democratic autonomy associates itself with notions of a democratic republic, participatory citizenship, democratic confederalism and a democratic nation, which separates democratic autonomy from the type of autonomy demonstrated by federalism. This raises very important structural questions about the political model of democratic autonomy, especially whether it is ethnic and territorial, and thus capable of drawing sharp boundaries between it (i.e. democratic autonomy) and other types of autonomy – federalism in particular. The discussion of autonomy further intensifies when we turn our attention to cultural rights, especially considering the latter's limits. Thus, to clarify the types and principles of the political models that the Kurds demand, this chapter provides the theoretical framework for the autonomy, federalism, democratic autonomy and cultural rights, respectively.

Autonomy

Autonomy is one of the most supported political models used when aiming to deal with the Kurdish question. The Kurds' search for autonomy aims to address the Kurdish question through the reinstatement of their ethno-cultural rights without separation, through the primary means of autonomy. Yet, since autonomy is very different inside from outside, and it is applied in different forms in practice, there is divergence among Kurds regarding the type of autonomy they look for. The variations in the models of autonomy can be classified as non-ethnic and non-territorial, non-ethnic territorial and ethnic territorial in a broader context, and these differences can be implemented over a range of diversities such as ethnic, religious, linguistic or cultural. It is from this angle that the two current political demands of the Kurds, democratic autonomy and federalism, can be considered within the context of autonomy. To an extent, the concept of autonomy could also be compatible with the Kurds' demand for cultural rights (cultural autonomy); however, the majority of the Kurds who are in support of gaining cultural rights reject the concept of autonomy altogether.

Autonomy, derived from the Latin words 'auto' (self) and 'nomos' (law) (Eide 1998, 251), is used to regulate the social, cultural, economic and political relations between the central state and local units and/or minorities in a broader sense. Under the provision of autonomy, a certain level of independent status is granted to minorities, thereby allowing such groups to arrange their internal affairs (Pratchett 2004, 362). Autonomy in this regard reflects a political system of shared power between the central state and local groups, allowing these groups to obtain the right to self-govern. The European Charter of Local Self-Government defines this separation of power as 'the right and the ability of local authorities, within the limits of the law, to regulate and manage a substantial share of public affairs under their own responsibility and in the interests of the local population' (European Charter of Local Self-Government 1985, Article 3 (1)).

Autonomy thus significantly varies in nature and in practice and can be applied in several forms. The varying nature of autonomy has raised countless discussions on its theoretical context (Kirişçi and Winrow 1997, 222). The existing literature provides various approaches to explaining the forms, principles and degrees of autonomy that local groups have over the central state. In his approach, Henri J. Steiner classifies three forms of autonomy that recognize local groups as independent powers in their relation to the central state to some extent: 'power sharing', 'territorial autonomy' and 'personal law'. Steiner's 'power sharing' model prioritizes the rights of local groups to be represented equally in a central state. This model gives local groups the capacity to 'veto' and 'quota' central state suggestions, which provides the local groups with a level of power to challenge the central state's decisions if they are perceived as negative (Steiner 1991, 1541–42). Steiner's second form of autonomy is based on territorial character and territorial autonomy. Territorial autonomy issues collective rights to the local groups concentrated in a particular territory and which have distinctive cultural, ethnic and/or religious identities granted by the central state (Steiner 1991, 1542). The notion of territory occupies a significant place in determining the level and content of power given to minorities. Territorial autonomy in this regard provides minorities a political status and the right of self-governance (Heintze 1998, 18) by allowing them control over their internal affairs, including education, traffic, housing and agriculture issues, and in some cases the use of economic resources, the right to tax collection and the deployment of their own local security forces (Rothchild and Hartzell 2000, 259). The devolution system in the UK, which grants a significant amount of power to Scotland, North Ireland and Wales; regional autonomy in Spain, particularly in the case of the Basques; Kurdish federalism in Iraq; and the Quebec case in Canada are all examples of how this model system fits into territorial autonomy form, although the specifics of how these devolved systems function do vary from case to case. Steiner's final categorization of autonomy recognizes 'personal law', specifically the 'religious law' of members belonging to an ethnic community in a majority. In this form of autonomy, Steiner considers 'personal law' as a necessity for building relations between local groups with diverse ethnic and religious identities and the central state. Countries which best represent this type of autonomy include India and Israel (Steiner 1991, 1542).

Along with deliberations made on the notion of autonomy, the principles of autonomy have also been a topic of discussion, with particular focus on the degree of power local groups have over the central state in their relations. Gordon L. Clark refers to two principles in his classification of autonomy – 'power of initiation' and 'power of immunity'. Clark explains that how much local groups gain from autonomy is dependent on these two values. The 'power of initiation' idea rests on the right of 'legislation' and 'regulation', while 'power of immunity' alludes to the 'power of localities to act without fear of the oversight authority of higher tiers of the state' (Clark 1984, 198–99). By combining these two principles, Clark divides the concept of autonomy into four typologies of local autonomy. In the first type, local groups possess both 'initiative' and 'immunity', and so, in a sense, they have a high level of autonomy – political territorial entities could be included within this definition. In Clark's second type of autonomy, local groups only possess 'initiative', and in the third categorization they have only 'immunity'. Therefore, in his second and third classifications, local groups are given a limited degree of autonomy because they are left without either 'initiative' or 'immunity'. Finally, in Clark's fourth classification, local groups are deprived of both 'initiative' and 'immunity'; thus, they categorically lack autonomy. This represents centralized cases, to an extent, due to the denial of minorities' demands for the acknowledgement of their cultural, ethnic or religious rights, as well as the potentially severe response this could elicit from the state (Clark 1984, 199).

Clark's principles are indicative of the clarification of the degree of autonomy in regard to local groups' values of 'initiative' and 'immunity'. However, his approach places the state at the forefront, and thus neglects to highlight the influential role of local groups' power in determining central state policies. Clark also neglects to mention the role of identity in determining autonomy. Mentioning the gap in Clark's approach, Pratchett (2004, 363–67) developed three separate understandings of local autonomy. 'Freedom from higher authorities' is Pratchett's first approach, which 'defines local autonomy as the degree of discretion that local authorities have from central government' (Pratchett 2004, 363). 'Freedom to achieve affect particular outcomes' is Pratchett's second approach, by which he discusses the power of local groups over the central state. Here Pratchett highlights the local groups' potential effect on central state decisions and authority (Pratchett 2004, 365–66). In his final approach, 'reflection of local identity', Pratchett focuses on and explains local autonomy through local identity. He defines local autonomy as 'the capacity to define and express local identity through political activity' (Pratchett 2004, 366). With this understanding he emphasizes the power of local groups to obtain a large degree of autonomy from the central state (Pratchett 2004, 366–67).

Federalism

Federalism derives from the Latin words 'foedus' (Elazar 2006, 5) and 'foederatus', with close links to the concepts 'foedus' (treaty) and 'fidere' (trust) (O'Duffy 2009, 202). Like autonomy, it is a quite contentious and ambiguous concept (Dare 1979, 34–35; Jinadu 1979, 13–14). Federalism positions itself against centralist administrative and political structures, meaning it is based on the idea of decentralization and the handing over of power to local units, which can be political, administrative or both in a broad context (Amoretti 2004, 10; Proudhon 2014, 68). The constitutional recognition of federalism dates back to the American Constitution of 1878 over administrative criteria (Dare 1979, 26). However, the model soon became an important alternative form of political governance, particularly to satisfy stateless minorities (Horowitz 2008, 102). Particularly, as Maiz (2000, 35) notes, nation states' over-reliance on a particular identity and homogeneous and assimilationist policies have strengthened federalism as an alternative political and administrative model in managing tensions and providing stateless groups with their ethno-national claims through unity with the state.

Territorial autonomies' strong reliance on a power-sharing principle here provides minorities with the ability to practise and protect their identity in their homelands (Amoretti 2004, 9). Federalism's reliance on the distribution of power and the constitutional division of sovereignty between a national state and local governments (Aroney 2009, 33; Clark, Golder and Golder 2009, 603; Hague and Harrop 2004, 228) could provide a ground for the latter to protect and improve their shared differences within the host state's unity (Heintze 1998, 24). The federal idea thus endeavours to 'accommodate, preserve, and promote distinct identities' (Burgess 1993, 3) through a territorially decentralized interpretation, which, along with the granting of minority rights, also aims to hold together these groups within the host state (Maiz 2000, 51). This is also the idea behind the power-sharing and decentralizing characteristics of federalism (Adegbite 1979). In doing so, federalism delivers stability and balance between central state and territorial groups (Gagnon 1993, 26–27), and provides 'political integration' (Elazar 2006, 2). The culmination of these factors, as noted by Stepan, leads to the assessment that federalism is a 'holding together' model (Stepan 2004, 444).

One of the primary aims of federalism thus became the satisfying of stateless groups and the removal of their need to establish their own independent states.

Accordingly, based on the protection of internal varieties, a greater understanding of federalism will deliver to local groups, especially stateless minorities, the power and authority to rule the regions they reside in. In doing so, territorial local groups are able to make better use of social and economic resources, provide security and, most importantly, to live openly with their identical differences within the state's unity (Blondel 2004, 234; Elazar 2006; Jinadu 1979, 15, 20). Hence, although it depends on the case and the form accepted, federalism can provide territorial minorities with the authority to generate their own capital, assembly, constitution, policies and legislative and judicial powers, and make them eligible for their own flag, march, anthem, local budget and local security forces (Özer 2009, 681–86).

Forms of federalism

The analysis and context provided above give a general outline for the rise in the demand for federalism and the main principles of its authority. However, the various existing forms of territorial autonomy, most of which are considered federal samples, and the noticeable differences between federalism forms indicate that further specification and clarification of federalism are required. Therefore, with a particular reference to Clark, Golder and Golder (2009) the following two sections will reflect on federalism under the categories, 'federalism in structure' and 'federalism in practice'.

Federalism in structure

With 'federalism in structure', Clark, Golder and Golder stress three main principles of federalism: 'geopolitical division', 'independence' and 'direct governance'. By the principle 'geopolitical division', they class a country as a federal country if it has more than one territorial unit, and if these units are constitutionally recognized or have a status 'that cannot be unilaterally abolished by the national or central government'. With their second principle, 'independence', they place emphasis on the importance of having 'independent bases of authority' between central government and local units. In this regard, their third principle, 'direct governance', focuses on power sharing between national and regional governments. This principle, therefore, implies that both parties – regional and central government – should act independently, 'at least in one policy realm' from each other (Clark, Golder and Golder 2009, 605).

To further elucidate the distinctions between federalism's structural forms, this section will also use the following sub-federalism categorizations: Congruent (Mono-Ethnic or Administrative) and Incongruent (Multi-ethnic), and Symmetric and Asymmetric Federalisms.

Congruent (mono-ethnic or administrative) and incongruent (multi-ethnic), and symmetric and asymmetric federalisms

Although they are still subject to questions and criticisms, most types of federal applications are currently practised throughout the world. It is estimated that nearly one-third of people are living under a form of federal autonomy (O'Duffy 2009, 201). Almost all forms of federalism rely on federalism's core principles, but in each case the application also has its own principles. Despite the broad use of federal models when put into practice, they can be grouped into ethnic and administrative federalism based on fundamental characteristics (Sharma 1979, 24–25). To begin with the latter, administrative federalism – which is also known as cooperative federalism (Laselva 1996, 175) or mono-national federalism – consists of only one ethnic group or nation (mono-nation). In this classification, local groups and the central state belong to the same ethnic identity or share the same social boundaries (O'Leary 2004, 161). The former classification (ethnic federalism) entails more than one ethnicity or nation (multi-national). In ethnic federalism, local groups, or minorities, are mostly located in particular regions and share a diverse identity with the host state (Heintze 1998, 25–27).

Arend Lijphart organizes this classification under 'congruent' and 'incongruent federalisms'. To clarify distinctions between 'congruent' and 'incongruent' federalisms, he compares the social and political boundaries of territorial units, such as ethnic minorities. Lijphart points out that 'in incongruent federations these boundaries tend to coincide, but they tend to cut across each other in congruent federal systems' (Lijphart 1999, 196). Exemplifying existing federal cases in light of the discussed categories, the mono-nations (single nation cases), such as Germany and the United States, represent administrative federalism samples (Özer 2009, 686), while Belgium, Spain, India, Iraq, Canada, the former Yugoslavia and the Soviet Republic, composed of numerous ethnicities (multi-national) concentrated in a particular region, are characteristic samples of ethnic federalism (O'Duffy 2009, 216–17). Both kinds of federalism are applied in most cases; however, evidence shows that, presently, ethnic (incongruent) federalism is most common, as is also the case with the

Kurds who call for federalism. As mentioned before, the increase in self-rule requests from stateless groups makes federal ideology preferable. Reflecting on the main principle of federalism, as Elazar (2006, 10) highlights, provision of 'group pluralism and individual liberties' illustrates that ethnic federalism is the ideal unit to accommodate identical claims of stateless groups and to resolve any conflict present between them and the state.

The framework drawn above gives general categorizations of 'federalism in structure'. Although all applications of federalism contain a few essential principles, there are distinct differences between them, as they each also consist of other principles. To further clarify this point, certain federal applications will be examined in relation to their principles.

Taking into account some of the current federal countries, the United States is characterized by congruent federalism because the individual states and the national government share the same ethnic identity or social boundaries (Clark, Golder and Golder 2009, 611). The cantonal federal model in Switzerland, on the other hand, is an incongruent form of federalism, as social and cultural boundaries, particularly with regard to language, are not strictly held within the country (Lijphart 1999, 196). Multiculturalism and multilingualism constitute the two main pillars of the cantonal federalism model in Switzerland because ethno-cultural and linguistic identities are factors in the construction and function of cantons (Bachtiger and Steiner 2004, 40–41). Like Switzerland, incongruent federalism is also in place in Belgium (Lijphart 1999, 197). With tensions between Walloons and Flemish people running high, federalism was introduced into the constitution in 1993 for its political and administrative characteristics (Hooghe 2004, 55). The structure of federalism in Belgium is made up of specific 'regions' and 'communities' – while Flemish-, French- and German-speaking people comprise the three linguistic communities, Wallonia, Flanders and Brussels are the regional side of the Belgian federation (Beland and Lecours 2007, 409). Each region in the Belgian federation makes use of autonomy and is in control of its internal affairs. Through linguistic and regional decentralization, Belgian federalism manages the relations between the central state and people attached to separate regions, or who have their own language (Hooghe 2004). Canada is another incongruent federalism case (Lijphart 1999, 196), centred on language and regional diversifications. Federal units employ a significant amount of independence in Canada (Simeon 2004, 99), but the Quebecois province raises questions about the true success of federalism since there is demand for separation from some Quebecois. As Keating (1997, 695) explains, in particular, Quebec nationalism has had an influence on communities – the idea of establishing its own state has increased among individuals.

Along with administrative (mono-ethnic) and multi-ethnic classifications of federalism, some also fit under the categories 'symmetric' and 'asymmetric federalisms' (Clark, Golder and Golder 2009, 612). In symmetric federalism, all local governments carry a similar status or are considered equal in political and economic terms by the national government (state), for example the United States (Ishiyama 2012, 213). Asymmetric federalism is simply based on the idea that some regions gain more power in comparison to the other regions in a country (Martinez-Vazquez and Boex 2001, 4; Wheatley 2010).

Federalism in practice

The study has already clarified that in order to consider a case as 'federal in structure' it has to illustrate three key principles: 'geopolitical division', 'independence' and 'direct governance'. However, despite their substantial power some federal countries do not demonstrate these three principles together. They exhibit only some, and therefore cannot truly be considered as 'federalism in structure' cases. Such cases, as outlined by Clark, Golder and Golder, will be classified under 'federalism in practice', which they also consider as decentralization 'that refers to the extent to which actual policymaking power lies with the central or regional governments in a country' (Clark, Golder and Golder 2009, 612).

Spain is a prime example of a 'federalism in practice' case. The country consists of several ethnic and linguistic groups, of which the Basques and Catalans are the most noteworthy. During the period of Franco (1939–75) the central state imposed its own identity and applied harsh policies to suppress minority groups, resulting in internal conflict (Aktoprak 2010, 282–300). In order to end this tragic internal tension, minority groups' claims had to be recognized, and thus Spain accepted federalism in its 1978 constitution (Beramendi and Maiz 2004, 123–24). The second article of the Spanish Constitution 'recognizes and guarantees the right to self-government of the nationalities and regions of which it is composed and the solidarity among them all' (Spanish Constitution 1978, Article–2, 10). Based on this principle, regionally located groups, such as the Basques, obtained the right to control the majority of their internal affairs (Llera 2000, 104). However, federalism in Spain does not meet the 'geographical division' condition since, as Clark, Golder and Golder (2009, 609) highlight, the central government has the right to retain some of the power unilaterally given to the regional governments.

India is another case which includes several ethnic, religious and linguistic groups that transitioned to a federal structure by acknowledging their differences. 'Power-sharing', 'cooperation' and 'accommodation' are the three main values the Indian case abides by, and which were substantially successful in resolving most of the internal conflict in India (Kohli 2004; Majeed 2009). However, Clark, Golder and Golder argue that the case of India also cannot be classed under 'federalism in structure' since it does not display 'geopolitical division'. They state that the national government has the right to intervene and change regional entities' boundaries, which contradicts the idea of 'geopolitical division' (Clark, Golder and Golder 2009, 610–11).

The devolution system in the UK is a slightly different type of autonomy, namely devolution that 'occurs when a unitary state grants powers to subnational governments but retains the right to unilaterally recall or reshape those powers' (Clark, Golder and Golder 2009, 609). With decentralization, Welsh, Irish and Scottish people are granted a large degree of territorial autonomy and have the power to manage most of their internal activities (Keating 2004, 167–68), although they each employ different levels from autonomy (Hannum 1990, 458; O'Duffy 2009, 204). Although devolution shares most of its values with a federal structure, it is not labelled federalism, in order to remove any separation concerns (Leopold 2009, 247–48). Secondly, and most importantly, it does not meet the 'geopolitical division' criteria because the central government 'retains the unilateral right to recall or reshape the powers that it has delegated or devolved to the regional governments' (Clark, Golder and Golder 2009, 609).

Overall, the discussions on autonomy in the previous sections and on federalism above show they are similar in some ways, but also demonstrate significant differences. First, as Hand J. Heintze states, 'autonomy is always a fragmented order, whereas a constituent state is always part of a whole. The latter participates in decision-making through organs of the federals state' (Heintze 1998, 25). He adds that federal units' affinities are more powerful than those of autonomous structures because federalism mostly concentrates on the following dynamics: territorial division, economic structure, the historical background of regional groups and relations with the central state, and ideology (Heintze 1998, 25). Taking the idea of federalism in that sense, as P. King (1993, 97–98) points out, federalism does not prioritize the granting of cultural values or rights only; it takes the notion of territory as a whole into consideration and recognizes rights in this sense. This provides a relevant framework for the type of federalism that Kurds demand.

Democratic autonomy

The term 'democratic autonomy' was first proposed by Abdullah Öcalan, the leader of the PKK, with the aim to find a solution for the Kurdish issue by developing a new theoretical and practical understanding. The model is relatively new and has been developing over time, and therefore academically it has not been discussed at great length. Despite this, democratic autonomy can be defined as non-state aimed at political and administrative model with strong reference to democratization of state (democratic republic), radical democracy, participant citizenship and the organizing of society in confederalist form. The model in this regard is based on the paradigm of a non-state aimed at being self-organizing and self-ruling within the state's territorial unity.

Since its birth, democratic autonomy has gained popular support among many Kurds. In particular, it has inspired the PKK and legal Kurdish organizations, in particular the BDP/HDP, DBP and all the other groups that gather under the KCK. Soon after the model was proposed, the BDP in particular was one of the first actors that officially accepted democratic autonomy as the political model to solve the Kurdish question within the context of the democratization of Turkey (Barış ve Demokrasi Partisi Tüzüğü 2008, Article 3(c)). The BDP has since dissolved, on 14 July 2014, and been replaced by the HDP, which is recently the main actor constructing its vision of democratic autonomy across Turkey. One of Öcalan's key arguments is that in dealing with the Kurdish question, democratic autonomy needs to be established within the social environment of radical democracy and participant citizenship (as will be examined later). It is within this context that the HDP has proposed the creation of local assemblies, within the establishment of locally and regionally autonomous areas (HDP Parti Programı 2014). Bearing a nationwide presence, the HDP receives support from various ethnic and cultural backgrounds and a wide range of Kurds, and therefore holds a beneficial position in being able to relay and construct the idea of democratic autonomy across Turkey. Contrary to the HDP, the DBP, which is active in Kurdish areas, chose to establish a model that is confined within Kurdish territories. The DBP preferred to emphasize the notion of 'democratic nation diplomacy', aiming to provide a platform for the Kurdish union both within the Kurds in Turkey and in the Middle East, while refusing the idea of a nation state. Trying to overturn a political system starting from the root of what it regarded as the problem, the DBP sees itself as the pioneer organization in the construction of democratic autonomy in the form of democratic confederalism in the Kurdish areas (Demokratik Bölgeler Partisi Tüzüğü 2016). Different Kurdish organizations have contributed to and interpreted the concept of democratic autonomy in varying different ways and to different extents, but they all agree on the fundamental principles of democratic autonomy proposed by Abdullah Öcalan. So, the discussion on democratic autonomy will be provided through its main principles with particular reference to Abdullah Öcalan.

In proposing democratic autonomy, Abdullah Öcalan's ideological transformation, especially his criticism of socialism and the state, has a decisive place. Dating back to the 1990s, Öcalan's desire to offer a non-state solution for the Kurdish issue first stems from his ideological criticism of Soviet socialism (as will be examined in Chapter 4). Especially following his kidnapping and arrest in 1999, Öcalan made a sharp ideological and paradigm change in his approach to the Kurdish question, and thus further refined his ideas within a non-state aimed paradigm. His time in solitary confinement in the Imrali prison allowed him to formulate his ideas and develop the concepts of democratic republic, democratic confederalism, democratic nation and democratic autonomy, bringing them under a new paradigm, namely democratic modernity (as an alternative to capitalist modernity), in order to define Kurdish demands and provide a long-term strategy within the idea of a pluralist democratic system, with reference to radical democracy. These concepts are intertwined (as will be argued later), and are 'political projects function as a "strategic dispositif": ideas and means through which Kurdish political demands are (re)defined and (re)organized' (Akkaya and Jongerden 2012, 6). For Öcalan, the aim was not to gain the Kurds a piece of territory that belonged to them; it was to replace an entire paradigm, namely capitalist modernity, that was seen as the root of many issues, including the Kurdish issue. Therefore, his objective was to develop a political model that reflected democratic autonomy, redirecting power so that the Kurds would be granted the rights of self-rule and self-organization (in the form of democratic confederalism) while being in a relationship with the state, within the idea of a democratic republic and participant citizenship. All of this was formulated within the concept of democratic modernity, being an ideological and organizational base for the construction of democratic autonomy. An understanding of democratic autonomy therefore first requires a clarification of the concept of democratic modernity and its key components.

Democratic modernity: An alternative to capitalist modernity

When Abdullah Öcalan used the term 'democratic modernity', he was referring to a paradigm that opposed the existing capitalist modern system that, to Öcalan, is the main source of societal, economic and political issues. The characteristics and fundamental features of capitalist modernity are not only the source of political, economic and societal problems, in his opinion, but also fundamentally obstruct the existence of society's communal values. These communal values are 'summarized as the socialization based on gender, life compatible with nature and society based on communality and solidarity' which underlie Öcalan's 'conception of democracy in the form of democratic confederalism' (Akkaya and Jongerden 2012, 7). Framing capitalist modernity through the concepts of capitalist modern society, the nation state and industrialism, Öcalan proposed the term 'democratic modernity' as a viable alternative. In stark contrast to capitalist modernity, Öcalan proposed a society founded on the basis of a moral and political society, with society organized in the form of democratic confederalism and eco-industrialism. In order to understand why Öcalan introduced such a radical conceptualization of democratic modernity, we can look at some of the criticisms he held of the existing capitalist modern system.

Öcalan's first critique of capitalist modernity stems from his consideration of capitalism as an exploitative system (in social, political and economic terms), which destroys moral and political society. With his concept of a moral society, Öcalan is referring to the communal and natural values of society (Öcalan 2013b). Within the context of political society, Öcalan frames the role of politics as being self-governing in nature, with society's active participation in the decision-making process (Öcalan 2013b, 89-92). Departing from this point, Öcalan's largest issue with capitalist modernity is that it politically and economically benefits a particular group, namely the bourgeoisie or capitalist class, while the majority of the population suffers. Despite the initial appearance that it shares a similar outlook with the socialist view of capitalism, Öcalan actually extends his framework for understanding capitalist modernity – criticizing Marx for failing to take into consideration the capitalist system beyond the economic level. The framework for understanding the capitalist system must therefore also be considered at the political, military and societal levels, since the alliance between the political, military and economic forces establishes a monopoly over society. These additional aspects of capitalist modernity, especially the political and military aspects, overlooked by Marx, are what fundamentally define its values. Taking this into consideration, Öcalan regards capitalism as the enemy not only of society's economic values, but of its social and moral values as well (Öcalan 2013a, 107–17). Öcalan articulates the latter issue through what he calls the isolation of society from its communal and moral values, which happens when it is required to obey the state's rules and positive laws instead (Öcalan 2013c, 270). The consequence of this is that individuals and society turn into objects for obeying the state's rule and laws, without having any sort of agency to express their existential moral and communal values. The reason why this is detrimental, according to Öcalan, is because communal values are replaced with the state's hegemonic, class-positivist laws – which are therefore not laws for the people (Öcalan 2013b, 92–205). Claiming that society is political through its natural values, Öcalan asserts that society's isolation from natural values damages its political character (Öcalan 2013c, 350). Thus, looking at capitalist modernity through the lens of the state's rules and positive laws, society becomes ideologically occupied, since its moral and political values are destroyed, leaving society vulnerable to all types of exploitation (Öcalan 2013b, 92–205). Öcalan is thus highly critical of capitalist modernity, since it not only damages society's moral and political character, but also replaces them with state-formulated positivist laws.

Directing our attention to the main instrument responsible for the regulation of capitalist modernity, Öcalan identifies this as the nation state, which constitutes the second pillar in his critique. Öcalan defines the nation state through the notions of hegemony, monopoly and capitalism. It is precisely through the capitalist system that the state is able to establish a monopoly authority over society (Öcalan 2013c, 243). Deeming the nation state to be a capitalist product, the function of the nation state is thereby to regulate politics, the state of the economy and society, in favour of a particular class. To Öcalan, those utilizing the nation state are members of the capitalist class, whose desire is to establish their hegemony and monopoly over society – to their own benefit and not that of the general population (Öcalan 2013a). Öcalan intensifies his critique, this time turning on the bureaucratic structure of the nation state and its role in isolating the population from politics, understood as a de-politicization of society (Öcalan 2013c, 350). Öcalan argues that the fundamental nature and communal values of societies are eradicated and replaced with a new standard of rules as a result of the state's hierarchical and bureaucratic structure. The prevalence of a hierarchy decreases society's influence on the decision-making process (Öcalan 2013b, 244–45). Not only does this hinder the ability of citizens to actively partake in the decision-making process but it makes them passive citizens and in a passive society. Looking at the centrality of the nation state in capitalist modernity, Öcalan notes that nation states pacify individuals and society while sacralizing themselves, which results in individuals' and society's de-politicization. Thus, the largest detriment to society is fundamentally rooted in the fact that society's moral values are replaced with a hierarchical bureaucracy, through the nation state (Gürer 2015, 195–96). Öcalan here also heavily criticizes representative democracy, and liberalism in general, for its intense emphasis on the notion of individualism and its lesser concern for and affiliations with the notion of society and/or collectivism (Öcalan 2013b, 37–38). Öcalan even argues that representative democracy can be considered to directly prevent people's collective participation in decision-making (Öcalan 2013b, 255–56). Based on this, Öcalan often refers to radical democracy and people's direct participation in the decision-making process and their contribution to the politicization of society.

The third cornerstone defining capitalist modernity is industrialism, and Öcalan brings our attention to two points: how capitalist markets allow for the establishment of monopoly, and the development of unplanned (conurbation) urbanization. The former refers to surplus value, where the capitalist class is seen establishing its economic monopoly over the people. Second, Öcalan criticizes capitalist industrialization as responsible for destroying the environment and ecology, especially through the development of unplanned urbanization (Öcalan 2013b, 5:437–38).

Following his critiques of capitalist modernity, Öcalan offers democratic modernity as a viable alternative. There is no doubt that capitalist modernity has flourished, dominating social, political and economic life for a long time. Yet to Öcalan, capitalist modernity has still not been able to eliminate democratic modernity completely. Therefore, despite capitalist modernity's dominance, democratic modernity has continued to survive to a certain extent (Öcalan 2013b, 235–37). Öcalan bases democratic modernity upon three pillars: moral and political society, democratic confederalism and eco-industrialism. Taking a closer look at these pillars allows us to understand the foundations and interrelated nature of these concepts and how they create an ideological and organizational base for democratic autonomy.

The building of a moral and political society comprises the first pillar of democratic modernity for Öcalan. He talks about a moral and political society as an alternative to capitalist modernity's capitalist societal understanding. The moral and political society is the notion he uses to understand the importance and relevance of democratic commonality and solidarity (Öcalan 2013c, 241). This understanding of communal values is the alternative to capitalist modernity's societal values. Öcalan's approach to society is deeply rooted in his belief in the foundational values which he considers essential for a moral and political society. With his concept of a moral society (as noted earlier), Öcalan is referring to the communal and natural values of a society. Öcalan likens a society that has lost its existential values and practices to a 'fauna/animal society'; therefore, foundational values, Öcalan says, are essential for the survival and continuation of a moral and political society (Öcalan 2013c, 90). Because a political society, in Öcalan, concerns itself with the active participation of society in matters of politics, Öcalan argues that society's role in the political process has a determinative role in the type of policy outcomes that are formulated.

Related to the first principle, Öcalan's second principle concerns the reorganization of society based on democratic confederalism, which he sees as an alternative to capitalist modernity's nation state organization. Democratic confederalism implies society's non-state, bottom-up self-organization, 'or democracy without a state' (Öcalan 2017, 21). Öcalan defines democratic confederalism as a political organizational form of democratic modernity and democratic autonomy, and therefore is the best organizational form for the participation and politicization of society (Öcalan 2013b, 253–57, 350). In effect, democratic confederalism concerns itself with how society should be socially and politically organized. In this case, democratic confederalism is underpinned by a horizontal organization of society, regarded as a bottom-up organization of society through the idea of radical democracy and participant citizenship (Akkaya and Jongerden 2012).

Democratic confederalism is by far the most ambitious principle underpinning Öcalan's systemic approach to ethno-national minority matters. In stark contrast to capitalist modernity, in particular its organizing of society thorough nation state form, the defining feature of democratic confederalism is that it proposes a communal-based organization, centred around the interaction of society's members and their own communal values. In other words, making references to the ideas of American anarchists and to the libertarian socialist Murray Bookchin (Öcalan 2010a), Öcalan puts forward a democratic confederalist structure that effectively eradicates the need for a capitalist modernist nation state form (Öcalan 2013c, 253). This structure is intended to erase the nation state's severe, bureaucratic and vertical organizational structure while restoring the communal and natural values of society: in other words, restoring the moral and political society. This type of bottom-up political organization relies on the participation of society at all levels and aspects, representing all classes and identities within the idea of participatory citizenship. In practical terms, the organization of society through democratic confederalism starts from the villages, towns, neighbourhoods and cities. Encouraging the inclusion of all identities (ethnic, religious, gender, cultural, etc.), democratic confederalism facilitates the establishment of local assemblies, organized by the citizens themselves from the local to the regional levels (Öcalan 2010a). A fundamental feature of democratic-confederalist organization is that all identities will first have their own self-organization, but will also be in close interaction with each other and will gather under a supra-organization. Proceeding from this foundation, local assemblies will take part in higher assemblies, which will derive authority directly from their citizens. The organizing of society through democratic confederalism in this regard can be at the local, regional and national levels.

For example, in the Kurdish region, Kurdish and other ethnic religious groups will be required to organize themselves at the local levels, but they will also come to interact in an upper-roof organization such as a city council. In addition to this, there will also be a roof assembly that represents all city councils, sub-assemblies and NGSs. The BDP-/HDP-/DBP-run municipalities and groups gathered under the KCK will establish youths, women, peasants, workers and different communes and assemblies in the neighbourhood, villages, district, city and region in Kurdistan (Yeğen 2016, 378–79). To illustrate the organization of society at the regional level, the DTK, for instance, will become the main representative body and represent the upper assembly for the Kurdish region, since it represents all sub-assemblies and/or diverse cultures and civil society organizations. The benefit of this structure is that each group will be truly representative of their population and be able to directly participate in the decision-making process.

Going back to an earlier critique, Öcalan explains how capitalism's representative democracy has hindered the ability of people to directly participate in politics or the decision-making process. Whereas with democratic confederalism the organizational structure accommodates each group, allowing them to directly participate in the decision-making process, by emphasizing radical democracy as the viable alternative to capitalist modernity's representative democracy (Öcalan 2013b, 255–56) Öcalan highlights that democratic confederalism takes its power from radical democracy in comparison to representative democracy. Democratic confederalism in this sense becomes society's non-state-aimed self-organization, which can be constructed without the support of the state. Based on this, Öcalan considers the following as democratic confederalism's main principles.

- The nature of democratic confederalism is versatile in that it is multi-layered and open to diverse identities (ethnic, cultural, linguistic, national and religious) and political formations.
- Its values rely on the moral and political principles of society and strongly oppose any type of capitalist, feudalist, industrialist or consumerist societal engineering projects.
- It relies on democratic politics. This idea of democracy is based on the democratic confederalist understanding of politics that runs contrary to the nation state's centralist, linear and bureaucratic administrative understanding. Based on this understanding of democracy, ideas of decentralization and self-rule are accepted.
- The system relies on enacting the principle of self-defence. This does not imply the creation of a military regime or monopoly of power. Rather, this understanding is based on society's internal and external security needs, which should aim to form self-security defence forces under the tight control of democratic bodies. Therefore, the goal is to protect the moral and political society and its democratic will, safeguarding it from any internal and external threats.
- By nature, it opposes hegemony in general and any sort of ideological hegemony in particular. Based on the idea of pluralism, democratic confederalism does not allow for the formation of any ideological hegemony. Democratic confederalism opposes the hegemony of any nationalist, fundamentalist, positivist science and sexist ideologies. It therefore welcomes all ideological diversities, unless they seek to damage the society's moral and political values and run to form their own hegemony and/or monopoly over others.
- Finally, contrary to the UN and similar structures, which are dominated by super-hegemonic powers, democratic confederalism chooses to rely on the national societies' organization, the World Democratic Confederal Union. The latter is considered more safe, peaceful, ecological, equitable and productive (Öcalan 2013b, 215–18).

Constituting the third pillar of Öcalan's democratic modernity, eco-industrialism is the alternative to capitalist modernity's idea of industrialism. This concept can be more usefully separated into two parts, industrialism/the economic system and ecology, in order to understand the interaction between these concepts. Öcalan challenges the idea of capitalist accumulation, since the system advocates a monopoly over people and surplus values. According to

Öcalan, the presence of a market is not a problem, provided it does not turn into an establishment that becomes controlled by a group's hegemony – thereby holding an unjust monopoly over the majority of society. Öcalan prioritizes the environmental well-being of a society, and therefore uses the term 'eco-society' as an alternative to the capitalist economy. In an eco-society, ownership is not the priority in economic relationships. Öcalan uses the term 'ecology' to highlight capitalism's destruction of the environment and development of unplanned urbanization. Here he gives foremost importance to the environment and ecological system, and severely criticizes its destruction by unplanned urbanization (Öcalan 2013b, 246–51).

Based on the principles discussed, democratic modernity aims to provide an alternative logic for organizing society. Most importantly, it places society's existential values first while making them key actors in politics; it also minimizes the harm capitalism causes to the environment and it organizes society (mode of organization) through the commune system. The principles discussed are fundamental in that they bring together the notions of direct democracy, ecology, feminism and communal forms of organization.

Within the framework provided, then, Turkey is quite obviously a nation state that epitomizes a capitalist modernity. Furthermore, it is based on a clear hierarchal, bureaucratic and centralist structure which by nature doesn't allow Öcalan's democratic modernity. It is within this context that the question is asked: How then can a society, or for the case under consideration the Kurds, formulate their political will (self-ruling and self-organizing) within the context of democratic modernity in Turkey? In particular, on what social, political and legal terms and bases can the Kurds develop relationships with the state, while at the same time constructing democratic autonomy under the paradigm of democratic modernity? Öcalan acknowledges the hurdle, and argues that, first of all, the state should obtain a democratic character and avoid relying on any particular nation. Thus, in order for democratic autonomy to be established, the state should democratize, in other words become a democratic republic, and it should rely on the idea of becoming a multi-nation, namely democratic nation.

Democratic republic and democratic nation

Understanding the prerequisites for building democratic autonomy, Öcalan acknowledges the barriers for the establishment of such a political system in nation state. Despite refuting the idea of a nation state, democratic autonomy is pragmatic in that it is not trying to remove or enact resistance against any existing nation states. At this point, democratic autonomy deems democratization of the Turkish state, or construction of a democratic republic, as the only and most relevant way for the solution to bring about the practising of democratic autonomy. It is from this perspective that democratic autonomy 'is neither a state-building nor a state-destroying project' (Draft Submission for a Democratic Autonomous Kurdistan 2011, 17). Therefore, democratic autonomy has no intention of closing its doors to nation states, but instead claims that democratic autonomy and nation state can actually compromise and act together over principled grounds. But this sort of interaction is subject to the basis that Turkey is democratized, which means the transformation of the existing state into a democratic republic. This transformation is crucial, since the existence of a democratic autonomy will unavoidably come into direct conflict with an existing nation state structure. Considering a nation state's centralist and identity-based nature, the two models would not be compatible. Thus, by separating the republic from the nation state, Öcalan considers the former more adoptable, and more open to differences and to democracy (Öcalan 2013c, 212–15). Democratic autonomy here aims to sensitize the state to democracy and transform it into a democratic republic, and thus make it more adoptable for the construction of a democratic autonomy (Draft Submission for a Democratic Autonomous Kurdistan 2011). With a democratic republic, diverse identities could develop a relationship and compromise with the central authority through mutual consent (Öcalan 2013b, 245–46). This is because, in comparison to the nation state, which practises and articulates a particular identity where members are forced to identify with it (Öcalan 2013c, 87), a democratic republic will refuse to affiliate itself with a particular culture, ethnicity, religion and/or identity. Becoming a democratic republic therefore assumes the transitioning between a state's centralist structure through decentralization into a more horizontal organizational structure (Jongerden 2017, 253). A democratic republic in this context implies the state's reliance on a multi-national understanding, and, based on this, Öcalan here offers the concept democratic nation, which is crucial to democratic autonomy.

The most fundamental nature of democratic autonomy (as will be argued later) is that it is multinational, and is thereby formulated as a democratic nation within the context of a democratic republic. The concept of democratic nation in this regard does not refer to a particular ethnicity. Highlighting this, Öcalan specifies his view of a nation by saying, 'I suggest that we understand nation only as another term for country and that we separate it from any ethnic connotations' (Öcalan 2011b, 79). From this perspective, a democratic nation recognizes all ethnic, religious and linguistic groups' identities as equal within the idea of citizenship. Democratic nation in this regard is not 'defined on the basis of ethnicity or language but on the basis of citizenship in a democratic republic' (Akkaya and Jongerden 2012, 5), which shows similarities with Ernest Renan's definition of a nation in which he harshly objects to using territorial and ethnographic affinities as a basis or component for defining a nation (Renan 2004, 32–36). The most coherent way of visualizing a democratic nation is therefore that it is seen as a roof nation.

Öcalan highlights the benefit of a democratic nation, which is that 'a nationhood brings unity'. Consequently, individuals living in a democratic nation are able to truly express their individual and collective rights, which as result complement one another (Öcalan 2012a, 17–20). A democratic nation is in position to manage and construct peaceful affiliations between varied groups, which thus prevents the domination of one nation over the others (Serxwebûn (July) 2011, 9–10). The following principles are regarded as the nine dimensions of a democratic nation. Since democratic confederalism is the organizational form of a democratic nation, there are some overlaps between the two ideas.

- *The free individual-citizen and democratic communal life:* this dimension emphasizes that a democratic nation relies on the idea of free individual citizenship and communal life. The latter challenges the liberalist notion of individualism, which instead considers individual freedoms to be 'freedom in the communality of society'. By emphasizing that 'without a commune or communal life, the individual cannot be fully realized', a democratic nation gives primary importance to the collective aspects of society.
- *Political life and democratic autonomy:* this dimension emphasizes the need for the construction of political society in line with its moral values, which could be acquired through democratic autonomy.
- *Social life:* this dimension emphasizes the transformation of society through a democratic nation. Capitalism tends to exert policies that destroy society and aspects of society, whether it be education, gender or any other social issue policy. A democratic nation aims to restore this imbalance by emphasizing society's and individuals' freedoms.
- *Free partner life:* moving on to the personal and collective aspects of quality of life, this dimension puts significance on the construction of a free life, with particular attention given to gender equality.

- *Economic autonomy:* having discussed the detrimental impact of capitalism earlier, this dimension emphasizes the minimizing of capitalist profit, accumulation and the presence of capitalist hegemony in the market.
- *Legal structure:* this implies the application of democratic laws which rely on the principles of diversity.
- *Culture:* this relies on cultural pluralism and the idea of co-existence.
- *Self-defence:* this dimension refers to the formation of local armed forces for the limited purpose of protecting the existence of the society within the context of the democratic nation.
- *Diplomacy:* the formation of common platforms among the Kurds, and between them and other nations. The diplomacy of a democratic nation relies on peace and solidary (Öcalan 2016, 32–59).

In connection to these principles, Öcalan makes the link between a democratic nation and a democratic autonomy, saying, 'when a democratic nation is the soul then democratic autonomy is the body' (ANF News 2010). Hence, democratic autonomy becomes the main body for the construction of a democratic nation in a democratic republic.

Democratic autonomy: Main pillars

Democratic autonomy is the concept used to define the status of the Kurds in the light of the democratic modernity paradigm. The model is a non-state-aimed social and political paradigm that rests on the development of interactions both among the Kurds and between the Kurds and the state. These interactions include the development of social, cultural, economic and political interactions, while avoiding territorial border changes (Bilim Aydınlanma Komitesi 2009; Öcalan 2011a, 33–34). The model precisely defines the type of relationship (particularly at the legal and political levels) that it wishes to enact with the state (Akkaya and Jongerden 2012, 7). Based on this understanding of democratic autonomy, Öcalan argues for the right to self-determination, but not within the traditional context of territorial self-determination and establishing a Kurdish nation state. Criticizing Lenin's concept of self-determination, who conceptualized it within the framework of state formation (Lenin 1998), Öcalan equates the right to self-determination with the formation of the Kurds' own democracy and non-territorial self-rule in a decentralized political system reflecting that of a democratic republic (Jongerden 2017, 246–55).

Democratic autonomy and a republic work in parallel with each other insofar as a citizen would be a part of both the republic and a democratic autonomous region. In this regard, democratic autonomy argues for a new type of citizenship. Organizing society in the form of democratic confederalism's bottom-up structure, democratic autonomy offers participant citizenship within the idea of radical democracy (Gürer 2015). Thus within the idea of participant citizenship, democratic autonomy signifies the Kurds' status and the type of relationship they would formulate with the state. In the context provided, democratic autonomy is established through eight main dimensions: political, legal, self-defence, social, economic, cultural, ecological and diplomatic.

Political dimension recognizes the priority of the political status of Kurds' collective rights, which aims to secure their national status. This is very important, since democratic autonomy claims it is capable of projecting the Kurdish issue as a national issue. By this very logic, democratic autonomy opposes the narrow focus on individual and cultural rights alone, and therefore projecting the issue nationally allows for the recognition of Kurds' collective rights and national status without drawing ethnic-territorial boundaries (Akat Ata 2012; Draft Submission for a Democratic Autonomous Kurdistan 2011, 18–21; Ersanli and Bayhan 2012, 204).

Thus, the formulation of a political dimension implies that Kurds will be free to self-govern themselves wherever they live in Turkey. For this to occur, Turkey would have to be administratively restructured into 20–25 regions (Serxwebun 2011, 4; Yeğen 2011, 96). Öcalan proposes the establishment of twenty-five provinces in autonomous regions, where seven of these regions will be established as Kurdish, with the remaining eighteen regions belonging to the rest of Turkey. Each region will be allocated its own local parliament, in a similar fashion to the system carried out in Germany (Kapmaz 2010, 316). Each province would therefore establish its own assembly comprising local people, to ensure that all aspects of the decision-making process involve the participation of the people. The Kurds, namely the DTK, have actually established this model in Diyarbakır city, which is composed of a local parliament representing the Kurds and other groups in Kurdish areas.

Legal dimension provides assurance that the Kurds' political status is constitutional. By providing that the system of democratic autonomy has legal status, it provides Kurds with a guaranteed protection of their rights and status on a constitutional basis. Furthermore, Kurds are provided with an assurance of their rights and political status within the context of international laws (Draft Submission for a Democratic Autonomous Kurdistan 2011, 21–24).

Self-defence dimension is the most contentious dimension presented by a democratic autonomy. Since armed forces have become so vitally imbedded within the conception of a nation state, it propagates feelings of uneasiness. This is due to the fact that any armed force has the potential to lead a group, and thereby declare its independence, in the right conditions. The acquisition of armed forces also bears the question: what kind of character does a democratic authority wish to externalize, and would it impede its characteristics as a soft power? Despite these concerns, self-defence is regarded as necessary for the protection of a society's physical, moral and political values in democratic autonomy. Self-defence in this instance does not necessarily imply the existence of an army, as it does with a nation state. Recognizing that any sort of means of physical protection will be used within a defensive context is important in articulating the principles of democratic autonomy. The organization of this defence will, for example, vastly differ from the centralized, state-controlled army used by nation states. In this regard, all villages, towns and cities will have the opportunity to act in self-defence in response to threats, such as the formation of local people's defence forces (Draft Submission for a Democratic Autonomous Kurdistan 2011, 24–25).

Cultural dimension concerns itself with the preservation and protection of the Kurds' historical, cultural and artistic values. This dimension primarily concerns itself with the identity of the Kurds. Alongside the Turkish language, Kurds wish for the Kurdish language to be encouraged in education and recognized as an official language in places where Kurds flourish. In addition to this, it requests that original Kurdish region names (which have been replaced with Turkish names) and Kurdish symbols be returned, including their flags, colours, customs and anthems (Draft Submission for a Democratic Autonomous Kurdistan 2011, 25–27).

Social dimension is concerned with building organizations that represent the people on multiple levels. These organizations can, for example, be city, town and village councils, and also assemblies among various classes, such as the democratic workers congress and democratic women and youth organizations (Draft Submission for a Democratic Autonomous Kurdistan 2011, 28–31). Democratic autonomy places particular importance on women's issues. Under this model, women will be able to hold the power to create independent organizations, as well as own their own armed forces, as formulated by the Women's Liberation Movement in Syria and in the PKK. The latter implies that men seemingly dominate any type of organization, and so to ensure the prevention of oppression against women, women will be able to protect themselves from internal and external threats.

Economic dimension seeks to create a self-sufficient economic system, emphasizing that people should have authority over their tax collection and their overground and underground resources (Draft Submission for a Democratic Autonomous Kurdistan 2011, 31–34). The main aim behind the economic dimension is to promote an economic system that is self-sufficient, thereby eradicating the need to rely on the state. Furthermore, it aims to prevent the establishment of a monopoly over the economic market.

Ecological dimension prioritizes an overlooked aspect of society, that being the environment. Unlike a nation state, a democratic autonomy would prioritize the conservation of nature. For instance, it would challenge the expansion and the construction of dams, which are considered harmful to surrounding wildlife (Draft Submission for a Democratic Autonomous Kurdistan 2011, 34–36). In addition, it would challenge the construction of unplanned urbanization.

Lastly, *diplomatic dimension* concerns itself with providing the institutional space for Kurds to manage their affairs at the regional and international level (Draft Submission for a Democratic Autonomous Kurdistan 2011, 37–38). Through the use of institutions and committees, democratic autonomy aims to aid the development of relationships between Kurds in all nations, namely Turkey, Iraq, Syria and Iran.

Taking a closer look at the logistics of a democratic autonomy operating in a new state structure (that being a democratic republic), delegation of authority would be divided between the central state and regional autonomies. By this division of power, the central state will be in control of matters concerning foreign affairs, defence and treasury issues. Autonomous regions, on the other hand, will concern themselves with the domestic politics of the region, such as the maintenance of local education, sport, tourism, cultural and social issues, public improvements, social insurance, and issues concerning women's rights. (Özer 2009, 710–11). Identified as a model that provides further decentralization of power, the state's role in everyday domestic affairs will be reduced significantly, while the capacity of the people to make political decisions will increase (Draft Submission for a Democratic Autonomous Kurdistan 2011, 15–16). Precisely summarized, a democratic autonomy focuses on 'less state (and) more society' (Serxwebûn (October) 2010, 9) within the context of democratic self-governance and self-organization.

Having outlined the details of a democratic autonomy, one may raise the question of whether a democratic autonomy could possibly be considered within a territorial autonomy framework. There are some significant overlaps between the two models, which could suggest that they are compatible to some extent.

In particular, when looking at the formation of a regional parliament, creation of regional/local security forces, collection of tax, establishment of international diplomatic committees and demands for self-governance, it does seem possible for a democratic autonomy to exist within the confines of an ethnic territorial autonomy framework. Despite this, when comparing the criteria for a democratic autonomy model (as listed above) with those for ethnic territorial political models, there are significant differences across most major aspects. Democratic autonomy's ambition to restructure Turkey into 20–25 regions, regardless of ethnic concentrations, highlights the extent of these dissimilarities. Contrary to ethnic territorial political models, democratic autonomy seeks to distance itself from the idea of affiliating with or representing a particular ethnicity. A democratic nation's refusal to rely on a particular ethnicity greatly contributes to this idea.

Cultural rights

Culture in a broad sense can be defined as a 'collective cast of mind', a set of norms and values with close connection to the term 'identity' (Kupper 1999, 227–37), particularly in the context of ethnicity and nationality (Gurr 1994, 348). The strong connection between culture and identity greatly influences and comprises the collective of a group (Cole 2014). The term 'culture' in this regard implies the collective beliefs and ideas of a particular group or society, taking the following characteristics into consideration: language, tradition, conventions, customs, faith and lifestyles (Abercrombie, Hill and Turner 2006, 92–93). Its close links with society have resulted in many seeing culture and society as complementary (Friedman 1994, 68).

Although the notion of culture subordinates various disciplines in the literature, a significant use of it is through the term 'right'. With reference to this, culture has been regarded as equating to people's substantial rights (Cowan, Dembour and Wilson 2001, 2–4), but it was not considered as such for a long period because many feared that culture could initiate separatist political claims among minorities. Cultural rights, therefore, were formally first accepted in 1966, to some extent similar to the concept of human rights (Robbins and Stamatopoulou 2004, 427).

The focus on culture and cultural rights grew as tensions began to escalate because minority groups collectively made claims to protect, practise and manifest their cultural values (Robbins and Stamatopoulou 2004). Cultural rights therefore offer a level of satisfaction to minority groups by recognizing their cultural identity and, consequently, resolving the dispute between them and the central state (Kymlicka 1995). Weighing up cultural rights in this sense, Sancar, reflecting on the previous considerations, relates cultural rights to the political and legal recognition of minorities (Sancar 2011, 24). Gellner (2001, 177) adds to this by explaining that cultural rights seek to protect variations in society and reach 'political and economic resources on the basis of cultural difference'.

Examining cultural rights in the light of the above discussions, it is evident that the principal objective is to protect and respect differences in society. Recognition of cultural rights is wholly based on the protection of minorities' values within a majority culture. And with this aim, cultural rights are focused on even more, and tackled as a 'human rights' issue as the hostility between minority groups and the central state heats up; and as a result, cultural rights are a priority of many international covenants (Symonides 1998). The United Nations Educational, Scientific, and Cultural Organization (UNESCO) was the first among these organizations. It highlighted cultural rights in its 2001 conference and declaration. Article (4) mentions 'cultural diversity (as) an ethical imperative, inseparable from respect for human dignity', and Article (5) declares that 'cultural rights are an integral part of human rights, which are universal, indivisible and interdependent' (UNESCO 2002). As a general rule, cultural rights are identified as a 'unified arrangement of practices and meanings'(Cowan, Dembour and Wilson 2001, 8). Nonetheless, despite such attention paid to cultural rights they are mainly dealt with at the individual level, and most international covenants,[3] and states are reluctant to recognize them at the collective level (Hamelink 2003, 7).

Reluctance to consider cultural rights at the collective level brings up the question of whether cultural rights should be recognized at the individual level or group level and brought to the forefront. According to Wall, collective rights imply further 'power', 'immunity' and 'liberty' for a group of people. Wall uses three perspectives to define collective rights under his three factors. First, there are collective rights or factors concerning the interests of more than one person. Secondly, he considers collective rights as a political fact that requires the right of power over a specific region. Finally, also relating to the second point, Wall associates collective rights with the notion of territory and the demand to manage the 'public environment'. Thus, he emphasizes that 'collective autonomy rights, then, are genuine collective rights and not mere shadows of individual rights of freedom of association' (Wall 2007, 236–38). Levey also widely discusses the notions of individual and collective rights. Levey classifies cultural rights as either personal (individual) or collective (group); personal cultural rights seek to provide freedom for individual autonomy, while collective (corporate) cultural rights relate to collectivity and acknowledgement of political autonomy (Levey 1997, 237–38). Given the deliberations on individual and collective rights, Will Kymlicka develops a different standpoint, and states that collective rights are extensive and 'so unhelpful as a label for the various forms of group-differentiated citizenship' (Kymlicka 1995, 45). Kymlicka therefore examines minorities' rights through freedom for individual autonomy (Kymlicka 1995).

2

Kurdish Identity

Ethnicity, as one of the main social and societal units, is one of the principal sources of identification. Especially with the formation of the nation state, ethnic identity became a source of power for solidarity and self-identification in social and political relations, and so resolving traditional and existing feudal socio-cultural affinities (Parsons 1975). Ethnicity starts to work as a unifying element among the group members and for building a sense of collectivity (Melucci 1996). Thus, contrary to arguments stating that ethnicity would lose its importance, as Bell (1975, 169–71) highlights, ethnicity has in fact become one of the key determinant factors in clarifying social and political relations.

Despite its growing importance, ethnicity is still one of the most contentious notions in social science (Enloe 1996). There are several ethnicity theories; however, the two contradictory views, primordialism and social constructionism (instrumentalism), have substantial weight in the literature (Somersan 2008, 75). The primordialist approach focuses on the ideas of birth and genesis. Primordialism considers ethnicity through kinship, with a particular emphasis on biology (Van Den Berghe 2005). According to this approach, ethnic affinities are, therefore, not chosen but given at birth (Geertz 1996; Grosby 2005; Isaacs 1975). Unlike primordialism, instrumentalism considers ethnicity as a socially constructed fact, and its boundaries are subject to change with the course of events (Keating 1997, 690). Instrumentalism thus rejects genetics and blood affinities as contributors of ethnicity, and emphasizes that ethnic identity is not a rigid or static phenomenon, but rather is socially constructed and has permeable boundaries (Brass 1996). Despite an ongoing discussion on its nature and development processes, ethnicity in a broad context can be identified through a shared name, culture, language, ancestry, myths, symbols, solidarity, history and, in some instances, territory (Hutchinson 1996, 6).

Ethic identity is determinant in the construction of the social and political reactions within Kurds; aware of this, the chapter frames Kurdish ethnic identity through its main components.

Two nationalist approaches to the Kurds

The Kurds were unable to form their own state when the notion of nation states began to be exercised in the modern period. The disintegration of the Ottoman Empire further fragmented the Kurds, and consequently they were ruled by four neighbouring countries, Turkey, Iraq, Iran and Syria, and experienced severe fragmentation and assimilation. They were prohibited from writing their own history; instead it was either completely denied or written by the powers who dominated them for a long time (Aksoy 1996). Discussion of the Kurds in this regard was dominated by the ruling states' ideological stance for a long time. Therefore, despite the recent academic focus, the Kurds were mostly considered only in a political sense for a long time, which brings the terms 'Kurds' and 'Kurdistan' into discussion.

The arguments relating to the Kurds, including their history, territory and ethnic origin (descent), can therefore be classified into two groups in Turkey. Both groups' views show clear differences from one another. The first argument relies on the state's official ideology, such as *Türk Tarih Tezi* (Turkish History Thesis)[1] and the *Güneş Dil Teorisi* (Sun Language Theory)[2]; these arguments refuse to recognize the ethnic identity of the Kurds, since they consider the Kurds to be of Turkish origin (see Yilmaz and Akagündüz 2011). This state-ideology-based approach tried to disassociate the notions of Kurds and Kurdistan from the Kurds' ethnic connotations. They strongly maintain the idea that, historically, the terms 'Kurds' and 'Kurdistan' either did not exist or were not used in relation to the Kurdish ethnicity. The main objective was to remove the central constituents of the Kurdish ethnic identity, in line with their policy of denying Kurdish ethnicity. Turkish official ideology therefore started to use propaganda to convince the Kurds that they are of Turkish origin – this became state policy for decades (Kürdoloji Çalışmaları Gurubu 2011, 93). Most Turkish scholars share the state ideology, published in many books and articles in support of this argument. These studies consider the Kurds to be subsumed within the Turkish identity, or as proto-Turks (see Seferoğlu and Türközü 1982).

This argument still generates interests among some Turkish scholars; however, with the PKK's struggle, and also the emergence of academic studies on the

Kurds, especially since the 1990s, among Western scholars, it has lost ground at the state level. The overwhelming majority of studies accept the diversity of the Kurds' ethnic identity. Nonetheless, the first argument provoked some not only to counter it, but also to oppose the nationalist agreements among some Kurdish nationalists in their approach to the Kurds. The Kurdish nationalist argument rejects all aspects of the Turkish state-ideology-based standpoints regarding the Kurds, and has developed a nationalist viewpoint on the Kurds. They consider the Kurds mostly through primordial affinities, with a strong reference to the notions of history, territorial concentration, and blood-based lineages and affinities (O'Shea 2004, 129; Vali 2005, 84–87). Highlighting the role that history (Cohen 2004, 88), territory (Aktoprak 2010, 23–24) and lineage play in the construction of ethnic identity (Kedourie 2004a, 104–6), Kurdish nationalists regard these constituents to be decisive in their approach, and to defining the Kurds (O'Shea 2004, 163). In such a nationalist and primordial reading, the Kurds are regarded as an ethnic community, with their current history dating back to the ancient period (see Bender 1991; Bois 1966, 10–11; Ekrem Cemil Paşa 1995; Meho 1997). The Lulu, Guti, Elam and Kassite clans of the time (present in the BC period) are thought to be the ancestors of the Kurds (see Bois 1966, 1–11; Ekrem Cemil Paşa 1995). The Kurdish nationalists' approach to the Kurds in this regard mostly relies on nationalist perspectives rather than verified data (O'Shea 2004, 56–57). Such a view, in other words, as Hirschler says, is an inverted copy of the *Turk Tarih Tezi* that was explained earlier, contrary to proven and reliable facts based on a Turkish nationalist narrative and state ideology (Hirschler 2001, 150). As Özoğlu (1996, 8–9) rightly argues, the existing literature does not provide reliable and sufficient data for relating Kurdish history to BC. Therefore, like Turkish nationalists and the state's official ideology, Kurdish nationalists' claim also could not generate sufficient interest.

History, Kurds and Kurdistan

Putting aside discussions on the Kurds' ethnic origin and ancient period history, Arabs have been found to be one of the first nations to have used the term 'Kurds', back in the seventh century (Minorsky, Bois and Mac Kenzie 2004, 11). Upon converting to Islam, the Kurds interacted more closely with Arabs. As a method of identification Arabs named the Kurds *Ekrad*, so it was easier to distinguish between the Kurds and Arabs. The use of the name *Ekrad* is a clear indication that boundaries between the two communities were present. However, as notions such as ethnicity and ethnic consciousness were not commonplace at the time, and as tribal affinities and religion were the two dominant forms of identification, it still remains unclear as to whether Arabs used *Ekrad* in an ethnic sense or to define the Kurds as a separate ethnic group (Burkay 1992, 47). Arabs used the name *Ekrad* for a long time, yet the Kurds' other neighbours mostly used the name Kurds – albeit not with an ethnic sense until the nineteenth century.

Like the term 'Kurds', discussion of the name Kurdistan also varies, especially on whether it hints at any ethnic connotations since the use of the term *Ekrad*. Data from previous researches indicates that neither the Kurds nor the authorities with which they interacted mentioned the term 'Kurdistan' for a long time. Despite the prevalent use of the term 'Kurds' in history, the Kurdish region (presently known as Kurdistan) was not referred to or named as such for a very long time. The name 'Kurdistan' was first notably used by the Seljuk sultan, Sanjar, in the twelfth century (McDowal 2004, 6). However, as with the term 'Kurds', there remains some uncertainty as to whether the use of Kurdistan during that period had an ethnic connotation. Izady indicates that the label 'Kurdistan' was used within an administrative context in the Seljuk period (Izady 2004, 109). In support of this, Bazil Nikitin also proposes that the notion of Kurdistan initially appeared in the Seljuk period, and like Izady, he too contests that there was an ethnic association in its use. Instead, to Nikitin, the Seljuks used Kurdistan as a geographic definition. To further strengthen this argument, Nikitin also underlines that there was a huge distinction between the Kurds' boundaries during the Seljuk period, the Ottoman Empire and modern state as it is today. Therefore, he states that the ethnic definition of the Kurds might not have coincided with the region labelled Kurdistan throughout history, since the Kurds' ethnic proliferation shows differences (Nikitin 1994, 56–58).

Considering the overwhelming dominance of tribal affinities and religion in the determination of the Kurds' social and political relationships until the late nineteenth century, Nikitin's and Izady's explanations provide relevant grounds for saying that the term 'Kurdistan', rather than having ethnic connotations, was mostly used in a geographic and administrative sense. On the other hand, use of the term 'Kurdistan', either in an administrative or geographical context, most probably covered many of the areas home to Kurdish tribes of the time, especially when considering the Kurds' divided tribal structure. However, there is further evidence to say that, although it was not used in a directly ethnic sense, the term 'Kurdistan' implies more than a geographical identification. Looking at the contextual-based discussions made on the term 'Kurdistan', James highlights that the Kurdistan entity was used for 'more than one reality and social representation', such as life-styles (nomadic-settled) and different social statuses, in medieval times (James 2011, 63).

Following the Seljuk period, the terms 'Kurds' and 'Kurdistan' once again appeared, during the Ottoman Empire. Ottoman authorities used the name 'Kurds' to identify Kurdish-speaking nomadic and settled tribes (McDowall 2004, 13). Making reference to language in identifying a group is without doubt important when understanding its ethnic identity – although it is not a sufficient condition by itself. Therefore, although the use of the Kurdish language as a method of identifying the Kurds is significant, the Ottoman rulers continued to dismiss the term 'Kurds' in an ethnic sense (McDowall 2004, 13). In the Ottoman Empire, Kurdistan was also used in a geographic sense. In 1847, the Ottoman Empire named the Kurdish region Kurdistan (*Kurdistan eyaleti* – Kurdistan Province) (Kürdoloji Çalışmaları Gurubu 2011, 93–99). Despite the limited number of sources regarding the Kurds in the Ottoman Empire, the emir of Bitlis, Sharafkhan (1543–1604) wrote a text called *Sharafname* in 1597, one of the first and most reliable sources regarding the Kurds and Kurdish history. In *Sharafname* he uses both terms 'Kurds' and 'Kurdistan' widely, and gives extended details about Kurdish history by mentioning famous Kurdish leaders, dynasties and tribes. He puts especial emphasis on Kurdish culture and collective identity, and associates them with the term 'Kurdistan' (Şerefkhan (*Sharafname*) 2006). From this point forth, it seems safe to say that despite the Ottoman authorities' use of the term in a non-ethnic sense, Sharafkhan builds links between Kurdish culture, history and the term 'Kurdistan'. This was further extended by the Kurdish philosopher Ehmedê Xanî, who used the terms 'Kurds' and 'Kurdistan' in the sixteenth century to define a diverse ethno-national group. In his acclaimed book *Mem û Zîn* (1695), Xani highlights the political status of the Kurds and notes their diversity and distinctiveness from neighbouring countries (Ehmedê Xanî 1990).

On the other hand, despite ongoing discussion on the meaning that the terms 'Kurds' and 'Kurdistan' implied, before and during the early modern period, it would not be wrong to say that territorial and historical consciousness made a significant contribution to the occurrence of Kurdish ethnic awareness. Loyalty to a specific part of a territory has been shown as making a massive contribution to the development of Kurdish collectiveness. Territorial consciousness in this regard became decisive in the development of Kurdish ethnic identity and also the Kurdish national movement (Romano 2010, 20). Territory's influence on Kurdish ethnicity became particularly prominent when associated with the notion of history. Especially within Kurdish nationalist literature and a primordial reading of Kurdish ethnicity, territory and history are considered to be two key factors in its construction and continuation as we have seen (see Bender 1991; Meho 1997, 7). Historical and territory hence contribute to Kurdish ethnic identity awareness.

Kurdish language

Language, as one of the key elements in ethnic and national identification, is significant in drawing ethno-national Kurdish identity boundaries. The Kurdish language, however, is not homogeneous, and this, as revealed through the fieldwork, influences the variations and markings of language within Kurdish cultural boundaries. Kurdish language, which includes various dialects, is a branch of Iranian and belongs to the Indo-European language family (Blau 1996, 20). The sheer volume of dialects has been a subject of many discussions. This has also raised the question of whether each of these dialects can be regarded as an independent language. This became far more important given that some internal Kurdish groups, especially the Zaza, consider language and/dialectical differences as a condition for being identified as a separate ethnic identity, or as non-Kurdish.

Mehrdad R. Izady divides the Kurdish language into two groups, Kurmanji and Pehlewani, in a wider context. In Izady's classification, Kurmanji also branches into two dialects, North Kurmanji (*Bahdinani*) and South Kurmanji (*Sorani*). North Kurmanji is common among the Kurds who live in eastern parts of Turkey and western parts of the Iraqi Kurdistan region. South Kurmanji, on the other hand, is mostly spoken in the city of Sulaymaniyah of the Iraqi Kurdistan region, and by some of the Kurds settled in Iran (Izady 2004, 299–307). Izady highlights that, like Kurmanji, Pehlewani also comprises two dialects, Zazaki (*Dimilki*) and Gurani. Zazaki is prevalent in the cities of Tunceli, Adiyaman, Bingol and Elazig, and in some areas of Bitlis and Diyarbakır in Turkey. Gurani, on the other hand, is widely spoken by Kurds who reside in Iraq and Iran (Izady 2004, 307–8). Similar to this, Van Bruinessen (1992, 27) suggests that the Kurdish language actually consists of four dialects: Kurmanji, Zazaki, Sorani and Gurani.

In addition to classifying these dialects, there is also a high degree of dispute on whether they should be considered within the Kurdish language or as independent languages, which became significant when drawing up Kurdish cultural boundaries. Discussing this point, Minorsky (1988, 74–75) indicates that the Kurdish dialects Zazaki, Sorani and Gurani vary from one another. In light of these questions, some, including Hassanpour (1997) and Aristova (2002, 26–27), have analysed these differentiations as being within language variation (i.e. dialectical differences). However, others, especially Turkish scholars, for example Çay (2010, 167–88), do not consider the Kurdish language and its dialects as a language at all. However, Ziya Gökhalp, one of the first scholars to focus on the Kurdish language, also looking at this issue, indicates that variances between Kurdish dialects are sufficient to identify them as independent languages. In other words, Gökhalp considers Kurdish dialects as independent languages and not parts or dialects of Kurdish (Gökhalp 2011, 30). This is an important point when considering the identification of individuals who separate themselves from Kurdish ethnicity – they refer to their dialect as an independent language, especially in the case of the Zaza. Presently, some Zaza identify themselves as a distinct ethnic group by specifically mentioning their separate language, *Zazaki* (Mutlu 1996, 519).

Despite such variations, the Kurdish language makes a prominent contribution to the formation and influence of the Kurdish identity. Being different from their neighbour nations' language, the Kurdish language has become one of the causative elements in the establishment of ethno-cultural boundaries between the Kurds and the surrounding nations since the sixteenth century (Sheyholislami 2010, 290). This influential role played by the Kurdish language, according to Blau (2006), has become greater throughout the modern period, and is a critical factor in identifying the Kurdish ethnic identity. The Kurdish language has contributed to the development of the Kurdish ethnic and cultural identity in various ways. As highlighted by Amir Hassanpour, the Kurdish language's influence on Kurdish culture and literature here has been decisive. In agreement with Hassanpour, the Kurdish philosopher Ehmedê Xanî (1650–1707) and the Kurdish poet Hacî Qadrî Koyî (1816–94) had long shown interest in the Kurdish language itself, and by relating it to the development of Kurdish identity in literature they had clearly illustrated the contribution of Kurdish language to identity. Xanî, in his famous book Mem û Zîn (1695), and Hacî Qadrî Koyî, through his poems, attempted to identify the Kurds and establish their political rights through the Kurdish language. They stated the importance of language in the identification of the Kurds as a separate ethnic group (Hassanpour 2005, 147–74). Ehmedê Xanî in particular made use of the Kurdish language in an ethnic sense and regarded it as a significant element in determining Kurdish ethnicity (Blau 2006, 105). Hence, despite dialectical variation from within, language has a prominent role to play in the construction of Kurdish ethnic identity. The importance of language in this became far more prominent at the beginning of the twentieth century and thereafter.

Religion and the Kurds

The Kurds in general are known for their religiosity. Since converting to Islam, religion has turned into a determinant dynamic in their social and political affairs. Religion has thus contributed to their social and cultural development and influenced their ethno-cultural identity, especially during the time of the Ottoman Empire and the early decades of the Republic (Kamal 2001). Particularly during the late Ottoman period, religion became decisive in building Kurdish consciousness in reaction to Armenian nationalism and missionary activities (Bozarslan 2002, 844–45; Yavuz 2001, 5).

The Kurds follow the Sunni school of Islam, which is common among many Middle Eastern communities. Consequently, religion may not serve as a contributory condition for determining ethno-national boundaries between different societies. However, as the majority of the Sunni Kurds pray according to the Shafi (Şafilik) school of jurisprudence, which differs from other laws of Islam such as the Maliki, Hanbali and Hanafi Schools of Jurisprudences, following the Shafi school 'contributes to a sense of Kurdish identity', since it draws boundaries between the Kurds and the others to some extent (Kreyenbroek 1996, 93). Combining such judicial variances together with Kurdish culture allows us to talk about Kurdish Islam to some extent. Kurdish Islam's nature displays the extent of its difference from the other Islamic understandings of the Muslim world. Having a separate culture could be regarded as an influential dynamic in the emergence of such differences; this contributes to the shaping of the Kurdish identity when compared to other groups. Making reference to this, Acker holds Kurdish Islam's 'syncretistic nature and incorporation of elements from older cults' responsible for its influence on Kurdish identity, which to Acker shows clear differences from other Islamic communities (Acker 2004, 101). Thus, despite sharing a common religion with many Middle Eastern communities, the distinct religious school they follow, the Kurdish culture and the resultant religious nature that defines them suggest that religion has contributed to the construction of Kurdish identity in some Kurds. However, as the following explanations reveal, their religious beliefs are not uniform, and the fact that they follow different religious forms with different *maddhabs*/denominations has had a destructive impact on some Kurds and Kurdish identity, as this has prevented unity between them.

Kurds in general follow various beliefs and religions. These may be categorized under four headings: Orthodox Sunni Islam, Heterodox Alevism, Yazidi and A/ Ehli Haq beliefs; these will be explained in relation to their interaction with and or influence on Kurdish identity respectively.

The lack of reliable and official facts regarding the Kurds' different religions makes tracing their religious map rather difficult. However, it is estimated that nearly two-thirds of Kurds are Orthodox Sunni (Andrews 1992, 153). Religion, particularly with Sunni Kurds, has tended to be organized through Sheiks and tariqas for a long time. The most popular tariqas who have been most well-organized within the Kurds are Qadiriyya and Naqshbandi (Kreyenbroek 1996, 95). Qadiriyya tariqa was established in Baghdad in the twelfth century by Abd al-Qadir al-Jilani (1077–1166), and by the fifteenth century had spread throughout the Middle East (Mojuetan 2005, 7). Another tariqa, Naqshbandi, is prevalent in the Middle East. Even though its origin may date back further, Naqshbandi obtained its central orders from Kawaja Bahu-ud Din Naqshbandi (1318–89) in the fourteenth century, and was passed on to succeeding generations by the tariqa's Sheiks and Caliphs (Gunter 2009, 141; Zelkina 2000, 80). Naqshbandi tariqa is largely popular among Middle Eastern Muslim communities, and even more so with the Kurds. The tariqa was introduced to the Middle East in the early nineteenth century by Mawlana Khalid, a Kurdish Sufi (White 2012, 52–53). Soon after its introduction to Ottoman lands, the tariqa was met with considerable interest by the Kurds. Even many of Qadiriyya sheiks converted to Naqshbandi tariqa, and some of them led the later Kurdish rebellions. Van Bruinessen explains Naqshbandi tariqa's popularity among the Kurds, first with reference to Khalid's Kurdish origin, and second because of the many Kurdish religious authorities he assigned, such as Sheiks, as Caliphs (Van Bruinessen 2000a, 26).

Soon after finding a place among the Kurds, both tariqas, especially Naqshbandi, have been an influential force on Kurdish society. Likewise, the Sheiks's supra-tribal identity and success mediating between Kurdish tribes and handling conflicts, and the traditional respect for religion already present among the majority of Kurds, confirmed them as political leaders, along with the religious authority they gained following the elimination of the Kurdish Emirates (Bulut 2009, 339–40; McDowal 1992, 12; Natali 2009, 42). Thus, with their new-found political leadership and religious power they strengthened their control of the Kurdish communities (Taşpınar 2005, 70). In the late nineteenth century, Kurdish Sheiks led many of the ethno-national Kurdish rebellions. The rebellions of Sheik Ubeydullah in 1882, Sheik Sait's rebellion in 1925 (see Olson 1992), Sheik Mahmoud Berzenci's rebellions over the period 1918–30 (see Hilmi 1995) and Mullah Mustafa Barzan's rebellion continued for decades, and are the most well-known Sheik-led Kurdish rebellions (see Jwaideh 1999). Sheiks were successful in gathering masses to fight for a common political claim. Their religious authority was an obvious cause of their success, and reason behind the construction of a common political demand among the Kurds. Religion (especially the Sunni school of Islam), through the use of religious figures, has therefore been highly influential in Kurdish politics (Van Bruinessen 2000b, 25) and Kurdish identity (Bozarslan 2002, 844–45).

Alevism (*Alevilik*) is the second widespread belief among the Kurds (the Kurdish Alevis). Alevis broadly name their belief Alevism (*Alevilik*), which in essence is of Anatolian origin and has strong historical roots (Kıeser 2001, 89). Alevism has a broad use, not only because of its variations but also due to the differences in its ethnic identification (as described by outsider). Yet it was originally named *Qizilbash* (red hat)[3] and its followers generally referred to as 'Ali worshippers' (Van Bruinessen 2000a, 21). Because of the lack of reliable data, the exact number of Alevis is still a contentious issue in Turkey, but it is believed that approximately 20 per cent of Turkish citizens identify as Alevi (Shakland 1999, 136). Kurdish Alevis comprise roughly one-third of all Alevis (Leezenberg 2003, 197), and make up nearly 25 per cent of the Kurds in Turkey (Romano 2010, 20). The majority of the Kurdish Alevis reside in and around the regions of Elazig, Bingol, Mus, Adiyaman, Erzincan, Sivas, Maras, Malatya and Dersim. Because of their political and economic motivations, most Alevis also migrated to the western parts of Turkey, especially Mersin, Izmir, Ankara and İstanbul. As is the case with Sunnis, the Kurdish Alevis also vary in the language they speak. The majority of the Kurdish Alevis speak a Zazaki dialect, but Kurmaji is widespread in some regions (Van Bruinessen 2000a, 88–89; Vorhoff 1998, 232; White 2003, 21–22).

On the other hand, despite sharing the same name, there are considerable differences between the Kurdish and the Turkish descendant Alevis. David Shankland underlines the fact that, unlike the Turkish descendant Alevis' complex relationship with Islam, the Kurdish descendant Alevis are more distant from mainstream Islam, particularly its Sunni school (Shakland 2003, 18–19). This has become far more evident in recent years, especially with the state's and the Sunni religious communities' intense efforts to integrate and assimilate Turkish Alevis into the Turkish national identity, as well as the Turkish state system's attempts in a wider context, such as the Cami-Cemi project, although these have met with considerable resistance from the majority of the Kurdish Alevis (Milliyet 2013). Such attempts, on the other hand, raise the question of whether Alevism is part of Islam or a separate religion. However, the conception(s) of Alevism in relation to Islam, especially whether it is a branch of Islam or an independent religion, is a contentious issue among many (O'Shea

2004, 25). Alevis themselves do not have a consensus on that point. And, rather than being approached theologically, discussion on the *definition* of Alevism is predominantly based on a political perspective. While some Alevis consider Alevism to be an independent religion (Geaves 2003, 53), for others it is a belief within Islam (Hirschler 2001, 157). Because of the minimal academic focus on Alevism, therefore, it is difficult to state whether Alevism is a religion or not. Yet one thing is for sure: that Alevis' rituals and practices significantly differ from the Sunni schools of Islam (Van Bruinessen 1996, 7). Because of tensions between Alevi and Sunni identities throughout history, and also the majority of Kurds' Sunni beliefs, Alevis' relationship with and influence on Kurdish identity are more complex and limited. It became, as the later chapters examine, even a determinant motivation behind some Alevis' distancing from Kurdish identity, especially as a reaction to the dominance of Sunni Islam in it.

Lastly, Yezidi and Ahle-Haqq (or Kakai – People of Truth, and Yarsani) religions are also adopted by some Kurds, mostly located in Iraq, Iran and Armenia (Acker 2004, 99–100). Compared to the other Kurds, the Yazidi population is quite small and has decreased considerably. The majority are located in the Kurdistan region of Iraq, but some also reside in Turkey, Syria and Armenia (Jwaideh 1999, 40). Many Yazidi people speak Kurmanji dialects of the Kurdish language, and it is widely accepted that they are of Kurdish origin (Fuccaro 1999). Yazidi belief is based on an understanding that God is inaccessible. However, referencing Gstrein, according to the Yazidi belief, despite the fact that Tawsi Melek (*Peacock Angel*) is considered to be the right hand of God, in reality Tawsi Melek is actually considered as God itself (Gstrein 2009, 56–59). The holy leader of the Yazidi belief is Sheik Adi Bin Misafir, and their holy book is the Black Book or the Book of Revelation. The majority of the Yazidi people reside in Shingal (also known as Sinjar) in Iraqi Kurdistan, but following the ISIS's attacks, a considerable number of Yazidis left their homeland.

Ahl-e Haqq, despite the small number of followers, is another belief held in the Kurdish world, particularly in the Kurdistan part of Iran. Ahl-e Haqq is a syncretic religion with a principal belief that 'the divine essence has successive manifestations in human form' (Mir-Hosseini 1994, 267). Ahl-e Haqq has a strong esoteric (*batin*) character (Mir-Hosseini 1994, 267), which is most probably further intensified through its interaction with Shi'ism, since esotericism, as noted by Henry Corbin, is central to the Shi'a faith (Corbin 1993). Being practised mostly by the Kurds in Iran, and also sharing some points with Shi'ism, provides the ground for considering Ahl-e Haqq as being part of Shi'ism. However, its main theological principles and practices massively differ from Shi'a Islam (Mir-Hosseini 1994, 267), which has led to tensions between the followers of both faiths (Van Bruinessen 1992, 29).

The contribution of religion to the development and shaping of the ethno-cultural Kurdish identity, especially within the Sunni Kurds, was noted earlier in this section. Religious division among the Kurds, especially through the Sunni and Alevi faiths, became one of main reasons preventing Kurdish unity. Religious identity in a way became a supra identity preventing ethno-national identity and unity among the majority of the Kurds for a long time, and this is still the case for some Kurds (Abdulla 2009, 116–17). Religion in this sense became the primary constituent in the identification of some Kurdish groups. As will be highlighted later, some Kurdish Alevis identify themselves through their religious identity, not ethnicity. Like Alevis, for example, some Sunni Muslim Kurds identify themselves through their religion (Islam) first and then their ethnicity (Kurdish); this, as will be covered in the analysis chapters, is still the case for some Kurds, and leads to differences in their political demands.

Tribalism

Tribes are a common social unit in the Middle East. Although a considerable number of Kurds do not define themselves through tribal identity, they do still possess a tribal structure. The research conducted by KONDA shows that 21.2 per cent of Kurds still consider their tribal membership as part of their identification (KONDA 2011, 140–41).

As collective social organizations, several factors contributed to the emergence of tribal structures. Considering the group-level situation, factors such as war, defence and harbouring are some motives that led to the development of tribes or tribal communities, since these situations demanded collective action and the diverting of collective power to the group (Hay 2005, 72; Özer 2003). Steen has examined major tribes and tribal confederations of the nineteenth century, particularly those originating from the near east, as forming 'a segmentary social structure based on an accepted patri-lineal lineage system, consisting of families and clans bonded by a system of sodalities or social networks that crosscut the clan system' (Steen 2009, 105). Tribes in this context could be regarded as multi-layered and highly complex structures. Continuous amendments and alterations in the modern period have continued to present tribes as complex in the modern day (Lapidus 1990, 26; Özoğlu 1996, 6). This is relevant for the Kurdish tribes as well.

Kurdish tribes included both nomadic and settled groups. However, the social and political developments which took place in the modern period led to most of the Kurdish tribes settling (Dahlman 2002, 276). When considering Kurdish tribal structure, it is evident they are not homogeneous entities. They have a heterogeneous structure that includes various sub-tribal units under different names. 'Kabile', 'taife', 'asira' (Poladyan 1991, 90), 'family', 'tire', 'ocak', 'mal', 'sülale', 'kehl' and 'hoz' are a few of these categories (Jwaideh 1999, 56). These groups are not common to all Kurdish regions, and they have various meanings which alter according to tribe and geographic location (McDowal 2004, 13). This, as Jwaideh (1999, 55–56) rightly states, makes it difficult to find a common terminology to categorize all the Kurdish tribes' sub-units. Hence, despite certain similarities between mentioned sub-tribes' units, they have further fragmented, and each sub-category has an independent organization, leadership and structure (Barth 1953, 34–40). Kurdish tribes in this regard have more than one social form (Barth 1953).

Many of the elements can be viewed as having had an impact on the construction and shaping of the tribes; however, the territorial concentration and loyalty to a particular territory and ancestry are both quite determinative in the identification of tribes (McDowal 2004, 14). This became especially evident in the Kurdish case because of the tribes' strong lineage affinities (Barth 1953) and attachment to territory, alongside their language and culture (Nikitin 1994, 306–7). These factors are decisive in classifying the Kurdish tribes and in shaping in-group and inter-group relations (Beşikçi 1969a). Because of their primordial structure, particularly with regard to the strong blood affinities and resilient attachment to language and culture, the prominence of tribal structures protected the dissolution of Kurdish identity, at least at the local level (Nikitin 1994, 306–7). The formation of tribal confederations (emirates or principalities), which ruled the Kurds with semi-autonomous status for almost three centuries during the Ottoman Empire, could here be considered to show how tribal structure turned into union at the local level and contributed to protecting the Kurds' cultural values (Lazarev et al. 2001, 105–15). Despite this, most of the Kurdish tribes acted independently in politics and were either in conflict or in rivalry with one another. Their tribal structure in this regard also caused conflict and prevented the formation of larger units and unity within the Kurds.

In this regard, examining Kurdish tribes through an anthropological and historical lens, and paying close attention to their fragmented structure and construction of confederacies, it is probable that tribal structure had reciprocal effects on Kurdish society and Kurdish identity. As Kutlay also emphasizes, on the one hand, since tribes had their own agenda and put their tribal interests first, the tribal structure impeded a national Kurdish unity formation, but on the other hand, their strong reliance on primordial affinities protected against the assimilation of Kurdish culture and identity, at least at the regional/local level (Kutlay 2006a, 9).

Tribal affinities still exist within the Kurds to some extent, especially in rural areas. However, the strong influence of Turkish modernization, the emergence of leftist and national Kurdish movements, especially the PKK's armed struggle, and the migration of nearly half of the Kurds to Turkey's western parts have either dissolved or weakened the tribes' structure and their influence on the Kurds. Tribal affinities have largely been replaced with the religious and ethno-national ties.

Kurdish ethnicity

Explaining Kurdish ethnicity in view of the ethnic identity constituents provided previously, we can see that a common name, along with a shared history, descent, language, culture, territory and religion – principally the Shafi school of Islam – are some of the determining components which assisted in creating Kurdish ethnic identity (Asatrian 2009, 10–45). Almost all of the mentioned constituents have contributed, but at various levels. Most of them, particularly culture, have been recognized by the majority of the Kurds, have been used in socio-political life, and have protected the 'material cultural integrity' of the Kurds (Aristova 2002, 316). Despite this, Kurdish ethnic awareness has developed late compared with neighbouring nations. There was some individual or intellectual awareness during the early modern period, but this has not reached the collective level. Ehmedê Xanî's focus on Kurdish language, history, character and statelessness in the sixteenth century, and his protest that as a diverse nation Kurds should be entitled to their own state, could be regarded as indicative of Kurdish ethnic awareness at the individual level (Van Bruinessen 1992, 38–39). Xanî's awareness, however, did not echo throughout the Kurdish masses for a long time. Kurds were incapable of constructing a unified identity until the late years of the Ottoman Empire. Tribal structure, conflict and competition between tribes, and their loyalty to the ideas of Islam and Ottomanism, were definite factors which prevented them from forming a unified ethnic identity at the group level (Chaliand 1994). Nonetheless, the political developments in the last century of the Ottoman Empire and the Middle East began to sensitize many people to their ethnicity. The intensified ethno-national claims in the Ottoman Empire's Balkan subjects and the migration of Turks from Caucasia are two key developments which raised the ethnic awareness of the Turks (McDowal 2004, 91–92). Mounting ethnic awareness in the empire's lands, especially that of the Turks, in the late nineteenth century sparked Kurdish intellectuals' ethnic sentiments. These intellectuals, most of whom were based in İstanbul, began to show mass interest in Kurdish ethnicity, and formed organizations around this identity (McDowal 2004, 92–93). Kurds' ethnic awareness advanced and developed into a territorial issue during the later years, but particularly subsequent to the collapse of the Ottoman Empire. The defeat of the empire and the new political alliances and formations in the Middle East were two central developments of the time, which led to greater open discussions and further divisions among the Kurds regarding their political status. For instance, forming an intellectual group, and pioneers in the Kurdish struggle, most members of the Cemilpashazade and Bedirkhan families openly called for Kurds' independence (Süreyya Bedirhan 1994; Malmîsanij 2010). Moreover, one of the well-known Kurdish leftist intellectuals, Abdullah Cevdet (Strohmeier 2003, 49), and a leading religious figure, Sayid Abdulkadir, called for autonomy (Bozarslan 2005, 206). Taking the development of Kurdish ethnicity in this light, it could be implied that it progressed into a new phase with the formation of modern Turkey. The creation of modern Turkey over a homogeneous national identity and its reluctance to include the Kurds resulted in further counter-reactions from the Kurds, thereby contributing to greater Kurdish ethnic awareness in particular subsequent the PKK's struggle (Beşikçi 1993). Based on this, as Izady (2004, 321) also points out, even if the Kurds have heterogeneity, their strong social cohesion, historical consciousness and material culture allow them to identify with a nation rather than an ethnic group. This is, however, as the following section examines, still an ongoing process.

Kurdish national identity formation

Nation is a decisive concept in changing social and political relations, yet, like ethnicity, it is also one of the most controversial ideas, and continues to be questioned in the relevant literature (Arnason 2006). There are several approaches pertinent to categorizing nation, but the three leading theories in nation studies are primordialism, modernism and ethno-symbolism.

Primordialism identifies nation over ethnicity by claiming that nations 'have their roots in pre-existing ethnies' (Van Den Berghe 2005, 113). Contrary to primordialism, the second approach, modernism, considers nation as a modern product (Anderson 2006; Gellner 2006), with a particular focus on nationalism (Eriksen 2002, 155–60). According to the modernist approach, the concept of nation grew as a result of socio-cultural, political and economic developments, which came into existence during the modern period (Breuilly 2005; Hobsbawm 1990). Here, Benedict Anderson regards nation as an 'imagined community' of the modern period. In establishing an 'imagined community', prime importance is given to the progression of 'print capitalism'. According to Anderson, 'print capitalism', for example the wide distribution of newspapers and books, created a level of connection between individuals with a common language because it provided a platform for those who did not even acknowledge each other to actually consider the same ideas presented in printed form. Thus, he says, people initiated the creation of their own 'imagined community', termed a nation (Anderson 1997, 2006). Ernest Gellner particularly focuses on the subjective constituents of nation, and stresses the particular importance of industrialization. According to Gellner, people create their nation through their 'beliefs', 'loyalty', 'solidarity' and 'culture' (Gellner 1997, 2006, 77–78). From Gellner's point of view, with the transition from an agricultural society to an industrial society people were forced to restructure and redesign their socio-cultural and political norms and organizations. He states that with the introduction of the new (industrial) society, a homogeneous culture developed over time, which in turn led to the construction of nation. Based on this, Gellner examines the transition to industrialization as the period of nation building (Gellner 2006, 117–19).

In light of the considerations of nation presented by the primordialist and modernist approaches, especially the paradoxical notions, an alternative method is ethno-symbolism. Ethno-symbolism presents a somewhat balanced position between modernism and primordialism. As with primordialism, ethno-symbolism holds ethnicity accountable for the development of nation; however, it also gives a level of importance to modernization (Smith 2005). In that sense, ethno-symbolism asserts that a nation's ethnic boundaries are a pre-modern construction; or they have existed for centuries but only obtained their political form (through the politicization of ethnicity) in the modern period (Smith 1996, 2009, 23–40). Taking the idea of nation within this specific context, it shares some common components with ethnicity, such as language, descent, culture and history, and the boundaries between them are permeable (Fenton

2003, 52). Despite such commonalities, while nation has a close affiliation with the state and the means to self-govern, ethnicity lacks these understandings.

Focusing on the relationship between ethnicity and nation in the Kurdish case, the first point to note is the complexity of the issue. As the Kurds still possess a tribal, ethnic and national structure, it is difficult to explore the interactions and transitions between them. Although presented with some difficulty, Miroslav Hroch's 'three-frame steps (A, B, C)' model could be helpful in understanding the expansion of the development of Kurdish national identity as a result of the emerging Kurdish national movement. Hroch uses the 'three-frame steps' model to analyse the changes in the national movements of the European nations. According to Hroch, in its development process a national movement has three separate structural phases. The first phase, 'A', he bases on intellectual studies regarding the group's language, culture and history. In the second phase, 'B', priority is given to the creation and spread of national identity in the light of a political programme. In the final phase, 'C', the national movement obtains a mass character (Hroch 1996, 63).

Considering the Kurds in terms of Hroch's phases, the Kurdish national movement was in Phase 'A' at the end of the nineteenth and early twentieth centuries. During that period, Kurdish intellectuals were focusing on the Kurdish language, history and culture in order to search and re-examine Kurdish identity. Publication of the first Kurdish newspaper in 1898, 'Kurdistan', illustrates the success of intellectual studies on the Kurds, and is also an indicator of Hroch's Phase 'A' (Strohmeier 2003, 25). Notably, many socio-cultural and political organizations were established soon after 'Kurdistan' was published. These organizations were mostly based in İstanbul; of these active Kurdish organizations, the most notable contributors were those Kurds who were either educated in Western countries, or had simply spent a considerable amount of time in the West, such as the Bedirkhan family members; Kurdish religious figures, including Sayyid Abdulkhadir and Said-i Nursi; and some Kurdish tribal leaders and individual intellectuals like Abdullah Cevdet, Ishak Sukutu and Memduh Selim Bey. Throughout this period, although many of the Kurdish political authorities' and intellectuals' political claims were cultural, they made a conscious effort to develop the Kurds at the organizational level and increase Kurdish identity awareness (Bozarslan 2005, 203–4).

Although a Kurdish ethnic awareness began to develop among some Kurds during the last decades of the Ottoman Empire, it only turned into a political arrangement following the First World War. This was, as Taşpınar explains, mostly a result of the reactions against 'Turkism' (*Türkçülük*) and due to influences from the politicization process among the empire's other subjects. The aim to create a homogeneous Turkish nation and the increase in Turkish nationalism have largely influenced Kurdish political identity (Taşpınar 2005, 77–82). This also enters into Hroch's second phase, 'B', where Kurdish intellectuals tried to spread national identity across large areas of Kurdish society via a framed political programme which for some Kurds later turned into demands for independence (Bozarslan 2005, 205; Strohmeier 2003, 25–26). In his article in the first issue of the magazine *Roji Kurd* (1331/1913), for instance, Abdullah Cevdet, a well-known intellectual involved in the Kurdish national movements during the Ottoman period, called upon the Kurds to make their own history and increase their national identity awareness. Cevdet demanded that all Kurds have an 'ideal' for their own nation in the future (Cevdet 1913, 17–18). Along with Cevdet, many Kurdish intellectuals began to call for Kurds to be given territorial independence after the First World War. Even, as a later chapter covers, the Kocgiri rebellion of 1920 and the Sheik Said rebellion of 1925 called for Kurds' territorial rights, including independence.

With defeat of the rebellions, Kurdish political activism went silent until the 1960s. The rise of several Kurdish leftist and nationalist movements between 1960 and 1980 strengthened the Kurdish ethnic identity consciousness through collective activities, especially with the formation of Kurdish organizations and their activities such as Eastern Meetings (*Doğu Mitingleri*), held between 1967 and 1969. As a result of these groups' activities and the emergence of 'collectivity', most Kurdish intellectuals deemed themselves 'more "Kurdish" in a social-psychological sense' (Somer 2002, 78). The growth of Kurdish collectivism increased both ethnic awareness and national sentiment among the Kurds. This allows us to regard the Kurdish national movement within Hroch's 'C' phase to some extent; however, the lack of a mass character among a large segment of the Kurdish community, and also the lack of a national consciousness for a large number of Kurds, prevents us from doing so until almost the late 1980s.

The PKK's struggle, as the next chapter examines in detail, has considerably accelerated the nationalization process. The increased demand for the construction of a common future within a high number of the Kurds was especially displayed via the PKK (Aydın 2005, 239; Beşikçi 1993). Nevertheless, the term 'nation' cannot be classed as being the only or even the most powerful social and political unit in the Kurds' social and political relations. As will be argued in following chapters, an ethno-national awareness among some of the Kurds has progressed as a result of the increasing level of conflict between the PKK and state security forces. However, a considerable number of the Kurds continue to prioritize their tribal or religious identity over their national identity, and some do not even acknowledge their national identity (Kirişçi and Winrow 1997, 33). Bearing this in mind, as O'Shea (2004, 129) highlights, despite attaining the basic criteria to be recognized as a nation, the Kurds now still need to create their own 'imagined political community'. Therefore, even though they have successfully gone into Hroch's 'A' and 'B' phases, whether the Kurdish national movement has reached the 'C' phase is debatable. In other words, the idea of national consciousness is still in the process of formation among the Kurds.

3
History of Variation in the Kurds' Political Demands: 1920–80

Variations in the Kurds' political demands are not a new issue. As is the case now, throughout recent history their political demands have demonstrated significant differences. Even during the last decades of the Ottoman Empire, while most of the empire's subjects were seeking independence, the Kurds failed to propose a common political agenda or political demands. Kurdish political elites of the time were split into two groups: autonomy seekers gathered around Sayyid Abdulkhadir and those who were calling for independence, mostly organized through Bedirkhan family members. This fragmentation was most intensified in what is modern Turkey. The main objective of this chapter is to provide a historical account of the political demands of the Kurds up to the 1980s.

The Kurds' political demands during the War of Independence (1920–23)

The collapse of the Ottoman Empire during the First World War triggered serious turmoil in Kurdish society. Following the war, the Kurds faced harsh social and economic conditions (Ahmed 1992, 36–50). Pitched battles were fought in their territories, and there was continuous fighting on many fronts, all of which led to massive social, economic and demographic destruction of the Kurds (O'Shea 2004, 90–92). This situation naturally laid the foundations for the re-formation of new social and political structures in Kurdish society and left them with two options: fight to form their own state or fight for autonomy under the rule of the Ottoman or the British Empire. Therefore, similar to the situation before the war, the Kurdish authorities once again split into two main groups according to their political demands: those who wanted independence and those who called for autonomy (Kurubaş 1997, 37). At that time, several Kurdish intellectuals organized in the KTC, especially those gathered around the Bedirkhan and Cemilpashazade families, and defended the idea of independence, although they were few in number and lacked mass support (Silopi 1969). In spite of this, most Kurds, especially those close to Sayyid Abdulkhadir in the KTC, demanded autonomy for the Kurds under the Ottoman Empire (Kutlay 2012a, 20). Kurds' religious respect for and loyalty to the Caliphate were by and large the main reasons for their resistance to the idea of independence (Aydın 2005, 235). However, concerns about the Armenians, especially the breaking out of tensions between the Kurds and Armenians in certain areas before and during the First World War, Kurdish fears about the formation of an Armenian state on territories previously shared by Kurds and Armenians, and their socially and politically fragmented structure and lack of sufficient power, also turned them against the idea of Kurdish state formation. These reasons pushed the majority of the Kurds to form alliances with the Turks under the leadership of Mustafa Kemal (Atatürk) during the Turkish National Liberation War (McDowal 2004, 125–27).[1]

Yet the Kurds' support for Mustafa Kemal was not unconditional or just to save the Turks. Their cooperation with Atatürk was based on the condition that they would be granted limited autonomous status following the war (Arokan 2014, 145; Olson 1992, 46; Yeğen 2013, 110–12). Aware of this, Mustafa Kemal also used the War of Independence as a platform to win over the Kurds and to instil in them greater confidence that they would be granted their political rights under an autonomous structure (Aydın 2005, 236). The promise of autonomy, despite the Turkish state's refusal to honour it, or even their decision to ignore it, is very clearly mentioned in certain official documents and in Atatürk's statements, such as in the Amasya Protocol (20–23 October 1919), a bill discussed on 20 February 1922 at the Turkish Grand National Assembly, his speeches at press conferences on 16 and 17 January 1923 in Izmit and during some of his interviews (Özer 2009, 289–92; Parlar 2005, 634–37). Following Mustafa Kemal's positive messages and promises, the Kurds formed an alliance with the Turks and participated in the Turkish National Liberation War; however, almost all his promises were forgotten with the Lausanne Treaty of 1923.

The forgotten promises and the policy of denial

The political history of the Kurds once again dramatically changed and moved into a new phase upon the creation of modern Turkey. Following the

Liberation War, relations between the Kurds and the newly founded Turkish state quickly began to deteriorate, mostly because of the state's reluctance to fulfil the promises given to the Kurds granting them their political rights under an autonomy status. The Turkish state's stance towards the Kurds began to alter when they won the War of Liberation and established relations with the British and French governments. This meant that the newly founded state achieved one of its main aims: to be considered by the Western powers. Relations between the British and French powers and the newly founded Turkish state led to international recognition with the Treaty of Lausanne on 24 July 1923. Lausanne underlined religious minorities' cultural rights and their protection, but there was no mention of Muslim ethnic minorities. The treaty that recognized the foundation of the modern Republic of Turkey therefore left the Kurds without a status. The Treaty of Lausanne, therefore, is seen to have brought destructive results for the Kurds, since it left them without political status at both the national and international levels (Gürbey 2006, 161). And, being given such international recognition, but with no reference to the Kurds, intensified the Turkish authorities' confidence, in line with their denial of the Kurds' political claims (Yeğen 2013, 112). Lausanne, therefore, provided the Turkish state with a strong political ground, and also encouraged it to establish its Kurdish policy upon the denial of Kurdish ethnic identity. The Turkish state abandoned its promises regarding the recognition of the multi-ethnic structure of society, and its approach to the Kurds completely altered after the Lausanne treaty was signed (Gunter 2005, 222). To put it another way, Atatürk merely toyed with the Kurds during the War of Liberation (McDowall 1992, 14), and when he had built the Republic on solid foundations he began to get rid of the Kurdish ethnic identity and political claims.

Policies issued later by the state, particularly 'Turkification' and a homogeneous nation creation project, clearly revealed the Turkish authorities' intentions. As a method of assimilating non-Turkish Muslims, but essentially the Kurds' ethnic identity, the state launched a 'Turkification' policy (Arokan 2014, 146–47; Bali 2006). Related to this, the Turkish state introduced a homogenous nation creation project intending to assimilate non-Turkish Muslim ethnicities into the Turkish national identity boundaries as defined through Turkish culture, Turkish language and the idea of Turkism (Bali 2006, 43), and Turkish nationalism (Kasaba 1997, 16–17; Köker 2010, 53). With the aim of creating such an 'ideal' and 'nostalgic' Turkish national identity and imposing it on others – i.e. non-Turks – the Turkish state showed no hesitation in utilizing extreme and violent methods (Akçam 2004, 56), including forced migration and changing the Kurds' demographic structure (Kirişçi 2004, 277). This intention to remove Kurdish ethnic identity in the Kurdish regions was significant for the Turkish state's aim to build a new nation state by way of Turkish national identity (Lundgren (2007, 45). With this policy, the Republic sought to eliminate Kurdish ethnic identity, and offered the Kurds no choice other than to accept and acknowledge Turkish national identity. Attempts founded on the assimilation and dismissal of the Kurds were made to enforce this, involving projects such as the Turkish History Thesis (*Türk Tarih Tezi*) and the Sun Language Theory (*Güneş Dil Teorisi*) (Beşikçi 1991; Hirschler 2001, 147).

The Kurds' concerns and discontent with the Turkish state greatly intensified when the state began to follow secular policies and implement some restrictions on religion, as well as begin the removal of the Caliphate on 3 March 1924. In line with this intention, and to eliminate the Turks social and cultural loyalties to the Ottoman Empire, Turkish state issued a series of reforms. Thus, as Bali also underlines, Atatürk tried to remove any connections between his new nation design and the Ottoman Empire by ensuring religion had no place in his understanding of nation (Bali 2006, 43). In support of this argument, Lewis explains that Mustafa Kemal sought to turn citizens' loyalty away from the Ottoman Empire and Islam to the idea of Turkish national identity (Lewis 1968, 358–59). The state's elimination of religion from the public sphere and oppression and denial of Kurdish identity outraged the Kurds and worsened the relations between both parties (Romano 2010, 58). The Kurds reacted to the Turkish state's deliberate policies through a number of rebellions. The rebellions of Sheikh Said-1925, Agri-1927–30, Koçgiri-1920 and Dersim-1938 are four which had a significant influence on the Kurds in many aspects.

Kurdish rebellions

Sunni Kurds' revolts: Sheikh Said and Ağri rebellions

The escalating concerns of the Kurds were brought about by the Republic's restrictions on religion, in particular the dismissal of the Caliphs, and its failure to provide the Kurds with the autonomous status that was promised during the War of Liberation. The Kurds were disappointed by the Republic's approach to, or rather restrictions on, religion and Kurdish identity. The anxiety and frustration of the Kurds were manifested in the rebellion of Sheikh Said in 1925 (Oran 2002, 875). Although Sheikh Said led the rebellion, it was the Azadî movement[2] that determined and structured the technical and ideological aspects of the rebellion from the beginning (Keiser 2003, 189). There is no specific date for the foundation of the Azadî, but it is estimated that it was established in 1923 by some Kurdish notables, intellectuals and Kurdish officers who were members of the Hamidiye corps, and was headed by the former Hamidiye corps officer Cibranli Halit (McDowall 2004, 192). The central cadres of the Azadî movement shared secular and nationalist views and their primary aim was Kurds independence (Oran 2002, 875). The movement, therefore, by following a national agenda, sought to bring the Kurds together and mobilize them for a common political purpose (Olson 1992, 76; Romano 2010, 60).

On the other hand, since the Azadî's core cadres shared a secular identity, they well knew that the rebellion might not reach or mobilize the masses simply through a nationalistic agenda or the demand for independence unless commanded by a religious and notable Kurdish leader (Oran 2002, 875). Therefore, following the detainment of Cibranli Halit just before the outbreak of the rebellion, Sheikh Said of Palu was appointed as the leader of the rebellion, mainly because of his Naqshbandi religious identity, charisma and authority (Aydın 2006, 60–61; Oran 2002, 875).

The Sheikh Said rebellion commenced earlier than planned, and thus was unable to secure mass support from many of the Kurds who might have supported it (Kutlay 2002, 268). However, the rebellion also clearly highlights the religious and linguistic divisions among the Kurds. The majority of the Zaza Kurds, because the Sheikh was also a Zaza Kurd and Naqshbandi, joined the insurrection, while the mainstream Kurmanji-speaking Kurds and the Alevi Kurds refrained from showing support (Ekinci 2011, 43; Kutlay 2002, 264). The competition, conflicts and religious differences between the Kurds, especially between the Alevi and Sunni Kurds, destroyed the prospects of them coming together for common action (Romano 2010, 61). Therefore, the rebellion failed to reach the majority of the Kurds, which was its aim. After Sheikh Said's arrest, the rebellion lost significant power, and as a result was almost completely over by 1925 (Sever 2010).

The fact that it was most popular amongst the Zaza and the Sunni Kurds, however, raised questions about the rebellion's character and purpose. For instance, Zurcher (2004, 171) differentiates between the purpose of leader cadres from those of the other ranks who were involved in the rebellion, asserting that, despite the leaders' calls for independence, the supporters mostly acted through religious inspiration and wanted to bring the Caliphate back to power and restore religious law. However, most view the Sheikh Said rebellion as the first large-scale and strongly religion-based Kurdish nationalist rebellion, known as an ethno-religious rebellion (Davison 1998, 150; Gunter 2004, 200; Van Bruinessen 2003, 387).

Following the suppression of the rebellion, Turkish's violence, which had already begun soon after the Treaty of Lausanne was signed, became a vicious mass attack. The Republic was already waging a war against the Kurds who had any connection with the rebellion, but their harsh methods also now extended to those Kurds who did not join or help the rebellion. Along with Sheikh Said, many leader cadres were executed, thousands of Kurds were killed and thousands more were put on trial and exiled from their homeland (Celîl et al. 1998, 163; Robins 1993, 660; Van Bruinessen 2000c, 143). The Sheikh Said rebellion provided the Republic with a basis from which to perform its suppression, assimilation and pacification policies on the Kurds. For instance, they formed an independence tribunal court which started to exact punishments in the Kurdish region (Jwaideh 1999, 399–401). In addition, soon after the revolt the foundation of the new Kurdish policy of the state was systemized with the Eastern Reformation Plan (*Şark Islahat Planı*) dated 24 September 1925. The Eastern Reformation Plan was issued in order to prohibit the use of the Kurdish language in a public space, force the Kurds to emigrate to western cities, bring Turkish immigrants back to the Kurds' homeland, punish or exile the families of those who had participated in the rebellion, supply more military precautions in the region and take full control of the region by constructing new roads, bridges and railways (Bayrak 2009, 35–40). All these steps indicate that the Turkish state used the Sheikh Said rebellion to legitimize the implementation of its homogeneous nation creation project, and for this aim it became necessary to eliminate the potential threat to this identity – the Kurds.

The Sheikh Said rebellion created an increased sense of trepidation within the newly founded Republic. Removing the conditions that might lead to another rebellion of this nature against the Turkish Republic became imperative. Along with the previously underlined harsh measures implemented at the community level, the state sought to eliminate Kurdish notables, including religious and tribal leaders and intellectuals. As part of this plan, after the Sheikh Said rebellion a great number of Kurdish notables involved in the rebellion were exiled, most of whom chose to settle in Syria (Ekinci 2011, 46). Syria had become a new centre for those Kurds who escaped the persecution of the Republic. To carry out their political and cultural activities, some of these Kurds established the Xoybun organization in 1927 in Syria, which had a secular and nationalist view of Kurdish identity (Alakom 1998, 21-23; Celil et al. 1998, 175). Xoybun was thus established as a national organization fighting for the independence of the Kurds, by fighting 'against the Turks until the last Turkish soldier is cleared out from the holy Kurdish land' (Celîl et al. 1998, 175). For that purpose it soon joined the Ağri rebellion, which had initially broken out separately from Xoybun in 1927, and took its organization and declared independence (Sureyya Bedirkhan 1994).

The Ağri rebellion grew soon after Xoybun was launched, but the two were independent entities, as noted previously. Angered and frustrated by the Republic's oppression and exile policies, the Kurds in the city of Ağri, particularly Dogubeyazit, initially revolted under the local leaderships of Broyé Heski Telo (Kalman 1997, 25-26). With the rising conflict between the local Kurdish forces and the Turkish army, Xoybun then actively joined and led the Kurdish rebellion under the direction of İhsan Nuri Paşa (Çelik 2012, 245). Xoybun's involvement with the Ağri rebellion meant that it was well planned and determined in its demands for independence (İhsan Nuri Paşa 1992). Xoybun made intensive efforts to reach large numbers of Kurds and awaken their national spirit and hope to establish an independent state; to do so, it used all national instruments belonging to the Kurdish community to mobilize them (Chaliand 1994, 37-38). Xoybun's identity meant that the rebellion did not have an overall religious character or purpose. This, therefore, makes the Ağri rebellion different from the previous Kurdish rebellions (Ciment 1996, 46).

The revolt was mostly supported by Kurds who resided near Ağri and the regions surrounding it, and it lasted for three years (1927-30). The subsequent defeat of the rebellion was caused by its inability to attract the majority of the Kurds, the betrayal of some Kurdish tribes, technical deficiencies and Iran's support for the Turkish Republic (McDowal 2004, 206-7). As with the post-Sheikh Said rebellion period, the Republic responded to the failed revolt by applying greater pressure on the Kurds. In this era, punishment was again not restricted to those Kurds directly involved in the rebellion. The Republic also destroyed many Kurdish villages and killed many civilians: for instance, the Republic's military operation in the Zilan district of the city of Van in 1930 resulted in the deaths of thousands of Kurds (Kutschera 2001, 125). Suppression of the Ağri revolt and the Republic's subsequent tough policies broke the Kurds' will to resist for a considerable number of years. Xoybun was also seriously affected by this defeat and lost its political and organizational power among the Kurds.

Kurdish Alevis revolts: Koçgiri and Dersim revolts

In order to clarify the Kurdish Alevis' political stance, especially in relation to the Turkish state and also their Kurdish identity, this section explores the Koçgiri and the Dersim rebellions, both of which have a significant place in the construction of the collective memory of the Kurdish Alevis.

Despite the importance of the timing of the rebellion, its sociological character and political claims, there is minimal literature on the Kocgiri rebellion. The rebellion, which is notable for its Kurdish character, was the first Kurdish Alevi rebellion to take place, in 1920. Since at this time the newly founded Ankara government was still involved in the War of Liberation, and discussions were still being made on the Treaty of Sevres, the fate of Kocgiri was critical for the Kurdish case (White 2012, 111). The Kocgiri rebellion took place in mostly Kurdish Alevi concentrated cities, including the Sivas, Erzincan, Dersim and Elazığ districts (Keiser 2003, 184). The objective of the rebellion was to provide the Kurds with autonomy status (Bayrak 2010, 132–33). The other demands voiced by the Koçgiri rebellion, conditional on the autonomy of the Kurds, were 'acceptance by Ankara of Kurdish autonomy as already agreed by İstanbul', 'the release of all the Kurdish prisoners in Elazığ, Malatya, Sivas and Erzincan jails', 'the withdrawal of all Turkish officers from areas with a Kurdish majority' and 'withdrawal of all the Turkish forces from the Koçgiri region' (cited in McDowall 2004, 185).

The Kocgiri rebellion most probably was an unexpected development for the Ankara government at the time because, like the Sunni Kurds, the Alevi Kurds were also fragmented, and there were no a strong nationalist sentiments among the Alevis at the community level. The Turkish state refrained from interfering with the rebellion, primarily because it was already occupied with the National Liberation War, and it only agreed to the conditions laid out by the rebellion to buy more time (Olson 1992, 57). The Kocgiri rebellion had a high possibility of achieving its goal since both the government in İstanbul and the Kemalist campaign were very weak at the time. However, when the political and material conditions were right, Turkish forces intervened and the rebellion was defeated quickly in April 1921 (White 2012, 112). Olson explains that the rebellion was unsuccessful because of the Kurds' tribal structure; the disagreements between the tribes involved in the rebellion; the rebellion's failure to receive widespread support from different Kurdish segments at the community level, particularly from the Sunni Kurds; its lack of foreign support; and variations in the rebels' beliefs and religions (Olson 1992, 56–62).

The Kurdish Alevis' defeat at Kocgiri silenced them until another Kurdish Alevi defence, based on insurrection, rose up in 1937-38 – the Dersim insurrection. It broke out in and around the Dersim region as a reaction against the Republic's policies over the Dersim region (Çelik 2012, 246). Dersim had had a semi-independent status since the Ottoman period (although not in political terms), and it wanted to keep the advantages of this status in the republican era. However, the Republic was adamant about removing the de facto semi-independent status of Dersim, and focused on the region following the suppression of the Ağri rebellion (Lazarev et al. 2001, 245; White 2012, 123-24). In line with this purpose, the Republic constructed new outposts, roads and bridges, and deployed numerous soldiers to besiege the Dersim region from 1934 onwards (McDowall 2004, 208). As a continuation of its aim to destroy Dersim's de facto semi-independent status and, in effect, implement an assimilation policy to abolish the Kurdish identity, especially by destroying the Kurds' demographic structure and territorial concentration, the Obligatory Settlement Law (*Zorunlu İskan Kanunu*)[3] was enforced on 14 June 1934 (Beşikçi 1977, 132-46). With this policy, as Bayrak also underlines, the Turkish state aimed to eliminate the main components and basis of the Kurdish identity (Bayrak 2009, 83).

The Kurdish Alevis of the Dersim region objected to these activities enacted by the Republic because they deemed them as an assault on their religious and ethnic identity. Thus, in order to halt the siege of their region and defend themselves, they united under the leadership of Sayyid Riza. Despite lacking sufficient military material, Dersim fought against the Republic's military forces. However, their defence was ultimately broken down and Dersim was almost completely destroyed between the years 1937 and 1938 (Jwaideh 1999, 418). The Republic's forces applied very harsh military methods in their attacks against the Dersim resistance and killed thousands of people (Kutschera 2001, 156). Their methods did not only involve the killing of thousands; it is estimated that thousands of Kurdish Alevis were also exiled (Jwaideh 1999, 419). Bayrak states that the Republic intended to cleanse the region of its ethno-religious identity by applying 'Tedip' (Civilise), 'Tenkil' (Punishment), 'Temdin' (Turkish Islamization) and 'Tasfiye' (Elimination) policies (Bayrak (2011, 225).

The suppression of the Dersim revolt allowed the Republic to secure power and enforce its authority on almost all areas of the Kurdish region. It placed the Kurds and their region under tough military control. Following the end of the revolts, Kurdish national movements went into deep silence until the 1960s.

Kurdish politics between the 1960–80s

Between the years 1924 and 1946 Turkey was governed by a one-party system, the CHP, also referred to as an authoritarian one-party regime (Aydın 2005, 96; Zürcher 2004, 176). The Republic persisted with single-party rule until 1946, yet internal and regional developments, especially Turkey's growing attachment to the Western world after the Second World War and increased reactions from inside the country, forced Turkey to transition into a multi-party system (Ahmad 2003, 99; Szyliowicz 1966, 275). Soon after, the Democrat Party (DP) entered Turkish politics in 1946 (Karpat 2010, 485).

The formation of the DP was welcomed by a large number of Kurds; it received considerable support from them during elections (Güçlü 2006, 31–32). Although most of the DP cadres transferred to the party are from the CHP, the Kurds' experience of tough punishment and assimilation since the Republic was established led them to have faith and hope in the DP, especially with the expectation that some steps would be taken to remove restrictions on their both ethnic and religious identities (Tan 2009, 316). However, there was no change in the Republic's approach to the Kurdish identity during the DP's rule. The DP did not make any effort to alter the state's homogeneous nation creation project, and even began to embrace the Republic's mentality on the Kurdish issue, for instance arresting fifty Kurdish intellectuals, students and some leading figures to eliminate potential Kurdish national activities and/or inclinations, in 1959 (Çamlıbel 2007, 22–23; Köker 2010, 58; Kutlay 2012a, 30; Tan 2009, 317). The DP tried to manage the Kurdish issue through the Kurdish tribes and religious leaders by empowering them in the party and providing them with economic opportunities, thereby integrating and assimilating the Kurds through religious and economic attachments (Ekinci 2011, 54–58; Kutlay 2012a, 365; McDowal 2004, 398–401). These attempts created new classes within the Kurds and integrated some feudal Kurdish groups into Turkey's political and economic system, but it failed to handle the Kurdish question and integrate the majority of the Kurds into the Turkish identity. Nonetheless, all these policies contributed to the fragmentation of the Kurds' political demands in later years.

The period in which the DP ruled, which amounted to almost ten years, ended with a military coup d'état on 27 May 1960. The coup removed the DP from power, and its leader, Adnan Menderes, and two of its ministers, Fatin Rüştü Zorlu and Hasan Polatkan, were arrested and executed, with the accusation that the party had violated the constitution of 1924 (Davison 1998, 179–80). The coup ended the DP era but caused further problems for Turkey's internal dynamics and politics. Following the coup, the military considered itself as the central defender of the Turkish Republic and the principles of *Kemalism*, or the state's founding ideology, and so it intervened in civil politics through various methods, including the direct seizing of power and by putting pressure on governments, and by bringing in its own policies (Hale 1994). After the coup d'état, a new constitution was drafted in 1961 by a committee which was assigned by the Military Coup Council (Committee of National Unity). Despite making clear references to the previous constitution's principles regarding the Turkish nation and the rejection of non-Turkish Muslim groups, particularly the Kurds, the 1961 constitution issued certain legal regulations which allowed the formation of leftist organizations (Çelik 2012, 246). Taking into account the military coup, the 1961 constitution and the removal of the DP, it is evident that nothing improved or changed in the Republic's approach to the Kurdish issue and Kurdish identity. In fact, oppression of Kurdish identity was toughened (Çelik 2012, 246). Because of the legal and political barriers, most Kurds took part in the Turkish leftist movements.[4]

The TİP,[5] formed in 1961, was one of the first to have had a significant role in the history of Turkey's socialist movements, and also in bringing the Kurdish question forward through a social and economic framework (Şener 2007). Most of the leftist and nationalist Kurds joined the TİP and took an active role in almost all ranks of the party, including leadership cadres. The TİP became a voice for those Kurds who wanted to retain both their leftist and ethno-national identities (Bozarslan 2007, 1175). Compared with previous parties, the TİP was almost the first political party which boldly took the Kurdish issue into its agenda, proposing the economic development of the region and recognition of cultural rights in its solution – this, however, became one of the significant reasons why it was outlawed (Aybar 1988, 64–66). Therefore, despite its good intentions, the TIP could not play a massive role in the solution of the Kurdish issues, and the party lost ground in Turkey overall, but amongst Kurds in particular.

On the other hand, although many of the leftist Kurds found shelter in the TIP and in later Turkish socialist organizations, most of the conservative Kurds, particularly those with a nationalist agenda, begun to organize through a Kurdish identity. Therefore, unlike Kurds with a socialist ideology, Kurds who shared a conservative and national opinion formed the TKDP under the leadership of Faik Bucak in 1965 (Ekinci 2011, 67). The TKDP established its policy upon a national agenda and welcomed Kurds from various socio-cultural and ideological backgrounds (Burkay 2002, 183). In line with this agenda, the TKDP defined its basic political demands as recognition of Kurdish identity and acceptance of the Kurdish language as an official language, the halting of settlement plans which aimed to destroy the Kurdish region's demographic structure and allowing the Kurds representation in parliament in accordance with their population density (Epözdemir 2005, 24).

The TKDP took action soon after its foundation and obtained considerable backing from the Kurds in many Kurdish areas, meaning that it was almost the first Kurdish mobilization following the repression of the Kurdish rebellions. However, only a few years after its foundation, political conflict and competition arose in the movement. One group acted alongside Dr Şivan (Sait Kızıltoprak) and withdrew from the TKDP, establishing the T-KDP in 1970. The T-KDP fought for the Kurds' right to determine their own fate, and demanded equal rights for Turks and Kurds (Bozarslan 2007, 1177–78). The T-KDP's solution to securing Kurds' basic rights and independence was to propose armed conflict, but this suggestion was met with disapproval from some Kurdish powers (Arik 2011). The T-KDP claimed that an armed people's war was necessary for the Kurds of Turkey to obtain their political rights (Büyükkaya 2008, 24). The T-KDP's strategy also prepared the foundations for the Kurdistan Workers' Party (PKK), which emerged later (in 1978).

The Kurds' political awareness advanced as leftist political activity in Turkey increased after 1965. The number of Kurdish workers, intellectuals, students and ordinary people who were concerned with the Kurdish issue and the Kurds' socio-economic conditions rapidly grew (Akyol 2007, 144–46). In most parts of the Kurdish region, Eastern Meetings (*Doğu Mitingleri*) were organized between 1967 and 1969 by the TİP and the TKDP for the purpose of increasing awareness of these issues (Karadoğan 2006). At these meetings, Kurds vocalized their ethno-cultural rights, along with demanding improvements to their social and economic conditions. Eastern Meetings, in this regard, clearly showed how Kurds' political claims involved more ethnic components, and had been transformed into demands for self-determination (Bozarslan 2007, 1176–77).

An increase in national awareness among the Kurds also resulted in growing discussions in Turkish leftist movements regarding the Kurdish issue of identification and proposed solutions (Yeğen 2007a). The DDKO was created in response to these discussions by some Kurds, most of whom had left Turkish leftist organizations following the 1969s (Ekinci 2010, 601–2). The DDKO was the Kurds' first legal organization in modern Turkey, and therefore made a great contribution to the Kurds' democratic legal struggle and further politicization (Maraşlı 2010). The DDKO, along with its socialist and nationalist ideology, garnered significant support from the Kurds in a short period of time

(Buran 2011, 71). The political and national awareness of the DDKO affected its political claims, and, as Güçlü (2005, 133) suggests, although there was a common agreement to end the denial and assimilation of the Kurdish identity, it was two political demands, independence and federalism, which found particular place among the DDKO's members.

Only eleven years after the military coup d'état of 27 May 1960, Turkish military forces once again intervened in the political sphere, on 12 March 1971. With a military memorandum, many of the Turkish and Kurdish leftist organizations were closed down, and a number of their members were either arrested or fled Turkey. The military memorandum considerably weakened the Turkish and Kurdish leftist movements' organizational structure and activities (Ciment 1996, 49; Kutschera 2001, 400). Despite this disintegration, following the release of these movements' cadres from prison, along with the general amnesty of Bülent Ecevit in 1974, many Kurdish organizations were founded once again. The most prominent among these movements was the TKSP, set up under the leadership of Kemal Burkay in 1975 (Ekinci 2010, 866). The TKSP carried a socialist ideology, and proposed for Kurds that they have equal status in a federal structure; still, it did not close the doors to independence, which it considered as an alternative political model for the Kurds (Çay 2010, 498).

The establishment of the TKSP saw many other Kurdish leftist and national organizations develop. The KUK in 1975, Beş Parçacılar and the KİP, also known as Péşeng, in 1978, are only three of them (Bozarslan 2007, 1190). The KUK, Özgürlük Yolu and the KİP coordinated and established the National Democratic Coalition (Ulusal Demokratik Güç Birliği-UDG) in 1979; however, it was active for only one year and disbanded in 1980 (Burkay 2010, 169–71). In the years that followed 1975, the number of Kurdish political organizations almost doubled. Rizgari in 1977, KAWA in 1976, Tekosin in 1978, Yekbun in 1979 and KSH in 1980 were some of the other Kurdish political organizations established just before the military coup d'état (Romano 2010, 76). Along with the varied organizational structures, practices and, to a certain extent, ideologies, the organizations also presented different political claims. For instance, while the TKSP, DDKD and KIP made demands for the recognition of federations, later groups including Tekoşin, Rizgari, KUK, KAWA (Özer 2009, 583–84) and Péşeng prioritized the creation of an Independent United Socialist Kurdistan (Çay 2010, 498–99).

By 1980, with another military coup d'état in place (September 12), almost all of the above-mentioned Kurdish groups, except for the PKK, had disappeared.

Analysis: Variation in the Kurds' Political Demands

The Turkish state's policy of denying Kurdish identity and of using violent methods to oppress Kurds' political claims has had dire consequences for the Kurds' social, political and economic structures, alongside their psychological impact. The Turkish state has clearly shown that it will not tolerate the Kurds' basic political claims, and will not avoid taking every measure to prevent them. The state's application of brutal physical and psychological violence, including the torture and killing of the Kurdish prisoners in Diyarbakır prison, which is still fresh in many Kurds' memory, has proved the Turkish state's toughness in their approach to the Kurdish issue. The PKK's commencement of armed struggle in such an environment, therefore, was a milestone in Kurdish political history and in the determination of their political demands, because the PKK's armed struggle has created a hope within some Kurds and has significantly contributed to the transformation of the Kurds and Kurdish identity, from its tribal-religious roots into an ethnicity. The PKK in this sense has over time contributed to the politicization and ethnicization of the Kurdish identity, yet this has not been sufficient for the Kurds to gather around a common political agenda. Following the PKK's struggle, the Kurds have further divided in terms of their political claims. This part of the research, composed of four chapters, attempts to analyse in an inductive way the reasons behind such variations.

4

Demand for Democratic Autonomy

The groups supporting democratic autonomy

The PKK

Democratic autonomy, first proposed by Abdullah Öcalan, was soon accepted by the PKK, BDP/HDP, DBP and affiliated legal and outlawed organizations. The PKK, as a political and sociological force in the Middle East, has successfully gained sympathy from a considerable numbers of the Kurds. The group has the power to influence the political balance relating to the Kurds in Turkey, Iraq, Syria and Iran to a certain extent. The PKK's power became particularly evident after the Syrian uprising (2011), when the PYD, which shares Abdullah Öcalan's ideas (Khalil 2017), and its armed organization, the YPG, took control of the Kurdish areas, known as *Rojava*, in northern Syria. The YPG's successful fight against ISIS in Syria, particularly during the Kobané resistance (September 2014–March 2015), and the PKK's rescue of thousands of Yazidis from ISIS in the Shingal region in Iraq have influenced the group's popularity further. Therefore, although the PKK is a Turkish-born movement and has campaigned for the Kurds' rights to live in Turkey, it is well organized in other Kurdish areas, including in the Kurdistan regions in Iraq, Syria and Iran, and receives considerable support from the Kurds. The group is also well organized in the Kurdish diaspora in Europe. Thus, contrary to Turkey and several other countries, including the European Union and the United States, which have put the movement on the terrorist list, a considerable number of the Kurds deem the PKK to be a legitimate Kurdish national movement.

The PKK in a broad context is the result of the unsolved Kurdish question, but the political developments that took place both in Turkey and in the Middle East following the 1970s also had an enormous influence on its emergence and organizational and ideological shaping. Soviet Communism, the rising up of social movements and the national liberation struggles in other regions have strongly inspired Kurdish youths, particularly at the universities, since the late 1970s. Turkey's denial and military oppression of the Kurds further created a fertile ground for Kurdish youths' interest in the Kurdish issue and later formation of the PKK. Specifically, the military coup d'état on 12 September 1980 and the state's militaristic approach to the Kurdish issue have had a decisive impact on the formation and strengthening of the PKK.

The PKK was founded on 27 November 1978 by Abdullah Öcalan and some of his friends (Balli 1991, 204). As a political and practical movement organized in line with the terms set by its leader (Öcalan 2011b, 50), the PKK was formed in reaction to the unstable political atmosphere of the time, in which the state had placed tough restrictions on the recognition of Kurdish identity (PKK Kuruluş Bildirgesi 1984). Therefore, the PKK used this intense atmosphere to initiate some social and political changes, and to strive to obtain the Kurds' ethno-national rights within an ethnic territorial and Marxist-Leninist ideological context (Beşikçi 1992). Öcalan suggested that the Kurdish issue had to be considered independently, and not grouped with the Turkish leftist movement's 'revolutionary solution' (Imset 1992, 9–10). This idea was in line with many of the Kurdish organizations of the time, because of their concerns regarding the Turkish leftist organizations' strong ideological stance and the refusal either of the Kurds' territorial claims or the consideration of the Kurdish issue as of secondary importance (Romano 2010, 75–78). Despite this, the PKK's stance was tougher than that of other Kurdish groups, since the PKK aimed to reach its goals through a national armed struggle. The PKK's harsh criticisms therefore were not restricted to only Turkish leftist movements, but also extended to other Kurdish political organizations, especially the KUK. Despite sharing (almost) the same political and ideological inclinations, the PKK criticized the Kurdish leftist and national organizations as being 'feudal', 'state agents', 'collaborator-slaves' and/or 'agent-provocateurs' (Imset 1992, 206). The PKK's stance in this way was doubtlessly not independent of the group's desire to become the sole power in Kurdish politics, which was challenged by many of the Kurdish groups. The power competition between the PKK and other groups soon progressed into a conflict, resulting in many deaths from both sides (H. Bozarslan 2004a, 96; Burkay 2010, 159–63). But, as the latest developments have shown, the PKK has become the main actor in Kurdish politics, while the KUK and almost all of the Kurdish organizations mentioned previously have either dissolved or markedly depleted. The reasons behind this are varied, but in the case of the PKK, the group's ideological pragmatism and nationalistic emphasis on Kurdish identity benefit decisively from the political conditions and opportunities in Turkey and the Middle East.

The political and ideological environment that Turkey was going through after the late 1970s and the emergence of the socialist and national liberal movements strongly influenced the determination of the PKK's ideological and political principles. Marxism-Leninism and nationalism in this regard constructed the two main pillars of the PKK's ideology, particularly during its initial years (Olson 2011, 1). The group's relationship with both ideologies has been more pragmatic in later years. In particular, nationalism, despite the PKK's refusal of being defined as nationalist (Serxwebûn (August) 2000, 6–9), is one of the central instruments in the group's national struggle, since it significantly contributed to the politicization, recruitment and mobilization of the Kurdish masses (Barkey and Fuller 1998, 24). Relying on its Marxist-Leninist and nationalist ideology, the PKK's initial aim for the solution of the Kurdish issue was the creation of a socialist, united, independent Kurdish nation state (PKK Kuruluş Bildirgesi 1984; PKK Programı ve Tüzüğü 1995).

The Kurds' demographic and territorial divisions and the denial of their ethno-national identity were two central themes in the PKK's call for an independent Kurdistan nation state, because, to its movement, only in this way could the Kurds be liberated (Balli 1991, 207). Based on this idea, the PKK aggressively challenged the solution of the Kurdish issue through autonomy models during its initial years by alleging that this would damage the development of the Kurdish national struggle (White 2012, 209–10). The PKK thought that establishing a socialist Kurdistan was the only means of freeing Kurds, and this, the movement believed, could only be achieved by an armed struggle. The region's unbalanced political character and strong reliance on military power led the PKK to believe that only an armed struggle could end Turkey's physical and cultural domination of the Kurds and rejection of Kurdish ethnicity (Karayılan 2012). Making a stand on this, the PKK launched militarized resistance against the Turkish security forces in 1984. Yet the PKK did not limit its war to resistance against the Turkish security forces; the movement also commenced attacks on the Kurdish feudal class, particularly the *aghas* and tribal leaders, since the movement alleged that these Kurds have close relationships with the state and had played a major role in the integration and assimilation of the Kurds (Karayılan 2012, 99–105; Öcalan 1993, 121–22; PKK II Kongresi Çalışma Raporu 1984, 35–36). The PKK's declaration of war against these classes diminished these groups' power in society to some extent, but on the other hand it caused further fragmentation among the Kurds since the rival Kurdish tribes and religious authorities took part on opposing sides – meaning that they sided either with the PKK or with the state (White 2012, 226–28). This outcome provided the ground and certain advantages for the Turkish state to eliminate the Kurdish political organizations, or at least to create an internal conflict within them.

In line with this aim, and aware of the disjointed structure of the Kurds, Turkish state formed a paid army from within the Kurds, namely the village guards (*Köy Korcuları*),[1] to fight against the PKK (McDowall 2004, 423–25). With the new threat from the village guards looming, the PKK responded soon after the formation of this paramilitary army. The PKK harshly attacked the village guards, killing many of them, which in turn further intensified the divisions and enmities amongst the Kurds (Lundgren 2007, 48). This grew worse during the 1990s over the PKK's declaration of *serhildan* (similar to the Palestinian *intifada*), which intensified and spread the war all across the Kurdish areas, with the PKK calling for Kurds to completely divorce themselves from the state.

Paradigm shift in the PKK's ideology and political demands

Soon after its foundation, and with the breakout of war against the Turkish security forces (1984), the PKK started to gain popularity amongst the Kurds. Many Kurds, from various social, cultural, economic and political backgrounds, joined the movement, including a considerable number of women, from all Kurdish regions, but especially from Turkey and Syria (Westrbeim 2010, 40). The PKK's focus on the importance of the Kurds' ethno-national identity and stance against the state's militarist approach to the Kurdish issue and its engagement with nationalism greatly contributed to the popularity of the movement with Kurds. To receive support from the religious Kurds, the group has also begun to distance itself from Marxist-Leninist ideology to a certain extent (Aras 2014, 76). Because the majority of Kurds did not have more problems with the PKK's emphasis on Kurdish identity, the group's initial ideological concerns and distance from religion placed barriers separating both sides. The revised policy has allowed the group to gain popularity with a wide range of religious Kurds since the 1990s.

The PKK's distance from Marxist-Leninist ideology became more of a necessity as a result of certain external factors, particularly the weakening of the socialist bloc, the collapse of Soviet Communism and the end of the Cold War (Barkey and Fuller 1998, 25–26). In line with this development, the movement's leader, Abdullah Öcalan, stated that they had to develop a new approach to understanding socialism. Mostly after the 1990s, Öcalan began to criticize the practice of Soviet socialism and put more emphasis on the notion of democracy in his approach to ethno-national issues (Ballı 1991, 287–89; Serxwebûn (Ekim) 1995, 12–13). Öcalan's initial critique of socialism was based on socialism's extreme focus on the idea of the state that in a political struggle everything should be done for the people and for humanity, not for the state itself (Serxwebûn (Ekim) 1995, 12–13). His ideas reveal that he aimed to put the people at the centre of his struggle and not the state, because to Öcalan, forming a state would not result in ultimate freedom for stateless nations. Öcalan here talked about intellectual and moral freedoms and deemed them the substantive means for the freedom of the people, before considering the creation of their own state (Balli 1991, 231–33). He further developed these ideas and took them as the basis of his approach to the Kurdish question following his arrest in 1999.

This ideological shift soon prompted a change in the PKK's initial goal – i.e. the foundation of a socialist Kurdish state. The PKK then began to revise its approach to the creation of a Kurdish nation state. As Öcalan abandoned his idea of the creation of a socialist united Kurdish nation state, he instead initiated a new understanding of socialism in his movement and begun to formulate his approach to the Kurdish issue within the context of democracy and citizenship (Akkaya and Jongerden 2013, 204). This understanding of socialism is more compatible with radical democracy, while growing ever more distant from the idea of territorial national self-determination that is fundamental to Marxist-Leninism's approach to ethno-national issues. In line with this ideological transformation, the PKK reduced its demands regarding independence and proposed a non-state-aimed alternative political model.

The PKK's approach to the idea of the nation state and a solution to the Kurdish issue changed course once again with the kidnapping of Abdullah Öcalan in Kenya in 1999. Following his arrest, Öcalan intensified his criticism of nationalism and the creation of a nation state even more, and even went as far as to challenge the solution of the Kurdish issue through territorial political models, particularly the creation of a Kurdish nation state and even ethnic federalism (Öcalan 2009). He strongly rejected both the nation state and ethnic federalism models for solving the Kurdish issue; instead, he began to focus on democratic solutions, and proposed granting the Kurds' democratic rights within the constitution (Güneş 2012, 126–29). Öcalan thus abandoned 'pan-Kurdish' tendencies (Akkaya and Jongerden 2013, 204) and began to put emphasis on the development of a radical democracy, a democratic republic, democratic confederalism and democratic autonomy under the paradigm of democratic modernity to resolve the Kurdish question. Emphasizing these ideas illustrates Öcalan's determination to distance his movement – the PKK – from the existing socialist experiences and state-aimed political demands. Öcalan's rejection of territorial political claims was not welcomed by certain Kurdish groups (see Marcus 2007, 288; Akkaya and Jongerdin 2013, 248), but the overwhelming majority of the PKK accepted most of Öcalan's proposals without objection.

The PKK and the politicization of Kurdish identity

The PKK's U-turn from the creation of a Marxist-Leninist Kurdish state doubtlessly surprised many, and raised the question regarding the movement's handling of the Kurdish issue, and even its national character. Despite this, the PKK has had a considerable influence on the politicization of the Kurds and Kurdish identity, and the development of the Kurdish ethno-national identity.

The conflict between the PKK and state military forces instigated a massive socio-cultural, political and economic assault on the Kurdish people. It is estimated that the conflict between the PKK and state military forces, particularly the latter's violent coercion, left more than 50,000 dead, including 17,500 unsolved murders, the arrests of tens of thousands of Kurds, the evacuation of 3,500 villages, and the migration of more than 2.5 million Kurds from their own homes (Olson 2011, 3–4). In its fight with the PKK, the Turkish state also intensified its pressure on the Kurdish identity, harshly punishing any demands regarding the Kurdish identity. The state's severe approach to the Kurds was in line with its struggle against the PKK, and most of the time turned into conflict with civilians. Particularly during the *Newroz* (new year) celebrations and other civil demonstrations, the state security forces came down heavily on the masses, which resulted in many dead, wounded and arrested. To avoid accepting any official responsibility for the killing, kidnapping and forced migration of the Kurds in the fight against the PKK, some within the security forces came together to establish a clandestine paramilitary group called the JITEM, which was involved in a massive number of crimes (see Uslu 2010).

All these acts of violence naturally led to mounting outrage among the Kurds against the state, and even generated the 'disintegration of some Kurds from the Turkish state and society' (Yalçın-Mousseau 2012, 55) because the state's actions actually caused the Kurds' trust and confidence in the state to fall (Imset 1992, 242). The Turkish state's militaristic approach and constraints on the Kurds' ethno-national claims helped to generate a counter-reaction against the Turkish state and led the Kurdish masses to become increasingly aware of their ethno-national identity, and this drove considerable numbers of Kurds to the PKK (Bozarslan 2004b, 84–85; Van Bruinessen 2000a, 115–16). By taking this into account, the PKK greatly intensified its struggle, and strove to show that it was the sole power able to save the Kurds from state violence, and free them (Romano 2010, 128). In line with that purpose, the PKK began to organize the Kurds into civilian groups and prepare them for armed struggle. The PKK organized social and cultural activities, formed associations and tried to reach all aspects of Kurdish society through a common national discourse and purpose. Their efforts were successful, as many Kurds worked intensively to create their own socio-cultural, political and economic organizations. For instance, they established radio and TV stations to create a national awakening of the political struggle and to advertise their demands for collective rights (Gürbey 1996, 21–22). The PKK aimed to create a platform to mobilize the people to demand their political rights (Beşikçi 1992; Romano 2010). Their activities soon brought results, and catalysed the movement in most parts of the Kurdish region. The 1990s saw a number of *serhildan* protests in regions densely populated by Kurds (Gunter 1990, 90–91; Gürbey 1996, 23; White 2012, 236).

The PKK's efforts resulted in the Kurds collectively voicing their political claims for the first time, following the defeat of the Kurdish rebellions which took place in the first three decades of the Republic and following the collapse of the Kurdish national movements established between the years 1960 and 1980. The PKK in that sense was responsible for repairing the Kurds' self-confidence with respect to Kurdish national identity, which had been denied subsequent to the foundation of the Turkish Republic. Thus, the PKK instilled in the Kurds awareness of their 'status-lessness' (Beşikçi 1992). This, as a result, 'radicalized the Kurdish population' (McDowall 2004, 428) and initiated the politicization of Kurdish ethnic identity and the growth of Kurdish nationalism (Gürbey 1996, 17–18; Romano 2010, 230–31; Yalçın-Mousseau 2012, 55). This subsequently caused the further radicalization of the Kurds and intensification of their political claims (Keyman and Özkırımlı 2013, 48). Secessionism then became the next step as Kurdish nationalism continued to intensify (Yavuz 2001, 11).

Hence, the Turkish state's denial of the Kurds and the war with the PKK made many Kurds conscious of their collective identity, leading to the creation or imagination of their own national identity. This further moved forward with the formation of Kurdish political parties on legal platforms.

From the HEP to the HDP and the DBP: Kurdish political parties

The creation of legal Kurdish platforms, particularly political parties, dates back to the 1990s. The PKK's struggle and the Kurds' growing interest in their ethno-national identity were undoubtedly the primary motive behind the formation of the Kurdish political parties. However, the fact that the current Turkish political parties either supported the state's actions, or had no interest in the Kurdish issue or of the serious human rights violations in the Kurdish region, ultimately made it essential for Kurds to take part in the democratic process, since this would allow Kurds' voices to be heard in wider society. Yet other external factors also provoked the Kurds to pursue their struggle thorough legal and democratic platforms. The collapse of the Soviet Union and Western countries' growing interest in the Kurdish issue were two factors, but the fact that Western countries placed the PKK on their list of terrorist organizations and their insistence that Kurds pursue democratic ways to achieve their goals were also decisive in forcing Kurds to take part through legal channels. Furthermore, the PKK's ideological transformation, moving away from the idea of the creation of an independent Kurdish nation state, and, most importantly, the Kurds' growing interest in their ethno-national identity and political rights, extended the Kurdish issue beyond the boundaries of the PKK. The PKK fully understood that the Kurds could not achieve their goals by violence alone, because, despite the fact that a considerable number of the Kurds were becoming more aware of their political rights, most were still avoiding being linked with the PKK's ideology and legacy of armed struggle. The state's extremely tough stance increasingly raised the Kurds' concerns, since it became clear that it would be difficult to defeat the Turkish state and secure the Kurds' political rights simply through force alone. And the PKK's violent approach, especially the killing of some civilians, was also damaging the legitimacy of the Kurds' struggle and preventing them from receiving support from Western countries (see Yıldız 2005a). Considering all these elements, sorting out the Kurdish issue together, through democratic means, became a necessity for the Kurds.

However, neither the state nor the Turkish military and Turkish political parties wanted the Kurdish issue to be discussed democratically. Because of this, the state did not want Kurdish political organizations which prioritized Kurdish ethnic identity to develop (Watts 1999, 631). To prevent this, the state also adopted legal measures. For instance, the Turkish legal system closed all the doors to political parties which were 'based on regionalism and ethnicity' (Güney 2002, 122). Despite the strictness of the state's policy, the Kurds insisted on carrying out their battle through legal channels, because this was a necessity for dealing with the issue in a democratic way. The Kurds' insistence on using democratic means to secure their political rights resulted in the formation of the HEP on 7 June 1990 (Watts 1999, 632). The HEP included Kurds from various social and economic backgrounds, but the party strongly relied upon a socialist ideology. The party made particular efforts to bring the Kurdish issue into the public agenda, and to provide a political and legal basis for discussion. In their proposal for a solution to the Kurdish question that was both legal and could be debated in a civil and democratic manner, the HEP made clear references to the Universal Declaration of Human Rights (Watts 1999, 636). The HEP in this regard primarily called for constitutional recognition of the Kurdish national identity, and wanted the state to take decisive steps towards developing human rights and a democratic process, especially for the Kurds, including progress on freedom of expression, education in their mother tongue and Kurdish broadcasting (Ölmez 1995, 161).

The HEP participated in the 1991 general election soon after it was formed. However, the 10 per cent election threshold meant that it ran on the ticket of the SHP and secured twenty-two seats in parliament. Although the HEP did not obtain this success in its own name, the election of Kurdish MPs who were sensitive to the Kurdish issue was remarkable, since it provided the opportunity of bringing the Kurdish question onto parliament's agenda. This coalition was also important for bringing the Kurdish and Turkish politicians or politics together, in order to tackle the Kurdish question through joint endeavour. Since the TIP experience, it was almost the first time Kurdish politicians had taken part within another Social Democrat party by stressing their ethnic identity. However, the cooperation between the SHP and the HEP did not last long, due to speculations that the HEP maintained ties with the PKK, which led to reactions from SHP members causing in Kurdish parliamentarians to sustain their time in the HEP (Güney 2002, 124). Because of the strong reaction against the HEP both within and outside the SHP, the party toughened its stance against the Kurdish MPs, and this reached its peak with the expelling of seven of them who had attended a panel titled *The Kurds: Human Rights and Cultural Identity*, organized in Paris in 1989, because of the claims that the conference had links with the PKK. As a result of this controversy, all the Kurdish MPs and the party's many Kurdish members resigned from the SHP in the Kurdish regions.

Despite its limited power and the split from the SHP, the HEP played a considerable role in increasing the awareness of the Kurdish issue among the public. Yet, through its actions, the issue was to some extent brought forward to the Turkish parliament in a civil and democratic manner for the first time. The HEP is, therefore, considered to be a revolutionary party for politicizing the Kurdish issue in the public sphere (Ölmez 1995), and also a party that raised questions on Turkish political and judicial structures. But its focus on Kurdish identity and activities, and its positive remarks on the PKK, instigated its closure by the Turkish Constitutional Court in 1993. The Constitutional Court declared that the party was a focal point for terrorism against the indivisible integrity of state because of its links with the PKK.[2] Despite the HEP's rebuttal, the Constitutional Court refused to acknowledge the Kurds' claim to be a minority group with reference to the Lausanne Treaty, which recognizes that religious communities have a status. Taking this as a base, the Constitutional Court claimed that the HEP damaged the unity of the nation by mentioning an ethnic group which is not included in the Lausanne Treaty, and outlawed the party (Koğacioğlu 2004, 447–48). To put it simply, the HEP's political activities, particularly its emphasis on Kurdish ethnicity, were perceived as a challenge to the wholeness or homogeneous understanding of Turkish nation by the Constitutional Court.

Given the reasoned decision for closing the HEP, it is possible to suggest that Turkey was not ready to recognize Kurdish identity on a legal basis. The authorities did not accept the public recognition of the Kurdish identity and, as in the case of the HEP, punished those who attempted to pushed for that recognition at that time. On the other hand, like the state, the Kurds were also not deterred from pursuing their legal struggle, and took a firm stand in the fight to obtain their ethno-national rights. It is even plausible to imply that the state's aggression against Kurdish identity further encouraged them to continue their activities. With this determination, the majority of the Kurds who took part in the HEP set up the DEP on 7 May 1993, soon after the HEP was banned (Güney 2002, 125). As the successor of the HEP, the DEP was also a secular, left-wing party which prioritized the Kurdish issue, and which fought for recognition of Kurdish identity. The majority of DEP members were of Kurdish origin, but the party initially also included a considerable number of members of Turkish origin. However, the DEP was unable to retain most of these Turkish members because of the party's strong focus on the PKK; it therefore can also be considered as a Kurdish-origin party (Alınak 1996, 67–73). As with the HEP, and as noted previously, the DEP also attempted to bring the Kurdish issue to the attention of the Turkish public and parliament, yet this approach was soon challenged by the Turkish state both in political and legal terms. The Turkish authorities first wanted the HEP declare the PKK as a terrorist organization, and second distance itself from the notion of Kurdish ethnicity (Watts 1999, 647–48). The first demand was not realistic, since the HEP and the PKK shared almost the same sociological background. The DEP, therefore, instead concentrated on creating a dialogue between the state and the PKK, since it deemed the latter to be one of the main actors in attempting to reach a solution of the Kurdish issue. The second demand was the HEP's main founding purpose – granting the Kurds' ethnic identity. Refusing that meant denying their own reason for existing, because, in addition to the DEP's understanding of the Kurdish issue and proposals for securing Kurdish political rights, the main objective of the party was to solve the Kurdish issue through recognition of Kurdish ethnic identity (Gürbey 1996, 26–27). Therefore, the DEP neither disassociated itself from the notion of ethnicity nor recognized the PKK as a terrorist organization, in spite of the state's huge pressure on and reaction to it (Watts 2009, 648).

Accordingly, because of the state's rejection of Kurdish identity, the DEP also soon faced a closure case from the Constitutional Court, and was officially terminated on 30 June 1994. The actions of the state were spurred on by the allegations that the DEP had links with the PKK and sought to destroy the unity of the state.[3] Yet the collapse of the DEP, as with the HEP, did not dissuade Kurds from their political fight to be included in Turkish politics with their own identity. It was because of this aim that a new political party, the HADEP, was established in May 1994 (White 2012, 246). Although the state closed down the DEP and arrested many of its members, including forcibly taking some of its MPs from the Turkish Grand National Assembly, an overwhelming majority of the DEP's members joined the HADEP. The Kurds' efforts in organizing the HADEP illustrate that they were adamant about solving the Kurdish issue and continuing their political struggle through legal platforms, despite all the state's obstacles.

In its political life, the HADEP participated in the 1995 and 1999 elections. In the first election it won only 4.2 per cent of the popular vote and could not pass the national electoral threshold of 10 per cent (Turkish Statistical Institute, 11). The majority of the votes went to the conservative WP.[4] Many reasons can be considered to explain the HADEP's defeat in Turkey and the RP's success in the Kurdish regions, such as the Kurdish feudal classes' close relationship with the state and Kurds' social and economic integration within the Turkish identity and PKK's armed struggle. However, mostly it is believed that it was the HADEP's secular identity that prevented it from finding favour with the majority of the Kurds, particularly religious Kurds (Güney 2002, 127). The HADEP also participated in the local and national elections of 1999, gaining only 4.7 per cent of the popular vote (Turkish Statistical Institute, 11). Again, the HADEP thus failed to reach the 10 per cent threshold in the general election. However, it gained some success in the local elections by securing thirty-six municipalities, including the municipalities of the cities with a high population of Kurd communities – Diyarbakır, Ağrı, Batman, Bingöl, Hakkari, Siirt and Van. The HADEP's accomplishments in the local elections and gaining a sizeable number of votes in Kurdish cities proved that it was one of the leading powers among the Kurds, and also the party representing 'Kurdish ethnic votes' (Güneş-Ayata and Ayata 2002, 139).

To deal with the Kurdish issue, the HADEP considered taking democratic, political and economic steps. To achieve this, it proposed decentralization, the strengthening of local units, education in the mother tongue, election of governors and local police chiefs by local residents, prevention of torture, freedom of expression, use of the Kurdish language in the public sphere and the reclaiming of original Kurdish village and town names (Güney 2002, 129). The Turkish state reacted negatively to the HADEP's claims, and the party was even accused of seeking separation. As can clearly be seen through these highlighted demands, the HADEP did not run on a platform of seeking a Kurdish state. The party's primary focus was granting the Kurds basic cultural rights within the context of a decentralized and democratized Turkey. Yet despite HADEP's, as well as previous Kurdish political parties', political messages and focus on resolving the Kurdish issue through democratic methods and/or on legal grounds, the state did not alter its view on Kurdish identity. Instead, the state adopted a tough stance against anyone who expressed their own Kurdish identity, or Kurdish identity in general; this resulted in the killing, kidnapping and arrest of many party members, and the party was closed down on 13 March 2003 (Ciment 1996, 158). The HADEP's emphasis on Kurdish identity and its political activities quickly caught the attention of the Turkish Constitutional Court. Like previous Kurdish political parties, the HADEP was outlawed on the grounds of having suspected associations with the PKK, and promoting separatism against the unity and territorial integrity of the state.[5]

Because of this, after the HADEP was outlawed, almost all of its party members joined the DEHAP, founded on 24 October 1997, as an alternative party. The DEHAP was the party of coalition between the Kurds and a few small Turkish socialist parties, particularly the EMEP. The DEHAP joined the 2002 election, but, like the HADEP, it also failed to pass the 10 per cent national election threshold, achieving approximately 6.2 per cent of votes in total (Kurubaş 2008, 34). Following the election results, which were insufficient to elect the party to parliament, the DEHAP dissolved itself in 2005, and most of its cadres joined the DTP, which had been established on 17 August 2005. As a replacement for the previous pro-Kurdish parties, the DTP also prioritized the Kurdish issue by adding it to its agenda and joining the 2007 and 2009 elections. In the 2007 elections, the DTP ran with independent candidates in order to pass the 10 per cent electoral threshold by procuring twenty-two seats.[6] Considering the Kurds' political choices in the general election of 2007, it is also worth noting that more than half the Kurds in Kurd-populated areas voted for the AKP; this shows that the DTP was still not successful enough to secure all the Kurds' support (Tayiz 2014, 12).[7] As was case with the HADEP, the Kurds were torn between their religious and ethnic identities. Given the AKP's religious identity, as Karlsson (2008, 168) underlines, it is likely that a large number of Kurds identified themselves primarily through their religious identity and separated themselves from the secular Kurdish party, the DTP, further illustrating the impact religion plays in shaping some Kurds' political choices. Religion, as the coming chapters will cover, continued to be one of the defining dynamics in determining some Kurds' approach to the Kurdish origin parties and political claims.

Similar to previous Kurdish political parties, the DTP also placed the Kurdish issue as a primary concern in its agenda. However, with reference to Kirişçi (2007, 19), two separate understandings at that point developed in the party: while the first one proposed a solution to the Kurdish issue through a pluralist, democratic understanding, the second looked towards federalism for a resolution. As with such political claims, ties with the PKK also became a contentious issue within the party. In regard to this separation, Olson underlines that while some members of the party strongly suggested establishing relations with the PKK and Abdullah Öcalan while continuing to wage an armed struggle, others proposed ceasing the violence and PKK's armed struggle (Olson 2009, 39, 70). This debate, as later development has shown, was favourable for those who did not want to end the PKK's armed struggle until the Kurdish question was resolved This, in turn, had a significant effect on Kurdish politics because, given that the state had closed down all the legal platforms available to the Kurdish parties and had outlawed them, most of the Kurds had begun to consider the PKK as the sole actor in the Kurdish public sphere. Having a common social ground between the PKK and the DTP in this sense greatly increased the PKK's influence on Kurdish politics. The DTP met the same fate as its predecessor, the DEHAP, and was eventually outlawed by the Constitutional Court in 2009; the main accusations being that the party orchestrated the central events against the inseparable unity of the state, the country and the nation.[8] Soon after it was closed down, almost all cadres of the DTP decided to join the BDP, which was established in 2008 and gave emphasis to the Kurdish issue by proposing a democratic autonomy model, which will be covered in more detail in the upcoming section.

In line with Abdullah Öcalan's ideological perspectives, particularly the idea of democratic autonomy, Kurdish politicians decided to run their policies through two different parties, the DBP (active particularly in the Kurdish regions) and the HDP (active all across Turkey). Based on this, the BDP dissolved itself on 11 July 2014 and continues as the DBP, and all of the BDP's mayors joined the DBP. The DBP is active in the Kurdish regions, and its main priority is the constructing of democratic autonomy through idea of democratic confederalism (Demokratik Bölgeler Partisi Tüzüğü 2016). The DBP in this regard established many organizations from village communes to city councils. The party, however, faced severe oppression from the state. The party's co-leaders and more than half of its mayors were arrested. The government also appointed 106 trustees to the DBP's mayor-run municipalities.

To run politics across Turkey, the HDP was founded on 15 October 2012. The party shares a left-wing ideology with emphasis on social democracy, secularism, feminism, minority rights and pluralism (Halkların Demokratik Partisi Tüzüğü 2014). The HDP supports democratic autonomy as the most applicable political model to solve the Kurdish issue (HDP Parti Programı 2014).[9] Relying on the idea of *Turkiyelilesme* (i.e. being a party representing all Turkish citizens from diverse backgrounds, not only the Kurds), the HDP also includes a considerable number of Turkish leftists in its ranks. The party is ruled by co-leaders, with one from the Turkish leftist movement or ideology. The party hence avoids identifying itself only with the Kurds and the Kurdish region, although the majority of its members are of Kurdish origin and the party takes the Kurdish issue as its priority. The HDP ran in the Turkish general election that took place on 7 June 2015 and won eighty seats (13.2 per cent). The party's success was the most historic event in legal Kurdish politics since the HEP. Yet its success also raised serious concerns within the AKP: first, the party (AKP) failed to form a government on its own, and second there was the Kurds' considerable support for the HDP. Following the AKP's failure to form a government, Turkey once again went to the polls, and an election took place on 1 November 2015. The HDP once again pass the 10 per cent threshold and won fifty-nine seats (10.76 per cent), losing twenty-one seats. Several issues strongly influenced the HDP's losses at the November 2015 elections: the AKP's running of a special military campaign against the HDP,[10] the start of the conflict between the PKK, Turkish security forces and the PKK-affiliated youth groups known as the YDG-H, and the digging of ditches in some Kurdish districts and city centres and the state's violent response to it,[11] which resulted in the deaths of more than 2,000 civilians and the complete destruction of some Kurdish cities and districts (BBC Türkçe 2017). The majority of the Kurds, including HDP supporters, criticized the PKK's 'Revolutionary People's War' strategy and the digging of ditches in some districts and city centres where the PKK received considerable support.[12] The HDP's failure to stop the digging of the ditches resulted in some Kurds distancing themselves from the party to some extent.

Following the elections, the AKP further intensified its pressure on the HDP. The government-affiliated media organizations, and particularly its leadership Recep Tayyip Erdogan, have not avoided affiliating the HDP with the PKK, and thus tried to marginalize the party. Along with the HDP's co-chairs Selahattin Demirtas and Figen Yüksekdag, many of the party's MPs and more than half of the provincial and district heads and executives, and thousands of party members and sympathizers, were arrested. The pressure on the HDP and DBP further intensified following both parties' strong challenge to the Turkish state's military operation in Kurdish areas in Turkey, and especially in the YPG-ruled Afrin canton in the *Rojava* region of Syria (in January–March 2018). Challenging the AKP's policies and criticizing Turkey's military operation, including through social media, resulted in the arrest and taking into custody of hundreds of members of both parties.

Motivation behind the demand for democratic autonomy

Democratic autonomy – although it is a new political model – is demanded by a considerable number of Kurds. By considering the data collected from the interviews and other primary sources, this part brings to the forefront the reasons for this demand among the Kurds who support the HDP/BDP, DBP and who have sympathy with the PKK. At the same time, the section also explains why supporters of democratic autonomy reject alternative solutions presented by other Kurdish groups and organizations.

National political status and the protection of Kurdish identity

The Kurds who call for democratic autonomy put emphasis on the Kurds' national character and how this contributes to obtaining political status. As is the case with the majority of the Kurds' demand for ethnic territorial political models, the supporters of democratic autonomy also distrust the state and believe that because they have not been given a national status, as their national identity is not recognized and protected by the constitution, their ethno-national identity is being assimilated, and even those political achievements they have already obtained may be taken away from them. Consequently, they argue that only through constitutional recognition of Kurdish national status (at the collective level in political and legal terms) can their concerns be truly eliminated. Thus, they rationalize democratic autonomy model within the context of national status first.

Taking into account the concerns and claims of the Kurds, the associations between political status and national identity are conveyed in the main principles of democratic autonomy. Democratic autonomy deems constitutional acknowledgement of the Kurds' national status as its primary objective: 'Democratic autonomy is the way to express that the Kurds refuse the political status based on the Turkish state's denial and destruction policies and are willing to reach a new status that allows them to live in freedom and democracy' (Draft Submission for a Democratic Autonomous Kurdistan 2011, 14). The model, therefore, signifies the Kurds' political status.

The belief that the Kurdish ethno-national identity is still denied and is under the risk of assimilation further makes obtaining a political status of great importance for these Kurds. The Kurds' distrust of the state here makes the achievement of a political status a more evident goal. This was a very common concern alluded to during the fieldwork. As expressed by Kudret Gülün, the BDP İstanbul Esenyurt district co-chair, most of the Kurds believe that they do not trust the state, and therefore claim that without the acquisition of a political status, Turkey will continue with its assimilation policies towards Kurdish identity.[13] For most of these Kurds, as noted by Arif Erol, who is also the BDP's İstanbul Esenyurt district co-chair, the state has progressed in its assimilation policies in order to remove or at least weaken the Kurds' national will. The lack of an official mention of Kurdish identity, for instance, is deemed to be proof of their concerns.[14] This apprehensiveness regarding assimilation was also highlighted in an interview with Hasan Yildiz, who is a consultant for some BDP-affiliated organizations. Hasan Yıldız often stressed the intensity of the assimilation processes taking place amongst the Kurds, because many did not have the opportunity to organize themselves and protect their ethno-national values. This resulted in the disintegration and 'disidentification' (*kimliksizlesme*) of the Kurdish identity.[15]

The Turkish state's systematic assimilation approach to its minorities, in line with its homogeneous nation-creation project (Beşikçi 1991, 1993), adds extra weight to Kurds' concerns, and therefore they believe that this can only be stopped if Kurdish national identity is constitutionally recognized and protected. The denial of the Kurds' status means a 'non-bloody genocide' of Kurdish culture, said Rahime Kanilga, who is a HDP Çanakkale executive and was the HDP Çanakkale municipality co-mayoral Candidate in the Turkish local elections held on 30 March 2014. Rahime defined the assimilation policies in Turkey in the following words:

> Assimilation is not a strategy (*policy*)[16] that is only applied to Kurds. Assimilation is a state policy that is applied to all nations in different forms and to different degrees. But, the assimilation has been applied to the Kurds is more than other nations. This starts with the national pledge during primary school. This is a non-bloody genocide that was revealed with the formation of republic and intensified later, by banning education in the mother tongue, banning Kurdish publications, and forbidding Kurdish names and places. This is an absolute must for colonialism.[17]

The Kurds who call for cultural rights, which will be analysed in the following chapter, consider the aforementioned anxieties as unrealistic, or at least exaggerated at the present time. Nonetheless, the negative stance held by the political authorities towards acknowledging the Kurds' political status supports this argument of the exponents of democratic autonomy to some extent. For instance, the CHP parliamentarian Birgul Ayman Guler's remark that 'Kurds cannot be equal to the Turkish nation' in her speech at parliament in 2013 (Sol Portal – 11 January 2013) and similar ideas were considered by many Kurds who witnessed them as voicing the state's official ideology.

The field research revealed that the anxieties of the Kurds (about implicit assimilation) escalated further with the existence of and then a string of references to nationalism in the current government's policies. Turkish nationalism's[18] negative reaction to and position against diverse ethno-religious groups, particularly the Kurds (Kentel 2014), are one of the most prominent causes for an increase in Kurds' anxiety and doubt relating to the state's approach towards their national identity. Emine Ayna's (BDP Diyarbakır MP), in the following citation, expresses the distrust that Kurds who call for democratic autonomy feel towards the state, and because of this, the importance of their struggle to obtain political status. In this matter she argues that state authorities, for example Prime Minister Recep Tayyip Erdogan, are Turkish nationalists and do not want Kurds to have national status:

> Erdogan, in reality, believes Turkish-Islamic syntheses. He is, essentially, a Turkish nationalist, he is an ultranationalist, and he has roots in the MHP. He

is both a radical Turkish nationalist and has roots in the Turkish nationalist movement. Because of that, Erdogan never wants the Kurds to have their status. He does it only if he has to. Not because he wants to. [...] Therefore, we talk about the right to self-governance or status for the Kurdish identity and Kurdistan people.[19]

Similarly, the BDP Diyarbakır MP Altan Tan spoke out, saying that that the current government, the AKP and its leader do not want to recognize the Kurds' national status. Altan said:

The Republic of Turkey, including Tayyip Erdogan, has not had good intentions from the start. Initially, the public regarded Recep Tayyip Erdogan and the government as conservative Muslims who also suffered from the regime and were imprisoned at the hands of the state. Therefore, people hoped that they would eliminate *Kemalism*, establish a democratic Turkey and grant rights to the Kurds. But it appears that Tayyip Erdogan and his colleagues are not able to go beyond the Turkish-Islamic nationalist paradigm. They will never acknowledge Kurds as a different people, as a nation.[20]

In the same line, in response to the question, '*so they will never acknowledge Kurds as a nation?*' Tan specified:

They will never see and will never consider Kurds on equal terms as a nation, an ethnic group or as a people. What I mean is that they will never do so voluntarily. This can only happen if Kurds seize their rights. As they say, rights are never granted, but obtained. That will be the case for the Kurds.[21]

Altan Tan and Emine Ayna's quotes indicate that these Kurds do not trust the state or the current government – the AKP – and there is fear among them that without political status their ethnic identity will become vulnerable; even their already attained political and cultural achievements will also be under threat from the Turkish state if the Kurds' political status is not granted. For instance, compared with the past, although limitations remain in place, currently Kurds can use the Kurdish language in public, print Kurdish newspapers (Azadîya Welat), broadcast in Kurdish (TRT-6), form social and cultural organizations and have the option to take selected Kurdish courses in universities. On top of these achievements, the BDP won 103 municipalities in the 2014 local elections on 30 March[22] and the HDP won 81 and 59 seats at the 7 June and 1 November 2015 Turkish general elections, respectively. However, the Kurds who defend democratic autonomy, as Fırat ANLI, member of the DTK and the Diyarbakır Metropolitan municipality's current co-mayor (elected in the 2014 election) highlighted, believe that most of these achievements are not protected through a legal system and are thus under the firm control of the state.[23] According to Fırat ANLI, the Kurds obtained these successes only through an arduous and bloody struggle, with unforeseen costs. He argued that the success of the BDP has a direct correlation to the Kurds' struggle. However, he asserts, there is no guaranteed protection of their achievements, as they are under the tough supervision of the state apparatus, such as governors and district head officials, meaning that the successes of the Kurds can easily be taken from their hands.[24] He openly said they do not trust the state when asked *how he considers the negotiation between the state and PKK*, namely the peace process,[25] which aimed to find solutions for the Kurdish issue in 2013–14. Fırat ANLI openly verbalized his concerns about and mistrust of the government;

> When the current situation with the peace process is considered, the Kurds are hopeful but cautious at the same time. […] Because of their previous experiences, so much disappointment has been seen. So many reversals have been experienced. I am talking about this by considering similar experiences, such as Habur and Oslo. There is always a feeling of failure in this process.[26]

The points highlighted by ANLI and other Kurdish politicians came true with the AKP's later policies. The AKP made a U-turn in its approach to the Kurdish issues and began to eliminate or at least weaken the Kurdish political will in every sense. The party started this with the rejection of the democratic initiatives that were part of the peace process. For instance, Recep Tayyip Erdogan stated that he did not accept the wording of the 'Dolmabahce Agreement', 28 February 2015, which aimed to solve the Kurdish issue through a democratic pluralist understanding in a broad context (Daily Sabah 2015). The agreement was drafted by the HDP and Abdullah Öcalan on the Kurdish side, and also the AKP, under the guidance of Deputy Minister Yalçin Akdogan with the implicit knowledge of Erdogan (Cumhurriyet 2016). Despite this, Erdogan rejected the Dolmabahce Agreement and launched a fight against the HDP, DBP and PKK.

It is widely believed that the main motivation behind Recep Tayyip Erdogan's refusal of the Dolmabahce Declaration was his fear of losing support from some Turkish conservatives and nationalists.[27] To the HDP Igdir MP Mehmet Emin Adiyaman, by initiating peace talks the AKP aimed to buy itself some time, and when it realized it would cost the party the election it began to return and implement a 'wartime ideology' which the state applied against the Kurds in the 1990s. To Adiyaman, therefore, the AKP was never sincere in its approach to the peace talks or to the Kurds,[28] although this view was challenged by non-

HDP affiliated Kurds to a certain extent. For instance, according to Hak-Par general vice president Arif Sevinç and Hüda-Par Şanlı Urfa provincial chairman Lokman Yalçın, neither the AKP nor the PKK was sincere in their approach to the peace process. To these Kurds, both parties approached the peace process with an eye to their own political benefit.[29]

Democratic autonomy supporters' concerns became far more apparent once the AKP began following nationalist policies and cooperating politically with the Turkish Nationalist Party. The AKP and MHP coalition resulted in the launching of military attacks and destruction of many Kurdish cities, districts and towns in 2015–16, and the arrest of thousands of HDP and DBP members. The AKP's nationalist policies ultimately resulted in Recep Tayyip Erdogan's rejection of the Kurdish issue by saying that 'there is no such problem in Turkey anymore, you cannot explain this to anybody. There is a terror problem in Turkey' (Hürriyet Daily News 2016). Furthermore, following the failed 15 July 2016 coup d'état, the AKP government closed hundreds of democratic and Kurd-affiliated social, cultural and media organizations, including TV channels, radio stations and newspapers including Turkey's sole Kurdish language daily Azadiya Welat.

The policies demonstrated by the state confirmed the anxieties of the defenders of democratic autonomy and consequently led them to claim that political status on a legal base was a necessity for the protection of Kurdish identity and Kurdish achievements. Gaining political status was regarded as 'a method of defence of Kurdish ethno-national identity and removal of the legal base that legitimize the state's assimilative rules'.[30] Sako, a DÖKH activist, openly articulated her concerns regarding assimilation by the state through well-organized and planned methods directed against the Kurds. She pointed out that even if the state did not apply forced assimilation policies or openly refuse Kurdish ethnic identity, this would not mean that the Turkish state had abandoned its aim to remove the Kurds' ethno-national identity over time.[31] Hence, to alleviate the fears of assimilation and the distrust that the Kurds for the state, the democratic autonomy model, which was intended to provide Kurds a national political status, should be embraced as an effective solution. As Seydi Fırat, a member of the DTK's Permanent Council and a Peace Assembly executive and spokesman, stated, constitutional recognition of the Kurds' status was in fact equivalent to granting the Kurds their national identity and minimizing their concerns.[32] This status, as highlighted previously, was demanded within the context of democratic autonomy and could be practised all across Turkey. To these Kurds, their national status 'is Kurdish people's status, but it is not only the status of those Kurds living in the Kurdish region'. This status also includes the Kurds who live in the western parts of Turkey,[33] and Kurdish internal minorities such as the Alevis.[34]

Within the framework discussed above, and as the fieldwork conducted clearly revealed, being a distinct nation, and having concerns about and distrust of the state's approach towards Kurdish national identity and the Kurds' achievements contributed significantly to the rise in demand for democratic autonomy.[35] To these Kurds, the granting of their national status in legal and political terms could alleviate their worries about the assimilation of their ethno-national identity. In this regard, as the deliberations conducted above reveal, the Kurds who support the HDP/BDP, DBP and PKK believe that democratic autonomy will provide such a status for the protection of Kurdish national identity.

Collective rights and self-governance

Demand for constitutional acknowledgement of Kurdish ethno-national identity is also a significant reason for democratic autonomy advocates to justify their refusal to support the granting of their ethno-cultural rights at the individual level, by highlighting the collective aspects of Kurdish identity. Democratic autonomy considers the resolution of the Kurdish issue only through individual cultural rights as being a denial of the collective aspects of Kurdish identity. Approaching the Kurdish issue only through individual cultural rights implies negation of their nationality. Therefore, they aim to sort out Kurdish issues within the context of collective rights and self-governance, which comprise the core themes of democratic autonomy.

Throughout the empirical research, many of the proponents of democratic autonomy were asked about the issue of individual and collective rights, with a particular focus on their insistence on gaining collective rights and their rationale for refusing cultural rights at the individual level. The fieldwork revealed that these Kurds want to self-govern as a nation, but expressed that this was impossible if only individual cultural rights were granted.[36] On this matter Selim Kurbanoğlu, the BDP Diyarbakır Yenişehir municipality mayor, stressed that the Kurds' status must be considered in terms of their national character. He put emphasis on the collective rights and aspects of Kurdish identity, and directly confronted the idea of acknowledging the Kurds' national will and identity through granting them their individual cultural rights alone. Approaching Kurdish identity only through individual rights, Selim Kurbanoğlu said, is intended to prevent the Kurds' demand for identical collective rights.[37]

This view was expressed on numerous occasions during the fieldwork. In support of this, Jiyan, a political and women's rights activist in the Kurdish diaspora in London, made reference to the national side of the Kurdish identity and stated, 'It is shameful that we are still talking about individual rights, or authorities talking about solving the Kurdish issue through individual rights.' She added that in spite of the fact that the Kurdish national struggle had continued for over a century, the Kurds are still deprived of their collective national rights. Jiyan also underlined that the Kurdish people will never give up their demand for national identity because their national identity is at the heart of their being – as already seen, they would rather give up their lives than give up the struggle for their national identity. This is because, she said, 'demanding only individual cultural rights for the Kurds' would mean 'denial of Kurdish national identity'.[38]

Rebuttal of their collective rights, to these Kurds, denotes the state's attitude to the Kurds as individuals who need to be governed. In other words, the state's aim is to prevent the Kurds from gaining the right to self-govern, as is the case with the current (AKP) government's policies. The following statement from the BDP Diyarbakır MP Altan Tan demonstrates the Kurds' attitude towards the current government's (AKP) refusal of their self-governance demand (collective rights) – the AKP's goal is to have control over the Kurds:

> Kurds, like Arabs, like Albanians, like Georgians, are a separate nation; they have a right to learn in their mother tongue and to govern themselves. Kurds and Turks are brothers and sisters. The two peoples will live together not in separate states, but in one state. Yet the government's mindset is different. They see Kurds as a minority to be governed, or at best, a younger sibling. The big brother who controls the money and has the power to govern can act as it wishes; it can beat the younger sibling or give pocket change to the younger sibling, who has no say in anything anyway.[39]

In light of this argument, the democratic autonomy supporters proclaim that the Kurds as a nation cannot be without a status which will grant them collective rights and the right of self-governance.[40] And so, they consider democratic autonomy as a political model which is able to provide them with a political will and status to gain their collective rights (Çelik 2012a). In this respect, as Ülsever (2011, 88–89) clarified, with democratic autonomy Kurds want to be considered as a nation and largely manage their internal affairs independently. That is also the main reason why these Kurds challenge the idea of resolving the Kurdish issue through their cultural rights only. However, the model also refuses the ideas of the nation state and ethnic federalism in dealing with the Kurdish question.

Rejection of the nation-state and ethnic federalism

The Kurds who defend democratic autonomy, although they seek for Kurds to be granted their collective identity and their right to self-govern, they make no reference to the nation state or ethnic federalism. They clearly detach themselves not only from nation state but also from ethnic federalism because they consider it as a projection of the state. Therefore, they do not have any interest in separation or the creation of an independent nation state, or ethnic federalism for the Kurds. Their quest for self-governance thus does not imply a desire for territorial self-determination. The observations collected from the proponents of democratic autonomy showed that the Kurds' demographic distribution and integration (dispersion), their fragmented structure (existence of Kurdish internal minorities), the consideration of territorial models as the crux of the conflict and decline in national boundaries are all supposed causes for the rejection of territorial political models in favour of democratic autonomy.

Dispersal of the Kurds across Turkey

The physical distribution of the Kurds around Turkey and their social, cultural and, particularly, economic connection with the Turks are one of the deciding conditions in the rejection of territorial political models and the consideration of democratic autonomy as an alternative, predominantly because the latter can be applied throughout Turkey.

Many of the interviewees addressed the Kurds' demographic distribution and its influence on their political demands. As can be seen in Figure 4.1, Kurds consist more than 20 per cent of the population in many of the Turkey's metropolises.

Emphasizing demographic distribution, the DÖKH activist Sako reiterated that more than half of the Kurds had migrated from their homeland, and now had close social, cultural and economic interactions with the Turkish community. Because of these interactions, Sako stated that the Kurds had been integrated into Turkey's ethno-national identity to a certain extent, and no longer had a yearning to return to their traditional homeland. Therefore, a substantial number of migrant Kurds felt more a part of the region they lived in, thus making it ever-more difficult to solve the Kurdish issue through ethnic territorial political models.[41] The point Sako emphasized was repeatedly alluded to by the other democratic autonomy adherents. BDP Diyarbakır MP Emine Ayna's following point stresses the same argument and explains why the Kurds

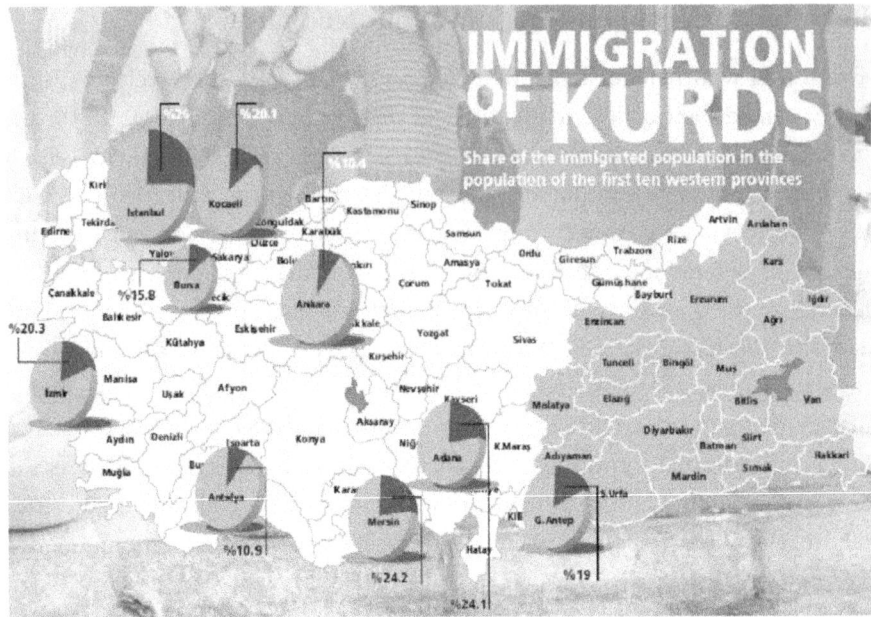

Figure 4.1 Immigration of Kurds: Share of the immigrated population in the population of the first ten western provinces. Source: (Sönmez 2013).

who call for democratic autonomy find the application of territorial political models rather challenging considering the Kurds' current physical distribution:

> Kurds and the minorities of the Kurdish region do not only live in Kurdistan. They are populated all around Turkey. For instance, the Kurds in Iraqi Kurdistan live in a particular region. [...] However, the Kurds in Turkey do not reside in a particular region. If you approach the Kurdish issue using a federal model, that means you exclude the Kurds who live in İstanbul, Ankara and Izmir.[42]

Supporting this, Altan Tan, a BDP Diyarbakır MP, explained that there are intensive interactions between the Kurds who migrated; the Kurds who settled in Kurdish regions; and people of other communities, for example, the Turks and the Arabs. The Kurds' socio-cultural and economic relations with the 'others', Altan says, cut across Kurdish regional boundaries, and so the conditions for forming territorial structures, particularly the creation of a new state, have become difficult (Tan 2009, 553–54). With reference to this and to the Kurds' current demographic distribution, Hasan Yildiz, a lawyer and consultant for some Alevi and BDP-affiliated organizations, underlined that 'proposing federalism or a nation-state for the Kurds would result in severe consequences for them'. Consequently, Hasan added, because of the distribution of the Kurdish population as well as its socio-cultural and economic integration within Turkey, the idea of territorial boundaries for most Kurds has been removed, most notably for migrated Kurds.[43] This is because to these Kurds ethnic territorial political models, both nation-state and ethnic federalist models focus on the Kurdish region and don't propose plausible solutions either for migrant Kurds or the diverse identities in the Kurdish region.[44]

Mentioning this, the BDP Diyarbakır Yenişehir municipality mayor, Selim Kurbanoglu, argued that democratic autonomy satisfies all Kurds, particularly those who do not inhabit Kurdish regions, by granting protection to all their ethno-national rights through unity with Turkey. Kurbanoglu therefore added that 'we [i.e. the Kurds] do not propose any political model which makes reference to a particular ethnic group or identity. That means conflict. Because of this, we suggest democratic autonomy'.[45] The democratic autonomy model defined here becomes an alternative because it can be applied across Turkey. Consequently, although democratic autonomy seeks to cater to all Kurds because it can be applied throughout Turkey by establishing local and regional structures, it also attracts migrant Kurds and groups who categorize themselves through different identities (Serxwebûn 2012a, 148). Democratic autonomy supporters make reference to democratic autonomy and its organizational form, democratic confederalism, which allows the Kurds and other minorities to organize all across Turkey. Mentioning this, Emine Ayna proposes the creation of local assemblies and councils over territorial political models because with these structures each cultural, ethnic and religious group will have equal opportunity for representation wherever they reside. Ayna added:

> If you propose an autonomy which could be applied for the whole of Turkey then each region would find the opportunity to have its own parliament and other mechanisms. [...] These parliaments or local assemblies will provide every group the right to representation, including the Kurds as well. Accordingly, the Kurds who live in other parts of Turkey, such as İstanbul, Izmir or Manisa, will be able to take part in the local assemblies of the regions where they are located.[46]

Considering Ayna's words, democratic autonomy proposes restructuring Turkey into 24–26 regions across the country. In these regions, Kurds as well as other ethnic and religious groups will have the ability to practise their identities, and to independently organize where they live through local councils and assemblies provided by democratic confederalism's bottom-up organizational structure. Hence, unlike the definition of a particular region and ethnicity, the application of democratic autonomy all over Turkey is one of the notable ideas that separate democratic autonomy from territorial political models, says Emine Ayna. In addition to this, she added:

> This is the point that differentiates our autonomy model from federalism and other autonomous models. In our model, the Kurds will be represented wherever they live. There are Kurds in almost all parts of Turkey, which means they have the right to take part in decision-making and rule themselves wherever they live. We do not restrict democratic autonomy only within a particular region. [...] That is the difference between our system and federalism.[47]

In this sense, the Kurds first of all will be recognized as a nation, and, based on this, in those regions where they make up the majority they will have their own parliament (which will be a supra-organization over the autonomous regions majorly settled by the Kurds), and the Kurdish language will be the official language; furthermore, there will be the creation of other social, cultural and political organizations determined by the eight dimensions of the model (Draft Submission for a Democratic Autonomous Kurdistan 2011). In regard to this, Ayla Akat Ata highlights the unifying characteristic of democratic autonomy: that it is a model capable of bringing the Kurds, Turks and other groups together, further enhancing the social, cultural and economic interplay between them by granting them their identical differences and thus decreasing the state's intervention into peoples' affairs (Akat Ata 2012). Consequently, to these Kurds, the application of democratic autonomy across Turkey makes it a preferable political model, but also an alternative option to nation state and ethnic federalism.

Kurdish internal minorities and the fragmented structure of the Kurds

The Kurds show a significant degree of variation at the linguistic and religious levels and this influences their political demands. The research conducted with democratic autonomy advocates, particularly with the Alevi and Zaza Kurds, clearly demonstrated that another reason why they refuse territorial political models is the fragmented structure of the Kurds. The individuals interviewed stated that Kurds' linguistically and religiously heterogeneous structure and their resultant status as internal minorities make implementation of territorial political models difficult, since these models take a specific territory and ethnicity into account. On the other hand, although the proponents of democratic autonomy alluded to the negative consequences of territorial political structures on the Kurds they, especially the Alevis and Zazas, also underlined the possibility that there would be further assimilation and oppression of the Kurdish internal minorities within the Kurdish and Turkish identity, and a greater division of the Kurds due to ethnic and religious tensions. During the interviews, these Kurds underlined the belief that in order to protect the Kurdish internal minorities' differences in Kurdish unity, these minorities (Alevis and Zazas) should construct their own autonomous regions, something which the democratic autonomy model largely considers.

Thus, the majority of the Alevis and Zazas who vote for the BDP/HDP identify themselves within the Kurdish ethnic identity and call for a democratic autonomy model. Despite their concerns, which will be covered below, the fieldwork research revealed these Zazas and Alevis are not alienated from the Kurdish ethnic identity. However, some Zazas and Alevis, who support the AKP and the CHP and currently demand the cultural rights only model, were isolated, which will be discussed in detail in Chapter 5. This chapter thus covers only the Zazas and Alevis who vote for BDP/HDP and demand democratic autonomy.

Observations of these Zaza and Alevi Kurds uncovered that they feared assimilation into the overall Kurdish and Turkish identity and feared the thought of being oppressed. Because of the lack of opportunities, the Zazas and the Alevis emphasized this risk of assimilation into both majority Turkish and also majority Kurdish identities (Partiya Serbestiya Dersim Program Taslagi 2009). A vast majority of Zaza-speaking Kurds, as highlighted by Hidir Çelik, president of Zaza-Der, are apprehensive about the loss of their language because it faces constant assimilation into the Kurmanji-speaking Kurdish identity. Hidir Çelik's following words clearly reveal his concerns.

> We come together with various friends and constantly say that we are a dying generation, the last representatives of a language, and this language will disappear after us. This is the first concern, this is a very important concern: if this language disappears, the culture also disappears. As Confucius says, *'why cut the nation, destroy its language instead?'* It is enough. We start the struggle with this concern. Then there was criticism of the Kurdish political movement. This was the second reason, because the Kurdish political movement's common ground does not distinguish between Kurds. To them, the *'Zaza and Kurmanji are both Kurds. Both Zaza and Kurmanji are dialects of Kurdish. We all are Kurds. We need to fight for the Kurdish case'*. Saying something against this means dividing the fight, and represents a national betrayal. You know this discourse. However, when we discussed it with them, they could not answer the following questions:

> If Zazas are Kurds and Zaza is a Kurdish dialect, why do you invest everything in Kurdish (*Kurmanji*)? Since they both are dialects, the scales should be equal. Since they both are dialects, why do you put the weights on one side and not the other. [...] When I go to the south (*Iraqi Kurdistan*) they say 'shame on you, you do not speak Kurdish'. When I say, 'I know Zaza', they say, 'Kurdish is our mother tongue; a Zaza can learn Kurdish in four months'. But why doesn't a Kurd learn Zaza in four months? Is he stupid? That is not the case; this is actually a political position. [...] Actually, Zazas make a point of differentiating themselves from Kurds, as they are assimilated so quickly, meaning that integration into Turkish society happens quickly for them.[48]

Along with this language-based fear of assimilation and resulting fragmentation, the interviews revealed that there was another dynamic that contributed to increased tensions and divisions among Kurds, relating to the dispute between Sunni and Alevi identities. A vast number of the Kurmanji- and Zazaki-speaking Alevi Kurds do not trust others and feel insecure in themselves, as well as being sceptical of Sunni Kurds. This was repeatedly stressed during the fieldwork research. For example, an academic of Alevi origin, Zuhal, remarked on the Sunni's oppression of the Alevis and the resulting Alevis' fears, which have been transferred through the generations.

> Well the trust is like this: Alevis will actively create a space for themselves and will say 'we are here as a power'. If they build all the political organizations by themselves from the bottom to the top, if they manage this, only when they can say this organization is ours will this trust come about. Otherwise, it will not happen. It will never happen because there is a traumatic memory that has been passed down since the Ottoman Empire. It is strange, the fact that it has been passed down, very odd. It appears out of time – Memory won't go away even though the reality is not the same. [...] Trust is transferable. We are still in a transitional stage for gaining this trust; there is no transferable trust, but we are in the process of getting it.[49]

The anxiety expressed by Zuhal also came across in an interview with Hasan Yildiz, who is a Zaza-speaking Kurdish Alevi. According to Hasan Yıldız, the Alevi Kurds remember the Sunni Kurds' alliances (with the Ottoman Empire) and their attacks on Alevis. Hasan Yıldız often referred to Idris-i Bitlisi (1452–1520),[50] a notable scholar of Sunni Kurdish origin, and stated that Alevis have not forgotten him and the Sunni Kurds' attacks on the Alevi Kurds. To Yıldız, the Ottoman Empire and the Turkish state have always oppressed and provoked the Kurdish Alevis by using the Sunni Kurds.[51] Hasan Yıldız's thoughts on the Sunni Kurds' perception of the Alevis explicitly demonstrate that Alevis' fears are not restricted to their religious identity. In this regard, as stressed by the president of the Yüzleşme Foundation, Cafer Solgun, the Alevis believe that their Kurdish identity is also a reason why they have been subjected to discrimination in Turkey. It is due to their both ethnic and religious identity, Solgun explained, that the majority of Alevis have been singled out (Solgun 2008). To the Alevis and Zazas, the Sunni Kurds and Sunni Turks can cooperate on Sunni terms, despite both parties' ethnic tensions. This allows the Sunni Kurds to be accepted by the Turkish social, cultural, political and economic system, while lack of such a common ground with the Sunnis results in the Alevis' exclusion. The BDP Tunceli mayor, Edibe Şahin, commented on this.

> Well, a Sunni Kurd finds himself in this state because of his Sunniness and a Safi Kurd because of his *Şafiiness*. Maybe he/she might not see himself according to his ethnic identity but in terms of his belief and sect, and he finds a place in governance, in government, in the system. However, we have religiously, ethnically and linguistically suffered. We have our dialect, and it is one of the dying dialects in the world. Because of this we are always considered as society's 'others'.[52]

These concerns demonstrate that Sunni identity has the potential to make Kurdish Alevis who support the BDP/HDP increasingly isolated from Kurdish identity unless their identity finds protection soon. This is primarily because of the tremendous fear that the Alevis experience. Here, 'Sunniness, no matter whether Turkish or Kurdish, does not provide trust for Alevis', said a Kurdish Alevi-origin academic, Zuhal:

> Actually, the Sunni Kurds have a definition of 'Alevi' in their minds; we know what it is. There is an approach to Alevis. [...] They consider Alevis as a problem and an issue, and they (Sunnis) think they will tolerate and absorb them. This is not an equal approach. Alevis have their own self-confidence, their own legal norms that they define themselves, they have their own values, their own culture. They try to exist within it, but there is no such approach within the Sunni group that develops this argument, and no such trust. Sunniness, no matter whether it is Turkish or Kurdish, does not provide trust for Alevis. We should accept this. My family is in a position of being able to express its Kurdish identity very clearly, but when Sunniness is the issue, there is a distance. This is not a distance that we use to define them (the Sunnis), this is a distance that they use to define us. Sunniness is a state sect, state religion. It has the power. ... This is a point where the state, its political history, involves lynching. Mass lynchings. I do not know if that happened anywhere else in the world, but they burned the Alevi intellectuals of this country. This was resented. This government politically pays

off those to whom it will place its confidence in now. The Alevis will never ever trust it. They do not trust anything which represents Sunniness.[53]

Taking into consideration the Kurds' heterogeneous structure – the Kurdish internal minorities – and their concerns, a majority of the Alevis and Zazas demand status through establishing their own autonomous region. This is considered to be a necessity for the protection of their identities, or, more specifically, to be protected from both the Turkish and Kurdish Sunni identity's dominancy. Most of the Alevis and Zazas, as openly expressed in the Wise Man Commission's meetings in the city of Bingöl, stress their need for status and their desire to protect and practise their identical values freely.[54] These Zazas and Alevis want to establish their own autonomous region because of their fears of being assimilated within the Turkish and Kurdish identities (Partiya Serbestiya Dersim (PSD) Program Taslagi 2009). For instance, the formation of the 'Dersim autonomous region', where they are densely populated, will allow the Alevis and Zaza to protect their identity, explained Zubeyde Teker, a representative of the East Anatolia Wise People Commission.[55] Because 'this has a meaning: to erase the concerns of the Alevis who comprise more than 90 per cent of the Dersim population. Dersim is a centre for Alevis. Giving it a status is important for substantially removing their concerns.'[56]

In this regard, most of these Alevis and Zazas consider the creation of territorial political models (federalist and nation state) as a source of oppression, because they proclaim that these entities are based on a particular region, ethnicity and religion; this in turn makes democratic autonomy a viable model for them.[57] As a result, according to Emine Ayna, considering the existing diverse ethno-linguistic and religious minorities, the distrust among them and the strength of their political demands will only increase if separate or territorial federal regions are established. The divided structure of the Kurds and disputes between some Kurdish groups, according to Ayna, make the creation of territorial political models problematic. Ayna highlighted that forming a Kurdish nation state or implementing the federalism model cannot solve these groups' problems because these models are grounded in the ideology of one ethnicity or particular group, and take only a specific region into consideration. Thus, she suggested democratic autonomy as an alternative because it is not based on one ethnicity.

> If a federation or state is formed in the Kurdish region, it would be named a Kurdish state or Kurdish federal region ... We do not approve of this because we say that it is not only the Kurds who live there. We say this to oppose the nation state. ... We do support the understanding of a nation state, either for the Turks,

or Kurds, or for any other people. Also, we do not accept placing Kurdistan over Kurdish identity, as we do not identify Turkey through Turkish identity. We do not adopt an ethnic or national approach. That is also the reason why other movements, particularly Kurdish organizations, do not understand us. As they consider issues from this point of view, they do not understand us.[58]

Given the multi-faceted composition of the Kurds and the concerns of Alevis and Zazas, the KCK executive council member Mustafa Karasu explained that with democratic autonomy, if a population belonging to a different identity is densely located in a particular territory it will be entitled to form its own autonomous region or take part in regional assemblies. Therefore, diverse cultural, ethnic or religious groups would find the opportunity to be represented in the autonomous region's assembly if they represent a minority (Karasu 2009, 271–72). Democratic autonomy in this way aims to characterize and acknowledge all ethnic and religious groups' right to govern themselves by enabling them to form their own autonomous regions, or take part in city councils or people's assemblies (Draft Submission for a Democratic Autonomous Kurdistan 2011). Based on the mentioned framework of democratic autonomy, the model's proponents believe that democratic autonomy illustrates and suits the realities of the Kurds and Turks. To Hasan Yildiz, for example, it exemplifies the humane fundamentals of a democratic political model. Yildiz further added that 'democratic autonomy is a humanistic political model. Therefore, it is the political model I can propose to the whole Middle East'.[59] Making reference to democratic autonomy's decentralized structure, Halis Yurtseven, the BDP Bingöl provincial chairman, stated: 'I suggest democratic autonomy for all people, not only for Alevis, I propose it also for Armenians, Christians and all other minorities.' Consequently, he suggested that democratic autonomy should be used to address Alevis', Zazas's and other minorities' anxieties. With reference to this, Halis identifies democratic autonomy as a 'Cultural Revolution Project', because in his view the model deals with all cultures equally, and is thus the ideal means to settle their issues.[60] This should be formulated as a democratic nations confederation in Öcalan (see democratic autonomy in Chapter 2). Democratic autonomy thus here is regarded as the model that best fits Turkey's multicultural realities.

> This system is not the one that is consistently considered to be a danger to the unitary system of Turkey. This is an administrative system, but it suits Turkey's realities and answers these realities. With this political structure, which is shaped according to a provincial system, each province will have its own parliament.

Within its boundaries, each will solve its own interior issues; it will elect its own rulers. Issues relating to education will not be a problem anymore; it will get rid of the habit of giving full authority to the central state almost in every matter.[61]

Taking issue in this vein, the Kurds who support the BDP/HDP insisted that instead of creating a territorial structure which they considered to be out of date and unrealistic in addressing the conditions of the Kurds,[62] democratic autonomy recognizes and considers all identical differences in the Kurdish region by granting status to both the Alevis and Zaza.[63] This allows the decentralized structure of democratic autonomy to give separate ethnic and religious groups the capacity to form their own autonomous regions and thus protect their identity (Öcalan 2012a, b). Hence, as noted in Edibe Sahin, through democratic autonomy, internal minorities – the Alevis and Zaza – would be able to form their autonomous regions, organize themselves wherever they reside, and have close interactions with all the Kurds; this would subsequently encourage the development of Kurdish national identity among the Kurds. The appointment of some Kurdish Alevi-origin BDP MPs in Sunni-Kurd-dominated regions, Sahin highlighted, clearly proves this, since it had led to interactions between various Kurdish identities and was a step forward in removing some concerns and mistrust between Alevi and Sunni Kurds.[64]

Moreover, through democratic autonomy Kurdish identity would be recognized as a 'corporate identity' (*kurumsal kimlik*) by protecting the differences of internal minorities.[65] For instance, Sami Tan points out, 'If Zazaca wants to survive, it should not separate itself from Kurdish society.'[66] Thus, for many of these Kurds democratic autonomy is considered to be a political model that does not have any intention to assimilate and dictate to others, unlike the nation state and federalism. This is a fundamental factor for supporters of democratic autonomy: to protect their linguistic, religious and cultural differences within the unity of Kurdish identity.[67] Thus, with reference to the fieldwork results, a majority of the BDP Alevi and Zaza supporters who identify themselves with Kurdish identity demanded democratic autonomy because they believed it has the potential to protect the identity of all minorities in Turkey, particularly Kurdish internal minorities, within Kurdish national identity. This strategy, as BDP Muş MP Demir Çelik (2012b) highlight, will, first, encourage the preservation of the equal differences between Kurds, and, second, prevent the disintegration of the Kurdish identity as it meets the demands of internal minorities. This is one of the substantial motives which make democratic autonomy desirable for Kurdish internal minorities who want to preserve their differences within Kurdish national identity, and make it easier for them to reject territorial political models because they take a particular ethnicity, religion or region as a basis.

Consideration of the nation state as the crux of the conflict

A theoretical framework of criticisms against the ethnic territorial political models, particularly the nation state, is mentioned in detail by Abdullah Öcalan. He refuses the notion of the nation state and the Kurdish (nation) state on moral and ideological grounds relating to the connection between the nation state and democracy (Öcalan 2012a). This section will thus analyse the irrationality of the rejection of Kurdish nation state formation with a primary focus on the views of the model's creator, Abdullah Öcalan, and the empirical findings of the research.

Öcalan, as previously noted, considers the nation state to be a modern capitalist product and one of the main factors behind conflict between peoples. The nation state, to Öcalan, as mentioned earlier, essentially serves and functions in the interests of a small group or clique instead of the masses. To support this argument, Öcalan highlights the federal status of the Kurds in Iraq and points out that the consequences of this structure, with the creation of a Kurdish nation state in other Kurdish regions, will benefit specific small groups, which he calls 'Kurdish Capitalist Modernity'. Kurdish nation state formation will therefore not serve the Kurdish peoples, but benefit the powers that want to use the Kurds (Öcalan 1999, 87). Öcalan's interprets the refusal of the nation state to speak to the Kurds as being in a similar vein. BDP Diyarbakır MP Emine Ayna's following remarks fully support Öcalan's arguments for rejecting the nation state:

> We believe the state's mentality will improve the hegemony mentality, and an elite group will dominate the people living there and will hold onto the sources [of power]. This elite group will hold onto these sources and come into power. Therefore, we believe that it is necessary not to introduce our community to a nation state and not to identify our people with the nation state. Our model is based on an autonomous structure close to an idea of a people's assembly. Because of that, we also do not accept a federal state structure either.[68]

With reference to this, and comparisons with territorial models, Seydi Fırat, DTK and Peace Assembly member, strongly underlined that democratic autonomy is not a model that can be dominated by an elite group, nor can it function in said groups' interests. To Fırat, the structure of democratic autonomy does not allow this.[69]

Abdullah Öcalan also strongly critiques the nation state because it contradicts democracy and damages human values. He argues that the nation state does not prioritize democracy because the nation state itself is not founded on democratic values. The state's relations with power, its use of force, its aims to build a homogeneous nation and its denial of differences are some of the points mentioned by Öcalan to explain the nation state's incompatibilities with democracy (Öcalan 2009). To Öcalan (1999, 77), it is 'what is experienced in states where there is no democracy'. The following citation from Selim Kurbanoglu, BDP Diyarbakır Yenişehir municipality mayor, is useful in analysing the rejection of the nation state, because here he detailed the damage the state has caused to humanity.

> In politics, after the strategic changes we made, we said, we do not want a state. Why not? We saw the state's damage. Even if it is our state, we do not approve of a state that oppresses its own people; in other words, we do not approve of a structure that is ruled by a specific elite. [...] We think the state destroys nations in the long term; it does not work as people intend, it does not consecrate the people, nation, and community, but it consecrates itself. There are examples: this may sound a bit odd, but we say that during the last five thousand years of the traditional history of the state these kinds of bad things happened.[70]

Öcalan considers the nation state as centralist, hierarchical and conflictual in character (Öcalan 2012c), and stresses that the state's intention to maintain sole power and its strong desire to shape society in line with its interests initiate problems and conflict. Based on this, he underlines that even though certain matters were attended to, the state itself became the main source of the problem (Öcalan 2010b). Öcalan (2009, 101) goes a step further by linking the state with concepts of totalitarianism and fascism. Considering all these together, the nation state is regarded as a centralist, assimilative and oppressive power.

The ideas highlighted by Öcalan are shared by the model's proponents. The most common point in these Kurds' rebuttal of the nation state thus lies in their belief that its ultimate aim is to create a particular identity-based centralist and homogeneous nation and to assimilate other identities. Agreeing with this, Zuhal emphasized that due to the nation state's centralist and homogeneous character it would, she said, never allow all identities to freely exist according to their own values. The state could not avoid imposing a particular nation's values over diverse groups in an authoritarian way:

> The state is always a politically distant body for me. When you say a state you need to define its religion, flag and anthem. If you define those things, you will

always become a reactionary, it will always become an authoritarian structure. Therefore, solutions (*structures*) and political arguments made outside the state are always closer to me.[71]

The points emphasized by Zuhal were often highlighted during the fieldwork and regarded as causes behind the outbreak of conflict. To the supporters of democratic autonomy, the nation state's reliance on a particular group's values, such as ethnicity, flag, language and religion, naturally generates conflict within those groups not represented in the state. The nation state, to these Kurds, thus means the establishment of the hegemony of one particular group over the others (Karasu 2012). To the model's defenders, 'the source of a conflict over a hundred years old and of the war is the state itself. Therefore, territorial settlement means more conflict, violence and bloodshed. Because the territorial model is a pressure mechanism itself, solving the Kurdish issue with these types of models would be a disaster for the Kurds'.[72] For instance, Sami Tan, president of the İstanbul Kurdish Institute, highlighted that the creation of a Kurdish nation state in Turkey has the potential to lead to the killing of more than one million people.[73]

Often specifying the modern Turkish state, democratic autonomy supporters' claim that the nation state is the main obstacle to freedom and the co-existence of different identities. The formation of modern Turkey based upon a homogeneous Turkish national identity (one nation, one language and one religion), they believe, was a disaster for the country's multicultural structure and caused tension in the country, and affected the Kurdish issue as well.[74] The conflictual character of the nation state and its intent to create a homogeneous Turkish nation and state are regarded as the main motives behind the Kurdish issue (Draft Submission for a Democratic Autonomous Kurdistan 2011).[75] Highlighting this, Dorşin, a political activist in a pro-Kurdish organization, indicated that Kurds believe that it is not ethical to support the nation state because it already caused great distress for the Kurds in the last century.[76] The state is deemed to be the substantial reason for the suffering faced by the Kurds, and it is strongly believed that, just as in the past, the nation state still has the potential to instigate huge trouble for the Kurds and the Middle East in the future.[77] The creation of a Kurdish nation state will generate just the same troubles as the Turkish state created. Mustafa Karasu, a KCK executive board member, said that a Kurdish nation state would develop an authoritarian character and become a source of new injustice and conflict, causing further persecution of the masses (Karasu 2009, 268–69). Dorşin's words as follows are quite significant in understanding the rejection of the nation state by these Kurds.

> The state, inherently, is designed according to inequality and war. Because of this I do not find it right that Kurds move away from one unequal and dependent system and start living in a similar system, even if it is itself called a Kurdish state. Because this state will also be unequal and will restrict freedoms.[78]

Furthermore, the model's supporters, as the BDP Diyarbakır MP Emine Ayna clearly noted, believe that the 'nation state cannot be transformed into a democratic structure'.[79]

Based on the noted criticisms of the nation state,[80] the correlation between the nation state and democracy is largely covered in democratic autonomy. This political model, as mentioned earlier, distances itself from the nation state and aims to democratize the existing states (Draft Submission for a Democratic Autonomous Kurdistan 2011, 20). To the Kurds who support democratic autonomy, as BDP Muş MP Demir Çelik notes, the model restricts the state's power and develops a people-oriented rulership understanding, which, he claims, contributes to democracy. The relationship between the state and democracy is formulated as 'state + democracy' (D. Çelik 2012b). Put simply, democratic autonomy defines the model as 'less state' and 'more society' in relation to democracy (Serxwebûn 2012b, 135). From this point forth, Seydi Firat stated that by using the term 'democratic' for their model they aimed to affiliate democratic autonomy with democracy.[81] Accordingly, as stated by Karasu (2009, 276), based on its close connection with democracy, democratic autonomy supports and gives preference to grassroots organizations, all leading to an increase in local participatory mechanisms and the construction of local assemblies. Construction of city and council districts from bottom to top within the context of democratic confederalism and the development of various social, cultural and economic associations to heighten civil society understanding in these Kurdish organizations were clearly seen during the extensive field research in the Kurdish regions. The focus of democratic autonomy is thus unity between those of every ethnic and religious identity, and is not opposed to nor has any intention of removing existing states' national symbols. The model guarantees that all ethnic and religious groups will be free to have their own symbols and values, such as flags, colours and anthems (Draft Submission for a Democratic Autonomous Kurdistan 2011, 19–20). This principle of democratic autonomy can also be applied across Turkey and is not exclusive to one ethnicity, highlights Öcalan (2010b, 10–11). Thus, to these Kurds, as a KCK executive council member, Duran Kalkan, points out, while the creation of territorial structures (nation state and federalism) leads to conflict, assimilation and division between various cultural, ethnic and religious groups, democratic autonomy is thought of as a relief for the damage caused by these territorial models (Kalkan 2012).

To sum up, looking at the issue as such, and as the fieldwork also indicates, the concept of nation state and federalism leads to categorization and fragmentation of the people, and creates a hunger for power in special-interest groups. And this, according to democratic autonomy supporters, provokes conflict. This is one of the key reasons why proponents of democratic autonomy reject the notion of the nation state, the other main reason being the nation state's proposed ethnic and territorial borders. Thus, they consider democratic autonomy as the only alternative political model able to unify stateless groups with existing states, thereby creating a peaceful and democratic environment. Furthermore, unlike the hegemonic use of power in a nation state, democratic autonomy establishes itself on a horizontal organizational understanding and takes the will of people as its base.

Decline in national boundaries

Democratic autonomy's exclusion of ethnic territorial political models also has a close relationship with the model proponents' claim that national boundaries are vanishing.

In the interviews carried out with democratic autonomy exponents, interviewees alluded to the view that weakening territorial character of nation state in international relations also directly influences these Kurds' rejection of territorial political models. Thus, as the interview results indicated, Kurds who seek democratic autonomy reject the creation of a Kurdish nation state so as to keep in line with the modern world's attitude to national borders and nation states – to these Kurds, modern states have started to remove them. This, as noted by BDP İstanbul Esenyurt co-chair Kudret Gülün, leads the Kurds to socially, culturally and politically exceed their territorial borders and move forward with the changing world. To support this point further, Kudret Gülün stated: 'I do not think about and want an independent Kurdistan at the moment. The territories are vanishing, and in a place like this, if we remember how the state is an oppressive power, I deny the state as a "fact."'[82] In line with Kudret Gülün, president of the İstanbul Kurdish Institute, Sami Tan suggested:

> The thing that the Kurdish movement needs to do is to construct a system that will not cause problems and conflict, and construct a system in which they will be able to maintain their existence and identity. Maybe, with the emergence of supra-national structures, the Kurds could create their unity on the principle of

unity with the other Middle Eastern societies. This unity with Middle Eastern societies could be based on the principle of a supra-national understanding.[83]

In an interview with Baran, who was conducting the KCK's political activities in the Middle East, he highlighted that the people of the global world do not want to be limited to or constrained by their state's defined borders. Referring to this, Baran explained that people are in intense interaction with others, but territories become meaningless when people construct social, cultural and economic affiliations. He concluded by clarifying that territory no longer holds importance for them, and that henceforward the Kurds should stop trying to establish new territorial borders.[84] Abdullah Öcalan's following explanations are also rather instructive.

> Today, in the light of globalization, and in particular in view of a world market enforced by scientific and technological progress, national markets and the state itself have become obstacles standing in the way of development, behaving like the conservative feudal dynasties of old. We see more and more supranational political or economic entities, or regional federations. And they are increasing in importance. The international community has never seen stronger times. (Öcalan 2011b, 10)

In a similar vein, DTK and Peace Assembly member Seydi Fırat's following quotation also sheds light on why the Kurds who gather around the BDP/HDP and the DBP consider the decline in territorial borders to be a cause for demanding democratic autonomy:

> It is not proper to talk about territories these days. It is different when we look at Asia, America and Europe now. It is not realistic to talk about strict territories in the present day. The borders become indistinct. This is not something that we specifically made up. The state of affairs in the world is like that, and this is the right thing. The world's river flows that way. We also need to flow that way. As a bayou of this river, we also flow downstream. We cannot fantasize about deciding the whole world's destiny. The reality is, the water flows that way. [...] The world is trying to escape rigid territories. It creates bigger associations. The technological and economic developments ensure this as well. We also have to act together with the modern world, considering these global realities. We should act together with the people around us, taking a similar approach, rather than remaining within our territories.[85]

Looking at the issue in this way, the start of the decline in national boundaries is one of the conditions that led the defenders of democratic autonomy to put an end to the creation of new territorial borders, or a Kurdish nation state. They, as BDP İstanbul Esenyurt Co-chair Arif Erol cited, considered territorial political models to be synonymous with socio-cultural and economic isolation from the rest of the world, and therefore believed that 'there is no sense in constraining Kurds within a narrowly designated geography in a century where the boundaries in the world have vanished'.[86] In light of this, the creation of a Kurdish nation state for these Kurds, and as argued by Öcalan (2012a), is considered to be a source of isolation, and of dependence on hegemonic powers, rather than freedom. Accordingly, they challenge the assertion that each nation should, in the current conditions, have its own state (Karasu 2009). Consequently, democratic autonomy's mentality and structure – arguing against the idea of constructing boundaries between people and in favour of adopting the world's direction of flow – make this the ideal model for these Kurds.

5

Demand for the Cultural Rights Only Model

Those Kurds who ask that their basic cultural rights be granted ahead of federalism and Kurdish state formation are mostly associated with the AKP and the CHP. Both parties have a distinct ideological stance and receive support from diverse segments of society, as well as the Kurds.

The groups supporting cultural rights only

The AKP and the Sunni Kurds

Soon after its formation, a single party, the CHP, ruled Turkey from 1923 until 1945. The party held the same principles as the Republic's founding ideology. With the transition to a multi-party system in 1946, except for a short interregnum period, centre-right and conservative parties found considerable support from the public and took the opportunity to stay in politics as opposing or ruling parties. As a result, the Republic's secular and sui-generis modernization project did not secure much support from conservative individuals, particularly in rural areas. The Turkish Republic's forceful attempt to impose secular values further distanced these conservative and rural individuals from the central authority and made them potential grassroots members first for the Democrat Party and later for a number of conservative parties.

Most of the Turkish conservative parties that formed after the 1960s took ideological inspiration from the Democrat Party (Taskin 2008) and, in the words of Kuru, challenged the 'assertive secularist' understanding of the Republic, which was embodied by the CHP between 1923 and 1945. The Republic aimed to drive religion out of the public sphere, restrict religious identity and make religion a private entity. As Kuru explains, assertive secularism became a platform for the state to control religion in line with its ideal nation project

(Kuru 2007). Despite this secularist policy, religion continued to influence social and even political dynamics in Turkey. All the measures taken by the state could not prevent religion's influence on society. Religion continued to influence the majority of Turkish individuals' social, cultural and political choices in various forms and through diverse institutions and social groups and communities, especially tariqas (White 2002, 108-9). Most of these religious communities and organizations worked as alternatives to the state's assertive secularist understanding and were successful in keeping religion active in society and increasing its political power, thereby gathering the majority of conservatives around themselves (Margulies and Yildizoğlu 1997, 146).

Religion's power in society became even more obvious as the conservative parties and rural communities began to appear ever more frequently on social, economic and political platforms, and particularly when both started to interact more. Yet this, as noted by Nereid, brought about two results: on the one hand it provided new opportunities for rural people to represent themselves sufficiently in the political system, but on the other hand it provoked reactions from Republican authorities relating to the secular principles of the Republic (Nereid 1997). Concerns regarding the Republic's secularism doctrine led the Turkish military to take an especially severe stance – in general, a coup d'état – against the conservative parties. Therefore, many conservative parties were either stripped of power by this coup d'état, for example the DP in 1960, or were outlawed by the Constitutional Court on the grounds that their activities (allegedly) failed to follow the secular principle of the Turkish Republic, such as the RP in 1998 and the FP in 2001. Nevertheless, the state's pressure and tactics were unsuccessful in impeding the rise in religious values and the new conservative parties emerging in Turkish politics, such as the FP and AKP in 2001. Taking the election results into account, it seems that these parties gained considerable support from within society, for instance the RP, which emerged in 1997, and the AKP, which has had sole power since 2002.[1]

Turkish conservative parties also received noteworthy support from the Kurds during the elections. The Republic's pressure to acknowledge (and refusal to do so) of Kurdish identity and its strong reliance on assertive secularism prevented the majority of the Kurds from supporting the CHP, which shared the Republic's founding ideology, especially denying Kurdish identity. This made conservative parties an alternative for the Kurds, since these parties shared the Kurds' religious concerns and, at least on the ground, followed a corresponding approach to the Kurdish issue, unlike the Republicans' policy (Çaha, Toprak, and Uslu 2010). Religion therefore has been one of the vital factors that contributed to the Kurds' close affiliation with the conservative parties in Turkey. This association grew further once the RP, mostly popular among Sunnis, was established (Shakland 1999, 99). As a result, the RP became one of the most supported conservative parties among the Kurds prior to its successors. As White (2002, 126) also highlights, the RP's religious identity and the party's strong emphasis on the term '*millet*' (nation), which granted each subject the right of self-governance to a certain degree during the Ottoman Empire, were the two main motives for the immense support the party received from the Kurds. In this regard, the RP's actions in its approach to the diverse groups' identical differences were very brave for that time. The party, based on its religious understanding, avoided attaching itself to a particular ethnic identity. Thus the RP, by considering the power that religion exercises within both Kurdish and Turkish cultures, aimed to deal with the Kurdish question from a religious perspective, or, in other words, within a brotherhood context, with strong reference to the Ottomans' *millet* system (Duran 1998, 112). The party set out to achieve two key points in response to the Kurdish issue: recognizing the Kurds' cultural identity under the supra identity of Islam, and distancing the Kurds from territorial political demands, such as federalism and independence (Çalmuk 2001). The party in this regard called on the PKK to lay down its weapons and run its struggle through legal platforms (Çandar 2011). This approach to the Kurdish issue, compared to that of the previous conservative parties, was undoubtedly significant. However, despite this stance, the party could not distance itself from Turkish nationalism, and despite the party's Kurdish voters' strong challenge it entered the 1991 election in a coalition with the Turkish nationalist party, the MHP. This coalition met with a highly negative reaction from the Kurdish voters. Several of the party's Kurdish members, including provincial and district heads and executives in the Kurdish areas, resigned from the party.

The RP's survival in politics was cut short in 1998 when it was shut down by the Constitutional Court due to allegedly acting against one of the main principles of the state – secularism.[2] Following on from this development, another Islamist party, the FP, was formed in 1998. However, the FP had no serious politicization, and so was divided between traditionalist and reformist groups (Yavuz 2011, 101). The latter group formed the AKP on 14 August 2001. Despite the influence of Recep Tayyip Erdogan in the formation of the AKP, as a result of Erdogan's political ban it was Abdullah Gül who initially led the party. Soon after the removal of his ban, Erdogan began to lead and dominate the party. The AKP came into sole power following the 3 November 2002 election. The party's success caused an increased concern to the Republican authorities due to their sensitiveness about secularism. The AKP therefore was regarded as a threat to this fundamental principle of the Republic, which is a sensitive and even untouchable issue, even within the Turkish military. This became one of the main motives behind the Turkish military's intervention into politics during the AKP's rule, particularly during the party's first two terms in power (Jenkins 2006, 185). Aware of Turkish secular powers', particularly the military's sensitiveness, during its initial years the AKP avoided being linked to the RP particularly its *Milli Görüş* 'National Vision' ideology and strong reference to Islam. Because the conservative parties' previous experience, clearly showing that they could be banned for allegedly acting against the secularist principles of the Republic, the AKP therefore spent great effort not to be identified with the RP and labelled as Islamist (Akdogan 2006, 63). Such efforts, however, did not succeed in convincing people that there was no association between their respective ideologies or of accusing party of having a hidden agenda against secularism.

The AKP described and formulated its ideological stance upon conservative grounds, but with reference to democracy. The party defined itself as a 'conservative democratic party'[3] – by this, the party again aimed to show its ideological distance from the RP (Dinçşahin 2012, 619). According to this identification, the AKP developed the phrase 'conservative democracy', describing itself as a merger of 'democracy' and 'religion', 'modernism' and 'traditionalism', and 'state' and 'society' (Çağlıyan-İçener 2009, 606). Accordingly, considering the current perceptions of the politicization of religion at the time, Fuller (2008, 50) remarks that the AKP demonstrated the efforts it took to 'distance itself from any formal relationship with Islam'. The party's policies, particularly after 2011, however, further led to increased questions regarding its democratic character and distance from the notion of Islamism. Especially following 2011, the party has taken on more Islamist and nationalist inclinations and followed policies that are more authoritarian under the Recep Tayyip Erdogan leadership. Under the absolute power and control of Erdogan, the AKP rulers have severely punished their opponents, restricted civil liberties and freedom of speech and refused minorities' basic demands. Contrary to their previous stance, the party has recently not refrained from being linked with nationalism to certain extent.

The AKP's nationalist ideology and authoritarianism further intensified after the failed coup d'état, to the Turkish state, led by Fethullah Gülen movement–affiliated officers on 15 July 2016 (Türkiye Cumhuriyeti Cumhurbaşkanlığı 2016). By using the coup d'état as an opportunity, AKP government declared a state of emergency which has continued to this day. Under the state of emergency, the AKP government has bypassed parliament and the constitution and related legal restrictions and severely punished its opponents, especially the Kurds, which the next section covers.

The AKP and its approach to granting cultural rights

It has previously been stated that a large number of the Kurds who demand cultural rights coalesced around the AKP and have expected that the AKP will address the Kurdish question. The AKP took some significant steps regarding the Kurdish issue within the context of democratization of Turkey during its initial years. The party in this regard developed specific democratic packages, and particularly a 'Democratic Opening Process' in 2009. The AKP's proposals were founded on the understanding that the Kurds would be permitted their fundamental rights at the individual level. The party took into account the social differences between the diverse groups when considering implementing the various claims. The AKP's pluralist understanding, for instance, involved the following conditions: education to be taught in diverse languages in private schools, or to be taught as selective courses in state schools, broadcasting in various languages, and respecting and protecting the cultural values of all groups (AKP Booklet Demokratikleşme Adımlarının Bölgeye Yansımaları (2002–12), 2013). In line with this ideology, the AKP stressed the importance of national citizenship and presented it as the fundamental condition for uniting Turkey and their approach to various groups' ethno-cultural claims. These issues were openly highlighted by the leader of the AKP, Recep Tayyip Erdogan, during his speech on the state's and the AKP's approach to the Kurdish issue in Diyarbakır on 12 August 2005. Prime Minister Erdogan spoke of the state's misguided approach to the Kurds. He declared that the Kurdish question was in fact a 'Kurdish issue', and adopted it as his own concern. He went further by announcing that in response to the Kurdish issue, his party would distance itself from the nationalist approach and instead follow the principles of 'further democracy', 'further nationality law' and 'further welfare', in the hope of reconciling the ethno-cultural and ethno-religious groups' demands (Yenişafak, 2005).

In a step to settle the Kurdish issue, the AKP, as will be covered in detail shortly, released specific democratization packages, which included the use of the Kurdish letters X, Q, W in private school education, selective Kurdish lessons available in universities, the use of original Kurdish district names, political propaganda available in different languages and the removal of the student oath which had increasingly strong nationalist undertones.

In the AKP's approach to the Kurdish issue, religion played an instrumental role. The AKP here (especially during its initial years), as was case with the RP, handled the Kurdish question through the idea of a religious brotherhood, and considered the *Kemalist* secularist and nationalist ideologies as responsible for the nascent Kurdish issues especially (Yavuz and Özcan 2006, 103). The AKP well knew that behaving otherwise might alienate its Kurdish voters and also damage Kurdish–Turkish ties, leading to a rise in Kurdish nationalism (Yavuz 2011, 136). With this at the forefront of his mind, and to ensure that the promises made to the Kurds were met, as well as to meet the requirements for democratization and EU membership, the AKP launched a democratic initiative in 2009. In spite of the strong criticisms it received from various parties in Turkey, particularly the nationalist party the MHP (see Somer and Liaras 2010), the 'Democratic Opening Process' was a significant strategy to consider when analysing the AKP's understanding of the Kurdish issue. The AKP's intention for introducing the process, according to Yayman (2011, 447–70), was to democratically unravel ethnic and cultural issues and create some sort of dialogue between ethnic linguistic groups in order to meet the Kurds' cultural demands with the basic principles of democracy. The process in this regard was noteworthy in recognizing minorities' social and cultural rights at the individual level (Akdogan 2011, 20–21; Efegil 2011, 31–32).

As part of the 'Democratic Peace Opening', the AKP initiated direct talks and negotiations with the PKK's imprisoned leader Abdullah Öcalan and the PKK in Europe in 2009, known as the Oslo Talks (BBC Türkçe 2012). To avoid criticisms and potential challenges from Turkish nationalists and some conservatives, these negotiations with the PKK were conducted through the Turkish Intelligence Organization (MIT) and directly with the head of the organization, Hakan Fidan. Hakan Fidan met with the PKK officials (Mustafa Karasu, Zübeyir Aydar and Sari Ok) in Oslo, and in the leaked tape of this talk (in 2011) Fidan says he is the special envoy of Recep Tayyip Erdogan (NTV Haber 2011). The Oslo talks were doubtlessly bold steps in the AKP's approach to the Kurdish issue considering the Turkish state's taboo against the Kurds and the PKK. The AKP's 'Democratic Peace Opening' therefore was significant compared with the previous government's Kurdish policy. Despite this, AKP followed a one-step forward, two-step back policy. The AKP's incoherent policies led many Kurds to believe that the AKP was playing with the Kurdish issue merely to secure the Kurds' support in elections, and also gain time to further strengthen their position in internal politics and in their relationships with Western countries, especially because the AKP, despite the initiatives and the talks with the PKK, did not take any serious, practical steps for dealing with the Kurdish question. It attempted to reduce the Kurdish issue to individual cultural rights, and avoided granting the Kurds with collective rights, including the use of the Kurdish language in education. With the arrest of thousands of Kurdish politicians, students, unionists and journalists following KCK operations that started in April 2009, the Kurds became far more suspicious of the AKP's intentions and policies. The AKP's incoherent policies generated great anger and distrust of the party among the Kurds. The 'Democratic Peace Opening' therefore did not produce any concrete serious steps for sorting out the Kurdish issues, and it ended in armed conflict between Turkish security forces and the PKK in 2011. The conflict between Turkish security forces and the PKK further intensified in 2012, especially with the state's return to militaristic methods in their approach to the Kurdish issue and the PKK's adoption of a new tactic, known as the People's Revolutionary War, in line with its aim to establish territorial control in some Kurdish areas. Furthermore, it is worth mentioning that the Fethullah Gülen movement also spent great effort to end negotiations with the PKK. The group attempted to agitate and manipulate public opinion, and thus put pressure on the AKP to end negotiations with the PKK, which could clearly be seen in the group-affiliated media organizations' publication at that time. By using its power in the judiciary and police forces, the group also took legal action to prevent talks with the PKK. The Fethullah Gülen movement–affiliated prosecutors, for instance, issued an arrest warrant for Hakan Fidan in February 2012, accusing him of espionage and meeting with the PKK members (Daily Sabah 2014), which shows the group's efforts to end talks with the PKK.

On the other hand, despite the ongoing conflict between the PKK and Turkish security forces and the Fethullah Gülen movement's persistent efforts, the Syrian uprising created new grounds for the AKP's resumption of talks with the PKK. This uprising, and the PYD/YPG's taking control of the Kurdish areas in northern Syria, *Rojava*, once again provided the basis for, or, more accurately, pushed the AKP into restarting talks with the PKK through its imprisoned leader Abdullah Öcalan, roughly around 2012. It was almost the first time that the AKP government did not hide its meetings with Öcalan. The main motivation behind the AKP's reinitiating talks with the PKK was its aim to take the Kurds' political struggle in Syria under control, especially by including them on the Syrian National Council, to eliminate or at least weaken the potential impact of the Syrian Kurds' similar achievements in Turkey. The following few months' continual negotiations and meetings with Öcalan resulted in Öcalan's call for a ceasefire and for the PKK to lay down their arms, and for the state to create a democratic environment and take steps to solve the Kurdish issue in return. In his letter, read at the Diyarbakır Newroz festival on 21 March 2013, Öcalan stated that almost four decades of continued armed struggle was not confineable anymore. He called for the PKK's armed units to move out of northern Iraq and for the struggle to be continued through democratic means: 'A new phase in our struggle is beginning. Now a door is opening to a phase where we are moving from armed resistance to an era of democratic political struggle' (BBC News 2013). This was a historic moment for both the PKK and the state's approach to the Kurdish issue.

The talks and negotiations between the AKP and the Kurdish side (Öcalan, the HDP and the PKK) resulted in the Dolmabahce Declaration on 28 February 2015, which aimed to deal with the Kurdish question through a pluralistic democratic understanding, free citizenship, democratization of the state and the drawing up of a new constitution in a broad context (Milliyet 2015). The points highlighted in the Declaration were in harmony with Öcalan's previously mentioned democratic republican and democratic autonomy conceptualizations in a wider context. The Declaration therefore had a historical importance for redefining the Kurds' relationships with the state and solving the Kurdish question through democratic ways. However, soon after the Dolmabahce Declaration was declared, Recep Tayyip Erdogan called for its cancellation, and he ended the talks with the Kurdish side (Daily Sabah 2015). Given that all the steps and preparations had been taken with his full knowledge, Recep Tayyip Erdogan's renouncing of the Declaration was a surprise, and led many Kurds to become further suspicious of the AKP's intentions and believe that the party's main aim was to prevent Kurdish autonomy formation in Syria and disarm the PKK without sorting out the Kurdish question by granting them their collective rights. Thus, Turkey's failure to prevent Kurdish autonomy formation in *Rojava* and bring the PYD/YPG into the Syrian National Council, and the PKK's refusal to lay down its arms without the creation of a democratic political environment and constitution and take concrete steps to solve the Kurdish issue, in a way made the Dolmabahce Declaration meaningless for Recep Tayyip Erdogan. Along with these factors, Turkish internal political dynamics also contributed to Recep Tayyip Erdogan's negation of the Dolmabahce Declaration. Turkish nationalists and the Fethullah Gülen Movement's severe oppositions to talks with the PKK, and especially the latter's manipulation of the public, generated fear within the AKP that they might lose ground with nationalists and some conservative voters.

The AKP's stance towards the Kurdish issue and the Kurds was severed even more following the HDP's securing of eighty seats in the 7 June 2015 elections, when the AKP failed to achieve sole majority for the first time. To regain power, the AKP initiated an intensive war against the PKK with the aim to create an insecure environment and instability, and thus made themselves the only alternative power capable of ending the chaos. Then the party's main strategy was to convince public that there would be instability, tension and chaos if they were not in power. The AKP therefore successfully initiated a 'controlled-tension' strategy and succeeded in achieving a sufficient majority to establish a single-party government in the 7 November elections.

After regaining power to form a sole government, the AKP sustained its war against the PKK and legal Kurdish organizations, especially the HDP and DBP. Pressure upon both parties intensified further with the declaration of a state of emergency after the 15 July coup d'état. Since the coup d'état, the number of detained HDP executives, members and supporters has reached 11,631. The number of the arrested was 3,382 as of 9 March (Arti Gerçek 2018). Including the party's former co-chairs, Selahattin Demirtas and Figen Yüksekdag, the HDP's 11 MPs, 83 co-mayors (55 still in prison), 43 co-provincial heads and 201 co-district heads have been jailed, and trustees have been appointed in 94 of the 103 DBP-controlled municipalities. With these policies, the AKP aims to isolate and marginalize the HDP, and cut its ties with the majority of Kurds.

The CHP and the Alevi Kurds

The CHP has a long history in Turkish politics, and in its words represents the Republic's main principles or founding ideology, which relies on republicanism, nationalism,[4] statism, secularism, revolutionism and populism (Cumhuriyet Halk Partisi Tüzük 2012, Article 2). The CHP is the main vehicle for spreading a *Kemalist* ideology, with a firm focus on its secularism principle (Ayata 1992). The party programme thus also challenges the manipulation of religion in politics and the 'politicization of religion and religionalization of politics', which has been one of the most sensitive issues in Turkish politics (Cumhuriyet Halk Partis Programı 2013, 49). Firm focus on secularism allows the party to receive sympathy from the majority of Turkish and Kurdish Alevis[5] who have apprehensions about Sunni Islam, especially those who define themselves through secular values (Ayata and Ayata 2007, 220–21).

Reflecting on the discussed issues, it is evident that ideological motivations play a predominant role in pushing Alevis closer to the CHP for support. The Alevis' fears and anxieties about political Islam make them more inclined to side with the CHP (Grigoriadis 2006, 455). The rise in conservative Sunni parties and the possibility that those of Sunni identity may gain power and related political acceptance have been perceived as a form of opposition by Alevis – this has had a considerable influence in determining the Kurdish Alevis' political claims. As a result, the majority of Alevis supported the Republicans' secularism concept and voted for the CHP, which they saw as a political authority willing to protect the idea of secularism, which they generally believed to be under attack (Ayata and Ayata 2007, 221).

On the other hand, although the CHP is the first political party of modern Turkey, and has since come into power on numerous occasions, it did not consider the Kurdish issue for a long time. The CHP embraced the founding ideology of the Republic, which outright denied the Kurdish ethno-national identity, mentioned previously. However, with conflict between the PKK and state military forces underway, and the implications this had for Turkey, this provoked the party to alter its understanding of the Kurdish issue to some extent. The fact that the Kurds raised political mobilization, especially their discontent regarding the CHP's Kurdish and Alevi policies, led the party to take some steps to deal with the Kurdish and Alevi issues. The Kurds, and particularly the Kurdish Alevis, also wanted the CHP to take some steps to grant them their ethno-cultural rights. Many Kurdish Alevis taking part in Kurdish national movements since the 1970s, including the PKK, further pushed the CHP to reconsider its Kurdish policy. However, this was particularly challenging for the CHP considering the fact that it shared the state's founding ideology.

The CHP's change in attitude with regard to the Kurdish issue to some extent dates back to the late 1990s, particularly following the SHP's Kurdish report (*Kürt Raporu*), proposed in 1989. The SHP was founded on 3 November 1985 following the CHP's closure soon after the 12 September 1980 military coup d'état and based on the CHP's ideological roots; however, its Kurdish policy and declaration of the Kurdish report was a milestone in the political history of both parties considering their loyalty to the founding ideology. The report stated that the Turkish Republic did not prioritize its principles according to any particular ethnic or religious group, but presented itself as a state for all citizens. Therefore, as written in the report, if some parts of society referred to themselves as Kurds, then Kurdish cultural identity must be recognized. In that respect, the report openly proposed that all legal and practical obstacles preventing recognition of Kurdish identity should be removed – for example, use of the Kurdish language (SHP Doğu ve Güneydoğu Sorununa Bakışı ve Çözüm Önerileri Raporu 1989). Yet the points highlighted in the report only emphasized Kurdish cultural rights (Ayata and Ayata 2007, 217), and therefore were not satisfactory enough to grant the Kurds their ethno-national identity. Despite this, the report was a bold and significant step towards accepting Kurdish cultural identity.

The SHP joined the CHP on 18 February 1995, yet the party's Kurdish report pushed the CHP to alter its view of the Kurdish issue, at least on basic cultural rights. Although the CHP still avoids talking about granting the Kurds ethnic collective rights, the party has focused on ethnic issues and developed projects related to this, which are included in its programme, which makes reference to the Lausanne agreement of 1923 and highlights its appreciation and respect for the differences in identity of the various minorities recognized by the treaty (Cumhurriyet Halk Partis Programı 2013, 46). In relation to the Kurdish issue, the CHP refers to the Kurdish report published by the SHP to emphasize its approach to this matter, in this way also recognizing the cultural rights of minority groups. The party strongly underlines that it respects its citizens' differences, and acknowledges their individual rights in a unitary understanding of the state. In addition, the CHP, through the party programme, voices the idea that 'ethnic identities are the honour of a person' which must be protected and respected by the state (Cumhurriyet Halk Partis Programı 2013, 46). Contrary to its stance in the past, CHP asserts that ethnic and religious differences no longer pose a danger to the unitary structure of the state, and to ensure the construction of a common nation these groups' cultural rights at an individual level must be acknowledged (Cumhurriyet Halk Partisi Programı 2013, 47). The CHP, in that sense, as Ayata and Ayata (2007, 220) point out, challenges recognition of these rights at the collective level, and any other kind of political autonomy, but acknowledges the Kurds' cultural rights at the individual level. The CHP, within this context, shares almost the same approach with the AKP's proposals for the solution of the Kurdish issue, since both parties deem that granting Kurds their cultural rights at the individual level is the best option. This became evident in the case of migrated Alevi Kurds, since majority of them migrated to the Turkey's Western parts. As KONDA's following figure shows, more than half of Alevis live in İstanbul and other Western regions (Figure 5.1). Again according to the same figure, only around 7 per cent of Alevis live in Kurdish Southeastern Anatolian region.

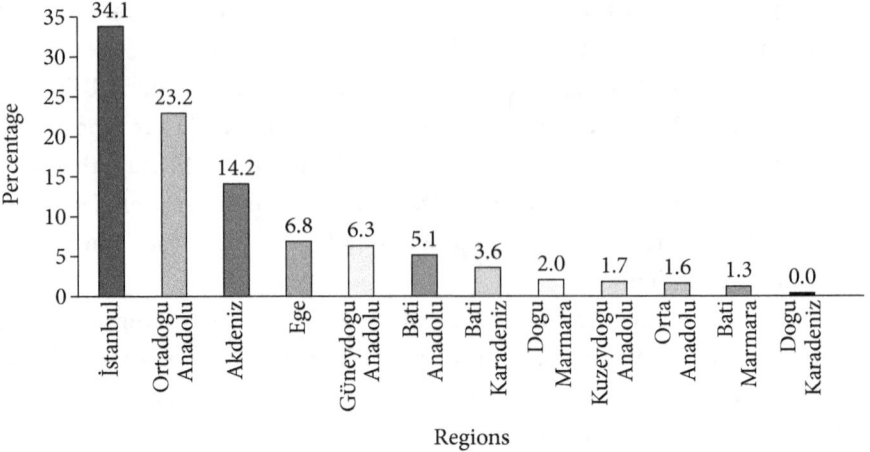

Figure 5.1 The geographical distribution of Alevis across Turkey. Source: (KONDA 2006, 24).

The factors underlying the demand for cultural rights

This section aims to explain the underlying causes behind the Kurds' demand for cultural rights over democratic autonomy, federalism and Kurdish state formation. Overall, the empirical findings of the research revealed that Kurds want to live in union with the Turks (without ethnic and territorial boundaries) and believe that gaining cultural rights would provide them with respect and repair the damage done to Kurdish identity, as well as restore relations between Kurds and Turks. This, in their view, would further contribute to interactions between the two peoples – the Kurds and the Turks – and strengthen Kurds' connections with Turkey. Granting cultural rights, therefore, is regarded as a necessity for building Turkey's unity.

Respect for Kurdish culture and the building of trust

The interviews conducted with the chosen Kurds showed that they consider recognition of their cultural rights as the initial step in removing the social, cultural and emotional destruction caused to the Kurds and Kurdish identity, as well as for maintaining relations between the Turks and Kurds. Acknowledgement of their cultural rights would first of all ease the pain of the Kurds on a psychological level, said AKP's Tunceli provincial party executive Riza Taskin.[6] Such a step would show that the state respects the Kurds' social and cultural values, and this would build a strong ground for Kurds to feel comfortable within the majority Turkish identity. Highlighting this point, Candaş Özçelik,

AKP Tunceli provincial party executive, stated: 'If cultural rights are accepted, the Kurds' dignity will be honoured.' Candaş added that the years of damage and destruction will be compensated, and empathy between two nations will be created. Therefore, 'the broken ties between the state and the nation will be repaired'.[7] Acknowledgement of cultural rights in that sense, as also noted by AKP Diyarbakır provincial deputy Adnan Nabikoglu, it was believed would establish a sense of respect for the Kurds, heighten trust for one another and strengthen integration between Kurds and Turks. He said:

> Social and cultural rights have to be granted. We were shy about speaking in the Kurdish language in the past. We thought we were going to be blamed. [...]My mother still cannot speak in Turkish. If you still deny that reality, how we can construct strong affiliations with each other?[8]

Acknowledgement of the Kurds' wish for cultural rights will protect their individual and human rights, and this, they believe, will lead to equality. Despite this sensitivity, they consider cultural rights at the individual level and claim that this will be sufficient to bring equality between Kurds and Turks, which was clearly underlined by CHP Bingöl provincial chairman Mustafa Kurban in the following statement:

> Today, all around the world, in America, Europe, Africa, everywhere, people support individual rights in order to be considered as individuals. [...]These rights sometimes could be for minorities, sometimes for small groups of people. What's important here is individual rights. [...]We support individual rights. Kurds, Turks, Alevis, Cherkes, Armenians; everybody can live together. None of the races have any value for me. ... For instance, one MP from our party said that, 'I do not consider Kurds and Turks equal'. This should not happen. When I go out onto the streets, people say, 'you still do not accept Turks and Kurds as equals, how can I join your party?' This caused a reaction. [...]This is not logical. It should not be said. [...]What we need to do is ... recognize everybody's rights. [...]For example, the new constitution should not be written based on the superiority of one race or belief.[9]

To clarify the connection between the protection of minorities' individual and human rights and the further demand for cultural rights, the interviewees were asked what they thought of education in the mother tongue – Kurdish. On this issue, Mustafa Kurban first of all openly stated that he did not pay much attention to his ethnicity. However, he highlighted that people's cultural rights should be granted because they form the basis of human rights and are essential for the construction of democratic understanding and society. He continued by referring to the education system in Turkey; if English, German and French education is available in Turkey, then Kurdish should also be accessible to the Kurds. However, this should be feasible without having to divide Turkey.[10] Suat Özdemir, the MASIAD Batman president, also supported this viewpoint:

> All people's cultural rights need to be granted, even if it is not right to say these have to be given, since they are already given at birth and we have to respect them. [...] people's rights to an education in their mother tongue, or whatever they are, should be granted. Not only for the Kurds, for everyone. Cherkes may want to live using their language. Why do you want to preclude this? You, as a man, do not have the right to prohibit a right that is given by God to another man. No one gives you this right. [...] This is a cruelty.[11]

The Kurds in question believed that by gaining basic cultural rights the Kurds would be freer, and, as highlighted by the CHP İstanbul Esenyurt district head Kemal Deniz Bozukurt, they believed it would bring equality between various groups, leading to fairer opportunities in Turkey.[12] Because by having rights they would gain respect for their values, the obstacles blocking the use of the Kurdish language would be removed, they would have freedom of education in their mother tongue and discrimination of the Kurds would largely be removed. In addition, the Kurds' cultural values would be protected.

Cultural rights will provide further integration and unity

Observations from the fieldwork conducted showed that granting Kurds their cultural rights is also considered to be one of the key factors that will affect the interaction and integration between the Kurds and Turks, and which will consequently renew the unity of Turkey. During the research, many of the interviewees immediately revealed that they refused to accept territorial political models, and explained their reasons for supporting cultural rights. For instance, during the interviews and conversations, Mirza Güçlü, a Kurdish businessman, frequently commented that the Kurds and Turks had been living together for more than 1,000 years, and that there was no real hostility between them. With reference to this, he explained they have common cultural values, history and unions through marriages. So, to Mirza, granting cultural rights would show the Kurds that their state respects them and regards them as equal citizens through recognition of their values, which he believed would further strengthen unity and interaction between their peoples.[13] Acknowledgement of cultural rights, to these Kurds, would create a platform in which the communities might co-exist in peace with respect for one another, and vice versa.[14] Therefore, recognition of cultural rights, to these Kurds, was regarded as a guarantee of unity in Turkey and without these rights there was potential for the state to become divided.

> All the Kurds' rights should be given within the framework of democratic laws. These rights also have to be given to all peoples, such as Cherkes; their freedom has to be recognized. The AKP does it. If I did not believe this I would not be in this party. [...]If these rights are not given, Turkey will become divided, weak, and there will be conflicts.[15]

As underlined in the quotation above, and also by many of the research participants, according to these Kurds, if Kurds' cultural rights are overlooked then Turkey would become divided. However, if their cultural rights are acknowledged, they will have no reason to disassociate themselves from Turkey. Aydin Karataş, CHP Tunceli provincial executive, gave more details on the link between acknowledging cultural rights and the unity of Turkey. He pointed out that by granting Kurds their cultural rights and freedoms, both communities would build greater solidarity and establish a peaceful atmosphere.

> Why we want to grant the Kurds their democratic rights is for Kurds to gain their freedom. A society which gains its freedom does not create danger. On the contrary, it will create integration. The Kurds and Turks would easily integrate. [...]We want the Kurds to be free. They need to obtain their democratic rights, which will not bring about any danger of the separation of Turkey. If the Kurds do not get their freedom, this country will be divided. If the Kurds' freedom is granted. [...] then there will be a peaceful atmosphere.[16]

Permitting Kurds their cultural rights, in their opinion, would prompt positive sentiments towards the state, because social, cultural and economic interactions between the two communities would be heightened, and thus the Kurds would feel safer.[17] Consequently, these Kurds believed that cultural rights would reinforce cooperation between Kurds and Turks, and the Kurds would no longer feel that their existence is denied, as it was during the last century, but would finally be appreciated by the Turks. And this, they believed, would significantly contribute to the integrity and unity of Turkey.

Rejection of territorial political models

The comprehensive interviews conducted with prominent group figures revealed the Kurds' social and cultural integration with Turkey, and the emphasis on their religious identity (Sunni and Alevi faiths) and ethnicity (refusal of ethnicity) as the two leading conditions which led them to reject territorial political models.

Socio-cultural integration

Data obtained from interviewing the Kurds associated with the AKP and CHP indicated that many Kurds shared the same viewpoints on the ideas which influenced their rejection of territorial political demands, specifically the intense social and cultural interactions and integration with Turkey. Reflecting on Kurds' integration within Turkey's social and cultural structure, these Kurds believed that applying territorial models (federalism and an independent state and democratic autonomy) would cause damage to the Kurds in many aspects, particularly their physical destruction.

During the fieldwork, many participants made reference to the interactions and integration between the Kurds and Turks. Many highlighted the widespread use of the Turkish language amongst the Kurds, particularly migrant Kurds, as an indicator of those Kurds who had assimilated into Turkish culture and community. Stressing this, MASIAD executive Mirza Güçlü disclosed that he had been living in İstanbul for more than fifteen years, and that although he could speak Kurdish he did not need to do so in daily life. For him, an individual's native language was important in many respects. Despite highlighting the significance of a person's mother tongue, he also revealed that his children do not communicate with him in Kurdish.[18] The Turkish language is not only used by migrant Kurds. Kurds living in Kurdish regions also use Turkish in their daily lives. Many of the interviewees explained that they have no need to use the Kurdish language or had any intention to learn it because they had a good command of the Turkish language. They were able to express themselves clearly in Turkish; therefore, there was no need to make effort to learn the Kurdish language, especially as it seemed to be a dying language. This was supported by AKP Diyarbakır provincial head Aydin Altaç, who explained: 'I can speak Kurdish, but not so fluently. However, I do not use Kurdish in daily life very often. I express myself well in Turkish.'[19] Most believed that they did not feel the need, or that they simply had no reason to learn or use the Kurdish language in their daily life.[20] Most of them, as AKP Diyarbakır Sur district executive Ahmet stated, believed that the Kurdish language would not make much difference to their regular day,[21] demonstrating their rational approach to the language. Some seemed unaffected by the idea that the Kurdish language is dying, most likely because they didn't use it every day and so it was of no significance to them.

Results from the fieldwork indicated that the vast number of Kurds emigrating from their homeland and becoming part of their new region's culture and/or society in turn influenced the large-scale interaction and assimilation of the Kurds within the majority group. In other words, these Kurds considered the migrated lands as their new home, and the majority of them don't consider the idea of returning to their homeland or the place of their birth. A substantial number of migrant Kurds revealed that they were welcomed and had happily joined Turkish culture or their new locality, and therefore had no urge to return to their homeland.[22] 'There are so many Kurds living in İstanbul, Izmir, Mersin, Antalya ... Why do the Kurds who live in Western Turkey go there after creating the Kurdish state? [...]I do not want to be separated from Turkey', said Kemal Deniz Bozkurt.[23] Echoing this idea, Adnan Nabikoğlu stated that the Kurds who had relocated to western parts of Turkey had no intention of returning to their homeland if a territorial political model had been established in the Kurdish region. He added that even his brothers and uncles, who held their Kurdish identity in high regard, would not return if asked.[24] To show how migrated Kurds had started to feel strongly part of Turkey, Mustafa Kurban, the CHP Bingöl provincial chairman, revealed that some of the Kurds wanted to be buried where they lived, and not in their birth place. For example, Kurban spoke of his father's experience: 'My dad lives in Izmir, he has 100 decare (acre) land in the village. I asked my dad: if there is a Kurdish state, will you return? He said, "son, I will stay in Izmir, I will not return ... Do not even take my corpse to Bingol."'[25] This noticeably shows how they integrated into Turkey. In these Kurds opinion a considerable number of the Kurds have already integrated into Turkey and feel themselves part of a major group identity, Turkish identity.

Given the high level of socio-cultural integration and a certain degree of assimilation, to the Kurds who only look for the granting of cultural rights, territorial political models are unrealistic both for the Kurds and for Turkey's conditions, and can potentially lead to conflict if established.

> We are intertwined. Look, here doesn't resemble Iraq, Syria or Iran. There, for instance, in Iran, Syria or in Iraq, the Kurds are generally located in a particular region. But here in Turkey it is not so. Most of the Kurdish population is not here, they live in western parts of Turkey. Despite that reality, if you declare federalism or democratic autonomy, then how will you bring them here? How will our Turkish and Kurdish brothers in the west accept this? [...] Because the Turks in western Turkey will tell you to go back home. This will cause conflict. We have to accept this reality.[26]

The view that territorial political models cannot be implemented in Turkey was often expressed throughout the fieldwork. Interviewees indicated that in the regions where ethnic and religious borders are dramatically separated or where there is less interaction amongst the societies, territorial models may be applied. However, in countries like Turkey, where social and cultural conditions and interactions are strong, but particularly because the connection between ethnicity and religion is so intense or there is no sharp ethnic and religious division between peoples, territorial models cannot be implemented successfully.[27] Because of these models' emphasis on a particular ethnicity and territory, interviewees believed that these models will lead to conflict and destruction under the current conditions in Turkey and similar countries; for instance, hostility between the Kurds and Turks in western parts of Turkey is likely to occur.[28]

With reference to this, the Kurds who demand cultural rights believe that establishing territorial political models could damage affiliations between various groups and disrupt the unity in Turkey because of the Kurds' demographic distribution and the high levels of integration that have already taken place. Therefore, territorial political models can also potentially lead to persecution of minorities, for example the Zazas.[29] In addition to this, supporters of the cultural rights only model explained that building territorial boundaries will not benefit the Kurds. One said: 'I will never allow Turkey to be separated. The boundaries do not have any importance. What I say is that for my happiness there should be no boundaries.'[30] In this vein, the observations made of these parties found that they were open to mixing with Turkish identity because it was a simpler way to gain status, a job or improved living standards.[31] This idea was shared by many Kurds, and led them to avoid defining the Kurdish issue in ethnic-territorial terms. The following explanation, from AKP Diyarbakır Sur district executive Ahmet, further emphasizes this:

> Our party base does not consider the Kurdish issue as an ethnic issue. They do not even use the term ethnicity. They do not need to use this term. We do not ethnicize (*etnikleştirme*) the Kurdish issue. Therefore, our party base does not consider ethnicity for solving the Kurdish issue. Accordingly, we do not think about the territorial political models.[32]

In that sense, they consider territorial claims to be an obstacle preventing integration, and also a use of social and economic resources.

> If I am happy in Turkey, and if the welfare level is better here, why should I ask for federalism or independence? More jobs, welfare and peace would make

my people and me happier. And so I say that Kurds' cultural rights should be granted, but we never want a federation or secessionism.[33]

The aforementioned discussions clarify that most of the Kurds who have a close link with Turkey or who have integrated into their culture and society are involved in the territory of their environment and are impartial about their own region – a strong indicator about their rejection of territorial political models. Moreover, many of these Kurds perceive territorial political models as the underlying cause of social, cultural and economic destruction and conflict in Turkey. For these Kurds, a cultural rights only model is appropriate because, they think, unlike with territorial political models, with cultural rights a level of respect for cultural values will be obtained, as well as stronger interaction and integration between Kurds and Turks.

Preferring religion to ethnicity

The Kurds are not a homogeneous community but have diverse linguistic (Kurmanji and Zaza) and religious (Sunni and Alevi) characteristics. Religion thus contributes greatly to their rebuttal of territorial political models and demand for unity with the Turks. Their beliefs also supersede their ethnic identity, which has an influence on their rejection of territorial models because these models prioritize ethnicity. This section now explores how religion influences the Sunni and Alevi Kurds' refusal of territorial models.

Negation of ethnicity through religious identity: The Sunni Kurds

Results from a survey conducted by SETA & Pollmark revealed the level of impact religion has on the relationship between Turks and Kurds. According to the findings, 26.7 per cent of the participants marked out religion from twelve other factors as the principal element which brings various Muslim ethnic groups and Turkey together. Within the same survey, 31.9 per cent of Kurds saw religion as a significant reason to live alongside Turks (SETA and POLLMARK 2009, 36–37). The interviews and observations collected during the fieldwork also exemplified the influence religion had on these Kurds' political behaviours. A high percentage of the participants highlighted religion as a decisive factor in their demand to live within the Turkish community. 'The common ground of Turks and Kurds is religion. If it is not understood well, there will be trouble. [...] In order to be together, it is very important that religion is a common ground between the two peoples, Turks and Kurds', said Adnan Nabikoglu.[34] Adile Gürbüz, the AKP Batman provincial vice-chairman, also presented a similar argument and identified how religion is a decisive common value between Kurds and Turks. To Adile Gürbüz, religion brings Kurds and Turks and the eastern and western parts of Turkey closer. She explained that the Kurds consider Turkey as their motherland. When asked, *'is it only religion that provides this?'* Gürbüz stated:

> At least 99% of Kurds consider Turkey their motherland because of religion. [...] We fought together in the battles of Gallipoli and Malazgirt. Salahaddin Ayyubi and Ahmed-i Xani are our shared values. We lived and protected everything together in the past. It was because of our Ummah understanding that we did all these things together. [...]Before anything else, we say Ummah; only then do differences come.[35]

For these Kurds, religious identity is essential for establishing their social, cultural and political in-group and intergroup relations.[36] In regard to this, AKP Diyarbakır MP Abdulrahman Kurt said: 'In my view, religion is not about performing daily prayers or fasting. Religion preaches that you behave in a certain way; for example, to be fair towards other people. This has direct implications for the rights of women, children and different ethnicities'.[37] Mirza Güçlü's following words illustrate how religion influences these Kurds' attitudes, in particular the shift in significance from ethnicity to religion (Sunni identity). Güçlü openly declared that he would rather live with pious Turks than non-religious or non-Muslim Kurds, such as the Yezidi or Suryani Kurds.

> Faith is very important for me. I feel closer to a Muslim Turk than agreeing with a non-Muslim Kurd. I get along with a Muslim Turk better. I have more in common with a Muslim Turk. I think religion is the thing that holds people together. [...]In my mind, the Kurds and Turks have to live together.[38]

On the whole, as outlined in the above discussions and as the results of the research suggested, the majority of the Kurds who demand their cultural rights place religious identity ahead of their ethnicity. Rather than their ethnicity, their religious (Sunni) identity is a determining factor in shaping their political demands, that is, unity with their religious fellows. This, in turn, contributes to their rejection of territorial models, since these models prioritize and consider Kurdish ethno-national identity as a supra-identity in specific parts of a territory.

Prioritizing of religious identity over ethnicity: The Alevi Kurds

Similar to the Kurds involved with the AKP, the Kurdish Alevis who support the CHP also prioritize their beliefs (Alevism) over their ethnicity. During the research study, most of the Kurdish Alevis in support of the CHP repeatedly stated that they identify themselves as 'Alevis' first. For instance, in response to the question, *'how do you define your ethnic identity?'* Yasar Demiralay answered, 'I am Alevi'.[39] Responding to the same question, many interviewees stated they preferred to identify themselves through their beliefs (Alevism), but explained that, if needed, they would class themselves as 'Kurds'. Most mentioned that they tended not to confirm their Turkish or Kurdish ethnic identity, nor their 'Turkishness' and 'Kurdishness', because their central identity was Alevi.[40]

The strength of their Alevi identity also significantly affected their political demands. Their concerns about Sunni identity, or, as they defined it, the growth of political Islam in Turkey, along with the other mentioned conditions, were the main reasons for their call for unity between the Turkish and Kurdish origin Alevis. The interviews carried out revealed that the Sunni identity (both Turkish and Kurdish Sunnis) was a threat for most Kurdish Alevis who supported the CHP. Kurdish Alevis were worried that Sunni groups would take any opportunity that may arise to control the Alevis.[41] The dispositions of both groups, therefore, further deepened the socio-cultural and political boundaries between them.[42] In particular, the Alevis had very little trust in Sunni identity and the Sunni authorities. For instance, in response to the question, *'the current government launched an Alevi opening process, why do you remain suspicious of Sunni identity or do not have trust in the current government, the AKP?',* a CHP İstanbul MP Muslim, Sari, responded:

> Well, there is no Alevi opening process. There is just a government that pretends that it deals with Alevis' problems. Well, Alevis' problems and their solutions are obvious. [...] The government otherizes Alevis. It strengthens its base through otherizing. It strengthens the Sunni identity. It creates an enemy (*Alevisim*), and through this enemy it strengthens its base. It employs such a strategy. The biggest other is the Alevis. The Alevis are *tukaka* (opponents) for this government. For the government, the Alevis do not have any problems to be solved. For them, Alevism itself is a problem. [...] Because there is a government shaped by Sunni Turkish ideology. [...] Because of this, Alevis are being otherized. This process now has gone one step further.[43]

The Alevis highlighted concerns that influenced their challenge to territorial political models, since these models take Kurdish ethnicity into consideration rather than Alevis' religious beliefs and anxieties. Analysing the anxieties of Alevis in that respect, as the CHP Bingöl provincial chairman, Mustafa Kurban highlighted, these Alevis mostly place emphasis on protection from the secular character of the regime rather than their ethnic and national identity. Mustafa Kurban, for instance, stated that 'the citizens here have concerns because of their sensitivity to the secularism which is artificialized in Turkey. They are worried that there might be a sharia state soon. They are worried, and think that if that happens, what will happen to the Alevis?'[44] The following statement from CHP's İstanbul MP, Muslim Sari, also gives some context to help understand the Alevis' concerns:

> There was the Alevis' call for equal citizenship in the constitution. [...]Without the possibility of securing these rights, Alevis' lives are in danger, especially after ISIS. People are being killed on the way to Cemevi in the eastern and southeastern regions by the police. Their living space is slowly narrowing. They tried to live in a specific area or neighbourhood.[45]

Moreover, another two reasons found to contribute to religious identity being prioritized over ethno-national identity, and to the territorial models being rejected, are increased Sunni-Alevi tensions and growing unity between Sunni Kurds and Sunni Turks, which in turn has strengthened Sunni identity. Throughout the course of the fieldwork, many Kurdish Alevis commented on their fears and apprehensions of Sunni Kurds. They openly expressed their concerns regarding the growing influence of religion on the world of politics, especially in the Kurdish region. A focus group discussion involving four Kurdish Alevis who emigrated to the UK almost fifteen years ago in an effort to escape the political oppression they faced in their homeland, and who were also currently active in some Alevi organizations in London, supported the former points mentioned. The discussion topic of the focus group was the prioritization of Alevi identity over Kurdish ethnic identity and the political model that they recommended would solve the Kurdish issue. The discussion started with the question, *'What do you think of the AKP's success in the 2014 local elections, particularly in the Kurdish region?'* Zeynep responded with:

> I voted for the BDP in previous elections. But, as the majority of Sunni Kurds voted for the AKP in the 2014 local elections I will not support any Kurdish origin party. It is the Sunni Kurds' religious identity and support for the AKP which scares me. Therefore, I call myself an Alevi not a Kurd.[46]

Kurdish Alevis' anxieties are not limited to this. They claim that religious groups or parties, like the AKP, consciously otherize Alevis to further strengthen and unite Sunni groups in Turkey, but particularly in regions with large numbers of Kurdish communities.

> Well, since the Ottoman period, even since the Republic, backward parts of Islam, and backwardness, have been supported in the Kurdish region. […]Now, certain Islamic groups and groups who struggle to implement Sharia exist. […] For 12 years the AKP government strengthened its power and … Sunnism. […] It approaches the Kurdish movement through this identity. This is what bothers us. […]That is why we are annoyed.[47]

Considering the issue in this vein, the close relationship between Kurdish and Turkish descendant Sunnis contributes to the Kurdish Alevis' growing fears and their doubts about Sunni Kurds, since they consider such relationships as Sunni coalitions in an historical context. Many of the political leaders interviewed from Alevi organizations and CHP branches in the Kurdish region associated the interaction between Sunni Turks and Kurds as an alliance between Sunnis, and as one of the central reasons for Alevis' fears.

> The AKP is in conflict with the basic principles of the Republic. It wants to remove the existing political structure. For instance, making regulation of the curriculum, formulated as 4 +4+4, is an example of this. With this, they aim to construct a religious society and want to raise a religious youth. They seek revenge. For instance, they strengthen the Directorate of Religious Affairs. The AKP does this with the support of the BDP. BDP supports them. […]They support each other.[48]

Although BDP did not provide any support for the AKP's regulation in the curriculum, most of the Kurdish Alevis in the CHP believe that both parties are in agreement, since the Sunni identity is a connection point between Sunni Turks and Sunni Kurds. A CHP Tunceli provincial executive, Aydin Karatas, explained this in the following words:

> The Sunni Kurds and Sunni Turks have common beliefs. Even though the people who live in the southeast are ethnically of Kurdish origin and a separate nation, they share the same life-styles and/or beliefs with the Sunni Turks. They pray with the same beliefs and in the same religious place, the mosque. They are similar to each other in this sense.[49]

The point highlighted in Karatas is common to many of the Kurdish Alevis gathered around the CHP. They conceptualize the relationship between Turkish and Kurdish Sunnis as a shared ideology of Sunni Islam or even brotherhood. The CHP İstanbul provincial MP, Muslim Sari, spoke of the relationship between Alevis and Sunni Kurds and Sunni Turks, and this illustrates the belief well:

Look – for instance, this ideology, the Sunni Turk ideology, plays well with the Kurds. Turks and Kurds get along well under the umbrella of Islam. We could call it a Turkish-Kurdish brotherhood. [...]But Alevism, Alevism's DNA and the Alevis' lifestyles are incompatible with this ideology.[50]

Kurdish Alevis' fear of Sunni identity and Kurdish politics, which was expressed in many of the interviews, has reached such incredible levels that they identify some of the relations between the PKK/BDP and state authorities as a compromise or alliance between Sunni Kurds and Sunni Turks. For instance, Abdullah Öcalan's letter written from Imrali prison[51] put emphasis on the Islamic solidarity between the Kurds and Turks and underlined the importance of Islam and its contribution to the close affiliation between them (Akşam-21 March 2013), and this caused trouble and provoked fear among many Alevis (Çıla 2013). During observations, many Alevis shared their thoughts about instigating talks between this jailed leader of PKK and the state, and also their apprehensions about the release of Öcalan's letter. The majority of these Alevis regard the talks between Öcalan and the state as marking a step in the direction of creating an alliance or cooperation between Sunni Kurds and Sunni Turks:

> The Kurdish movement had a discourse intended to protect Alevis' rights in the past, and especially Kurdish Alevis' rights. With the reconciliation after peace process, saying Kurds and Turks can gather under the umbrella of Islam principally means looking at the issue from the Sunni perspective. This annoyed Alevis a lot. Kurdish and Turkish Alevis are not in this equation. There are Sunni Turks and Sunni Kurds in this equation. This is troubling, this troubled Alevis.[52]

Kurdish Alevis' criticisms of Öcalan's letter were so intense that they regarded it as the fundamental factor which led to their distrust of Sunni Kurds, especially when taking into account their previous tension with Sunni Kurds.

> There is a previous history. [...]Because we received a nasty blow from Sunni Kurds and Sunnis, we deliberate [on the issues] now. We want to be sure. We have no power to take the slaughter and devastation anymore. [...]That letter, therefore, has a huge impact. In one sense, it is the reason not to trust (the Sunni Kurds).[53]

The observations of CHP party branch members, including the mostly Kurdish and Kurdish Alevi organizations which support the CHP, revealed that many Kurdish Alevis, as noted by CHP Tunceli provincial executive Mustafa Alabat, believe that 'Sunni Kurds and Sunni Turks would support each other from a common religious and political base and exclude Kurdish and Turkish Alevis'. Put simply, they believe Alevis would be left to their own devices and fates.[54]

Considering Alevis' anxieties in light of the discussions provided, the findings suggest that the social and political boundaries between Sunni and Alevi Kurds continue to grow and have already reached a significant level, especially with the formation of some radical Kurdish Islamic groups, for example Hezbollah.[55] This, in turn, has led to them to prioritize their religious identity over their ethnicity, more clearly unity between Alevis, for the protection of their beliefs, but most importantly of their security. Reflecting on this, CHP's Bingöl provincial chairman, Mustafa Kurban, stated that they do not place emphasis on their ethnicity because 'Alevis have fear of death, fear of death from the Sunnis'. In an explanation of their increased fears, he added that, currently, many people from the city of Bingöl are fighting for radical Islamist groups in Syria. Therefore, he explained, because Alevis anticipate their death they cannot prioritize their ethnic rights.[56]

The fieldwork demonstrated that because the Sunni identity of Sunni Kurds is a point of alarm for Alevis, they give priority to their religious identity – Alevism – and to the unity between Alevis of Kurdish and Turkish origin. In other words, examining the discussion between Kurdish ethnicity and Alevi identity in light of the above points, 'Alevi identity is very strong, so strong that it overcomes ethnic differences' (Shakland 2003, 18). As Leezenberg (2003, 197) explains, some Kurdish Alevis chose to distance themselves from their Kurdish identity and regard the term 'Kurds' to mean 'Sunni'. Kurdish Alevis, therefore, relate more to Turkish Alevis than Sunni Kurds (Seufer 1997, 172 cited in Houston 2001, 105). Thus, taking into account Alevis' concerns, it appears Alevism has become a common belief for most Alevis, meaning their liberation is dependent on harmony between Alevis-Turks and Kurdish Alevis. Most Alevis believe that their ethnic identity needs to be gathered under Alevism, which overrides Turkish or Kurdish identities.[57] They claim that the oppression of the Alevis 'causes gatherings of Turkish, Kurdish, and Arabic speaking Alevis'. In other words, it has turned Alevism into a 'supra identity'.[58] This, on the other hand, led to many of these Alevis rejecting the concept of territorial political models because they suspect it has the potential to damage any likely union between Alevis of Kurdish and Turkish descent. In addition to this, they believe territorial political models will reinforce Sunni identity in regions with a high Kurdish population, and give Sunni identity power over the Kurdish Alevis. Contrary to territorial political models, they stated that all ethno-cultural and ethno-religious identities must be respected and protected, as this will encourage harmony between Alevis in Turkey. And so, while acknowledgement of territorial claims increases fears of Sunni identity, oppression and inequality, recognition of cultural rights is regarded as a basic human right that will reinforce trust between Kurds and the state, as well as between Kurdish and Turkish Alevis in Turkey.

Rejection of democratic autonomy

The majority of the Kurds who seek cultural rights, as the previous section detailed, prioritize their religious identity (either Sunni or Alevi) over their ethnic identity, and because of this, reject territorial political models, since these models rank ethnicity first. Despite the proponents of democratic autonomy's claim that the model considers all ethnic and religious groups and can be applied across Turkey, many of the cultural rights adherents do not regard this as a genuine statement. First of all, they argue that the conditions of democratic autonomy are insufficient for Turkey.[59] Therefore, to these Kurds, 'declaring democratic autonomy and the right to self-govern is not realistic'.[60]

They also claim that the model is not 'sincere' and will not represent all Kurds on equal terms.[61] Therefore, many of these Kurds who participated in the study claimed that democratic autonomy will provide authority to only specific groups – the BDP/HDP and the PKK – and will offer nothing to others, such as the Alevis. This point was also brought up by Kemal Bozkurt:

> Neither the PKK nor the state gives us anything ... For instance, there was Abdullah Öcalan's explanation in his letter, what was he saying? He was sending his compliments to Fethullah Gülen. He was talking about Islamic unity and brotherhood. Öcalan did not mention the Alevis. Did he say anything about Alevis' rights? No. Was there any demand about Alevis' rights in the words of the people from the southeast? No. Some of the BDPs talk about Alevis' rights, when they come here, but just for the sake of conversation. There is nothing apart from this. Even if some of their MPs or high-level individuals have something to say about Alevis' rights, the people of southeast do not have such an idea.[62]

They believe that if any kind of autonomy, especially democratic autonomy, were granted to the Kurds in this region, serious problems would arise.[63] Because they claim that democratic autonomy will establish an authoritarian structure under the governance of the PKK and affiliated organizations, many Kurds, as also mentioned throughout the research study, believe democratic autonomy's structure and affiliation with the PKK and BDP will result in the persecution of the individuals who oppose this model.[64] Bingol Martyrs Family Association president Ziya Sözen, who lost his father to the conflict with the PKK, for instance, explained that democratic autonomy will only work to establish the PKK's authority in the region.[65] Highlighting this, AKP Diyarbakır Sur district executive, Hasan, spoke of the approach of the Diyarbakır Municipality, which was won by the BDP in the last election (2014), against opponents of the BDP and democratic autonomy. He explained that if you are not a relative of anyone who lost their life during the PKK's struggle, or anyone imprisoned because of their affiliations with the PKK, it is not possible to get any support from or manage your affairs easily with the municipality. He added that with democratic autonomy, Kurds are restricted when carrying out their internal affairs.[66]

These Kurds' anxieties greatly increased with the PKK-affiliated group when the YDG-H declared democratic autonomy in the HDP-/DBP-run municipalities and the digging of trenches to fight Turkish security forces in the civil settlements in 2015–16. Despite the state's extremely harsh reaction to the digging of trenches and the killing of many people and the destruction of many settlements, most of the AKP member Kurds did not avoid supporting the state's measures by claiming that if the PKK took control this would result in further destruction, as highlighted by AKP Diyarbakır provincial chairman, Muhammed Dara Akar.[67] Underlining the PKK-affiliated groups' declaration of establishing democratic autonomy by force, many Kurds, including non-AKP supporters, stated that this clearly showed how democratic autonomy is an authoritarian political model, not peaceful, and would not work to the benefit of all Kurds. It would provide authority only to the PKK. Hence, these Kurds believed democratic autonomy is not democratic. It would allow the PKK to establish its power over other groups by force.

6

Demand for Federalism

Federalism is one of the mostly referred to political models by the Kurds, especially those Kurds who are conscious of their national identity. The interviews revealed that through federalism, Kurds want to achieve recognition of their national status in their own territory, that is acknowledgement of their territorial national status, as was seen in the Kurdish case in Iraq.

The groups supporting federalism

Med-Zehra and Zehra Communities: Kurdish Nurcus

The Turkish Republic's strict policy of secularism and the subjugation of Kurdish identity prevented the Kurds from organizing through their ethno-religious identity. Most of the religious Kurds therefore took part in Turkish religious communities for a long time. Even now, a high number of religious Kurds take part in Turkish religious organizations and communities, especially the Kurds who put less importance on their ethnic identity.

The religious Kurds (Kurdish Nurcus) who founded Med-Zehra and later the Zehra community also initially took part in Turkish religious communities which followed the well-respected Kurdish-origin religious scholar Said-i Nursi's (also known as Said-i *Kurdi*[1] and Bediüzzaman) teachings (collected in *Risale-i Nur Külliyati*) for guidance. Following Said-i Nursi's teaching has been a decisive factor for the development of further relations between the majority of the Kurdish and Turkish Nurcus (Yavuz 2006, 130). The relations between the Kurdish and Turkish Nurcus and various understandings in the Nurcu movement continued without any serious dilemmas during the period when Nursi was still alive. However, soon after his death in 1960, diverse interpretations and dissenting voices began to appear among Nursi's followers. The first divisions took place around how they would spread Nursi's teachings, whether through use of Latin or Arabic script. This resulted in the emergence of two groups: *Okuyucular* (readers) who supported the spreading of Nursi's teaching through Latin and *Yazicilar* (writers) who demanded that they continued to teach in their original Arabic script. The disagreements within the Nurcus intensified later, especially around regional and ethnic identity, and over diverse interpretations of his teachings (Yavuz 2006, 152–58). The disputes on ethnic lines appeared within the Kurdish Nurcus because of their sensitivity on Kurdish identity, with particular focus on Nursi's approach to the Kurdish issue.

Nursi's religious identity was undoubtedly the primary cause that led the Kurdish Nurcus to respect him and adopt his teachings as one of the main guides in their approach to religious, social and political issues, but his Kurdish identity and approach to the Kurdish issue (which can briefly be formulated as granting the Kurds ethno-national identity with autonomous status) also had a considerable influence on the Kurdish Nurcus (Atacan 2001; Aydinkaya 2012). Because of their emphasis on Nursi's views on the Kurdish issue and his teachings, the Med-Zehra harshly criticized the Turkish Nurcus because they claimed that after Nursi's death some Turkish religious communities made changes to Nursi's teaching by replacing the terms 'Kurds' and 'Kurdistan' with others (Atacan 2001, 123). These supposed changes to Nursi's *Risale-i Nur Külliyati*, principally the aspects which focused on the Kurds and their regions, consequently generated discontent among Kurdish Nurcus (Dursun-Seyhanzade 1993, 27–47; 1998, 6–12). This is because, as the analysis part of this chapter explores, to most of the Kurdish Nurcus, Turkish Islamists try to ignore or even remove Said-i Nursi's Kurdish identity and play down his focus on the Kurds. To the Kurdish Islamists, in order to remove or weaken Nursi's Kurdish identity, some Turkish Islamists' efforts were not only restricted to making changes in *Risalei Nur*. They also persisted by attempting to associate him with the Arab title *Sayyid*, despite Nursi's family's and the Kurdish Nurcus' explanations that his ethnic identity was Kurdish and did not have any connection with the *Sayyid* title (Zinar 2011, 156–57).

The reasons mentioned above increased dissatisfaction amongst the Kurdish Nurcus, which further intensified over time. To the Kurdish Nurcus, the Turkish Nurcus remained close to Turkish nationalism and a form of 'Turkism' (DAVA Dergisi 1993, 12–13; Yavuz 2003, 175–76). For the Kurdish Nurcus, it was nationalism which prompted the Turkish Nurcus to overlook Said-i Nursi's Kurdish identity, as well as his opinions regarding the Kurds and his solution for the Kurdish issue (Canlı and Beysülen 2010, 239–41). Thus, also in relation to the political atmosphere in Turkey, the tension between both groups grew after the 1970s. This led the Kurdish Nurcus to take more interest in Kurdish identity and Kurdish issues by taking inspiration from Nursi's approaches (Yavuz 2006, 157–58). The Kurds' concerns regarding their identity and the Turkish Nurcus' disinterest in them, and even their attachment to Turkish nationalism, provoked these Kurds to search for and create their own organization (Aydinkaya 2012; Şengül 2004, 532). Thus, based on their criticisms of Turkish Islamists, especially the Nurcus, and their intentions to solve the Kurdish issue, the Kurdish Nurcus formed their own community in 1973, called Med-Zehra,[2] under the leadership of Mehmet Siddik Dursun (Seyhanzade) (Şentürk 2011, 270–71).

The majority of Med-Zehra's members were of Kurdish origin, and spent much more intellectual effort in creating public awareness of Kurdish identity and finding a solution to the Kurdish issue on religious grounds. Nevertheless, Med-Zehra did not describe itself only as a Kurdish-origin religious community, but adopted the teachings of Said-i Nursi with respect to his approach to Kurdish identity (Şengül 2004, 532) and took action to highlight Nursi's Kurdish identity. This strategy found a significant place in their official publication, *DAVA* magazine (published in 1989). In DAVA encompassed 'Med Zehra's dual Kurdish and Islamic identities' (Atacan 2001, 112). DAVA gave great importance to the Kurdish issue and Kurdish culture, identity and history, with respect to Nursi's interpretations. Many of the magazine issues published articles which exposed Turkey's oppression of the Kurds. In addition, most of the articles raised questions aimed at finding a solution to the Kurdish issue through an Islamic Ummah understanding, and often criticized the Turkish Islamist organizations' stance regarding the Kurdish issue.

Med-Zahra's formation in most senses was a significant step in the Kurdish Nurcus' approach to the Kurdish issue. First of all, they openly challenged Turkish nationalism and the nationalization of the Turkish Nurcus by highlighting Said-i Nursi's Kurdish identity and emphasis on the Kurdish issue. Second, they combined Kurdish identity with religion in their approach to the Kurdish issue. The group in this way 'attempted to maintain a balance between Kurdish nationalism and Islamism' (Yavuz 2003, 176).[3] The group in this regard became a main representative of Kurdish Islamic Movements (Atacan 2001).

Despite its significant contribution to the development of Kurdish Islamic identity, Med-Zehra experienced numerous internal struggles in 1990, mostly regarding leadership and governance issues. Med-Zehra was unable to resolve these issues and subsequently divided into two groups, Med-Zehra and Zehra. Some Kurdish Nurcus left Med-Zehra and founded the Zehra Education & Cultural Foundation under the leadership of Izzettin Yildirim[4] in 1990 (Şentürk 2011, 271; Yavuz 2006, 157–58). To Yavuz (2003, 176), the latter included mostly Kurdish Islamists with nationalist inclinations. Subsequent to its division, Med-Zehra lost almost all of its influence on society, and presently the Zehra community holds more importance.

Zehra community followers were largely of Kurdish origin, and they focused on developing a Kurdish ethno-national identity and settling the Kurdish issue, as well as stressing their Islamic identity. The community became a centre for the Kurds who wanted to practise their beliefs and ethnic identity together. Şahan, a prominent authority in the community, for instance, said that 'Kurdish identity expresses itself within us. Kurdish youths who do not want to be deprived of their religion, language, and ethnic identity consider us as a shelter'.[5] The Zehra community, following Med-Zehra's lead, published the Kurdish-Turkish language-based *Nûbihar*[6] magazine in 1992, which highlighted the Kurdish question in many of its issues. It was their main tool to reach out to Kurdish society and construct intellectual studies on the Kurds. Focusing on Kurds and the Kurdish issue, it became a platform for many to express their outlooks on the Kurdish issue and offer possible solutions.

The Zehra community continues its activities through student houses, gatherings around bookshops, in preparation schools, by publishing independent magazines and by establishing special publishers. The community is well organized in almost all parts of the Kurdish region, particularly in Diyarbakır, Van, Batman, Mardin, Sanliurfa, Bingöl, Mus, Igdir, Agri, Bingöl and Siirt. The group is also active in western parts of Turkey, particularly in İstanbul, Ankara, Izmir, Mersin and Bursa where there are a high number of Kurdish migrants.

From Hezbollah to Hüda-Par: Radical Kurdish Islam

Hüda-Par, founded on 17 December 2012, represents radical Kurdish Islamic views. Soon after it was established, the party organized itself in Kurdish areas and Turkey's western part, particularly areas rich in Kurds. Although the party is relatively new in the political arena, its roots trace back to the 1980s with the political and armed organization Hezbollah. Most of the party members, including some of its founders, had either been imprisoned or put on trial over alleged links with Hezbollah before the party's establishment. Hüda-Par, as the party's Diyarbakır provincial head Vedat Turgut clarified, shares the same grassroots origins with Hezbollah.[7] Therefore, it is evident that Hüda-Par is a progression of Hezbollah (Çağatay 2014, 5). Thus, in order to identify Hüda-Par, this section will first give a history of Hezbollah.

Although the exact date for when Hezbollah was established remains unknown, according to the book *'Kendi Dilinden Hizbullah; Mücadele Tarihinden Kesitler'* (Hezbollah in Its Own Words: Selection from the History of the Struggle),[8] published by the Hezbollah-affiliated Isa Baggasi (also known as Isa Altsoy), members started to come together between the years 1979 and 1980. To Baggasi, the group members came together to solve those issues that the Islamic world was facing which the organizations of the time were unable to deal with (Baggasi 2004). The social and political developments that both Turkey and the Middle East were going through had significant influences on Hezbollah's formation. Hezbollah explained these by offering certain historical reasons, and also Islamic liability (Tutar 2011, 115). The emergence of Marxist-Leninist leftist movements in Turkey in general and in Kurdish regions in particular, the Turkish Republic's assertive secularism, military coup d'états, the failure of existing Islamic organizations to tackle social and political issues, and certain regional developments, particularly the Iranian Islamic revolution of 1979, were certainly factors that created fertile ground for the group's formation and growth in later years (Baggasi 2004; Hizbullah manifesto 2012). As will be detailed later in this section, the Kurdish issue was not among the group's top priorities during its formation process.

Hezbollah members would gather around bookstores and small tea houses. It is still not clear whether the group was organized and/or had affiliates/members in how many cities during its formative years, but the group's leader cadres were certainly living in Batman and Diyarbakır. The idea of forming Hezbollah therefore was seeded in the cities of Batman and Diyarbakır around the *Ilim and Menzil*[9] bookstores, and almost all of the members were of Kurdish origin (Şentürk 2011, 593). And so, with reference to Isa Baggasi, as an Islamic movement Hezbollah is a Kurdish-region born movement, and it recruited mostly Kurdish-origin members (Baggasi 2004, 55); but the group also soon began to organize in Turkey's western parts and then launch its violent activities.

Before its formation, some Hezbollah members, including its leader, Hussain Velioglu, were active in the National Turkish Students Association (*Milli Türk Talebe Birliği-MTTB*) (Kurt 2015, 41–42), whose ideology was a mixture of Turkish Islam and nationalism. Despite such a background and certain similarities between them, Hezbollah's ideology and methods significantly differed from the existing Turkish and Kurdish religious groups. Because of the group's pragmatism, close affiliations with politics, violent methodology and warm acceptance of diverse religious sects, particularly Shi'ism, it is rather hard to define Hezbollah's ideology within a clear-cut framework. The group ideologically benefited from various Islamic scholars and schools of thought. The leader of the Iranian revolution, Ayatollah Khomeini's teachings, Salafi doctrines and Said Havva of the Muslim Brotherhood's opinions, had a significant influence on Hezbollah, at least during its formative years (Çakır 2011a, 249). Hezbollah also took aspects from Said-i Nursi's *Nurculuk* and Sayyid Qutb's and Ihsan Sureyya Sirma's understandings (Uslu 2007, 133); all three of them also share some doctrines, but significantly differ in terms of their methodology (*manhaj*) for running their cause (*dava*). Considering all these together, Hezbollah's theological stance can be placed between Salafi thought and *Nurculuk* in a broad context. By Salafism here I meant both militant, violent Salafism (militant jihadism) and non-violent Salafism, or, using Quintan Wiktorowicz's classification, Purists (non-violent, purist Salafism distanced from politics), Jihadists (violent Salafism with a particular interest in *takfir* – excommunication) and Politicos (non-violent Salafism with an interest in politics) (Wiktorowicz 2006). Hezbollah has gone through all of these three types of Salafism in practice. Benefiting from and/or applying diverse ideologies and teachings of these Islamic scholars has provided Hezbollah with substantial social and religious grounds for acting pragmatically. This, as will be explained later in this section, allowed Hezbollah to change their strategy by putting down their weapons and acting as a civil movement by opening various social, cultural and political organizations.

Given the conditions which led to the emergence of Hezbollah and the structuring of its ideological codes, religion is the underlying factor in its political identity and policy decisions. In line with its ideology, Hezbollah criticized the existing Islamic organizations' weakness and linked them with the state. In this respect, the group defined the main aim of its formation in the first years was to remove the secular Kemalist regime and form an Islamic state. The group found the regime to be the root cause of most problems in Turkey (Baggasi 2004). Once Hezbollah had established its ideology, its priorities were fixed on the development of the organization and propagation of its Islamic programme. The group labelled itself as a religious movement and avoided making any reference to ethnicity and/or other identities. Hezbollah therefore underplayed the Kurdish issue in its agenda during its initial years (Düzgit Aydın and Çakır 2009, 103). Despite this, some within the group, known as the Hezbollah Menzil, were more sensitive to Kurdish identity and placed more emphasis on the Kurdish issue by developing harsh criticisms of the state and Turkish Islamists, but this did not impact on or alter Hezbollah decision to avoid mentioning the Kurdish issue during its first years (Bulut 2009, 359). Evading mentioning the Kurdish issue was one of the main reasons for the group's success during their first years, since this allowed Hezbollah to escape the state's surveillance and oppression and receive support from the Kurds who were against of the PKK. The group's priority within the Kurdish region was to provide a strong Islamic understanding and way of life (Yavuz 2011, 217), and this was what the PKK and other secular Kurdish groups were fiercely challenging.

Hezbollah's pragmatism and avoidance of the Kurdish issue did not prevent the group from organizing in the Kurdish areas. Although the group was not formed as an armed organization, and initially focused on religious issues such as Dissemination (*Teblig*), Guidance (*İrşad*) and non-militant Jihad (*Cihad*) activities (Baggasi 2004, 40; van Wilgenburg 2012, 4), the outbreak and subsequent escalation of the conflict between the PKK and Turkish security forces in the Kurdish area strongly influenced its struggle and political priorities. With concerns over the PKK's growing popularity, Hezbollah intensified its activities in many Kurdish areas in small groups, especially in Diyarbakır, Batman, Siirt, Van and Mardin where the PKK was receiving considerable support (Siverekli 2008, 143). Hezbollah's focus on Kurdish identity entered a new phase and became a necessity for the movement, with debilitating repercussions – a conflict ensued between the PKK and state security forces in 1984, and the Kurds increased their interest in their ethno-national identity – a problem because Hezbollah well knew that it wouldn't be able to receive support from the majority of the Kurds without mentioning their ethno-national demands.

Hezbollah and the PKK's targeting of the same geographical and sociological base, the Kurds, soon brought both groups into conflict with each other. Hezbollah's intensifying of activities in PKK-dominated areas and the state security forces' overlooking and toleration of these activities in order to weaken the PKK's influence generated concerns and provoked strong reactions from the PKK. As had been the case with the Village Guard, the PKK well knew that the security forces would use Hezbollah against the PKK and its sympathizers in both political and military terms. There were also other reasons for both groups' political and armed confrontation. Ideological motivations in this regard comprised the first reason behind Hezbollah's challenge to the PKK, especially considering the latter's Marxist-Leninist worldview. Attacking the PKK's Marxist-Leninist ideology, Hezbollah declared the PKK to be an enemy of both Islam and Kurdish values (Baggasi 2004, 75). However, it was Hezbollah's desire to became the only power and voice of the Kurds that led the group to directly challenge the PKK. Therefore, Hezbollah resisted the PKK, attempting to prevent it from gaining sole power and control, and tried to join power in the Kurdish region, causing further hostilities between them (Nugent 2004, 70).

The trouble between the PKK and Hezbollah further intensified following the 1990s, with the PKK's activities mounting but Hezbollah also strengthening to some extent. At this time, both groups had a level of power within the Kurds. But while the PKK mostly organized in the Kurdish masses and also gave priority to legal activities, Hezbollah preferred to remain as an underground organization. The conflict between the PKK and Hezbollah in that sense led to a greater awareness of the group's activities. This made Hezbollah's name and power even better known, but also opened the door for the development of dirty affiliations between the group and a Turkish Deep State organization, JITEM, which committed many crimes in the Kurdish region. The Turkish state officially does not accept the existence of JITEM, yet, as part of the struggle against the PKK, JITEM has committed kidnapping, torture, forced disappearance and killing of many Kurds, which is a well-known fact among Kurds (Uslu 2007, 127). To defeat or at least diminish the PKK's power, JITEM used Hezbollah against the PKK by closing its eyes to Hezbollah's kidnapping and killing of PKK sympathizers (van Wilgenburg 2012, 4). None of Hezbollah's members who committed these crimes were arrested at that time.

The conflict between the PKK and Hezbollah took place in the districts and city centres in Kurdish areas and continued for almost six to seven years (in the 1990s), and gave rise to the social, political, psychological and economic destruction of the Kurds. It left hundreds dead; thousands of Kurds migrated and, most significantly, the political split between the Kurds intensified (Pekoz 2009, 325–27; Uslu 2007, 127). The battle between both parties also weakened their power in the region. The conflict in this regard was not sustainable for both sides. Thus, aware of the immense cost and crushing outcomes the conflict had for both parties, the PKK and Hezbollah came to an agreement in 1998 which ceased the physical conflict (Nugent 2004, 71). Following the truce, both sides stopped the fight; however, they continued to compete with and resent one another.[10] Particularly, because of Hezbollah's civil killings, and, most importantly, its method of killings such as the use of 'hogties' generated a huge reaction against the organization. Resentment against Hezbollah not only appeared within the PKK and its sympathizers. Religious Kurds also began to seriously challenge Hezbollah, especially because of its impetuous violent oppression of its opponents, including religious Kurds, such as the killing of the Zehra community leader Izzettin Yildirim and some other religious Kurds (BBC News 2000). I asked both Zehra and Hezbollah members about the killing of Izzettin Yildirim during the fieldwork. Zehra authorities without a doubt claimed that Hezbollah killed him, while the Hezbollah authorities accepted that they had kidnapped him for questioning, but refused to admit to killing him.

At the same time, a deep hatred for Hezbollah also began to develop within a vast majority of Turkish society once the group extended its area of activities and killings to include Turkish cities, particularly İstanbul, Mersin, Adana, Ankara and Konya. Hezbollah's recklessly violent oppression of leftist activists, intellectuals and feminists using the 'hogties' method provoked a severe reaction within Turkish society. Especially the killing of the Turkish Muslim feminist Konca Kuriş using this method generated massive hatred and reaction against the group. Despite the Turkish security force's clandestine relationship with and influence on the group, Hezbollah's expanding of its killing to non-PKK sympathizers and its organization in Turkey's western parts show that it had begun to act more independently. Hezbollah's truce with the PKK further revealed that the group's interests had begun to clash with the state's interests as well. All these matters encouraged the Turkish security forces to look over the policy of Hezbollah and to consider the group as a threat to its national security, and drove it to act against the movement (Van Wilgenberg 2012, 4).

In the first months of 1999 the state launched operations against Hezbollah, culminating in the killing of its leader, Hüseyin Velioglu, and the arrest of thousands of its militants and supporters. The state's intensive operations weakened Hezbollah's power considerably (Baggasi 2004, 145–46); however, it was unable to completely eliminate it. With the operations, the state aimed to get Hezbollah's power under control, rather than simply eliminate it; as later years showed, the state wanted to use Hezbollah and affiliated organizations against the PKK. As will be explained shortly, it is most probably because of this that the state opened all legal doors to the formation of Hezbollah-affiliated legal organizations.

Following the state's actions, Hezbollah put down its arms and concentrated on civil politics.[11] The state's operations against the movement and the negative image it had in society in a way led the movement to use legal platforms to conduct its struggle (van Wilgenburg 2012, 7). Hezbollah then gave precedence to civil methods and began to create legal associations. It started to open bookstores and publishers, and published books, all under different names, as well as daily/weekly newspapers and magazines (Düzgit Aydın and Çakır 2009, 104–5). In order to strengthen its struggle against the PKK and some Islamist groups in the Kurdish region, and also to gain grassroots support, Hezbollah began to use a nationalist discourse and further put Kurdish identity and the Kurdish issue onto its agenda, often as its foremost priority during its civilization process (Jenkins 2012). The movement at that point can be argued to have achieved some success. Highlighting Kurdish identity through a religious discourse allowed the group to gain sympathy with some religious Kurds. The group in this regard 'reinforced the Kurdish consciousness of Islamist Kurds' to some extent (Uslu 2007, 131). This has further led the organization to extend its grassroots support and also compete with the PKK in receiving support from the Kurds who are more sensitive to their religious identity.

In line with its civilizing and legalizing purpose, the creation of a political party became a prerequisite for joining power in the Kurdish region for Hezbollah and linked organizations. With this, and with the termination of the Hezbollah-affiliated faction Mustazaf-Der on 11 May 2012, the majority of Mastazaf-Der's founders formed the *Mustazaf-Der Movement* (*Mustazaf-Der Hareketi*) (Işık 2013, 219), and then the Hüda-Par party on 17 December 2012. The Hüda-Par's party programme gave priority to the causes which influenced the Kurdish issue and the urgent steps needed to be taken to settle it (see pages 8–10). To achieve this, it demanded constitutional recognition of the Kurds; consideration of the Kurds as a primary constituent of the founders of the Turkish Republic with the Turks; recognition of the Kurdish language as an official language along with Turkish; the removal of the Turkish anthem and similar symbols which refused the Kurds; the return of Kurdish city, town and village names; the removal of articles which place emphasis on the term 'Turk' in the constitution; the removal of the village guard system; further decentralization; and the election of local authorities/officials by local people (see pages 30–35). In that respect, it is suggested that Hüda-Par intended to fill the existing political gap in the regions densely populated by Kurds by recognizing their religious and ethno-national identity. In addition, it is implied that the party was initiated primarily as a mechanism to solve the problems in Turkey, particularly those regarding religion and the Kurdish issue (Hür Dava Partisi Programı 2012). To avoid potential pressure from the Turkish state, Hüda-Par did not openly mention federalism in the party programme, but during the fieldwork, as will be argued in the following section, the group used the term 'decentralization' within the context of federalism.

Hüda-Par is mostly active in the Kurdish region and districts inhabited by Kurds. A substantial percentage of its members and supporters are of Kurdish origin. Results from the 2014 local elections held on 30 March strongly support this, as Hüda-Par obtained a great majority of its votes from the regions largely populated by Kurds.[12] Hüda-Par did not secure any seat in parliament, and has not won any municipality so far. The party's votes were less than 1 per cent in total across Turkey. Nonetheless, the party succeeded in becoming the third power in many Kurdish areas after the HDP and the AKP. Hüda-Par in this regard is capable of changing the balance of power at the elections in some Kurdish areas, particularly where the HDP's and AKP's votes are close to each other (Çifçi 2014). Furthermore, the group is also quite active and in close relationship with society. It operates a variety of welfare and economic activities and is successful in bringing thousands to celebrate the Prophet Mohammed's birthday (*Mawlid*) event. Therefore, despite its failures in elections, Hüda-Par is quite an active and dynamic power within the Kurds.

Hak-Par

Hak-Par was formed on 11 February 2002 with the intention of solving the Kurdish issue (Hak-Par Programi 2002). Although Hak-Par is considered as a young party in politics, its ideological roots date back to some of the active Kurdish political organizations of 1960–80, such as the Kurdish Socialist Party (PSK) (Miroğlu 2012, 253–54). The party's ideology in this regard could be framed as mixture of nationalism and socialism, although the Kurds' national interests comprise the party's main priority.

Hak-Par gives prominence to the Kurds' national identity and collective rights. Its previous leader, Kemal Burkay, says that it emerged due to the political void in the Kurdish region and met the Kurds' desire for a national party. In the opinion of Burkay, Hak-Par was established because the PKK and pro-PKK legal organizations had disregarded the national interests of the Kurds (Burkay 2012b). The party in this regard is in a tough competition with the PKK, accusing the latter group of not being national, which will be argued in the following sections.

Hak-Par identifies itself as a Kurdish party, and in practice it is predominantly organized in the Kurdish region and its grassroots members consist largely of Kurds. Soon after its establishment, Hak-Par was at risk of being shut down, but instead was issued a dismissal of action.[13] To underline this, the party's political agenda is centred on the Kurdish issue and on efforts to find a viable resolution (Hak-Par Açılım Ve Kürt Sorunu İçin Federal Çözüm Önerisi Kitapçığı 2009,

3–4). In this respect, Hak-Par openly proposes federalism, which is based on equal constitutional recognition of the Kurds as a nation (Hak-Par Parti Tüzüğü 2002, Madde-3, 6–7).

Despite its deep roots in Kurdish politics and at an organizational level both in Turkey and in Kurdish diaspora in Europe, the party is organized in many of the Kurdish areas. Hak-Par has deep roots among the Kurds, especially in the Kurdish diaspora in Europe. Hak-Par is organized under the umbrella organization *Yekitiya Komelén Kurdistan* (Union of Kurdish Associations, Komkar), first founded in Germany in 1978, and has forty membership organizations in EU countries (Østergaard-Nielsen 2003, 62). Despite the political tradition it represents and its organizational structure, Hak-Par has not been able to achieve considerable support from the Kurds when compared with the HDP and the AKP, both of which receive significant support from the Kurds. Hak-Par's overall votes in Turkey and in Kurdish areas add up to less than 1 per cent. The party therefore does not have any seats in parliament, and won only one municipal mayoralty, Konukbekler, Muş, at the local elections in 2014. Despite this, the party receives support from the nationalist Kurds and Kurdish Alevis to some extent.

Kadep and T-KDP

Kadep was founded under the leadership of Şerafettin Elçi, the former Minister of Public Works, on 20 December 2006. With ideological roots in the Turkish Kurdistan Democrat Party (TKDP, founded in 1965), and also its close links with the Kurdistan Democrat Party in Iraq (KDP), Kadep represents the 'conservative democratic tradition' of the Kurds (Miroğlu 2012, 254). Like Hak-Par, Kadep also proposes the federal model as an answer to the Kurdish issue (Kadep Parti Programi 2006, 19). The party in this regard shares almost the same political principles with Hak-Par. However, like Hak-Par, Kadep was also unable to reach the masses in the Kurdish region. The party cooperated with the BDP in the 12 June 2011 general elections, and its charismatic leader, Şerafettin Elçi, was elected from Diyarbakır. After the death of Şerafettin Elçi on 25 December 2012, Kadep lost almost all its authority and consequently merged with the KDP-T in May 2016.

The T-KDP was founded under the leadership of Mehmet Emin Kardas on 28 April 2014. Like Kadep, the T-KDP also traces its ideological roots back to the TKDP of 1965. T-KDP represents nationalist democratic traditions of the Kurds. The party is majorly organized within the Sunni Kurds. The T-KDP has recently been active in some Kurdish areas, especially in Diyarbakır. In their approach to the Kurdish issue, the T-KDP underlines recognition of the Kurds' national status under federalism. The T-KDP in this regard takes the Kurds' federal status in Iraq as a model.[14]

ÖSP

The ÖSP was founded under the leadership of Sinan Çiftyürek on 21 December 2011. As a Kurdish democratic socialist party the ÖSP was founded upon Marxist principles and emphasizes democracy and socialism in its approach to social, cultural, economic and political matters. Challenging capitalism in this regard takes up a large place in its party programme (ÖSP Programı ve Tüzük 2011). Highlighting the democratization of Turkey, the ÖSP underlines the importance of the decentralization of dealing with the ethnic, religious and cultural minorities' identity problems. The party in this regard recognizes the Kurds' right of self-determination, and, related to this, proposes federalism, which is named the Kurdistan Federal Region of Turkey in the party's programme. Through federalism, the ÖSP claims that federal regions should have power to make decisions on internal issues, including health, education, security and local economic resources (ÖSP Programı ve Tüzük 2011).

The conditions influencing the demand for federalism

The groups which call for federalism vary in their historical and political background, ideology and social structure; however, these differences have not prevented them from making common political demands for federalism. Through federalism, these Kurds want to rule themselves (self-rule) within a defined territory, which they name 'Kurdistan'. To do so they require their own parliament, judicial power, local police forces, official recognition of the Kurdish language, power over tax collection and economic issues, and the right to manage their other internal affairs – transportation, housing, tourism, sports and so on. Reflecting on the comprehensive interviews with the mentioned groups' prominent authorities, together with the primary sources, this part clarifies the causes that lead to the demands for federalism and the rejection of other models (democratic autonomy and the granting of a cultural rights only model), respectively.

Reaction against the use of religion in the assimilation of Kurdish identity

The groups' search for federalism often pointed to the uncertainties of both the state and the Turkish Islamists regarding their approach to Kurdish identity. These groups stated that despite sharing the same religion, Turkish Islamists (such as religious communities, especially Fethullah Gülen, Süleymancilar, the Iskenderpasa movements and conservative parties) made no change to the founding ideology understanding of the state, which they noted continues to deny Kurdish ethnic identity. To the Kurds, Turkish Islamists' opposition to the state and/or Kemalist ideology only refers to Kemalism's secularism understanding, not the state's homogeneous nation creation project or the assimilation of Kurdish identity. Therefore, these Kurds specifically underlined the fact that, due to their shared religious beliefs and the dominance of Turkish culture, religion is either consciously used or involved somehow in assimilating the Kurds, particularly considering the intense social, cultural and economic engagement between Kurds and Turks. Consequently, the groups under consideration emphasized that only with a federal model will Kurds be able to protect their national identity, because only this model will give them the power to self-rule on their own territories and the opportunities to obstruct assimilation through religion.

In the context provided, Halis, who has a prominent position in the Zehra community, revealed that the Kurds were the main allies of the Turks during the time of the Ottoman Empire and the Turkish War of Independence. Halis repeatedly raised the matter of the religion-based alliance between the Kurds and Turks, and noted that despite all the policies issued by the secular Turkish Republican regime, Kurds continued to associate with the religious Turks. To Halis, the main aim of the Kurds was to remove this secular regime and construct a religion-based brotherhood ideology between the two nations – the Kurds and Turks. Nonetheless, he explained that the state and religious powers in Turkey never wanted the Kurds to obtain their national rights. To prevent the development of Kurdish national identity, he noted, these powers took every opportunity, and used every means – especially religion – to do so. For instance, he said, some clandestine powers in the state killed their leader, Izzettin Yildirim, using the hand of Hezbollah, because Izzettin Yildirim was seen as the figure responsible for merging the Kurdish religious and national identity.[15] An interview conducted with Tahir, who also has a representative position in the Zehra community, revealed similar sentiments. During the meeting and two days following it, Tahir continually made reference to how the state and Turkish Islamists disappointed the Kurds by refusing their ethnic identity, especially because they used religion as a tool to achieve this. He explained that Kurds' expectations of gaining their ethno-cultural rights by overcoming the secular and nationalist ideologies of the Republican regime had started to turn into a distant goal as the religious parties came to power. Contrary to the expectations they had of the Turkish Islamists, Tahir indicated that Turkish Islamists developed an 'artificial Islamic' understanding which did not involve an Islamic approach to the *kavims*' (nations) rights. To Tahir, this Islamic understanding did not want to recognize the Kurdish ethnic identity.[16]

Turkish Islamists' flirting with the state's and/or the state's ideology regarding the Kurdish issue here consists one of the central concerns for the Kurdish Islamists. These Kurds claim that despite their opposition to the Kemalist regime during the first few decades, Turkish Islamists cooperated with the state when the Kurdish identity became the central issue. Mentioning this, Şahan, who is (in a way) in a leadership position in the Zehra community, noted:

> Organizations like the Tasavufi (*Sufist*) groups and the Suleyman Hilmi Efendi (known as *Süleymancilar*) groups, which were formed during the period of Yeni Said (since 1925), turned to the community's culture and values. […]The organizations that were fundamentally against the system started to integrate into the system. By integrating into the system they turned against their origins. This caused problems. When these opponent groups integrated into the system, we did not like it.[17]

The point highlighted by Şahan played a fundamental role in the Kurds' suspicions about the Turkish Islamists and concerns regarding the instrumentalization of religion, particularly the assimilation of the Kurdish identity through religion. This, they say, further intensified through the strengthening of Turkish religious communities and political organizations. They regarded the associations between the Turkish Islamists and the state as a development of an 'artificial Islamic' understanding and assimilation of the Kurdish identity, as noted by Recep, who had vast experience of Turkish and Kurdish religious communities and is currently active in the Zehra community. Recep explained that Turkish Islamists have not stopped using religion to assimilate Kurdish ethnic identity, and did not oppose the state's use of religion for such a purpose.[18] To those demanding federalism, Turkish Islamists 'wanted to distance Kurds from their national purpose [pursued] through religion'.[19] In this regard, it was claimed that many of the Kurds have been alienated from their ethno-national identity, as religion significantly influenced their integration and assimilation into Turkish identity. They stated that Turkish Islamists had made a great contribution to assimilating Kurds through religion (Pekoz 2009).[20] Christopher Houston also supported the claim discussed by the proponents of federalism to some extent, stating that their understanding of religion in a national sense kept Turkish Islamists silent when the Kurdish identity was denied by the state (Houston 2001).

The point articulated above is significant in understanding the influence of religion in shaping of these Kurds' political demands. For instance, something that will be discussed further with reference to those Kurds who demand cultural rights, the Kurds' religious-based connection with Turkey prioritizes their religious identity over ethnicity and refuses any form of territorial political demand; for them, establishing territories between the Kurds and Turks will damage the unity of Islam and Turkey. However, contrary to the Kurds' demand for cultural rights, discussions with federalism adherents revealed that religion does not hold similar weight for these Kurds because they place emphasis on their ethno-national identity. Highlighting this, Murat, who had actively taken part in Hezbollah between the years 1990 and 2000 and is currently active in Hezbollah-affiliated organizations, mentioned that Turkish Islamists' insensitiveness towards the Kurdish issue and their disinclination to recognize Kurds' ethno-national rights, as the state does, has raised suspicions amongst them.[21] This led many Kurds to think that there are no more differences between the state and Turkish Islamists in their approach to the Kurdish issue.[22]

Based on this idea, many of the Kurds involved in the groups under consideration have doubts about the state and Turkish Islamists since this allowed the use of religion for political purposes, and this has brought the Kurds nothing despite their contribution to Islamic history. The following statement from Hüda-Par Batman, provincial head and candidate of Batman's mayoral local election (held on 30 March 2014), Aydin Gök, highlights this point by referencing other Muslim nations' considerations of Kurds as well.

> We have been servants throughout history. We have served, in other words. Well, really, truthfully we have served. We have not received anything in return. We can't see it. Some people have shown us Islam as a target. [...]Kurds have suffered a lot because of Arabs, Persians, and Turks. Kurds have really served throughout history.[23]

These concerns, as the empirical findings also revealed, prompted Kurds to take measures against the use of religion, as an influencing power, by their neighbouring Muslim nations, because to these Kurds, as Tahir noted, religion recognizes the equality of nations, with one not serving another. Reflecting on these thoughts, he believes more could be achieved by heightening an understanding of Ummah.[24] This would also influence their political inclinations. An interview with Enes, who was heavily involved with Hezbollah and later with legal Hezbollah-affiliated organizations, helps clarify how Turkish Islamists' approach to the Kurds and their lack of interest in Kurdish identity have affected the Kurds' political inclinations.

> I used to vote for the Welfare Party. Then I started to vote for the AKP. Of course, being a religious party and looking after the Kurdish issue in the beginning had a considerable influence on [me] supporting the AKP. Those days, recognizing cultural rights and living together like brothers made so much sense, because I wanted to believe in the sincerity of the Turkish Muslims. […]However, after seeing the AKP's and Turkish Muslims' attitudes to Kurdish issues and how they started to act and think like the state, a strong Kurdish identity started to develop in me. I focused more on my nationality. […]Let me give an example. When I looked in a library of one of the Turkish Muslim NGOs I saw only Turkish scholars. I saw Ömer Seyfettin's books, for instance. They got very angry at me when I asked, 'why are there no book related to the Kurds and written by Kurdish scholars?' This affected me a lot. At that moment I understood that Turkish Islamists are with us in terms of religion, but they do not want to recognize our ethnic identity. Anyway, I do not vote for the AKP or any other Turkish party any more. […]Our Turkish Muslim brothers did not act sincerely towards us. Therefore, I believe we have to be considered and have rights just like a nation has. A *Kavims'* (nation's) rights are already approved by our religion. Otherwise, it might not be possible to prevent future discrimination against us and assimilation of our identity.[25]

Recep's following quote is also illustrative in understanding how these Kurds' concerns in relation to the use of religion in fragmenting the Kurdish identity provoked a reaction in them, in a political sense. Recep underlined that Muslims have no hesitation about using religion as a tool to remove Kurdish ethno-national identity, regardless of the effect this has on Kurdish people. He added that this is because, as also mentioned by Enes above, Turkish Islamists place emphasis on religion but have no interest in acknowledging Kurdish identity:

> Belief is the reassurance to all races and cultures. However, when it comes to the Kurds, they used belief not as a reassurance but as an attack. They used belief to destroy Kurdish culture, and it was the Muslims who did it. […]God created all the races so that they would recognize each other, but Muslims, in general, used

belief to destroy the Kurds in this place; but there is no other belief like that. [...]Well, they deny the Kurds under the name of Islam. They, of course, use Islam. What I say is that, even if the students of Bediüzzaman stand against the Kurds' fundamental rights, this means they do not understand Bediüzzaman. [...] Denying the Kurds under the name of religion or Bediüzzaman means that you do not know religion and Bediüzzaman totally. Someone who knows these things should not be saying this. Because true belief does not say it. Bediüzzaman does not say that; *risale* does not say that. On the contrary, these three sources are a guarantee for recognizing Kurds' rights.[26]

Taking the criticisms and concerns of the supporters of federalism regarding the state and the Turkish Islamists' approach to Kurdish identity, Hüda-Par Batman provincial head Aydin Gök voiced this as discrimination against Kurdish identity. Consequently, as Gök's following statement indicates, political dispositions are impacted:

We deem this as racism. We start the fight from now; we will not be your servants. By starting the fight, we say we are not your servants anymore. We say you will saturate Islam. You will give the Kurds rights equal to those that the Arabs, the Persians and the Turks have.[27]

Thus, in order to stop the denial of Kurdish identity and in order to solve the Kurdish issue, the president of the Nûbihar association, Rauf Çiçek, highlighted they (Zehra community) have to take certain steps and develop the Kurds' national consciousness. Çiçek, for instance, expressed that as the state and associated religious communities wanted to remove the terms 'Kurds' and 'Kurdistan' from their memory, they first published *Nûbihar* magazine then opened the Nûbihar foundation in reaction to the state. Rauf Çiçek added that to settle the Kurdish question, develop the Kurds' national consciousness and remove their concerns, they must have the right to self-rule (self-governance). To Çiçek, this would prevent their neighbours from intervening in their affairs.[28] This idea was also supported by Aydin Gök, Hüda-Par Batman provincial branch head. He directly stated that they did not want to stay under the political authority of Turkey without a territorial status in line with Islam. Gök explained that the Kurds accepted Islam as an authoritative condition, but accepted living under it only with the prerequisite that they would gain national rights in one state. In addition, during the interview Gök reiterated that they challenged the Kurds' submission to other nations in the name of religion. He strongly affirmed that they would no longer tolerate Turkey's use of religion as its pawn. He explained:

Allah says we divide you into different races, groups, to know each other. We divide you not to fight with the world or with each other.[...] We divide you into *kabilas* (nations) to know each other. When we say that, we say that whoever appropriates Islam [does so] not to rule other races. There is an assumption that, because the Turks act like they inherited Islam because of the Ottomans, they consider that they can rule other races. We never accept this. Some people abuse this. [...]When we look at it considering Islamic references, it is not possible to have a race that is superior to others. We cannot accept this. We do not want to accept this either. We do not say that. Islam provides equal rights for everybody. Allah says, 'Verily the most honoured of you in the sight of Allah is (he who is) the most righteous of you'. [...]When a Turk expresses himself and his rights without any problem, a Kurd should also be able to do that. He should learn his language, his ancestry; he should have a political status. Kurds should self-govern. This status is necessary. [...]Therefore, whoever did something for this nation and country, it is good (*hayırlı*). We see this and consider them brothers.[...]However, we should add that although we accept the priority of Islam, we do not accept that it should be in the hands of Turks only. [...]You should stop it when someone imposes something on you. The idea that even if it is Islam, it should be in our hand, it is not Islamic and sincere. We do not do and accept this. Well, we are Kurds, we will do what Kurdishness requires. You cannot prevent this.[29]

With reference to this issue, according to the proponents of federalism, but particularly Kurdish Islamists, religion is clear about recognizing nations' right to self-rule under an Ummah ideal.[30] Based on this idea, but also with reference to Said-i Nursi's "'*Cemahir-i Müttefika-i Islamiye*'" (The United Republics of Islam) understanding, Kurdish Islamists thus take religion as their foundation in order to grant Kurds the right to self-rule.[31]

With regard to the aforementioned concerns and political claims, Azad Ayyildirim and Burkay Aslan, both Komkar executives and Kurdish politicians in the Kurdish diaspora in London, articulated that their demand for self-rule over their territories can only be accepted through federalism.[32] To put it another way, these Kurds believe that having no control over their own affairs will provide a strong ground for the state and Turkish Islamists to use religion as an assimilative force in subsuming the Kurdish identity.

Consequently, based on interviews conducted with the Kurdish groups under consideration, these Kurds suppose that continuous use of religion by Turkish Islamists and the state to assimilate Kurdish identity is one of the prominent conditions which reduced the power of religion in keeping Kurds without a territorial status in Turkey, and in turn, raising demand for self-governance, that is federalism. Therefore, as argued above, to these Kurds, but specifically the Kurdish Islamists, religion deems all nations equal and recognizes their social and political rights at the same level, and not through the assimilation of some nations by others. Accordingly, to these Kurds, acknowledgement of the Kurds' demand for the right to self-rule is the first necessity when considering Islam's approach to nations' rights, which in turn, they mentioned, has the potential to prevent the state from assimilating the Kurdish identity through religion. This is primarily because these Kurds believe that Kurds can prevent the use of religion from dissolving and integrating the Kurdish ethnic identity by adopting a federal model.

Ethnic territorial national status

Acknowledgement of the Kurds' national status is one of the main motivations behind the demand for federalism. As previously revealed, the proponents of the HDP/BDP, DBP and the PKK also consider the recognition of the Kurds' national status, which they name the national status of a democratic nation (with less focus on the notion of territory, and particularly ethnicity), as a primary factor in the rise in the demand for democratic autonomy. Federalism's defenders harshly oppose this because they consider territory and ethnicity (the construction of ethnic territorial self-government) as a necessary constituent in identifying and recognizing the national status of Kurds. In this regard, the outcomes of the research revealed that the desires to be acknowledged as having a national status and allowed to form an ethnic territorial authority are significant foundations that contribute to the demand for federalism.

In the context provided, two facts are essential in these Kurds' status request: ethnicity and territory. More clearly, they consider territory through ethnicity as contradictory to democratic autonomy's non-ethnic nation definition. Throughout the research study, many of the interviewees, including the PSK leader Mesut Tek, Azad Ayyildirim, a Kurdish politician and Kom-Kar executive, Tahir, an activist within the Zehra community and Cudi Dabakoğlu the Kom-Kar president, underlined that a nation can be thought of as a nation when it has authority over its own territory. They associated the term 'nation' directly with a particular part of a territory, which they named Kurdistan. They explicitly underlined that if a nation has a territorial concentration then it should be given right of power over its territory. Territory, in an ethnic sense, to these interviewees is at the forefront of Kurds' national identity and political claims.[33]

Despite sharing diverse ideologies, the Kurdish groups' search for federalism justifies their claim to territorial national status through both religious and non-religious terms. Referring to Islam, for instance, Ismail, who was an executive of the closed Hezbollah-affiliated Mustazaf-Der association, openly said that he considers *Medine Vesikasi*[34] (the Medina Constitution) as a factor in the recognition of Kurds' territorial claims. He explained that because the Kurds are a separate territorial nation, their status must be acknowledged in light of this.[35] The point highlighted by Ismail was further strengthened by the Kadep Diyarbakır provincial chairman, Ciwanroj Ceyhan. According to Ciwanroj Ceyhan, becoming a territorial nation makes self-governance a necessity, which he believed could be achieved through federalism. He associated the demand for federalism with territorial nation status as follows:

> Turkey needs to be ruled by a federal system because there are two nations. One is the Kurdish and the other one is the Turkish nation. This cannot be denied. We should not ignore this. Also, Kurds live in their own territories. They reside in their own homeland. Some people in Turkey sometimes twist this by saying there are also Laz, Georgians and Circassians. They are also nations, but their homeland is not here. This is not their territory. This territory belongs to the Kurds. This geography, this land is of the Kurds. It was also named Kurdistan in history. Because of that, we think the federal system is suitable. Two nations could live in such a common system. It could be within unified boundaries.[36]

This idea expressed by Ciwanroj Ceyhan was also voiced in another interview with the PSK leader, Mesut Tek. Mesut Tek disclosed that the territoriality of a nation had an influence on the demand for territorial political assertion, in this case federalism. He repeatedly highlighted that the Kurds are one of those nations that depend on territory for their national identity. He continued by explaining that the Kurdish nation cannot be described without their territory, in which they have lived for thousands of years. He argued:

> If there is a nation like Kurdistan, and a region like Kurdistan, why not a federation? It should be, because it has historical equivalence. […]This is a historical reality. They are the real owners of these lands. […]If there is a land which gave them their ethnic identity, why did they give up their territorial demands? If there is a federation that is based on territory, they will look at the future more securely.[37]

Taking the concentration of the Kurds in a territory in order to determine their national status, these Kurds, as DDKD Diyarbakır executive Halim İpek stated, claim that they have 'consciousness of their national identity', and therefore their relations and status in Turkey should be considered accordingly.[38] In this regard, they consider federalism, according to the terms of Halim İpek, to become the way they govern their territories.³⁹ Otherwise, Kurdish national identity will be dominated and so become fragmented and weak (Bozyel 2012, 28).

Thus, taking into account the empirical findings, they believe that the Kurds' national status needs to be recognized by acknowledging their territories, which they suggest is achievable through federalism because the model provides status without division.

Building equality

With reference to acknowledging territorial national status, another condition which contributes to the demand for federalism is these Kurds' request for equality between the Kurds and Turks. Having their territorial national status recognized in this way is considered a pre-condition for building equality between the Kurdish and Turkish nations.

Many of the research participants expressed the belief that the Kurds want to be treated as an equal nation, and this, they claim, can be built only through federalism. Mentioning this, Hak-Par president Kemal Burkay stated that federalism will provide political and status equality between the Kurds and other nations.⁴⁰ In other words, they believe it will provide equality between the Kurds and other nations in terms of recognizing the Kurds' political will (Burkay 2004, 75). By identifying the Kurds as a nation, also in support of the claim(s) emphasized by Kemal Burkay, the Nûbihar executive chief Süleyman Çevik also highlighted the necessity for building equality between nations – namely the Kurds and Turks. He explained that if the Kurds have a political and administrative status and authority over their territory, they can be classed as a nation and free people. If not, the Kurds will be labelled as *'second class citizens'* in Turkey. Çevik added:

> The ideal community is the community where all people are equal and independent; all people benefit from rights equally. But it seems it is not possible for Turkey's context. In Turkey, the problems are not solved by saying we are all brothers. When your language is not as free as his, when you do not have the same power in government that he has, when your governors do not have the powers that his have, you become a second class and he becomes a first class [citizen]. […]When you say we are brothers in Turkey, it does not mean that we are equal in rights, laws, and access to benefits. There is an understanding that we are equals, but you should be dependent on us. In circumstances like this, it is not possible for the Kurds to gain their rights, speak their language and live their culture.⁴¹

The statements and anxieties cited by Çevik were often mentioned by the other federalism seekers in the course of the fieldwork. Highlighting the inequality between the Kurds and Turks, the federalism adherents stated that this can only be removed through federalism. Mentioning this, İbrahim Güçlü, one of the founders of Hak-Par, regarded federalism as a necessary condition for protecting the Kurds' national identity and will, and ensuring the constitutional recognition of Kurds as an equal nation, both in status and in rights.[42] Otherwise, as Hüda-Par's Diyarbakır provincial chairman Vedat Turgut explained in the following statement, they believe that Kurdish national identity will be divided and separated further by the more politically and culturally powerful nation, a situation which they already faced within the last century from their neighbouring nations. Turgut stated:

> When dealing with the Kurdish issue, let us not be misunderstood: as our party leader says, we should be like the nail and the finger [i.e. *inseparable*]. However, they consider the Kurds as nails and themselves as fingers. The nail can be trimmed when the time comes; it may not be useful. Because of that, we say we do not want to be like nails and fingers – you always make yourself like fingers and us like nails. If there is justice and equality, we want to be like the equal teeth of a brush. Since you accept that there was genocide against the Kurds, assimilation, and injustice, in order to eradicate this suffering you need to make positive discrimination. At least in this way they can reach your level economically and culturally.[43]

The concerns mentioned by Vedat Turgut are commonplace for many Kurds. For instance, Halim Ipek spoke about the inequality between Kurds and Turks:

> We have been living together for 1000 years; we exchange daughters. It is true. We tried to live like brothers. But, we were not approached as brothers. However, imagine a brotherhood that does not give me any of my rights and puts me to one side if it is to its own benefit. If you are disturbed by my Kurdish identity, education in my mother tongue, some of my rights and so on, where is the brotherhood?[44]

In support of Halim Ipek's and Vedat Turgut's standpoints, the Hak-Par İstanbul provincial head, Semra Arcan, expressed that the starting point in politics for them are the terms 'Kurdish nation and territory'. According to Arcan, they make great effort to protect the Kurds' territorial national identity because this is the only way to defend the Kurds' free will and provide a sense of equality.[45]

In this regard, Kemal Burkay suggested that the principal way of achieving this is to gain authority over their territory, and so take their nation's affairs into their own hands. This ideal concept, he stated, can be supported by federalism: 'with federalism, equality would be provided between two nations, the Kurds and Turks'. If this were successful, Burkay added, there would be no need for separation because both nations could live together in peace.[46] This is because, they claim, federalism is the only model which has the potential to remove disparity between the Kurdish and Turkish nations and provide social, cultural, economic and political equality in Turkey at the national level (Ak 2010; Burkay 2012a, 15–16). Federalism thus will allow the Kurdish issue to be settled on an egalitarian basis (Bozyel 2012, 29) because federalism, to these advocates, is the model which is capable of deterring other nations from controlling the Kurds and establish equality between the Kurdish and Turkish nations.

Resolving ethnic tensions

Tensions between the Kurds and the powers that rule them date back to the second half of the nineteenth century. Following almost three centuries of continual semi-autonomous status for Kurdish principalities, relations between the Kurds and the Ottoman Empire started to deteriorate as the Empire introduced centralization policies and demanded control of the Kurdish region, particularly following the late nineteenth century. This predominantly intensified once modern Turkey was established because of Turkey's denial of the Kurdish ethnic identity. To instil recognition of their ethno-national rights, Kurds rebelled against the state numerous times to demand their independence, or at least their right to autonomy.

Although conflict between the Kurdish national movements and the state developed, a matter which was often highlighted during the fieldwork, there was no similar observation among Kurds and Turks themselves. An ethnic conflict has not taken place between the two people at the group level. However, most of the interviewees also referenced the growing tensions, mistrust and social division developing between the two peoples. These factors could at any point lead to an ethnic conflict, with discrimination (in social, cultural, political and economic terms) against the Kurds reaching new levels. The research conducted by KONDA in 2011 provided illustrative data on the growing social and cultural distance between the Kurds and Turks. Findings revealed that 57.6 per cent of Turks did not want to have a Kurdish spouse, 53.5 per cent did not want to have a Kurdish business partner and 47.4 per cent did not want any Kurdish neighbours. On the other hand, similar questions addressed to the Kurds yielded relatively smaller percentages: 26.4 per cent of Kurds did not want to have a

Turkish bride, 24.8 per cent did not want a Turkish business partner and 22.1 per cent did not want a Turkish neighbour (KONDA 2011, 106). The data revealed strong grounds for ethnic tension.

Highlighting this, Cudi Dabakoglu, president of Kom-Kar, demonstrated that the increased ethnic tensions in Turkey, predominantly seen in the intense discrimination against the Kurds, prompted these Kurds to develop methods and tactics to protect themselves from any potential attacks. He insisted that if their ethno-national identity were recognized by the principle of self-rule, in other words through a federal model, reasons for ethnic conflict would be removed, because the Kurds would be satisfied.[47] As Ibrahim Güçlü conveyed in the citation below, the Kurds who called for federalism argue that gaining authority over their territories will, ultimately, provide protection. He explained that this particular value of federalism would impede any potential ethnic conflict. To Güçlü:

> The relationship between Turks and us until now has not been voluntary and independent; we have been forced to have a relationship. This relationship is by force. It should not be like this. Before anything else, we should be equal nations. We should be equal in both rights and status. If this equality is not fulfilled as much as it is for the Turks, Arabs and Persians there will be more conflict. Let's consider a father who has five children: we say they are brothers. If you give more property to three of them, the other two brothers will create a dispute. [...] [So] the Kurds will fight if they do not obtain equal rights like other nations. For instance, why is Chechnya fighting? Because they say they want Chechnya to rule themselves. [...] Because it does not want to be dominated by Russia. [...] If this is not given, there will be conflict. This is the same for many nations. We do not want to shed blood, but it is shed.[48]

Considering this from the point of view of federalism's proponents, they declare that the conflict will not conclude unless their collective rights are recognized and they are recognized as a nation by giving the right of self-governance over their territory;[49] 'otherwise, there will be chaos, war or racism'.[50]

To clarify the contribution that federalism will terminate or considerably reduce ethnic tension, the DDKD executive Halip Ipek was asked, *how do you consider federalism as a political model in resolving existing tensions and preventing the outbreak of ethnic tension?* And *what will happen if federalism is not recognized?* Ipek responded with the following:

> Well, first we experienced an emotional crash. My brother has not recognized me up until now; if it continues like this, this emotional crash will be more fatal.

> [...]There will be a crash. Kurds will resist. They will bring civil disorder. They will rebel. Kurds will carry on their democratic political activities; this will cause a crash.[51]

Considering the 'emotional crash' between the Kurds and Turks noted by Halim Ipek, Ibrahim Güçlü explained that federalism is a necessity not only for ending the increasing tensions between the Kurds and Turks, but will also become a norm of Kurdish politics. He put it thus:

> Hostility will end with a federation. 100 years of dispute will end. The tension between Turks and Kurds will end. This will change the Kurds. The most important thing with federalism is that it will end the politics of ruling the Kurds which comes from *Kemalism*. Therefore, the Kurds will become a nation that rule themselves. Kurdish politics will be normal, it will be multiplied and democratic. Kurdish politics looks like the *Kemalist* model now.[52]

On another note, despite federalism supporters' claim that federalism will end ethnic tension, the Kurds who demand democratic autonomy as well as cultural rights proponents, as noted earlier, assert that federalism could repress minorities within the Kurds, and this will lead to tension. An interview conducted with Hüda-Par Bingöl provincial executive Orhan Açikbaş, who is also a Zaza, was particularly illustrative in understanding federalism's exponents' response to this claim. In response to this criticism, Açikbaş stated that if federal status were given to the Kurds, some Zazas might become anxious. However, the majority of them will not see it as an issue because, he explained, the state puts pressure not only on the Kurds but on Zazas and Alevis too. Therefore, Açikbaş noted that if Zazas' and Alevis' rights are also acknowledged, a federal structure would not pose a threat to their identity. He added that problems are only likely to occur if the Kurds use federalism in favour of a specific group, and assimilate others.[53] In this regard, Ibrahim Güçlü considers federalism as a political model which will re-obtain Kurds' internal minority identities. Güçlü underlined that with federalism, the Kurdish internal minorities, the Alevis and Zazas, and the Kurds will respect and recognize each other's identities and learn to live together.[54] In this context, federalism is also regarded as the model which eliminates tensions within the Kurds.

The discussion provided above, based on observations made among the Kurdish organizations, shows that these Kurds, by exploring the long-standing history of the conflict between Kurdish national movements and the state, believe the current tensions in Turkey are likely to develop into an ethnic conflict at the community level and spread through society. Aware of this possibility, the Kurds who support federalism stress that the only method for avoiding ethnic conflict in Turkey, but also for satisfying the Kurds, relies on the right of self-rule over their territories as a nation. To these Kurds, the distribution of power and the right of territorial self-rule, which federalism prioritizes, are essential points able to end the tension between the Kurds and the state and prevent the possibility of a community-level ethnic dispute. This idea, therefore, contributes to the increased demand for federalism among these Kurds.

Controlling local economic resources

The empirical outcomes of this research indicated that another reason for the rise in federalism demands among the Kurds under consideration is their request for power over their economic resources. These Kurds noted that although the Kurdish region has rich natural resources, the Kurds remain one of the poorest communities in Turkey because the state has failed to manage their economic resources and avoided taking steps to improve the Kurds' economy. As can be seen from the following figure, Kurdish areas are least developed comparing with rest of Turkey (Figure 6.1).

The Kurds who demand federalism describe the Kurdish region as being rich in underground and surface resources, and with sufficient capital; however, these resources have not been used in their favour, and they have faced economic

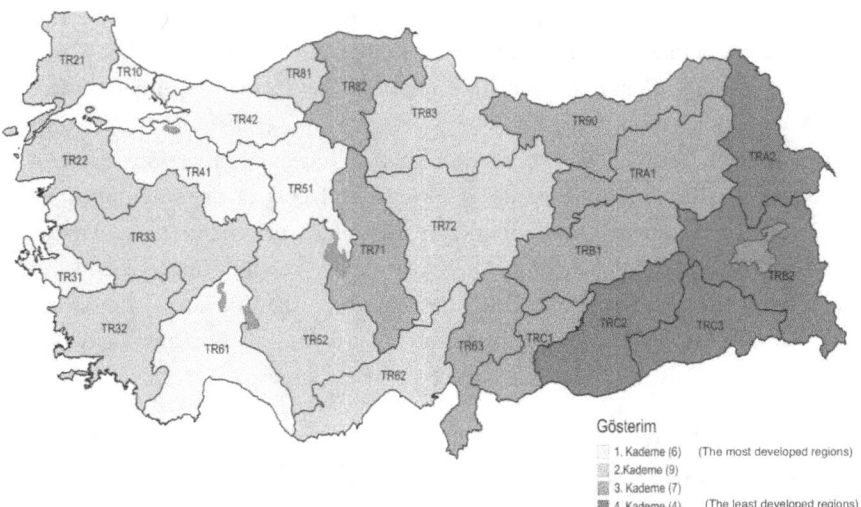

Figure 6.1 Socio-Economic Development Index (2011). Source: (T.C. Kalkınma Bakanlığı 2013).

discrimination and deprivation from the state.[55] The research found that federalism supporters believe that the state has consciously avoided developing the economy in their region. They claim that in order to prevent the development of national consciousness, the 'state either impedes the accumulation of capital in the Kurdish region or has transferred it to the western parts of Turkey'.[56] In the same vein, Güçlü pronounced that:

> With the current situation, the government thinks that if the Kurds develop economically and reach the economic standards of other nations they will demand their freedom, therefore, the state has left region without any development.[57]

This point was alluded to by the Hak-Par Diyarbakır provincial executive Eşref Çakan. He referenced previous economic policies issued by the state to help support this argument, because, as he said, these plans also did not prioritize the region's economic matters.[58] For instance, the ÖSP general vice president Aziz Mahmut Ak openly pointed out that they did not have confidence in the state when it comes to their financial matters, and demanded power over their economic sources and to manage their economic affairs independently to a large extent. To Ak, the state does not want the economy of the Kurdish regions to grow, so they intentionally use Kurdish regions' underground and overland resources to benefit Turkey's other regions. He dubbed this policy as the 'acquisition', 'plundering' and 'colonization' of the Kurdish region. Ak added:

> Kurdistan has its own underground and overland resources, has its own market. [...]Turkey applies colonial politics at the moment. Actually, with this, Kurds are an annexed and non-status colony. You know, in overseen dependency there is more colonization than in an annexed one. However, here, in the Kurdish region, we talk first about annexation, then colonization. Therefore, colonial politics is pillaging politics at the same time. Pillaging of riches. Ignoring its owners. For instance, Latin America is very much nationalist these days, it rejects imperialist pillaging in its country. They say, you mine underground and sell the riches somewhere else. This is the same for Turkey, actually. For instance, the industry is almost half the size of Kurdistan in the city of Izmit. Therefore, the raw materials and energy are carried in great volume from there.[59]

To the Kurds who demand federalism, economic self-sufficiency is a given, a fact which was often mentioned throughout the fieldwork research; however, they cannot use their own resources because of the state policy in place. As a result, they are left to live in the poorest conditions. Therefore, having right of power over their own resources is considered as a necessary condition for the

Kurdish region to develop economically, said the former president and current executive of the Kurdish Advice Centre (Kom-Kar), Burkay Aslan.[60] To justify their argument, many of the interviewees mentioned the economic development of the Kurds in Iraq. For instance, Cudi Dabakoglu explained that economic investment and economic development in the Iraqi Kurdistan region have increased since the region established federalism. He added that the case of the Iraqi Kurds illustrates very well the positive impact of having authority over their own economic growth and resources.[61] Reflecting on the Iraqi Kurdistan case, they pointed out that if they also had such control over their resources under the model of federalism, the Kurdish region would develop similarly. As in the Kurdish case in Iraq, Aziz Mahmut Ak expressed the importance of having the right to self-rule in their region, as well as control over economic resources in their development:

> When this is happening we have a mission to protect Kurdistan's under and over ground sources. As I said, this will happen with us coming to power. Just like it happened in the South (*Iraqi Kurdistan*); although oil is the matter of concern now, they gained the right to a great extent.[62]

In support of this, ÖSP leader Sinan Çiftyürek argued, 'Kurds should have the right to manage their own resources, which are rather rich. Kurds should decide how they use their resources.'[63] This is because, with the right to exercise power over their economic resources, this will subsequently create dramatic changes to their overall development. If they have authority over their territory through federalism, Hak-Par Diyarbakır provincial head Vasif Kahraman explained, capital will be stocked in the region mostly inhabited by the Kurds, and Kurds will be able to set up their own market.[64] Because power over their economic resources, Vasif Kahraman said, means their capital will remain in their region, their own market will emerge, and thus Kurds will have choice over how to use those economic resources.[65] Güçlü's following explanation also highlights the significance of federalism related to the points presented here. He stated that federalism will play a vital role in Kurds gaining the power to manage their economic resources, and therefore they will no longer be strongly dependent on the central state. Thus, they 'will benefit from underground sources, water, land and agriculture', which 'because of the state's colony politics' they cannot use, said Ibrahim Güçlü.[66]

Taking all of the points presented, collated from the empirical findings of the research, it was clear that the state deliberately precludes economic growth in the regions mostly populated by Kurds and does not use Kurds' economic resources for the welfare of the Kurds, but for its own gain. This, in turn, heightens Kurds' demand for power over their economic resources, and subsequently for the federalism model, which, they asserted, will provide capital, a national market and efficient use of resources in the interest of their own nation. Thus, by applying federalism, they suppose that the economy of the regions majorly inhabited by the Kurds will grow. This idea has made a significant contribution to the increase in the demand for federalism.

Rejection of other political models

Why not a national state

There is a close connection between federalism and the nation state since federalism is generally considered as a step towards the formation of a nation state. This raises the question of why the Kurdish groups cited in this chapter essentially demand federalism and not a nation state, even though they respect people's right of national self-determination. First, they believe that establishing a Kurdish nation state, considering the Kurds' social and political structure and the political conditions in Turkey and the Middle East, can lead to a conflict between them and the other states in the region. In other words, regional and international conditions may not allow the Kurds to have their own state at this stage. According to Osman Resulalan, highlighted in his article written for the Med-Zehra-associated *DAVA* magazine, the creation of a nation state would further complicate the solution of the Kurdish issue in the current conditions. Interaction between the Kurds and Turks, along with the regional powers' tough approach to the Kurds' independence demands, he says, could generate a massive conflict between the Kurds and the state. This, in turn, has the potential to negatively impact on the Kurds because they do not have sufficient power in present conditions (Resulalan 1991, 15). On this matter, the Kürt-Kav administrative committee member and veteran Kurdish politician Mehmet Emin Eren stressed that international and regional political conjuncture and the Kurds' neighbours' tough stance on the creation of a Kurdish state made it difficult to construct a Kurdish state because, in their view, such a demand could lead on to other problems such as conflict with their neighbours.[67] The concerns highlighted so far clearly became evident in in the Iraqi Kurdistan case. To determine their future, the KRG held an independence referendum on 25 September 2017, and more than 92.7 per cent of voters said 'yes' to independence (The Guardian 2017). Soon after the referendum, Turkey, Iran and Iraq put their all disagreements aside and employed severe political and economic sanctions on the KRG, along with the support of the Iran-affiliated al-Hasdh al-Shaabi paramilitary forces, followed by the Iraq army's invasion of the oil-rich Kirkuk and more than 40 per cent of Kurdish territories (Cockburn 2017). Because they challenged the referendum, the Kurds' Western allies, notably the United States, just watched the developments without intervening or supporting the KRG. This shows how regional and international conjuncture is not suitable for the formation of a Kurdish state.

Alongside the reasons provided, federalism adherents, especially Kurdish Islamists, highlighted the fact that separation could damage the relationships between Muslims. Thus, against the idea of constructing new borders between peoples and states, the Hüda-Par general vice president Necat Özdemir said:

> As Hüda-Par, we never support placing borders, walls, fences or mine fields between Muslim countries. We want them removed entirely. [...] Likewise, we want borders with Iraq, Iran, Syria, Georgia and Armenia removed as well. [...] The borders could be thought of as they are in Europe, where borders are becoming meaningless.[68]

Looking at the issue from the Kurdish Islamists' perspective, separating nations by states could damage the understanding of Ummah. For instance, according to Murat, who had affiliations with Hezbollah-linked organizations, their aim is to create unity, not separation, between Muslim nations. This is the fundamental reason for claiming federalism, because the model proposes unity of nations by granting all their political rights.[69] Nevzat Eminoglu, an academic and activist within the Zehra community, highlighted the same point by referring to Bediüzzaman Said-Nursi's *Cemahiri Müttefika-i İslamiye* (Union of Islamic Republics) project, which to Eminoglu acknowledges nations' rights. He noted that they want recognition of the Kurds' national rights along with those of other Muslim nations under the umbrella of Islam.[70] The points revealed in an interview with Enes also support Eminoglu's view.

> Allah created me as a Kurd. He deemed me suitable for this. I and no one else can object this. Why is it wrong to defend a nation's rights that Allah thought I am suitable for? It is wrong to deny that. Because of that I say, as Bediüzzaman says, I support the idea of '*Cemahiri Müttefika-i İslamiye*', and I believe this is the right thing to serve under the umbrella of Islam for my nation.[71]

As Enes' statement indicates, these Kurds, essentially Kurdish Islamists, consider the idea of Ummah as a model for protecting nations' rights. They therefore assert that the creation of a nation state can damage the ideal of Ummah.

Accordingly, within the context provided, federalism's backers believe that forming a Kurdish state can lead to conflict between the Kurds and neighbour states, since the current socio-political conditions of the region are not presently prepared for such a level of change. Furthermore, most supporters, especially Kurdish Islamists, avoid drawing sharp boundaries, since they believe this will damage Muslim unity. Federalism, therefore, is considered as the ideal political model to either remove or ease ethnic tensions between the Kurds and Turks by satisfying the Kurds' ethno-national sentiments in their union with Turkey. The idea of federalism, as the research consequences introduced, is thus regarded as a necessity for the elimination of separatist inclinations in Kurds.

Rejection of democratic autonomy

The arguments in previous sections have elucidated that achieving a territorial national status was significant in heightening the demand for federalism amongst Kurds. The liberation of the nation is conceived as the liberation of territory. This is also one of the crucial points which differentiate federalism from democratic autonomy, because, as noted in previous chapters, democratic autonomy does not strongly base itself on an ethnic territorial understanding. This leads federalism supporters to claim that democratic autonomy lacks national character, and therefore cannot meet the Kurds' national requests and/ or needs.

With reference to this, Azad Ayyildirim, a London Kom-Kar executive and political activist in the Kurdish diaspora, underlined that democratic autonomy is not a national project, and that it does not aim to achieve the Kurds' requests for a nation because 'democratic autonomy first of all is not based on a territorial understanding'. To justify his argument, Azad explained that because democratic autonomy does not clarify or mention Kurds' territorial borders 'it cannot be identified as a Kurd or *Kurdistani* model'.[72] Like Azad Ayyildirim, Ibrahim Güçlü also deems democratic autonomy as not beneficial to the Kurds or to their nation. To Güçlü, this project belongs to the state, with influence from the Kemalist powers to remove Kurds' national status demand and weaken their national mobilization. For Güçlü, therefore, democratic autonomy cannot provide Kurds with a national status.[73] Democratic autonomy's aim to re-structure Turkey into 20–25 regions, including the regions mostly inhabited by the Kurds, has in turn further provoked criticism of the model regarding its national character. Because, as noted by PSK leader Mesut Tek, federalism's exponents claim that democratic autonomy has the potential to divide the Kurds' homeland and Kurdish national identity.[74] With reference to this, these Kurds claim that since democratic autonomy actually divides society by re-structuring Turkey into 24–26 regions, it has the potential to further increase tension.[75]

Furthermore, federalism's proponents also share their criticism of democratic autonomy by highlighting that it is to some extent a social engineering project, and remains ambiguous. For instance, Hak-Par leader Kemal Burkay harshly criticized democratic autonomy when asked, *what are the differences between democratic autonomy and federalism and why do you refuse the democratic autonomy model?* during an interview when he visited Hak-Par İstanbul province:

> Now, they (*democratic autonomy's defenders*) say, 'we do not want land', 'We do not want borders'. But if you call for autonomy, then an autonomous region has its own borders. Just as a village has its own borders, an autonomous region has its own borders too. [...]You demand some rights for a particular region and a particular people.[...]Borders have to be defined.[...]But, in democratic autonomy, borders are not defined. [...]They say 'there won't be land, any borders'.[...]An autonomous region should definitely have a flag.[...]But they do not even say that. No border, no flag, no official language, they say 'unitary' about this. But if this happens, it will not be called autonomous. They say 'we will not touch the unitary structure', but if the unitary structure is to stay, there will be no autonomy. [...]Democratic autonomy is a monster.[...]Kurds will not gain any rights with this. Come on, do not deceive the Kurds. [...]Everything is societal engineering. It is not necessary to mess the Kurds around like this.[76]

Finally, most of the federalism proponents criticized democratic autonomy, claiming that the model is not democratic either in nature or in practice. To these Kurds, democratic autonomy is authoritarian, even a dictatorship. Highlighting the de facto declaration of democratic autonomy by HDP-run municipalities, Hüda-Par Bingöl executive Hamdullah Tasali stated that

> The HDP's self-governance understanding does not rely on the idea of self-governing. In their understanding of self-governance, there is no place for other opinions. In some way, this is similar to a dictatorship, such as a one-party ruled self-governance system like the CHP's one party ruled system of the 1930s [...]Kurds were previously leaving their homeland because of the state, such as the JITEM oppression, but now they are escaping from the HDP's oppressive democratic autonomy model. Because this model is not democratic.[...]They try to establish democratic autonomy through weapons.[...]Because of their oppression we can't open our party branches in Hakkari, Yuksekova or Tunceli.[77]

Democratic autonomy, it is believed, will not bring peace and stability to the Kurdish region; it will lead to economic destruction and the deterritorialization of the Kurdish areas.[78] Highlighting the de facto declaration of democratic autonomy and the digging of ditches in districts and city centres especially, T-KDP general president Mehmet Emin Kardaş underlined the pointlessness of digging ditches and the de facto declaration of democratic autonomy, particularly because of its destructive effects on the Kurds. To Kardaş, the YDG-H's war will bring nothing to the Kurds.[79]

Taking into account the fieldwork outcomes illustrated, critiques regarding democratic autonomy's nature and ethno-territoriality are the main factors which led many to refuse democratic autonomy and consider federalism. In other words, because the Kurdish issue is described as a nation's territorial rights, to these Kurds the solution is also tied to territoriality in an ethnic sense. This, in turn, is the main explanation for rejecting democratic autonomy – the model refuses to approach or consider the idea of territory in the solution process for the Kurdish issue.

Rejection of the cultural rights only model

Meetings with elites from the Med-Zehra and Zehra communities, Hak-Par, Kadep, T-KDP, Hüda-Par, Hezbollah and ÖSP and related organizations, revealed that these Kurds refer to the Kurds' collective identity and their association with the concept of nation. For this connection, they object to the recognition of the Kurdish identity simply at an individual level or merely for citizenship. They proclaim that granting only cultural rights would neither satisfy nor appreciate the Kurdish (group) identity in any respect.[80] In his article in the Med-Zehra community–affiliated *DAVA* magazine, Resulalan (1991, 15) highlighted that, as granting only cultural rights will not satisfy the Kurds' ethno-national claims completely, it also cannot resolve the Kurdish issue. As a result, as Dabakoğlu explained, Kurds will always struggle for their territorial national rights, which could drive the country into chaos.[81]

In a similar vein, these Kurds stated that there is a national belonging, national feeling, territorial integrity and historical memory within Kurds. Referring to these sentiments, Peköz argued that such objective and subjective parts of identity cannot be described just with reference to cultural rights. To Peköz, as Kurds are a nation like Turks, Arabs, Persians, Scots and Welsh, which have their own flags, symbols, parliaments and education in their native language, Kurds should also have the same advantages. Therefore, he reiterated that granting of cultural rights alone would not satisfy these same needs for Kurds.[82] The point declared here once again reiterates the importance and impact of being a nation on the political demands of these Kurds. In line with this, Ciwanroj Ceyhan professed that by securing cultural rights alone, Kurds will not have sufficient power and authority. However, the state can remove their rights at any moment. Kurds, therefore, are always at risk of losing their cultural rights if these rights are not assured with a federal status, added Ciwanroj. And so, Ciwanroj emphasized that by granting them only cultural rights, Kurds will not feel protected, and thus will lose trust in the state.[83]

Overall, taking into account the background provided in light of the interviews conducted, becoming a territorial nation contributes to a demand for collective rights. Federalism herein is conceived as a political model in which Kurdish identity is recognized by national status over a historical part of the land. This is considered as the primary approach in conceding the Kurds' rights at the collective level, and ensuring that equality between the Kurds and other nations is sustained, especially with the Turks. For them, the cultural rights only model does not provide this.

7

Demand for a Nation State

Despite the previously mentioned political models, some Kurds call for the creation of an independent Kurdish nation state. These majority Kurds gather within the Azadî movement, the PAK, KKH and the Kurds associated with Ismail Besikci Vakfi (IBV). The highlighted organizations support the Kurds' right of self-determination. This is also echoed by various extremist leftist organizations, such as the DHF and the Işçi-Köylü-Kızılbayrak group, that openly identify themselves through their socialist ideology. The Kurds associated with these groups come from various social strata. While the Azadî mostly include Kurds strongly associated with religion, other organizations include individuals from working class and peasant backgrounds, migrant Kurds, the Kurdish diaspora, those from socialist backgrounds and so forth.

The groups supporting independence

The Azadî initiative

The Azadî, also known as the Kurdistan Islamic movement, founded by some Kurdish Islamists on 6 November 2012, aims to sort the Kurdish question through the concept of self-determination. The group rises above religious ideology with a strong reference to Kurdish national identity. Based on this, the group took the name Azadî with reference to the Azadî organization that organized the ethno-religious Sheik Said rebellion of 1925.

The group is based in Diyarbakır, but also extends to other areas in the Kurdish region and has links with Kurds in western areas of Turkey. In its Declaration and Agreement Text, the Azadî describes itself as an initiative comprising Kurdish Islamists who look at Islamic strategies to find a solution for the Kurdish issue (Înîsiyatîfa Azadi (Metnèn Declerasyone û Mutabeqetè) 2012). Azadî identifies the Kurds in Turkey as a separate nation, names the

Kurdish region Kurdistan, considers this region the Kurds' ancient homeland (Înîsiyatîfa Azadi (Metnèn Declerasyone û Mutabeqetè) 2012, 27) and considers the two common dialects of the Kurdish language to be Kurmanji and Zazaki (Înîsiyatîfa Azadi (Metnèn Declerasyone û Mutabeqetè) 2012, 28). The group openly expresses the idea that the division of and rule over the Kurdish region by its neighbouring nations, Turkey, Iran, Iraq and Syria, have consequently stripped the Kurdish nation of any political status (Înîsiyatîfa Azadi (Metnèn Declerasyone û Mutabeqetè) 2012, 28). Azadî, therefore, highlights the fact that Kurdish people and Kurdistan are presently under the forced political domination of their neighbouring states, and, as a result, their social, cultural, political and economic rights have been denied, neglected or compromised (Înîsiyatîfa Azadi (Metnèn Declerasyone û Mutabeqetè) 2012, 29). With regard to this context, Azadî proposes that Kurds should have the freedom and right to make decisions on their social, cultural, political, and economic life. To elaborate, Azadî claims that Kurds should have the freedom to decide on their future and their 'right of self-government in Kurdistan' (Înîsiyatîfa Azadi (Metnèn Declerasyone û Mutabeqetè) 2012, 31). They base this ideal on the principles of national self-determination rights (Înîsiyatîfa Azadi (Metnèn Declerasyone û Mutabeqetè) 2012, 31–32).

Azadî, despite this religious ideology, allied itself with the HDP during the June 7 2015 elections. The initiative's secretary general, Adem Geveri (Özcaner), was elected as member of parliament for the city of Van, on the HDP list. Despite some challenges from within the group and following resignations (Rudaw 2015), Azadî still allies with the HDP on national grounds.

PAK

The PAK, under the leadership of Mustafa Özçelik, was founded on 19 October 2014 in support of an independent Kurdish nation state (Partiya Azadiya Kurdistane Program 2014). Founded on a national ground, the PAK has Kurdish members from various classes. The party was founded by the Kurds who came from the DDKO and DDKD's background, and shares close ideological and political orientations with the Kurdistan Democrat Party of Iraq. By using the slogan 'Kurdistan right now', the party aims to solve the Kurdish and Kurdistan issues (Partiya Azadiya Kurdistane Program 2014). The PAK clearly underlines that it is a Kurdish and *Kurdistani* party, and therefore insists that they are not a party to be defined within the context of *Turkiyelilik*, which is supported by the HDP. Thus, contrary to the HDP's non-state-aimed demand for the right to self-determination, the PAK seeks the creation of a Kurdish state (Partiya Azadiya Kurdistane Program 2014).

The PAK has branches in Diyarbakır, Van, Muş, Batman, İstanbul and Izmir.

KKH

The Kurdistan Communist Movement (KKH) is another Kurdish-origin party, which was founded in 1982. The KKH's main areas of focus are the mostly Kurdis-settled regions in Turkey, and seek to group these regions together as Kurdistan. In their struggle they often highlight the idea that the state has annexed the Kurdish region. Therefore, they consider the Kurdish issue as a matter of the nation's liberation (Yirmi Birinci Yuzyilda Özgürlük ve Sosyalizm Manifestosu 2008). The movement's members currently are mostly active in Europe.

IBV

Many of the Kurds' demands for the creation of a Kurdish nation state are active in various socio-cultural, intellectual and political organizations. The İsmail Beşikçi Foundation (İsmail Beşikçi Vakfı-IBV)[1] is a research organization, and provides strong intellectual support for a Kurdish state formation. Those who gather around the organization have a leftist ideology and base their demands for a Kurdish nation state both on this ideology and on the Kurds' national character. The organization's founder, İsmail Beşikçi, has been one of the leading scholars in Kurdish studies and conducted a wide range of research regarding the Kurds since the 1970s, underlining the Kurds' rights to self-determination. Beşikçi's interest in the Kurdish question resulted in his imprisonment for more than fifteen years, but his work and ideas have had a significant influence on those who are active in the Kurdish cause.

DHF

Presently, there are numerous active extremist leftist groups in Turkey. A substantial percentage of these groups include Kurd members. The DHF is a Marxist-Leninist and Maoist organization, which accepted İbrahim Kaypakkaya as founder and leader of the Marxist-Leninist Communist Party of Turkey. Kaypakkaya was killed under torture on 18 May 1973, but his resistance to the Turkish security forces in prison, 'choosing to die rather than give information', became a symbol of revolutionary resistance within the Turkish and Kurdish leftist organizations (MLKP 2017).

The DHF is quite active among Kurdish Alevis, especially in Dersim (Tunceli), İstanbul and Izmir and Ankara, and also in the Kurdish diaspora in Europe. The DHF publishes the biweekly *Halkin Günlügü* newspaper, and the magazines *Sinif Toerisi, Sanci* and *Demokratik Kadin Hareketi*. The group recognizes Kurds' right to territorial self-determination, with reference to Lenin's conceptualization of a nation's rights to have its own state (Lenin 1998).[2]

Kizilbayrak/TKİP

The Kizilbayrak group, also known as TKİP, was founded in 1998. Sharing a Marxist-Leninist ideology, the group receives considerable support from Kurdish Alevis. The group's approach to the Kurdish issue, as was the case with the DHF, is based on Lenin's conceptualization of a nation's rights to self-determination. Adopting a socialist perspective, the TKİP considers the Kurdish question as being a result of imperialism and the cooperation between the Turkish and Kurdish feudal and bourgeoisie classes, finding a solution in the salvation of the Kurdish peasant class. The group in this context recognizes Kurds' rights to territorial self-determination (TKİP Programı 1998).[3]

The demand for a Kurdish nation state

Despite the Kurds' failure to establish a Kurdish nation state in the twentieth century, this idea has continued to find interest among many Kurds. Alongside the fact that the Kurds are a territorial nation, certain conditions have also led many Kurds to claim that the creation of a Kurdish state is the only way to sort out the Kurdish issue. This part will analyse the primary data collated during the fieldwork research to address the contributory factors which led to the demand for a Kurdish nation state amongst the Kurds involved in the above-mentioned groups. In this regard, this part, consisting of two sections, will initially analyse the causative factors behind this demand for an independent state, taking safety considerations and territorial demographic weight as its causes. Following this, the motives for the refusal of other political models (federalism, democratic autonomy and the granting of cultural rights only) over an independent state will be investigated.

Safety consideration(s)

The interviews conducted with Kurds involved in the groups under consideration revealed that because of their mistrust of the state'(s) rule over the Kurds (Turkey and other regional countries, Iran, Iraq and Syria), they have dramatic safety considerations, including physical oppression, annihilation, mass arrests, torture and forced migration. The empirical outcomes of the research also indicated that the rise in ethnic and religious conflict in the Middle East further escalated their concerns. This is primarily because these Kurds believed that the state'(s) rule over the Kurds led to further attacks against the Kurds. However, for them, this fear could be removed if they were able to establish their own state; this will be the focus of this section.

Over the course of the fieldwork, many of the interviewees made mention of the state's approach to the Kurds over the last century. The following remarks from the Azadi initiative İstanbul representative, Mahmut Koyuncu, clearly demonstrate these Kurds' claim that the state intended to destroy the Kurds' demographic structure by applying various acts of violence:

> Just look at the state policies in the past, in the 1990s: the burning of Kurdish villages, towns, cities, and forced evacuations. The problem for the state was that most Kurds were living in Kurdistan.[…]If the Kurdish population was less than 60% of all the population settled in Kurdistan, the state would not have evacuated them or burnt down the Kurdish settlements. The state's main objective was to evacuate Kurdish villages and force the Kurds to migrate from their homeland and move to western parts of Turkey. Because Turkey believed that it would be easy to assimilate the Kurds in this way.[4]

Adnan Firat, of the Azadi initiative executive, noted that their past experiences comprised one of the main reasons behind their distrust of the state and demand for their own state because, as Firat indicated, statelessness was the main factor that led to their oppression:

> First, let's recap. Whatever happened to the Kurds is because they are stateless and without status. Whatever happened, over all the 100 years of exile, whatever we complain about now happened because we are a nation that does not rule ourselves, we have had no power. It is because we have had no words to speak about it. This is because we were not decision makers. It's entirely normal that people who have experienced this for 100 years want independence or a state. This nation's intellectual memory has been constructed through these experiences. It is normal if they want to form their own state. Both from the Islamic political and secular perspectives, people's rights and a nation's state

demands are legitimate. Especially if they have experienced all kinds of cruelties because of their national identity, demanding a state is compulsory.[5]

The state's previous attempts against the Kurds, as inferred in the above quotation, contribute to these Kurds' fears of living in union with Turkey, because to these Kurds 'the state still aims to destroy Kurds' demographic structure and their unity'.[6] The thoughts regarding the state's approach to the Kurds and their certainty that these are continuing were detailed in interview with Adnan Firat. To Firat, just as it was in the past, lack of status and state were still the main reasons behind their suffering and current fears:

> Look, yesterday one Kurd was killed, a student. Nationalists killed him. One was also killed in Diyarbakır. Look, how many people were killed in Roboski? The day before, someone else was killed. They did not even become news. It is very easy to kill Kurds. Almost the easiest thing. Why? Because Kurds do not have the power to decide. They do not have the power to resist this. Imagine if a Turk was killed at the Greek border while smuggling. What would happen? Would the Turkish state not make a big fuss? Yes, it would.[…] But every day, tens of Kurds are killed, but the state ignores it. That means we are an abandoned people. No one looks after our lives. Because of that we value our language, culture and identity. We value ourselves. We take life seriously. We are people who have dignity. How can I accept such things that have happened and are happening to the Kurds? Even for education in our mother tongue I do not know how many people will die.[…] We are not like them. As a nation, we have suffered too much because of our status-lessness. We have experienced all kinds of suffering. That is why our claim to independence is necessary. That is a human desire. It does not matter if you call it Islamic, humanist or civilized, it is a necessity. Look at it from another angle. The theoretical reference is obvious. Neither Islamists nor socialists nor internationalists can deny this.[7]

The conditions revealed in Adnan Firat's interview above were also highlighted by the DHF political activist Zelal, who experienced being taken into custody a number of times and was killed by Turkish security forces in a conflict in 2017. According to Zelal, there would never be a time when Turkey would recognize Kurdish ethno-national identity and end its oppression, unless it dissolved Kurdish identity. In the interview with Zelal, he often remarked that 'the Kurds should not trust this state; therefore, an armed struggle is necessary for the formation of a socialist Kurdistan and Turkey'.[8]

Taking issue on that point was Irfan Burulday, one of the founder members of the Azadi initiative, who highlights in his blog post entitled 'Free and Independent Kurdistan' that those Kurds who do not trust the state and adopt statelessness means defence-lessness and more suffering for them (Burulday 2013). This idea was expressed by many during the fieldwork. Numerous interviewees made reference to this and explained how it creates barriers between constructing their future with the Turks or under the political authority of Turkey. For instance, a prominent Kurdish politician, Ruşen Aslan, who is also the IBV executive, professed that these barriers literally and metaphorically block their union with Turkey, and this opinion is largely due to the state's attitude to the Kurdish issue. To Aslan,

> At this point the state has a disruptive role. That is why, if the solution is not based on that status being linked to the territory, the danger is always there. Disruption will grow and this will be enacted severely.[…]Now, look at the Kurds, they have been in a serious war for about 30 years. Nevertheless, they are not even given education in their mother tongue. Now, how can you confer your future or a nation's future to this state? How can you trust this state? And so, Kurds, in all cases, should obtain their own status.[…]Today, cyclically, a federation, but as a nation and a right, Kurds' independence is essential.[9]

The interviews conducted brought to the light that to these Kurds the state's approach and their own safety considerations were two of the main causes that pushed them to turn to demands for independence. Securing their own state, as Adnan Firat underlined in his following citation, will in their view halt the destruction of their people, territory and identity.

> I also say the same thing. This is not permissible. There are things that force you to claim independence. Your language is disappearing. Is there anything beyond that? Today there is huge assimilation in Kurdistan. Look at Diyarbakır Street, no one speaks Kurdish. Is there anything beyond that? Then new generation cannot speak Kurdish.[…]Beyond that, the Kurds already have national consciousness. It has been like that since Ahmedi Xani … Even during those days there was a nation between two empires. And even in those days these two empires used this for their benefit. Ahmedi Xani proclaimed this. Ahmed Xani said the only solution for this was, in the term current in his day, for the Kurds having their own Sultanate, or in today's terminology their own state.[…]He formulated this. We are now way behind the Xani period. At least there was no problem of education in the mother tongue. There were madrasas that carried on education in the mother tongue. There was no cultural rights problem.[…]but still they wanted their own state … These conditions are more pressing now. We need historical consciousness. We apply a bit of anachronism. We have history. […]If we know and read this extensive history that is available to us, and still do not do anything, this means we are insulting ourselves. Demanding a state is not only

the natural result of national consciousness, it is an emergent wish that is based on social and political conditions, or it is a form of independence, liberation.[10]

With reference to this, Irak, a Kurdish politician and activist in London, highlighted that 'as a majority of the Kurds are conscious of their national identity and ready to form their own state, it is now time for the creation of a Kurdish state. Because it could be too late for this state tomorrow'.[11]

The interviews with the organizations under consideration indicated that the safety considerations of the proponents of an independent state were not only a result of their distrust of Turkey, but also because of their mistrusts of the regional countries (Iran, Iraq and Syria). In addition, intensified ethnic and religious tensions in the Middle East alongside some of the violent attacks against the Kurds further contributed to their growing concerns and related demands for an independent nation state.

The interviews revealed these Kurds associate their statelessness with the attacks and assaults they suffer. In an interview, Vahit Aba, one of the founders of PAK, made reference to the ISIS's assaults on the Kurds in the Shangal district of Iraq and Kobani enclave in Syria, expressing that these attacks on the Kurds affirmed the need for the creation of a Kurdish state. To Aba, 'the Kurds will always be oppressed and tortured, and face cruelties, if they do not have a status and state or if they do not become their own masters'.[12] To further support that point, Dersim, who was arrested and harshly tortured during the 1980s, and who is currently a political activist in the Kurdish diaspora, spoke in a group conservation at a Kurdish organization in London and responded to the question asked by the author of research, *why has ISIS continuously attacked the Kurds?* by simply reverting to the fact they are 'stateless'. Without even waiting for the following question, *why?* he added that if the Kurds had their own army, heavy weapons and air force, neither the regional state(s) nor ISIS would dare to attack the Kurds.[13] The independent state proponents, therefore, believe that because the regional countries either oppress or show no attempt to ally with the Kurds, they (the Kurds in the Middle East) must merge to consolidate their power. This is, said PAK leader Mustafa Özcelik, the only possible way for them to protect themselves and became a strong power in the region. To encourage this idea, he referred to the cooperation between the PKK/PYD and Peshmerga forces of the Kurdistan Regional Government (KRG) developed in Kobani, and explained that if they have their own state, no authority can defeat or destroy the Kurds.[14]

Taking the assaults faced by Kurds into account, independent nation state supporters highlighted that 'Kurds should have right to merge with other

Kurdish regions'.[15] In this regard, they deemed existing boundaries as 'the political boundaries which separate the head and the body of Kurdistan',[16] and, as Fuat Önen, a Kurdish politician and intellectual, stated, they want 'to remove artificial territories between them' and enhance the idea of a united Kurdistan among the Kurds.[17] Therefore, the Kurds who called for independence openly expressed the hope that they will eradicate these boundaries as soon as an opportunity arises, because they want to live together with other members of their nation. Mentioning that point, Fuat Önen added:

> We, the Kurds, want to live with the Kurds on our land, Kurdistan. As a Kurd, I first want to live with a Kurd from Mahabat, Kobani, Hewler or other Kurdish parts, not with a Turk from Bursa city in Turkey. After the Kurds unite then we can live with a Turk from the city of Bursa. [...] The Kurds' political development and achievements in Syria and Iraq led us to hope and show that the Kurds in all parts will ultimately obtain their status. [...] Then they will remove the political borders drawn between them, and they will unite. Kurdistan part in Turkey with the largest territory and population will have a determining part in the construction of a united Kurdish state.[18]

Taking into account the Kurdish considerations and demands specified above, which were derived from the empirical findings of the research, for them, 'the backward-looking status quo will not be destroyed unless the Kurds manage to create a modern state formation on the land they inhabit'.[19] This is predominantly because, they believe, the 'state formation of Kurdistan will have a deterrent effect on terror and reactionary [violence]' in the Kurdish region and the Middle East, with particular stress on ISIS' and similar organizations' current attacks on the Kurds.[20] Otherwise, as Vahab, executive of the İşçi-Köylü group illustrated, the 'Kurds would be at risk of oppression, assimilation and violence in Turkey and in the Middle East'.[21] In this regard, they describe the Kurds as an oppressed nation, and highlighted that 'if a nation faces oppression and pressure, it has the right of national self-determination' in order to protect itself.[22] Therefore, based on this framework, as Kani Yado noted, they think 'within the current conditions of the world and the region, it is a necessity for the Kurds to be an independent state'.[23]

Territorial national demographic weight

The high volume of interviews conducted with Kurds of the groups under consideration also revealed the Kurds' demographic density, particularly the concentration on a specific part of a territory, as one of the main reasons for entitlement to the right to territorial national self-determination. They regard statelessness as one of the main motives behind the Kurds' territorial and demographic separation from Turkey, Iran, Iraq and Syria. This is especially significant when considered along with their safety considerations.

Over the course of the fieldwork research, most of the Kurds interviewed highlighted that the Kurds are the fourth largest stateless communities, with a population of 40 million in a particular territory in the Middle East alone. They associate the Kurds' demographic concentration in a particular territory with the right to the creation of their own state considering together with the Kurds' other national components, especially ethnicity.[24] Highlighting this, the veteran Kurdish politician Kani Yado noted that 'based on ethnicity and population, Kurds are the biggest nation of all the regional nations. Demanding the state formation of Kurdistan and its independence is the right of the Kurds as nation; it is the right of every Kurd.'[25] To Kurds, such a crowded population should not be managed or ruled by other nations, since they regard this as an insult to Kurds' will. From their point of view, being ruled by smaller countries, both in terms of territory and population, is unacceptable, but also the main causes behind their partition.[26] This idea is further supported by a prominent scholar in Kurdish studies, İsmail Beşikçi, who has a considerable intellectual influence on the Kurds' claims for the creation of a Kurdish state. Beşikçi argues that although the Kurds have a heavy demographic weight, as well as a historical piece of land, they currently remain without status both in Turkey and in international relations, having a divided socio-cultural and political structure (Besikçi 2013, 203–4). To Beşikçi, statelessness is the main reason for the fragmentation of Kurdish territories and, more importantly, their suffering (Besikçi 2013). He has further asserted that two significant motives for the Kurds to push for their own nation state are the idea of transforming themselves into a territorial nation and occupying a particular region for a length of time. To emphasize his argument even more, he has drawn attention to the huge impact of territory and demographic weight on nations and nation states with considerably smaller territories and populations than that of the Kurds. He explains that Kurds should have the permission and freedom of their own state because if these smaller nations are capable of gaining state status and authority over their territory, Kurds should also be so entitled. Finally, Beşikçi has clarified that if Kurds join other nation states they will no longer be governed by smaller states.[27]

The points underlined by Beşikçi were repeatedly mentioned during the fieldwork. Observations made exposed the belief that gaining territorial national status and securing demographic weight would provide extra motive for these Kurds' assertion of independence. For instance, the question, '*why do many communities made up of few thousand or million people, like Cyprus, Luxemburg, Kosovo or former Soviet republics, have their own state, while the Kurdism, of more than 25 million inhabitants, do not?*' was a common point drawn upon by most of the Kurds who advocated for the right to their own state. They openly stated that they did not want to be governed by a state which was territorially and demographically smaller than the Kurds.[28] That was an essential perspective that created a realization among the Kurds that they should have the right to decide freely on the future of their own nation and geography. Otherwise, they believed, the Kurdish question could not be solved, and other territorially and demographically smaller states would decide on their future.[29] They therefore highlighted that their demographic weight and concentration on a particular territory provided them with sufficient reason to be granted the right to self-determination.

Overall, the data obtained from the in-depth interviews suggested that having safety considerations (both internal and external) and demand for self-rule in the largest stateless community within the region were two (related) instrumental factors which led to a high demand for independence. To put it a different way, these two reasons generated demand for the right to territorial national self-determination, namely a state, in international relations. Based on this context, to these Kurds, in the words of Ruşen Aslan, 'independence is a right, and the Kurds have this right, to form their own state'. They will further be divided and suffer otherwise.[30]

Criticisms and rejection of alternative political models

Criticisms of the federalist model

It was previously reiterated that many of the Kurds fighting for an independent state also accepted a federal formation. However, they would consider federalism only for a transitional period, or as part of a steady transition towards a state. Consequently, most motives behind the increased demand for an independent state also applied to federalism. However, in their approach to Turkey, their degree of trust and safety considerations differed to some extent.

The issue of distrust towards the Turkish state is not a concern only among the Kurds who struggle for the creation of their own state. As Chapter 6 revealed, federalism supporters to some extent also do not have trust in the state. However, federalism adherents believe that the Kurds would be able to defend their national identity if they obtained political status in Turkey. They point out that with this status, Kurds will also be able to protect themselves from any physical attacks they may encounter. Therefore, since the Kurdish issue can be solved by the state which rules over the Kurds, they suggest there is no need to create an independent Kurdish state, because this will cause further trouble, conflict and chaos.

This idea proposed by federalism supporters is opposed by the Kurds who call for an independent state, because the latter believe that without their own state, Kurds as a nation do not have the means to protect themselves. Kurds' historical experience, as noted previously, has greatly influenced their lack of faith in the state and their consequent demand to establish their own state. Based on this, the academic Helin noted that 'it is a danger for the Kurds when the Arab, Persian and Turkish states, by whom they have been oppressed for many years, have the only say in the situations that relate to the Kurds'.[31] In simpler terms, they believe that since the state has oppressed the Kurds, and currently does not show many structural differences to its makeup in the past, they are hesitant.

These Kurds justified their idea by launching attacks on Kurds in the Iraqi Kurdistan region since 2011. They highlighted that although the Iraqi Kurdistan region has the most powerful federal structure, because it did not have modern and heavy weapons it was unable to impede ISIS from occupying some areas of the region, leading to a tragic scene in the Shingal district.[32] With reference to this, opponents of the federal model note that the federal model cannot provide the Kurds with sufficient power to guarantee their own safety. Their actions have affected all Kurds because federalism denies Kurds their own air force, strong international diplomatic network or central military army with heavy weapons.[33] In addition to this, federalism proponents want to invest in security. As a result of these restrictions, they criticize federalism and explain that only an independent state has the potential to deliver Kurds' needs because 'in their own state they will feel safe'.[34]

Within this framework, Mahmut Koyuncu explained that 'Kurds should not be told that they are going to be confronted with many problems if a Kurdish nation state is created' because their objective and subjective conditions for obtaining territorial status are secure. Furthermore, Koyuncu explained that although current political conditions make the creation of a Kurdish state to some extent problematic, it eventually has to be formed.[35] This is also the point that differentiates these Kurds from those demanding federalism, because they consider federalism as a transitional model to be gone through before eventually establishing a Kurdish nation state.

Refusal of the democratic autonomy model

Advocates of a Kurdish nation state formation severely challenge democratic autonomy primarily because it is less focused on territoriality or the drawing of Kurdish region boundaries and Kurdish ethnicity. A strong emphasis on the territorial side of Kurdish identity is one of the decisive points which separate independence demanders from those Kurds who call for democratic autonomy and cultural rights. This is because, as PAK leader Mustafa Özçelik underlined, for them the Kurdish issue is a national issue, requiring the right to self-govern and the right to self-determination.[36] Consequently, as democratic autonomy is not based on territorial recognition of the Kurds, Mahmut Koyuncu deems this model to be ambiguous, and underlines that such models 'weaken Kurds' power of resistance'.[37] Because of this, these Kurds severely challenge the idea of Turkiyelilesme.

Taking the issue in that sense, these Kurds claim that their past struggles to free their territory and the heavy price they have paid have made establishing their own state a necessity. They state that the Kurds made these struggles to rescue their nation and territory.[38] Therefore, rather than providing freedom to a nation without any consideration of its territory, the Kurdistan Communist Movement describes the Kurdish issue as a liberation of both the Kurdish territory and the Kurdish nation. Freedom for the nation and independence are thus also considered as freedom of territory; the reverse is also true (Yirmi Birinci Yuzyilda Özgürlük ve Sosyalizm Manifestosu 2008, 57). Territory in that sense is not classed merely as a part of a land for these Kurds: 'Territory is not only a piece of land. It is not only a border. It is the name of a state. If a nation lacks its own state and language, that means this nation does not exist.'[39] The connection between territory, nation and state is formulated as 'one of the conditions that makes a nation real; nation is the idea of a country', and therefore territory.[40]

Furthermore, another reason contributing to the rejection of democratic autonomy, for these Kurds, is that the model is unable to provide the Kurds with sufficient conditions and opportunities to protect their physical existence, as is the case with federalism. According to PAK leader Mustafa Özcelik, since democratic autonomy does not define the Kurds' status through territory, nor make mention of their national liberation, it cannot solve the matter related to the 'Kurds and Kurdistan'.[41] Therefore, they claim they will not have the authority to make their own decisions, and so their existence will always be in danger with democratic autonomy. 'If democratic autonomy is established, I believe there still will be a dependent and insecure environment for the Kurds. In other words, the national (*central*) government will decide what to do if there is any danger to the Kurds.'[42]

To further clarify this idea, the TKDP's leader, Mehmet Emin Kardaş, responded to the question '*If the Kurds in Rojava,*[43] *contrary to democratic autonomy, had their own state, would ISIS still attack them?*' by briefly expressing that 'no', they would not attack.[44] Accordingly, especially because of these Kurds' mistrust towards the state and other Middle Eastern powers, Fuat Önen asserted that other political models – democratic autonomy and federalism – could not prevent the Kurds from incursions:

> These models cannot provide sufficient instruments for the Kurds to tighten their security and to protect themselves from attacks. For instance, as the Kurds do not have their own state, they do not have heavy weapons, military forces and other instruments. Therefore, they could not prevent the seizing of some Kurdish regions in Iraq and Syria by the Islamic State of Sham and Iraq (ISIS). This terrorist movement seized the Shingal region of the Yazidi Kurds in Iraq, and now it is assaulting the Kurdish region in Rojava. Therefore, apart from the formation of a Kurdish nation state, other models cannot protect the Kurds from these offensives. These attacks may happen to the Kurds in Turkey as well. And so the Kurds should have their own state. That is the only way for the Kurds to protect themselves from the attacks of the states that rule them and from the other powers' offensives, like ISIS. Other political models cannot provide this because, as I said before, they will not provide the Kurds with sufficient weapons and power.[45]

Taking the Kurds' independence demands in light of the conditions previously mentioned the following questions need to be considered: '*How do they consider the alterations made to the Kurds' demographic structure?*' and '*Doesn't this make the creation of a Kurdish state impossible?*' In response to these questions, Mahmut Koyuncu stated:

> Although the majority of the Kurds migrated from their region, that does not mean that there is no Kurdish population in the Kurdistan region. Kurds still comprise the vast majority of people in Kurdistan … 90% of the people who live in Kurdistan are still of Kurdish origin.[46]

In response to the same questions, Kani Yado's following explanations are also significant, since he clarifies the reasons why the Kurds' demographic distribution is not an obstacle to the creation of a Kurdish nation state for these Kurds:

> It is obvious but not binding that some Kurds who migrated to the metropolises and obtained properties become anxious when Kurdish independence is

mentioned. Apart from these exceptions, the migrated Kurds' connection to their homeland is not cut off. On the contrary, it is very strong. In fact, it has not escaped attention that they are in favour of a more active struggle. When Israelis spread across the world, the same claim had been made, but now they take their position within a prestigious state as a strong country on their own land. The Kurds did not forget their language; the Israelis did, but their language is now one of the living languages.[47]

Taking issue in this sense, Ali, who is a member of the leftist Kizilbayrak group, stated, 'the Kurds should be entitled to the right of self-determination, since that is their more than 1000 years' old dream. That is why democratic autonomy is unrealistic and less demanding'.[48]

Overall, the discussions presented indicate that the Kurds who demand the creation of a Kurdish nation state have no trust in the states and powers around them, and believe that democratic autonomy will not provide them with sufficient rights and means to protect their ethno-national identity or defend themselves against any attacks. Consequently, they deem the creation of a Kurdish nation state as the only viable option for protecting the Kurds in every respect.

Rejection of cultural rights only model

As is found with regard to democratic autonomy, the Kurds in support of establishing independence strongly challenge granting the Kurds only their cultural rights. The interviews conducted plainly showed that these Kurds identify the Kurdish issue as a nation's demand for acknowledgement of their collective rights. Therefore, they stated that granting the Kurds only human or individual rights will not satisfy the Kurds or solve the Kurdish matter.[49] The following passage from an interview with Mahmut Koyuncu accurately illustrates why the Kurds reject the idea of granting cultural rights alone.

> I spent 35 years getting rid of Turkishness or the dirt that Turkish education caused. [...]If I waited or spent 35 years of my life to forget the epileptic seizure of the Turkish flag, the independence march, or the November 10th commemoration, you would think the rest.[...]A few days ago my daughter was punished by her teacher for not writing Ataturk's name with a capital first letter. Her teacher made her say, 'Ata, please forgive me' while clasping her hands. In a system like this, to demand cultural rights alone means the Kurds' assimilation. And it is only a waste of time.[...]Because they do not want to grant Kurds legal status. While Kurdish history is still fresh, there is no guarantee that people who do not give status to Kurds with sidesteps, will not do the same thing again. [...]We have a crisis, in that Kurds are denied. Kurds should create all of their

organizations based on their national identity. Otherwise, time works against them. The state also knows that.[....] Therefore, recognition of cultural rights alone means assimilation, and is a waste of time.[50]

The Kurds who demand the creation of a Kurdish nation state, as the findings of the research also suggest, hold territory as a key factor in the development of their independence struggle, but also refuse to accept the mere granting of their cultural rights, since this does not consider their territory. This, as Azadi Initiative's Press Secretary and Executive Adnan Firat cited, also explains why the Azadi movement identifies itself as a 'Kurdistani' movement and refuses the idea of acknowledging only the cultural rights of Kurds. Adnan Firat added:

> We are a Kurdistani movement. I underline this. Kurdistani means freedom of Kurdistan. I do not mean that in the sense of granting of cultural rights. I mean as a people and nation: freedom of the Kurds. We accept Kurdistan as a state, and we aim to struggle for it by achieving Kurds' national rights.[51]

Overall, the empirical findings of the research indicated that the Kurds' demand for an independent state stems from their distrust of Turkey and other regional states due to their previous political approach to the Kurds. Their concerns seem to have arisen especially after the recent attacks against the Kurds in Iraq and Syria. Because of their security considerations, these Kurds highlight that the Kurds in Turkey should form their own state, and in the long term they should unite with the other Kurds living in regional states, Iran, Iraq and Syria, because statelessness is considered the same as defencelessness. Therefore, they primarily reject the other political models, thinking that these models are not able to provide security for the Kurds. Among these models, democratic autonomy and cultural rights are also criticized for not targeting Kurds' territorial and ethnic concentrations. Because, according to these Kurds, the Kurdish question is a national issue, and it should be solved by recognizing their territorial national identity, which means being entitled to the right to national self-determination while also taking account of their security considerations.

8

Theoretical Analysis of the Research Findings

The motivations provided (by the models' exponents) to explain the Kurds' political demands and the variations between them are applicable to existing cases and theories. Some of them, however, are not supported. Thus, this chapter explains the empirical findings of the research in the light of relevant theories, to see how and to what extent they are valid to the relevant literature. It will first look at democratic autonomy and cultural rights before moving to examine federalism and the nation state.

Analysis of the findings regarding democratic autonomy

Democratic autonomy, as explored in Chapter 4, treats constitutional recognition of the Kurds' national identity (granting of political status) as its base. The model identifies the Kurds as a nation, and intends to provide them with a national status within the union with Turkey. This means constitutional acknowledgement of the Kurds' status and their equal attainment of political and economic resources within the idea of self-rule. This, as revealed through the fieldwork, is one of the substantive motives for which the model started to receive support.

Demand for the capacity to 'access state power' (Cederman, Wimmer and Min 2010) and to be recognized through their ethno-national identity – more specifically, a political status claim – has been raised by many national minorities throughout the modern period (see Mybury-Lewis 2002). Minorities' call for political status is, as Grimshaw underlines, the basis of their desire for recognition and equal rights at the social, political and economic levels (Grimshaw 2006, 327). Some ethnicities' success in forming their own state has further led these formerly stateless groups to demand equal use of social, cultural, economic and political resources and collective rights: in other words, to insist upon constitutional recognition (Thompson 2006, 116). Such recognition means constitutional acceptance of their ethno-national identity and its protection on a legal basis. Such political status demands made by ethno-national minorities were not welcomed by most host states. Most nation states attempted to assimilate minorities within their homogeneous nation- and state-creation projects (Canefe 2007; Eriksen 1992). Especially in the Middle East, most states are still reluctant to recognize ethno-national minorities' assertion of their political status. These states still implement a homogenization policy, with the intent to assimilate their minorities' identities. One such policy is the aim to create a common language, as a result of which most linguistic minority languages are facing the risk of extinction (Eriksen 1992). The consequence is that disregarding minorities' political status and oppressing them harshly have caused 'minorities to not perceive their current political status as legitimate' (Gunaratna, Acharya and Pengxin 2010, 17). This in turn has meant that gaining political status and collective rights became the main focus that many minorities chose in order to protect their identity (Casals 2006). This, as the last century witnessed, has led many stateless minorities to contest their nation states, especially their homogeneous nation-building projects, and so many regions saw conflicts and tensions break out (Gunaratna, Acharya and Pengxin 2010, 15–17; Kymlicka 2008; Ryan 1990). As a consequence, minorities' desire for equal rights and political status has triggered a national struggle against the states which rule them (Guibernau 2010).

Many ethno-national minorities have paid a high human price in pursuit of this goal, but it has also had an opposite effect: states have been forced to deal with minorities' political demands to certain degrees (Borchgrevink and Brochmann 2003, 96–97). As a result, it is currently difficult for most states to sustain their oppressive policies denying minorities' rights, at least to the same degree of severity and violence as they implemented in the past. This is primarily because the states ruling ethno-national minority groups are well aware that these groups are more conscious of the national identity and political issues that affect them, especially given their organizational and mobilization levels in the globalized world (Smooha and Hanf 1996). And so, present conditions make it difficult to keep an ethno-national group in a position without political status and suppress its claims through military means and violent methods, as most of the nation states did previously. This is also the case with the Kurdish question, since the 'status quo' which denies Kurdish ethnic identity cannot be sustained under current conditions, especially considering the Kurds' national organizational level and awareness, as well as regional and international developments (Barkey and Fuller 1998, 184).

Nation states that include minorities therefore have certain options for dealing with their minorities' demands and managing ethnic conflict: 'partition', 'ethnic democracy', 'constitutional democracy' and 'liberal democracy' (Smooha and Hanf 1996). Discussing the same point, Brochmann also argues that both the minority's and the majority's interests depend upon each other to some extent. Multicultural states therefore should accept 'a kind of nation concept that embraces ethnic groups and other groups by appealing to a sense of responsibility a cohesion within a delimited identity. Minorities are dependent on the majority community's glue to guarantee any special rights they enjoy' (Brochmann 2003, 10). The points highlighted by Brochmann require a new type of nation building (Brochmann 2003).

These arguments are also fundamental to democratic autonomy. This is because democratic autonomy underpins the necessity for the transformation of the state into a democratic republic and the formation of a new understanding of nation, namely a democratic nation, since both (i.e. democratic republic and democratic nation) rely on the ideas of pluralism, democracy and participant citizenship. These concepts became especially evident considering the Kurds' divided structure and their physical dispersion, which make the creation of ethnic territorial political models rather difficult (Öcalan 1999). On this issue, John McGarry and Margaret Moore express the view that 'non-territorial autonomy is useful for national minorities that are too dispersed or few in number to exercise or to aspire to territorial autonomy' (McGarry and Moore 2005, 71); this further supports democratic autonomy proponents' demand for constitutional recognition without reference to ethnic territorial political models. Democratic autonomy supporters' proposal for constitutional acknowledgement of the Kurds' political status in the light of the ideas of democratic republic, participant citizenship and, especially, democratic nation (which all imply a non-ethnic territorial context) is applicable to Turkey. In other words, democratic autonomy is ideal considering Turkey's fear of ethnic territorial political models. Refusal of democratic autonomy, therefore, as supporters of the model underline, means that the Turkish state aims to continue to deny Kurdish national identity and perform assimilation alongside various different methods, using policies to permanently integrate and assimilate the Kurds, thereby making their political status claims irrelevant over the long run. These claims are further supported by the current government's (i.e. the AKP's) ending of all democratic peace initiatives – particularly the Dolmabahce Declaration, which aimed to solve the Kurdish question within the framework of pluralism, democracy and citizenship – and immediately after the 7 July 2015 elections and the intensifying of the suppression of Kurdish politics (such as the arrest of thousands of Kurdish politicians), alongside the claim that there is no Kurdish question. The AKP's policies thus can be encapsulated as the state's 'one step forward, two steps back' policy in relation to the Kurdish issue (Walker 2013), and provide some indicators that force those demanding democratic autonomy to establish the constitutional recognition of their ethnic identity more relevant.

Democratic autonomy proponents' search for political status is more significant when considering the fragmented social structure of the Kurds (the existence of internal minorities). The majority of the Kurdish internal minority groups, the Alevis and Zazas, who call for democratic autonomy believe that their identities have been assimilated within the Turkish and dominant Kurdish identities, precluding them from seeking recognition of their own status, namely their internal minority status. In this regard, they consider that democratic autonomy is the most appropriate model for securing their status within the wider Kurdish identity, and that with new-found power to form autonomous regions, their concerns would subside. The condition of Kurdish internal minorities reveals that anxieties and status demands are common in many such cases. Although many minorities include diverse internal minorities, these internal minorities' demands and concerns are usually overlooked. But, as minorities become the newly dominant groups (especially in the regions they rule), the nervousness of internal minorities also grows, because many erstwhile minority groups can now withhold power from internal minority groups (Moore 2005). Remembering the contribution of the 'collective fears of the future' to fuelling minorities' anxieties and ethnic tensions (Lake and Rotchild 1996, 41), these problems can cause conflict within minority groups.

And so, taking the Kurds' fragmented structure and the anxieties of internal minorities, in particular the tension between the major identity group, the Sunni Kurds and the minor identity group, the Alevis, as a subject, we see that the application of democratic autonomy to the whole of Turkey makes it an appropriate political model because of its decentralized structure, which would allow for the creation of local autonomous regions. Democratic autonomy's proposal for restructuring Turkey into 20–25 regions and organizing society in the form of democratic confederalism, which would allow each group/identity to have their own organization and local autonomy, could remove Kurdish internal minorities' concerns and prevent tension between various Kurdish groups.

This discussion provides a valid context for consideration of democratic autonomy in dealing with the Kurdish question. Despite this, democratic autonomy contains certain ambiguities. First of all, although democratic autonomy strongly emphasizes the term 'nation' in the context of national status, this mainly refers to a democratic nation. The main reason for formulating the idea of nation to mean democratic nation within the context of democratic autonomy is because this model differentiates democratic nation from the existing dominant definition of nation; the latter, in a wider context, could be defined through other components: language, particularly a 'standardized language' (Anderson 2006); religion (Coakley 2004); territory (Aktoprak 2010, 23–24), race (Kedourie 2004a); ethnicity, culture, history, myths and symbols; memory; and the demand for constructing a common future with group members and involvement in a wider economic cooperation (Smith 1991, 14). The term 'democratic nation' shares some of these components, such as language, culture, myth, symbols and history (Bilim Aydınlanma Komitesi 2009, 103), but it separates nation from ethnic connotations (Öcalan 2011b, 79). Democratic nation in this regard shares to a certain extent Ernest Renan's understanding of nation; he harshly objects to using 'ethnographic' affinities and instead classes 'sentiments', 'soul' and 'spirituality' as the driving forces in the creation of nation (Renan 2004, 32–36). However, democratic autonomy's rejection of ethnicity, and its refusal to draw sharp territorial boundaries, clashes with the relevant understanding of nation, raising questions about the model itself, particularly about its reliability and practicability. Because nation in a broad sense, as Van Den Berghe (2005, 115) states, is a territorial, political organization, it is more clearly a 'politicized ethnicity'. The relation between territory and nation 'naturalizes the linkage between blood and soil' (Kaiser 2004, 230), two factors which are insignificant in the conceptualization of the democratic nation. In addition, as Schulze (2005, 195) notes, nation shares most commonalities with the state. Nation, in other words, usually has inclinations towards finding its identity in state form (Bruer 2010, 29–30; Weber 2004, 43). That is also the point which differentiates the perception of national status held by those defending democratic autonomy from the understanding of the supporters of the territorial political model, because democratic autonomy does not consider political status as specifically applying to a particular region, or to creating a state. Therefore, although democratic autonomy heavily emphasizes the idea of nation and the demand for a national status, it does not provide clarity on how it will secure these demands without involving the main components of nation, ethnicity and territory. The concept of the democratic nation therefore has not yet been accepted in a broad sense in the literature, nor has it been properly conceptualized.

Apart from ambiguity over its conceptualization, as the research revealed, the idea of the democratic nation is also one of the main reasons why the exponents of democratic autonomy reject ethnic territorial political models: because to democratic autonomy advocates these models, especially the nation state, are the main sources of conflict, since they prioritize a particular ethnicity and territory. The nation state, as often highlighted in Öcalan and by democratic autonomy advocates, is regarded as the main source of inequality and conflict.

The objection to the nation state in democratic autonomy is relevant to some extent; in particular, the idea itself is the main source of conflict. Ever since the idea of the nation state was introduced, particularly because of its intention to provide and maintain the political loyalty of all its citizens, these citizens have become the basis of trouble for many ethnic, religious or national minorities (Waller and Linklater 2003). In most cases, nation states developed to reflect a single ethnicity (Duncan, Jancar-Webster and Switky 2009, 65), and mostly by denying the identity of ethnic minorities. Nation states' oppressive rule and their homogenizing approach to ethnic minorities resulted in the massive destruction of most societies, including conflict, assimilation, forced migration, demographic change and poverty. This, whether 'to create a nation-state or to protect it', brought about the question of the 'legitimacy' of the nation state (Canefe 2007, 4).

The development of supranational governance, globalization, national territorial fragmentation, political apathy and new forms of lifestyle are also certain factors that raise further questions about the idea of the nation state (King and Kendall 2004, 3–6), especially the protection of territorial boundaries and how the state can meet citizens' varied and globalized needs, which leads to the idea that the nation state is in decline. The development of supranational organizations, such as the creation of the EU, for instance, as also often highlighted by advocates of democratic autonomy, demonstrates the ways individuals cut across their national boundaries (McGray and O'Leary 1996, 336–37). Globalization has raised even more questions: for instance, increased globalization in the areas of society, politics, culture and the economy not only highlights the boundaries being exceeded, but also shows that the nation state does not properly fulfil its citizens' needs (Gülalp 2006b). Put simply, people's needs intersect the nation state's boundaries, and therefore the fact of the nation state becomes a fundamental topic of discussion (Castless et al. 1996, 359–61). All these are certain indicators supporting the claim that nation states are in crisis to some extent.

The outline provided supports the hypotheses of those who support democratic autonomy that it will not be of benefit to the Kurds to draw territories around them in order to create a Kurdish state, so long as the model of the nation state is the main source of conflict, is incapable of meeting all its citizens' needs and also is in decline. Starting with the first of these, it is because most nation states deny or give limited recognition to their minorities' rights which has generated conflict in many cases. However, as can be seen in countries such as Switzerland, Canada, the UK and France, most of the democratic nation states have successfully handled tensions with their minorities. Therefore, contrary to Öcalan's belief that the nation state's nature is a source of inequality and conflict (because of his conceptualization of the state as a capitalist, hegemonic, monopoly and homogeneous structure), the emergence of conflict between a state and its minorities is more about the former's character. As for the second, although it is because nation states may not be capable of meet all their citizens' needs in a globalized world, it is still not certain that the nation state is at the stage of total annihilation, or even is dramatically declining. It is true that the nation state is more debated than before, but the idea is still powerful in many societies (Lewellen 2011, 278–79). In other words, 'despite all its shortcomings' and crises, to some extent the fact of the nation state is not in decline: quite the contrary, it is on the rise in many nations (Drucker 1997, 159), and it is still the main and most powerful actor in international relations (Nester 2010, 30). Moreover, many of the stateless nations continue to look to create their own state: the Iraqi Kurds', Catalonia's and Scotland's independence referendums (despite having territorial autonomous status) far support the notion of how the nation state is resilient on the ground. This contradicts the argument of proponents of democratic autonomy that national boundaries and, as a model, nation states, are in sharp decline.

Analysis of the findings on the demand for the cultural rights model

The research findings illustrated that, according to the Kurds who look for cultural rights, attaining basic cultural rights means that Kurds are no longer restricted, but have gained respect for their cultural values and ethnic identity, which over the last century they have been without. Acknowledgement of their cultural rights is, in view of this, necessary for removing the Kurds' mistrust of the state, and for strengthening the integration and common affinities between the Turks and Kurds, further supporting the union of Turkey.

Granting minorities their cultural rights is a relatively well-supported idea, highlighting the host country's respect for minority identities. This consequently means that states which rule minorities recognize their differences and do not have any intention of implementing assimilation policies that seek to dissolve minorities' or different groups' identities within a majority group (Alba and Nee 1997; Gordon 1964; Stavenhagen 2013). Granting cultural rights in such a way could work in removing ethnic minorities' concerns and their mistrust of the host state; accordingly, it can further help integrate minorities with the majority group, consequently strengthening the state's unity (Efegil 2011; Kirişçi and Winrow 1997, 239). Integration, which has a 'positive perception of ethnic differences' (Brochmann 2003, 4), is therefore significant in developing good relations between minority and major groups because it aims to sustain further dialogue and interactions between both groups and support minority groups' attachments to the host country, while maintaining their own values (Maliepaard, Lubbers and Gijsberts 2010). Intermarriages (Kalmijn 1998), education (Gijsberts and Dagevos 2007, 807; Iadicola 1981, 193), demand for the highest positions and status, access to all resources (Cook 2003, 91) or minorities' predisposition to assimilate into the dominant group at the individual level in order to be able to use the same benefits provided to dominant groups (Kónya 2005) are some of the key dynamics which have an influence on the integration process. Thus, relating the contribution of integration in the attachment of minorities to the host society to the idea of unity means that granting minorities their cultural rights acquires more importance, since this re-establishes minorities' trust of the host state.

Specifically linking the context provided above to the Kurdish case, there is a very high level of integration between the Kurds and Turks, as underlined by the cultural rights defenders discussed in Chapter 5. Currently, a high number of Kurds have been integrated through various methods in Turkey (Akyol 2007), such as through intermarriages. Despite the lack of specific statistics, it is estimated that there are roughly 3.5 million mixed Turkish and Kurdish people in the populace as a result of intermarriages (KONDA 2011, 91). Migration, particularly Kurdish demographic dissemination across Turkey, is also one of the crucial dynamics which have contributed to their integration. Substantial numbers of the Kurdish population do not presently reside in their traditional homeland: most live in western parts of Turkey, as well as in several other countries (Hassanpour, Skutnabb-Kangas and Chyet 1996, 369; Sirkeci 2000, 156–61). Kurds' physical dispersion, as underlined by Gezik, has made it hugely difficult for them to practise and develop their ethno-cultural values, but has also driven them to adopt the majority group's identity to various degrees. This, as he underlines, has further intensified the social and political gap between various Kurdish groups, such as between the Alevi and Sunni Kurds (Gezik 2012, 102). Thus, the migration of almost half of the Kurds from their homeland, but particularly their 'dispersed settlement'[1] across Turkey, has contributed further to their interaction and integration with Turkey (Karlsson 2008, 161). In light of this, territorial models could potentially devastate the social, cultural and economic structures of both Kurds and Turks (Akyol 2007). These models, along with the democratic autonomy model, as Efegil also notes, underline the possibility of emerging political tensions and internal armed conflict in general in Turkey, but particularly among the Kurds (Efegil 2011, 36).

The discussion provided above supports the cultural rights defenders' argument that a considerable number of Kurds have integrated into the state, and that, by securing their cultural rights, their previous suspicions of the state because of its assimilation approach in the past will eventually be eradicated. The granting of cultural rights in a sense has the potential to restore relations between the Kurds and Turks, and further attach the Kurds to the state (Akyol 2007; Pamak 2005; Türkmen 2009). In agreement with this idea, Kurds can hold back from adhering to ethnic territorial political models, especially the formation of a Kurdish state, when they recognize the Turkish state as their own and are granted cultural rights in return (Çandar 2013, 60). Otherwise, being deprived of recognition and representation in a state, denied their own values and restricted from accessing all resources may socially and politically distance minorities from the state (Nimni 2009). This has recently become evident for many Kurds since the state's refusal of the Kurds basic cultural rights, especially denial of their ethnic identity, which has had a substantial impact on the transformation and determination of Kurdish identity, with ethnicity as the core layer (Hirschler (2001). This has contributed to the Kurds' nationalization process and the transformation of their political demands: from acknowledgement of their cultural rights to ethnic territorial claims.

Therefore, taking the Kurdish question within the context of transformation in Kurdish identity, especially its achievement of an ethno-national character, two counter arguments are raised against the Kurds which limit their approach to the Kurdish issue, granting the Kurds their cultural rights only. There is evidence illustrating the idea that granting minorities their cultural rights protects their values to some extent; however, granting cultural rights alone may not satisfy politicized ethnic minorities in the long run (Kirişçi and Winrow 1997, 39). This is a significant point in the Kurdish question too, because of the politicization and ethnicization of Kurdish identity with strong reference to territory. As addressed in Chapter 2, territory and ethnicity are two of the main constituents of Kurdish identity, and both are influential in shaping their political demands. Consequently, as illustrated, cultural rights can satisfy some Kurds; however, these rights may not be sufficient to satisfy the identity demands of a considerable number of Kurds, considering the Kurds' level of politicization level and their consideration of the Kurdish question through an ethno-national lens. This became far more evident considering the Kurds' current territorial political achievements in the Middle East, with the implications these achievements had for the Kurds in Turkey (Taşpınar and Tol 2014). This is because the Kurds in Turkey (comprising the largest part of all the Kurdish areas in the Middle East) would not be satisfied by being granted their cultural rights only, while the other Kurds, especially the Kurds in Iraq and in Syria, had achieved territorial control in their areas.

The second objection to the cultural rights model asks how cultural rights can be adequate enough to protect against or prevent assimilation of the minorities' identity at the highest level of integration between major and minority groups, if minorities are not granted collective rights that have a lower place in the cultural rights granting model. Therefore, since the idea of cultural rights mostly concerns giving these rights at the individual level, ethnic minorities' integration and assimilation are likely in the long run. Looking at this in terms of the Kurdish case, the political parties the AKP and the CHP, which include the Kurds, advocate granting their cultural rights, and also consider recognizing these rights at the individual level. Acknowledging Kurdish cultural rights at the individual level, however, as some segments of the Kurds also argue, cannot prevent assimilation of the Kurdish ethnic identity, considering the Kurds' physical dispersal and fragmented structure and the high level of interaction and integration between the Kurds and Turks. Because, although integration on the one hand contributes to developing relations between the Kurds and Turks and heightens the Kurds' attachment to the state, on the other hand, assimilation of Kurdish identity over time is very likely. More clearly, close links between the Kurds, but particularly migrated Kurds, and Turks have the potential to develop over time, leading to the Kurds' assimilation in Turkey, if Kurds lack the opportunities to practise their collective identity. Even today, a considerable amount of migrated Kurds' ethnic identity becomes blurred over time, and they begin to identify themselves through the major group's values (Rubin 2003, 318; Tan 2009, 539–40). In support of this, most of the children born from intermarriages cannot speak the Kurdish language, and associate themselves more with Turkish culture and identity (Tan 2009, 539). This is considered a clear indication of Kurdish assimilation into Turkish identity.

In light of this, granting Kurds their cultural rights could increase, to some extent, their trust in the state, thus contributing to the idea of unity between the Kurds and Turks. But, because of the Kurds' demographic distribution, and following the inevitable strong association and interaction with the Turks, granting them their cultural rights at the individual level might not prevent their identity from dissolving into the major group's identity. Integration would consequently lead to assimilation in the long-term. Granting the Kurds their cultural rights at the individual level therefore would in a way mean assimilation of the Kurdish identity in the long run (Çiçek 2011, 24). This is one of the main the reasons to reject the idea of only granting the Kurds their cultural rights: to prevent the melting of the Kurdish identity.

The empirical findings of the research showed that another rationale for refusing territorial political models and considering cultural rights as an alternative model is the priority given to religious identity (Sunni and Alevi identity) over ethnicity, the latter being the basis of territorial political models among the Kurds' demand for cultural rights. Although the relationship between ethnicity and religion is controversial, religion can have a considerable influence on ethnic identity, especially in the cases consisting of diverse religions or beliefs, and has experienced religious tension to various degrees (Enloe 1996). In such circumstances, despite the competition between ethnicity and religion, strong alliances can develop, with both identities overlapping one another. Religion 'could provide a basis for group formation and for the mobilization of these groups for social and political conflict and co-operation' (Rex 1993, 19). Religion can thus have an effect on 'ethnic and individual self-definition' (Safran and Liu 2012, 273) and could be one of the prominent forms of ethnic identity-making components (Hammond and Warner 1993, 59). Therefore, given the affiliations between religion and ethnic identity in this sense, as noted in Geertz, religion as a primordial factor can have an impact on establishing group consciousness among the group members and contribute to group formation (Geertz 1963, cited in Rex 1993, 18). This outline shows that religion could become 'a defining feature of nation' (Veer 1999, 19).

Religion, however, as can be seen in the Kurds who advocate for cultural rights, may not have the same influence on ethno-national identity in all cases, particularly in cases where religion is shared. In such cases, the role of religion is seen as a supra-identity bringing distinct ethnic groups together. In other words, as Christiano, Swatos JR. and Kivisto highlight, having a distinct ethnicity does not crosscut religious affiliations since religion advances as a common identity of all the different ethnic groups. More clearly, social and political cooperation among similar religious groups overlaps ethnic separations under the umbrella of religion (Christiano, Swatos JR and Kivisto 2008, 160). 'Religion in this pattern extends beyond ethnicity, reversing the previous pattern, and religious identification can be claimed without claiming the ethnic identification' (Hammond and Warner 1993, 59). Religion under these conditions may be instrumental in dissolving ethnic identity boundaries, with some saying that 'religious homogeneity may not be the *sine qua non* of ethnic boundary maintenance' (Enloe 1996, 202).

The discussion made above provides a valid context for understanding how religion is a decisive factor in determining the social and political relations of the Kurds who seek cultural rights. The majority of the Sunni Kurds who demand their cultural rights currently identify themselves through their religious identity – with their ethnicity carrying second importance. Religion as a result, as the majority of the Kurds and Turks share the same belief (a majority Sunni identity), further provides interaction and integration between the two communities. Granting of cultural rights here heightens religious fellowship, in other words, removes Kurds' concerns, and substantially reinforces ties with the Turks (Pamak 2005). To highlight the importance of religion between both communities, for instance, Türkmen states that the Turks and Kurds have to deal with the Kurdish issue through an *Ummah* understanding (Türkmen 2009). More clearly, religion is prioritized over ethnicity, which has happened with some Kurdish groups in the past. For instance, although the Kurds were presented with opportunities to create their own state, they opposed it in order to retain the religion-based unity between the Turkish and Kurdish communities; as some put it, they prioritized their religion instead of their fight for ethnic or national identity (Özer 2009, 376–81; Tan 2009, 536).

Similar to some Sunni Kurds, some Kurdish Alevis also prioritize their religious identity (Alevism) over ethnicity. There are two dynamics which influence these Kurdish Alevis' preference for their belief – Alevisim – over their ethnicity. The first is the previous hostility between the Sunni and Alevi Kurds. The in-group conflict and tension between Alevi and Sunni Kurds in the past remain alive in many Kurdish Alevis' collective memory. For instance, Sunni Kurds' indifferent attitudes to the Kurdish Alevis' Kocgiri revolt in 1920 and the Dersim insurrection in 1938 (Keiser 2003, 184), and the Alevis distance from the Sunni Kurds' rebellion against Sheik Said in 1925 (Leezenberg 2003, 201), clearly indicate the tensions and the political gap which emerged between the two groups. Because of these tensions and gap in social and political ideals, the Kurdish Alevis' trust in the Sunni Kurds was damaged, and remains so. In other words, their collective memory contributes to their growing suspicions of the Sunni Kurds. Consequently, the Alevis' suffering, their collective memory and their historical consciousness constitute 'the background of Alevi identity politics' (Ulusoy 2011, 416).

The second and most important condition which contributed to them prioritizing Alevism over ethnicity, as the data obtained from the research also indicated, is the belief that political Islam intensified in Turkey, and that the rapprochement between the Sunni Kurds and Turks through a Sunni identity is underway. Their fear of Sunni identity created a platform which pushed a substantial number of Kurdish Alevis to prioritize their religious identity, Alevism, over their ethno-national identity and define themselves as Alevis (Leezenberg 2003, 203–4). Some Kurdish Alevis, therefore, primarily list their religious identity, Alevism (Natali 2009, 174), and were determined to have all Alevis in Turkey. This is because their safety, and the protection of their Alevi identity, is dependent on the Alevis collectively gathering in Turkey. Alevism has thus become a primary and supra-identity approach that the Kurdish Alevis take to the Turkish descendant Alevis, rather than to the Sunni Kurds (Arakelova 1999, 399). In that sense, there has been an 'emergence of a wider Alevi identity transcending the various Alevi communities, the efforts to reconstruct Alevi belief and ritual at the supra-level, and discourse on Alevis as a type of ethnicity' (van Bruinessen 2006, 40). The point highlighted clearly shows how some Kurdish Alevis, most of whom gather around the CHP, supersede their ethnicity with Alevism. This contributes to the refusal of territorial models, because they take ethnicity as their base. Consequently, territorial political models mean the supremacy of the Sunni Kurdish identity, since the Sunni Kurds comprise the majority and politically are more powerful among the Kurds than these Kurdish Alevis.

Analysis of the findings on the demand for the federalism model

Federalism has been one of the most preferable political models for stateless groups, since the model provides the latter with a significant amount of power to manage their internal affairs. This became particularly evident in cases where the minority identity was in tension with the host state and experiencing a significant degree of assimilation. The empirical findings of the research revealed that the four underlying motivations leading to the development of federalism claims from the Kurds who advocate the model are the fear of being assimilated, particularly through religion; the demand for the construction of equality between two nations – the Kurds and Turks; the idea that federalism will resolve ethnic tension; and the right to power over their economic resources.

To begin with the first, religion has the power to interact with and affect society and politics at most levels. The level of influence played by religion and the subsequent changes it generates differ with each case. In Muslim countries, religion either constitutionally or through its deep roots in society is a decisive power in determining social and political affiliations. Aware of the power that religion has in society, federalism's supporters claim that a common religion with the Turks and the power of religious identity amongst the Kurds present an opportunity for the state to use religion in integrating and assimilating the Kurds with the state. Their concern is supported by the relevant literature to certain extent.

Religion, despite certain constitutional restrictions, has been a decisive power in determining social and political affiliations in Turkey. Turan explains the effect of religion on political culture in Turkey in four aspects: 'identification of political community', 'provision of political legitimacy', 'construction of political ideologies' and lastly 'shaping of political values and wording/styles' (Turan 1991). The four aspects provided in Turan have been significant in determining the state's policy of religion, especially in the instrumentalization of its 'nation-building project' Houston (2001, 85). The state has used religion as a social order in controlling society through various ways and via specific institutions, particularly the TDRA (Shakland (1999, 44). Especially through the TDRA, the state has aimed to create a secular, Kemalist and Hanafi Sunni Muslim Turkish national identity (Yılmaz 2013).

Along with supporting the claim that the state uses religion for the purpose of taking citizens under its control and creating a homogeneous national identity, as federalism exponents also state, Turkish Islamists also use religion in line with their Turkish Islamist synthesis creation project. Based on the empirical findings of the research, federalism advocates stated that there is a close interaction between religion and Turkish nationalism in Turkey. As is recently also the case with the AKP government, the Turkish state has spent considerable effort on harmonizing religion with nationalism, which has generated the development of a religious nationalist understanding among a majority of Turks (Parla 1993, 207–10). The creation of such hybridization has found an important place in conservative parties too. To achieve the idea of unity in the nation, members of most of the tariqas and religious communities (Pekoz 2009, 406–10) and conservative parties, especially the RP and recently the AKP, have for a long time entertained religion, and this has significantly contributed to the attachment of the Kurds to the majority identity (Houston 2001; Tuğul 2010). According to a research conducted by the Strategic Research Centre, more than 30 per cent of Kurds in the Kurdish region have a connection with tariqas (Kırmızı and Bölme 2009, 116). The majority of these Kurds prioritize their religious identity and do not put stress on their ethnicity. This supports the claims of the advocates of federalism that the state uses religion to suppress the Kurds' views on Kurdish national identity and the Kurdish struggle, and that it has been successful to some extent.

On the other hand, despite using religion in line with this aim, generalizations made from the results cannot be made. As highlighted above, using religion to create close ties between the Kurds and the state has been effective for some Kurds. However, not all Kurds have been swayed. Here it is appropriate to underline that for those Kurds who are aware of their ethno-national identity, such as those who have connections with the Zehra and Med-Zehra communities, religion does not have an influence on their integration with the state or on their assimilation. The reason for this is, as the discussion presented in Chapter 5 indicated, has been a close relationship with the development of ethnic awareness and subsequent national consciousness among these Kurds. Ethnicization of Kurdish identity (*Kurdishness*) in these Kurds has contributed to the development of Kurdish national identity despite the state's efforts to deter this. In that regard, the Kurds who demand ethnic territorial political models emphasize their national character and its close interaction with territory. In other words, for these Kurds, Kurdish national consciousness reached a point that could only be satisfied either by their gaining independence or by securing territorial autonomy over their homeland. It is because of this that for the Kurds who call for federalism, religion does not supersede their ethnic identity. For these Kurds, 'ethnicity and religion in different forms have played a significant role in the formation of Kurdish identity and in their overlap, they appear to have strengthened one another' (Atacan 2001, 138). Thus, as Sarigöl also underlines, the idea that religious connection and consciousness will decrease ethno-national identity does not work for all Kurds. To Sarıgöl, religious consciousness does not obstruct the increase of ethno-national identity and such tendencies among the Kurds (Sarıgöl 2010, 542–43). This is because to those Kurds who emphasize their ethno-national identity, the idea of Islamic fraternity and/or brotherhood (which is often stressed by the Turkish state and religious Turks) should provide 'active support for the protection of ethnic difference, not its cancellations in some meta-Islamic identity' (Houston 2001, 178). Thus, although religion has contributed to the integration and assimilation of some Kurds into Turkish identity, it has not influenced all of the Kurdish communities in a similar way, at least those Kurds who are aware of their ethno-national identity and who demand ethnic territorial political models.

The second idea which contributes to demands for federalism, as noted earlier, is the demand for equality between the Kurds and Turks so that they become two equal nations in every respect. As the research outcomes revealed, for federalism's exponents, the federalism model is the best possible way to obtain opportunities to protect the Kurdish identity from dissolving, and for constructing equality between the Kurds and Turks in all aspects. Looking at the issue in that sense, federalism, as largely argued previously, aims to protect minorities' identity through the self-rule principle of the model (Elazar 2006). Federalism in that sense could well function and be useful mostly for the minorities that concentrate on a specific region (Kirişçi and Winrow 1997, 219). Therefore, as the model essentially considers a specific region, it may not do so successfully in ethnically intermingled cases (Kirişçi and Winrow 1997, 228), and may preclude the dissolving of migrated individuals' identity. In this light, because of dramatic alterations in the Kurds' demographic structure, federalism could fail, compared with certain cases such as the Basques (Eryıldız 2012), to meet migrated Kurds' concerns regarding the disbanding of their identity to major groups, and may not be capable of constructing equality between the Kurds and Turks.

As noted above, the idea that federalism can accommodate ethnic tensions between the Kurds and Turks and put an end to the heightened discrimination against the Kurds was another related reason which influenced the demand for federalism. Although no ethnic conflict between the Kurds and Turks at the community level has been noted, with conflict intensifying between the PKK and state security forces, an ethnic tension has arisen between the Turks and Kurds, at least at the individual levels (Kurubaş 2008, 32), and associations between the two communities have begun to deteriorate. With tensions evolving, the social and emotional distance between the two groups has further increased and, consequently, discrimination against the Kurds has escalated (Gambetti 2007; MAZLUM-DER 2008: 77–123). Taking into account the local-level ethnic tensions already in place, particularly with the migrant Kurds in western regions of Turkey (Saraçoğlu 2010) such as in the Inegol and Ayvalik districts of the city of Bursa, there is a high risk that existing tensions might grow into ethnic tensions in Turkey (IHD Araştırma Raporu 2010). Herein, the Kurds' contested history with the state as a result of their ethnic identity being denied has created suitable ground for such a conflict to emerge (Kirişçi and Winrow 1997). Accordingly, increased ethnic disputes in Turkey in general, but, more importantly, the intense discrimination against the Kurds, have the potential to turn tensions between Kurds and Turks into an ethnic conflict at the community level, particularly in the western parts of Turkey, which has a high density of migrated Kurds (Bozarslan 2004b, 79).

Reflecting on the aforementioned issues, federalism is highly regarded as a conflict-resolution model. Federalism has a determinant role in resolving conflict, which mostly emerges because of the 'conjunction of shared grievances with a strong sense of group identity and common interests' (Gurr 1993, 124), 'economic inequalities' (Malesevic 2006, 34), 'security dilemmas' (Jesse and Williams 2011, 46), emphasis on territoriality (Coakley 2003) or territorial cleavages between minorities and the host state (Amoretti 2004). The main principles of federalism – power sharing based on shared rule and self-rule, or, in other words, diversity in unity (Elazar 2006), and certain of its other principles – are effective in accommodating tensions between central and local units (Moots 2009). For instance, the UK, with a long history of tensions between minorities and the state, or Belgium, with a running dispute between Walloons and Flemings, has decreased these tensions and either removed or at least delayed secessionist leanings among minorities following the transition to certain types of federalism (Marchildon 2009). This discussion supports federalism demanders' assertion that federalism can halt the tension between the Kurds and Turks to a substantial degree.

Despite the success of federalism in resolving ethnic tensions between minorities and the state in certain cases, it cannot be said this is the case for all. There are also examples where federalism has failed to resolve ethnic issues and remove separatist inclinations among minorities (Kumar 2007). For instance, despite minorities' considerable autonomy in the Soviet Union, Yugoslavia, Czechoslovakia and Slovakia, federal cases have collapsed, and currently, in some federal cases, tensions continue, such as in Quebec in Canada (Kirişçi and Winrow 1997, 227–28). Furthermore, despite having federal status, the Iraqi Kurds' ethnic tension with the Iraqi central government and winning the independence referendum on 25 September 2017 shows the limits of federalism for dealing with the ethnic tensions. Both the successes and failures of federalism in settling ethnic tensions show that, even though federalism is not always effective in resolving all such tensions, the certainty in most cases is that it has either dealt with these disputes or at least reduced them, for example as is the case in India, Belgium, Britain and Spain (Conversi 2000; Marchildon 2009).

The final cause behind the demand for federalism is the model that supporters demand in order to secure power over their economic affairs, because they claim the state has either consciously prevented the economic development of their regions or it cannot successfully manage their economic resources. Kurdish regions in the Middle East in general, but in particular in Turkey, have rich natural resources (see Izady 2004, 389–412). Despite this fact, the Kurdish regions in Turkey remain the poorest districts.[2] The reasons behind this are varied, but one to note is that the state did not take any serious steps to improve the economic structure of the region (McDowall 2004, 447). Consequently, the per capita income of the Kurds in the region is proportionally low. Secondly, the state would not successfully manage the economic resources of Kurdish areas, which further worsened as the battle between the PKK and state military forces intensified (Yildiz 2006, 220–28). Taking into account minorities' economic deprivations, based on their concerns, federalism through self-rule and shared rule grants federal governments the right to power over their regions in most aspects (Maiz 2000). And so, taking federalism in a fiscal sense, the central state mostly takes responsibility for managing 'macro economic stabilization and income distribution', while federal regions have the power to provide 'goods and services' for their own population (Majocchi 2009, 425). Such power enables federal regions to independently manage their economic sources and 'carry the weight of their own financial decisions' (Maiz 2000, 56), which could remove ethno-national minorities' concerns relating to their resources and their grievances relating to economic deprivation. Federalism, therefore, could serve to satisfy minorities in an economic sense. Federalism in that sense could remove Kurds' concerns and contribute to their economic development.

Analysis of the findings on the demand for the nation state model

The creation of a Kurdish state (despite the difficulty of the conditions) has become a lifelong dream for many of the Kurds in modern Turkey. This became especially evident in relation to recent political developments in Turkey and the Middle East. Based on the findings of the research, those demanding independence argued that because the Kurds were ruled politically by Turkey against their will, and because the state's approach to the Kurds has always rested on denial, physical oppression and forced migration, the creation of a united Kurdish state is the only way in which their safety considerations can be removed so that they can be satisfied. ISIS's current assaults on the Kurds in the Middle East in that sense have further raised their safety considerations, and have become a reason to justify their demand for independence, because statelessness means defencelessness in all respects for these Kurds. In this regard, as revealed in Chapter 7, becoming a particularly territorial nation with specifically demographic weight and being under the risk of assimilation and physical oppression are two key linked motives which have bred the demand for territorial self-determination among these Kurds.

The conditions that enable minorities to secede from the host country and gain their right of self-determination have met with considerable interest in the related literature. Mentioning this, Buchanan states that if minorities are beset with 'discriminatory redistribution' policies, they have the right to secede from the host country. Based on this, Buchanan points out that 'discriminatory redistribution' can occur in three different forms: if the state runs an economy policy in favour of a particular group but to the disadvantage of others; if a minority's identity, culture, lifestyle or other values are under risk of extinction; and finally if the state is unable to protect minorities from internal and external attacks (Buchanan 1991, 38–45). In addition, Herber C. Kelman notes that facing physical assault, assimilation, annihilation, violation or many other forms of discrimination creates the means for minority groups to claim secession and to be entitled the right to self-determination. To Kelman, the right of secession could be considered under these identified conditions, but also by considering those groups (mostly the host state) that will be affected by this decision (Kelman 1997). With reference to this, as Miller highlights, the state's intention to remove minorities' identity and impose its own creates a national state as an alternative avenue for minority groups (Miller 1995, 88). Mentioning minorities' rights to self-determination, Lenin underlines that forcing a nation to be under the control of a state – he names it as 'annexation' – creates legitimate ground for seeking secession and self-determination. Thus, to Lenin, such a nation has the right to save its nation and free its territories from the state, or from those that forcibly rule it (Lenin 1998, 139–40). Most of the leftist groups who support the Kurds' demand for independence here make reference to the Marxist-Leninist literature.

The context provided above, particularly Buchanan's second and third conditions, is to some extent applicable to the Kurdish case in Turkey regarding their political history of the twentieth century, in which 'the Kurds officially did not exist until 1991; they were officially labelled "mountain Turks"' (Eriksen 1992, 326). The Republic sought to wipe out the Kurds' political will and ethnic identity from history, and political authorities took any means to achieve this (Besikçi 1990, 1992). The Kurds therefore were faced with various kinds of oppression. Especially the conflict between the PKK and the state security forces resulted in the destruction of the Kurds' demographic and even sociological structure (Çalışlar 2013, 30–36). The state's denial policy and militaristic approach left the Kurds with almost no option, except for secession from Turkey. Miller's comparison between the Kurdish and Catalan cases regarding the demand for independence is rather illustrative on this point. Although Miller does not consider the creation of a Kurdish state as the only way for reaching a solution of the Kurdish issue, he reveals that the state's tough policies left the Kurds no other way except for independence when he compares the Kurdish case with the Catalan case, where the Catalans did not face such a policy in Spain (Miller 1998, 66). The AKP government's previously mentioned specifically harsh policy towards the Kurds (not only those in Turkey, but in other Kurdish parts as well particularly in Iraq and Syria), significantly contributed to the Kurds' idea to seek independence. The AKP's very harsh stance against the Iraqi Kurds following the independence referendum and its military operation in the YPG-controlled Afrin enclave, taking control of it in January–March 2018, are some developments that raised concerns that the Turkish state was attempting to annihilate the Kurds' ethno-territorial claims in the Middle East. All these were justifiable reasons for encouraging the Kurds' independence demands, especially in the light of the theoretical framework provided above. Establishing a Kurdish nation state, therefore, as Besikci argues, was the only choice to protect the Kurdish ethno-national identity (Beşikçi 2013).

Along with their fear of assimilation, particularly with regard to safety considerations, the Kurds being a territorial nation and their demographic weight were also regarded as two other linked contributory factors driving demand for secession and encouraging a sense of entitlement to the right of national self-determination among independence advocates. Ghanem deems 'territorial concentration and demographic weight', 'internal cohesion' and 'the quality of leadership' as three determining 'auxiliary variables' that influence minorities' political demands (Ghanem 2012, 363). Because of the fragmentation in the Kurds' social and political structure (i.e. their existence as internal minorities), Ghanem's last two variables, as revealed in Chapters 4 and 5, prevented the rising demand for ethnic territorial political models (such as federalism or independence).

These two variables therefore cannot be considered as contributory factors in raising the territorial political models among the Kurds. However, Ghanem's first variable, 'territorial concentration and demographic weight', as stated previously, had an influence on the intensification of the Kurds' political demands. It can be considered as a significant variable(s) to be recognized along with the right of national self-determination by independence supporters.

According to Ghanem, 'territorial concentration' and 'demographic weight' together have an effect on the degree of minorities' political demands. Ghanem argues that historical links with a particular territory and its population density generate intensification of political demands and provide a greater advantage for ethno-national minorities to pressurize the host state to grant them their collective political rights (Ghanem 2012, 367). Coakly also considers the ideas of territory and group size as two significant conditions that influence minorities' political claims. Making comparisons between groups' 'territorial concentration' and 'ethnic cohesiveness of territory', Coakly categorizes minorities under four models: 'the locally weak, territorially dispersed group'; 'the locally weak, territorially concentrated group'; 'the locally strong, territorially dispersed group'; and 'the locally strong, territorially concentrated group'. Based on this classification, territorial concentration, especially in circumstances where the ethnic group is 'locally strong', intensely influences ethnic minorities' political entitlements and has the potential to act as a dynamic factor in raising territorial political claims (Coakley 2003, 8–10). Ghanem's third model closely matches the Kurds' current condition because although they comprise the majority in their regions, a high number of Kurds are dispersed.

Ghanem's and Coakley's suggestions provide us with a fundamental foundation from which to make further discussions on the demand for independence made by the Kurds in relation to the notion of territory, since this, as argued in Chapter 7, is not only a piece of land for these Kurds but a nation and state as well. As also noted in Storey, populating a particular area of land for long periods creates a strong attachment to it. As Storey puts forward, this connection to the land is heightened by experiences which occur while on the land, especially if they are at the cost of the people (Storey 2002, 109–10) such as war, death and suffering. With reference to this, Galnoor suggests that the existence of close bonds between territory and people establishes a strong 'emotional attachment' to territory. Territory becomes part of an 'individual and collective identity and, therefore, also of the nation' (Galnoor 1995, 9), and this in turn justifies minorities' 'claim to exercise continuing political authority over that territory' (Miller 1998, 68).

The discussion made here provides a valid context for explaining the motivations of those Kurds who seek independence. The idea of territory functions in a similar way, and is regarded as a main condition for the Kurds to gain the right of national self-determination when considered along with their demographic weight and safety considerations. Becoming a territorial community and having demographic weight are, no doubt, significant objective contributory factors behind the increasing demand for territorial independence. However, first, it is not necessary to claim that every nation should have its own state, or that the idea of nation should be identified with a state (Kalaycı 2008, 91), and, second, becoming a territorial national community and demographic weight are not sufficient conditions for causing an ethno-national group to demand its full independence. There are two more conditions that must be met in order to further argue a minority group's right of self-determination. Miller (1998, 69) explains them: that an ethnic group's request for secession can be recognized if it is capable of acting as a nation, and that it is capable of governing itself (practising power) on the territory where it is located. The point mentioned by Miller raises the question whether the Kurds are so capable, primarily because Chapter 3 clearly revealed that the Kurds' social structure does not only consist of the idea of nation, and that they are fragmented by their language and religion. More clearly, their social and political structure is also distinctly fragmented (some even refuse to be identified with their Kurdish ethnic identity, such as some Zaza). Therefore, can they act as a nation at all? And, because of their politically fragmented structure, how will they be able to rule themselves? Tensions between some Kurdish groups, for example between the Alevi and Sunni sects, or as armed groups between the PKK and Hezbollah and the PKK and the Village Guards, further make this question relevant. These stipulations make the Kurds' demand that they are entitled to the right of national self-determination rather problematic.

Overall, the discussion provided suggests that some factors, for instance having a high level of security consideration, taking into account the state's heavy-handed degree of oppression in the past and its current attacks on the Kurds in the Middle East, along with the Kurds' territorial demographic concentration to some extent, justify these Kurds' independence demands. However, the creation of a Kurdish state is still difficult because of the Kurds' fragmented social and political structure and, most importantly, because of the possible negative influences on Turkey and the Middle East as a potential consequence of their secession.

Conclusion

This research has studied the rationale underlying the variations among the Kurds' current political demands, which have been categorized into non-ethnic territorial (democratic autonomy), non-ethnic non-territorial (cultural rights) and ethnic territorial (federalism and an independent state), following an inductive methodology. In exploring the rationale motivating the variations in the Kurds' present political demands, the research study involved in-depth interviews with the chosen groups' representatives and activists. The main fieldwork was carried out between the years 2012 and 2014 in Turkey, Iraq and the UK, but, paralleling later developments in Turkey and the Middle East, especially in Syria and Iraq, and their potential influence on Kurds' political claims, I have updated the research, including a few more interviews in 2015–16.

Findings for the democratic autonomy model

The research showed that as an armed and political movement the PKK has a considerable influence on the political demands of the Kurds. The PKK's impact on the Kurds is driven by two key motives: the state's ongoing Kurdish identity denial policy in different forms and increasing political and military pressure on the Kurds, and the PKK's strong emphasis on the Kurds' ethno-national identity by instrumentalizing nationalism to a certain extent. The state's denial and oppression of the Kurds in addition to the latter pushed many Kurds to approach the PKK and make their ethno-national identity a prime focus. With the intensification of the conflict between the PKK and state security forces, the Kurds face severe persecution from the state, and as a result have become more mindful of their ethno-national identity. In other words, the conflict between the PKK and state security forces, but particularly as a consequence of the state's tough policies, has resulted in the politicization of Kurdish identity, particularly the transformation of religious and tribal ties into ethnic and national affinities to a considerable extent. In this regard, since its foundation the main aim of the PKK has been to create a sense of *Kurdishness* among the Kurds and make them really think about the questions *who are the Kurds?* and *how can they achieve political status?* To achieve this purpose, the PKK adopted intense ideological and practical methods. The group's relationship with ideology has been quite flexible and controversial; nevertheless, its ideology can be defined within a democratic socialist understanding, and with nationalism in a broad sense. Especially following Abdullah Öcalan's intense intellectual effort, the PKK has further adopted the idea of radical democracy in its approach to the Kurdish issue. Politicization of Kurdish identity and the transformation in the PKK's ideology have influenced the latter's approach to the Kurdish issue.

Related to this background, the research findings demonstrated that there is great emphasis on the term 'nation' among those Kurds who call for democratic autonomy, which they refer to as a democratic nation. Democratic nation refers to a non-ethnic, pluralist understanding of nation. Democratic autonomy puts democratic nation at the centre of the solution process for the Kurdish issue, and it proposes acknowledgement of the Kurds' national status (constitutional recognition of the Kurdish identity). The Kurds in support of the BDP/HDP and DBP and who consider the PKK persist with their claims for political status in order to remove the legal and political grounds for ethnic denial and acknowledgement of the Kurds as a nation. Therefore, one of the key agendas of the democratic autonomy model is the demand for a national status, which in fact is one of the instrumental factors for the demand of the model itself. This is also one of the main reasons behind the refusal of the cultural rights only model, because in this situation the Kurds' national rights are still overlooked. Democratic autonomy considers the Kurds to be a separate nation, and so they request that their political rights are acknowledged as collective rights at the national level, unlike cultural rights, which are mostly granted at the individual level.

On another note, it was also revealed that the Kurds demanding democratic autonomy, federalism and the nation state agree that their nation and political status need to be recognized at a collective level. However, democratic autonomy's understanding of nation is formulated in terms of a democratic nation, which does not draw sharp boundaries between nations or put emphasis on ethnicity, whereas the Kurds who demand federalism and the nation state underline the importance of ethnicity and territory in their understanding of nation and the approach to the Kurdish issue. Considering the issue in that regard, as noted by the Kurds who struggle for democratic autonomy, structuring territories along ethnic lines is of no benefit to the Kurds and cannot be applied. This is mainly because of the dramatic shift in the Kurds' demographic structure. Although Kurds have lived in distinct territorial areas for years, economic factors and conflict between the PKK and the state security forces have caused a massive change in their demographic structure. Therefore, to democratic autonomy supporters, extensive changes to the demographic structure of the Kurds complicate the establishment of ethnic territorial political models, because nearly half of the Kurds are spread all across Turkey.

The changes in demographics in this regard can impede ethnic territorial solutions for the identity concerns of migrated Kurds because ethnic territorial political models focus on a particular region, namely Kurdistan. This is a fundamental reason why HDP/BDP, DBP and PKK supporters suggest establishing a democratic autonomy model as an alternative, because the models can be implemented throughout the country by re-structuring Turkey into 20–25 regions. This means non-ethnic territorial decentralization of Turkey. With this structure in place, all diverse ethnic and religious groups dependent on their population quantity will either directly rule those territories or be represented in some form. In the case of the Kurdish region, since the Kurds are the majority group, they will have authority over the region. However, in western parts of Turkey they will be represented according to their population, because Kurds are the minority group in that case. Democratic autonomy's emphasis on radical democracy and participant citizenship and the organization of society in the form of democratic confederalism makes the model more applicable to a decentralized Turkey. Thus, in support of this, the empirical findings of the research showed that the democratic autonomy supporters use the case of the Kurds in Turkey to illustrate why this model is the most appropriate political model for protecting Kurdish national identity, regardless of their geographical location. This also revealed one of the reasons why supporters of democratic autonomy reject ethnic territorial political models.

This study also suggested that another reason why supporters of the BDP/HDP, DBP and PKK reject ethnic territorial political models for democratic autonomy relates to the Kurds' fragmented social structure (the existence of internal minorities). It was revealed that the majority of Alevis and Zazas, who define themselves through their Kurdish ethno-national identity, demand democratic autonomy because they believe this model offers them the capacity to create their own autonomous regions, which will provide rights and the ability to control their own internal affairs. It can be argued that this is their response to the years of oppression they faced from the state, and, to some extent, other major identities, for example, the Sunni Alevis oppressed by the Sunni Kurds to some extent. Herein lies their main reason for rejecting ethnic territorial models and seeking democratic autonomy instead. Ethnic territorial political models, to exponents of democratic autonomy, are predisposed to shaping diverse identities in line with the identities of politically and culturally dominant groups. Consequently, as the research outcome illustrated, many Kurdish internal minorities fear that their identity will be in danger with no opportunity offered to them to protect themselves if ethnic territorial political models are applied. The creation of a Kurdish nation state and ethnic federalism in this regard would, they believe, be a disaster for Kurdish internal minorities and the Kurds living outside of the Kurdish region, because this model prioritizes a specific region in an ethnic sense and so permits the dissolving of internal minorities' identities and the formation of a homogeneous Kurdish identity. Consequently, contrary to ethnic territorial models, democratic autonomy is identified as a decentralist structure where the state offers them circumstances to form their own autonomous regions in terms of their collective identities and geographical density. In other respects, democratic autonomy is deemed as a model able to protect Kurds' internal diversity within Kurdish unity.

Along with the above-explained objective conditions, the research's findings also specified that to the democratic autonomy proponents their ideological and moral standings also do not coincide with the ethnic territorial political models, which contribute to their rejection of these models. Abdullah Öcalan's opinions on this point are quite influential on these Kurds. Despite the close correlation between establishing a nation and the demand for a nation state or federalism, democratic autonomy rejects the idea of a Kurdish nation state. The model's supporters first of all claim that the nation state functions in the interests of an elite group only, and will not hesitate in inflicting oppressive measures on the majority of the society when the interests of both groups are at the forefront. Second, they put emphasis on the nation state's conflicted nature, explaining that it will contradict with the essence of democracy and therefore cause tensions within and between peoples. To these Kurds, since it was first established the nation state has plainly shown how it causes competition and hostility among peoples, especially in the case of the Middle East. In that regard, they deem the creation of a Kurdish nation state as source of conflict between both the Kurds and other Middle Eastern communities, because of the nation state's hegemonic nature and its aim to create a homogeneous nation and to assimilate and design other identities in line with this aim. Establishing ethnic territorial boundaries therefore has the potential to impact negatively on the relations among Kurds and between Kurds and other groups. Furthermore, questions on the state's national territories as a result of social, cultural and political developments in the modern world were also raised, and created further doubt for the model's supporters concerning territorial models, particularly a nation state for the Kurds. They questioned why the Kurds should isolate themselves to a small part of the region while the world discussed removing territories. In the light of the research findings, the aforementioned consequences further encouraged democratic autonomy's adherents to question the ideology of the nation state as well as federalism, because they highlighted that federalism also creates boundaries between people and is a state-oriented model.

On the other hand, despite its applicability to Turkey and its potential for sorting out the Kurdish question, democratic autonomy's non-ethnic definition of nation and its de facto declaration of nation (by the PKK-affiliated armed forces) in some Kurdish areas raise severe questions regarding the model's understanding of democracy. Despite the challenge of the majority of Kurds, the PKK-affiliated youth groups' declaration of democratic autonomy and the digging of ditches for the protection of these areas show that democratic autonomy may have little consideration for people's consent. This became of great importance, and raises questions regarding democratic autonomy's sincerity, since the model rejects the nation state because of its ignorance of the majority's will and because of its conflictual character. Therefore, although democratic autonomy can be regarded as an ideal model in theory, its practice exposes its true nature and ambiguities.

Findings for the cultural rights only model

The PKK's struggle, as previously noted, has been influential in determining the Kurds' political claims, especially in the Kurds' nationalization process, which is clearly seen in the case of democratic autonomy. Yet, although the PKK effectively created a national consciousness among some Kurds, it also widened the socio-cultural and political diversity among Kurds. This was predominantly due to the PKK's past conflict with some Kurdish feudal classes, its Marxist-Leninist ideology and its distance from religion. Its declared motives were further manipulated by the state, and thus have encouraged a number of the Kurds to distance themselves from Kurdish ethno-national identity. In contrast, these groups have further strengthened their ties with Turks. It is substantially easy for some Kurds to become part of Turkish identity because almost half of the Kurds had already migrated to western parts of Turkey and there has been considerable growth in social, cultural and economic interactions between them and Turks. Some Kurds even reluctantly integrated with and assimilated into Turkish national identity to varying degrees. The empirical outcomes of the research introduced the information that through integration and assimilation many Kurds have become part of the Turkish national identity and have become alienated from their ethno-national identity, especially from the idea of territory. Long-term integration, particularly when turning into assimilation, initiates the disintegration of Kurdish ethnic identity, which is one of the main reasons for the refusal of the assertion of ethnicity and territory. Despite this, most of the Kurds who seek cultural rights have been negatively influenced by the state's policy on the Kurdish issue and want to trust the state in all senses. Therefore, the Kurds who advocate for cultural rights only claim that if the Kurds are granted their cultural rights their mistrust towards the state will be removed and interaction and integration between the two communities will develop.

Building on this issue, religion has greatly influenced the development of close interaction and integration between Kurds and Turks, as well as the rejection of ethnic territorial political models by those Kurds advocating cultural rights. The historical alliance between the Kurds and Turks is one of the main dynamics that created closer relations between Sunni Turks and Sunni Kurds, and made religion their common identity in modern Turkey. By raising the conflict between the PKK and state security forces, these relations between some Sunni Kurds and Sunni Turks further intensified. As conflict emerged, some religious Kurds sided with the PKK and have emphasized their ethno-national identity, and currently demanded either ethnic territorial political models or their democratic autonomy. However, a considerable number have approached the state and the religious Turks. To these Kurds, the construction of ethnic territorial political models and democratic autonomy will result in further persecution, and their interaction and religious affinities with the Turks will be damaged. Thus, as the study's empirical outcomes highlighted, religion (essentially Sunni *madhhab*) in that sense becomes a significant measure of identity for the Kurds who gather around the political party the AKP and its affiliated groups. For the substantial number of Kurds who continue to identify themselves through their religion, ethnicity is either of secondary importance or has no relevance. In other words, religion has superseded those Kurds' ethno-national identity, and they consider ethnic territorial models destructive for the union of Sunni Kurds and Turks.

Therefore, it was discovered that most of the Kurds who call for cultural rights and gather around the AKP prioritize their religious identity over their ethnicity. In this light, rather than ethnic territorial models and democratic autonomy, they call for their cultural rights to be granted because they believe this will contribute to the strengthening of religious affinities between the two communities, and that this will contribute to the unity of Turkey.

Moreover, the research study also found that although religion (primarily Sunni *madhhab*) plays a crucial role in building close ties between Sunni Kurds and Turks, it also widens the social, cultural and political gaps between the Sunni and Alevi Kurds. In other words, it causes disparities within the Kurds. Because of past tensions between Sunnis and Alevis, Kurdish Alevis' collective memory distances them from Sunni Kurds but allows them to form associations with Turkish Alevis. The Sunni faith created a foundation for cooperation between Sunni Kurds and Turks, while Alevism created a common ground and social cohesion between the Turkish and the majority of the Kurdish Alevis who gather around the political party the CHP.

On another note, the increase in political Islam in Turkey in general, and among the Kurds in particular, such as Hezbollah, has escalated Kurdish Alevis' fears of Sunnis. Consequently, Alevism became their favoured identity. The unity between Alevis, as the study's outcome showed, is now a matter of life and death for most Kurdish Alevis. Consequently, Alevis who mostly demand democratic autonomy and territorial political models, consider the state as the main factor responsible for their ethnic and religious suffering. In addition, they believe Alevis will only be liberated if their ethnic identity is free. On the other hand, the Kurdish Alevis who demand the cultural rights only model prioritize their faith over their ethnicity because, based on the research outcomes, they believe the liberation of the Alevis depends on the idea of union of all Alevis in Turkey. Therefore, they refuse ethnic territorial political models and democratic autonomy because they foresee that these models will damage the common ties between Alevis of Kurdish and Turkish descent. As a result, and similar to the Sunni Kurds who support the AKP, they replace their ethno-national identity with their faith, Alevism, which makes the unity of all Alevis most prominent and their ethnic and territorial political models insignificant. To put it simply: because territorial political models and democratic autonomy in this case will be constructed and ruled by a Sunni majoritarian identity, these Alevis believe there will be a degree of pressure on them if the models are actually implemented.

Granting Kurds cultural rights will doubtlessly be a significant step in handling the Kurdish question. Dealing with the Kurdish issue within the context of cultural rights may also become sufficient for the Kurds who have migrated, or for the Kurds who have been integrated into Turkish society for a long time. However, it is clear that cultural rights will not satisfy the majority of the Kurds, considering the ethno-national character of the Kurdish issue and Kurds' politicization and organizational level and their growing political consciousness. Kurds' ethno-territorial achievements in Iraq and Syria make it extremely difficult to solve the Kurdish issue merely through granting their basic cultural rights.

Findings for the federalism model

It was previously highlighted that religion, principally the Sunni sect of Islam, played a crucial role in bringing a majority of the Kurdish and Turkish communities together and forging strong alliances. However, as also emphasized by federalism's proponents, particularly Kurdish Islamists, religion has been used in particular as an instrument for assimilating Kurdish identity into Turkish identity by the state and by the majority of the Turkish Islamist groups. Turkish Islamists became impartial to the Kurdish issue or, if they still maintained some interest, cooperated and acted in line with the state's approach to the Kurdish issue. The state, as also underlined by federalism's adherents, attempted to develop and spread the Turkish Islamic Synthesis, which they suggested in the long run would integrate and assimilate the majority of the Kurds within the Turkish national identity. Accordingly, the research consequences showed that to federalism's exponents, especially Kurdish Islamists, the repercussions of using religion as a tool to disseminate Turkish national identity, the development of the Turkish Islamic Synthesis and the assimilation of Kurdish identity, prompted them to question the role of religion as a unifying parameter between the two communities. In reaction to this, the research's outcomes revealed that the Kurds seeking federalism have begun to challenge the role of religion in their relationship with the Turks. Moreover, the research outcomes discovered that while religion previously created the opportunity for these Kurds to remain in Turkey without an ethnic territorial political structure in place, in current conditions, particularly with the development of a national consciousness among Kurdish Islamists, religion no longer has the same influence or power to keep them in Turkey without an ethnic territorial status. Kurds who demand federalism believe that this is because the state would no longer be able to use religion as an influencing power in the assimilation of the Kurds, and also because they will have the power to protect their own national identity.

The Kurds believe that federalism has the power to either eliminate or reduce ethnic conflict, and this is another motive for the demand for federalism. The state's denial of Kurdish identity and its repressive policies resulted in tensions in Turkey, although this did not reach the community level. However, following the intense armed conflict between the PKK and the state military forces, coupled with the mounting discrimination against the Kurdish identity, tensions gained an ethnic flavour with the potential to evolve into a widespread ethnic conflict. The increase in Kurds' ethno-national awareness, and the state's reaction to this further escalated the tensions in Turkey. Related to this, the fieldwork found that federalism's advocates believe that the only way to prevent further conflict is to satisfy the Kurds' national sentiments and convince the Turks that this will intensify Turkey's unity. To these Kurds, federalism's 'diversity in unity' principle can resolve existing ethnic tensions and prevent the possibility of a full-blown ethnic conflict, whereas other political models contribute to conflict.

The research conducted discovered that the Kurds' demand for power over their economic resources is another significant reason for their demand for federalism. Federalism exponents strongly believe the state either failed to meet Kurds' economic needs or consciously prevented their economic development in order to impede their national consciousness, which in turn has shown to have had a positive impact on economic development. Thus, these Kurds claim that to prevent the state from using Kurds' economic resources, and to raise Kurds' economic development, Kurds need power over their own economic resources, which, they believe, can be obtained only through establishing the federalism model through union with Turkey.

Along with the above-explained objective conditions, the research's findings also specified that there are many motives for federalism's supporters refusing other political models. To begin with, the model's supporters believe that because of the Kurds' social and demographic distribution, establishing a Kurdish state can lead to conflict, when considered along with the regional states' negative approach to the Kurds' independence demand. Secondly, although federalism proponents place emphasis on the territorial character of the Kurdish nation, they, in particular Kurdish Islamists, object to a Kurdish nation state because they believe it could damage their understanding of Ummah and the unity between nations. This is also the point that is challenged by the non-religious federalism supporters, since the latter put less importance on the idea of Ummah. This study found that both territory and nation are determinant dynamics in the emergence of the demand for federalism. The concept of nation is also stressed by the Kurds who demand democratic autonomy. However, as discussed earlier, they identify their understanding of nation as a democratic nation which doesn't take ethnicity into account and rejects drawing territorial boundaries between nations. The Kurds who demand federalism instead harshly challenge democratic autonomy because, to their mind, the model's fundamental ideology is ambiguous and unrealistic as a political model. Federalism supporters also pointed out that democratic autonomy's proposition to re-structure Turkey into 20–25 regions will in fact fragment Kurdish national identity further. They also explain that democratic autonomy can influence the integration and assimilation of the Kurds because it does not consider the Kurds' territorial concentration. It is also important to note that while democratic autonomy ideologically rejects structuring territories between nations, the Kurdish region and Kurdish nation are fundamental in the philosophy of federalism. Based on this, federalism's defenders don't see democratic autonomy as a national political model, and even believe this model has a destructive impact on the Kurds' national identity. Furthermore, and similarly to supporters of democratic autonomy, federalism's proponents challenge the cultural rights only model. They argue that Kurds are a nation; therefore, their political status has to be acknowledged through their collective rights; otherwise Kurds will not be satisfied, which will lead to further unrest.

Federalism has been one of the most applied models for satisfying stateless minorities. Most Western countries have dealt with their ethnic and religious minorities' identical demands through certain types of federalism. In the Kurdish question, too, federalism is an applicable model in terms of addressing Kurds' ethno-national satisfaction within the context of self-rule. However, federalism fails to provide a satisfactory solution to the migrated Kurds' identical concerns and internal Kurdish minorities' status demands.

Findings relating to the nation state model

Findings from the research study highlighted the Kurds' mistrust towards the Turkish state, and regional power is one of the main conditions for the formation of a Kurdish state. To the independence adherents, Turkey is still looking for ways to assimilate the Kurdish ethno-national identity and destroy the Kurds' social and political structure. The state's previous policies of denial and persecution of the Kurds, plus some of the violent attacks which occurred in recent times, are the basis for their claims that the state was either directly involved in or purposely did not protect the Kurds from these attacks. The

AKP government's recent pressure on the Kurds and Kurdish identity greatly contributes to the Kurds' concerns regarding the state's Kurdish policy and their own safety considerations.

The Kurds' safety considerations further intensified with the assaults on the Kurds in the Kurdistan region in Iraq and the Kurdish region in Syria by ISIS and by regional countries. ISIS's heinous attacks on the Kurds (in Iraq, Syria and Turkey), Turkey's seizing of the Afrin canton in the Kurdish region in Syria and finally Turkey-Iraq and Iran's cooperation to prevent the KRG's independence referendum and the seizing of Kirkuk from the KRG forces are some of the factors that have provoked anxieties in Kurds about their safety. Therefore, independence supporters believe that without their own state the Kurds will be defenceless. In this regard, they believe, the creation of a Kurdish state in Turkey and in other regions, plus their merging together, is essential in order to lay to rest the Kurds' safety considerations and provide them with security and protection of their ethno-national identity.

The two linked variables – that they are a territorial nation and have demographic weight – when regarded alongside their security concerns, are also significant in relation to the Kurds' demands for territorial national self-determination. The idea of territory here plays a fundamental part in the call for independence when considered in the light of its meaning to the Kurds' national movements in the past. Kurdish rebellions in the first two decades of the Turkish republic and the PKK's first decade of political activity noticeably supported the Kurds' battle for independence. The Kurds' territorial national struggle for independence, therefore, has historical continuity, which has contributed to the construction of a territorial Kurdish national consciousness. The historical background of the study showed that in this process of struggle, the liberation of territory overrides all other stages. The research findings indicated that territory, especially when considering the Kurds' demographic weight, is not only a piece of land for these Kurds. Territory comprises collective memory. In other words, territory here holds an essential meaning for these Kurds, and consequently strongly influences their demand for territorial independence: liberation of nation is equivalent to liberation of territory. Taking the issue in that context, to independence demanders, Kurds' territorial consciousness and demographic weight highlight the need for a Kurdish nation state.

The research also explored the significance of territory for Kurds demanding federalism. However, compared with the Kurds who demand the right to territorial national self-determination, federalists still want to live with Turks, but demand power over their region. The Kurds who demand federalism prioritize equality of nations over separation of nations in unity. As a result, Kurdish federalists do not focus on finding a solution for the Kurdish issue through formation of a Kurdish state, whereas independence supporters claim that federalism will not provide the Kurds with sufficient security, since they will still be dependent on the state in most aspects.

The research also found that democratic autonomy exponents place emphasis on the idea of nation (particularly democratic nation), whereas independence supporters see this model as insufficient to satisfy the Kurds' national demands and provide them with safety. To independence supporters, because democratic autonomy does not ground itself on an ethnic territorial sense it cannot provide the Kurds security nor prevent the dissolution of the Kurdish identity. Independence adherents also reject the cultural rights only model because they underline that the Kurdish issue requires the liberation of their nation and territory, not the liberation of basic cultural rights or individuals. Therefore, to independence advocators, granting cultural rights alone will result in the denial of the Kurds' national identity and the disintegration of the Kurdish identity. In addition to these outcomes, the Kurds will be defenceless, and therefore at risk of any form of attack.

Turkey's severe stance against the KRG's independence referendum and seizure of Afrin

Although the scope of the Kurds' political discourses is wide, it is still a fact that Turkey's recent political stance towards the Kurds in the Middle East has the potential to weaken the Kurds' physical and emotional ties with Turkish society and coalesce them around a common political agenda and set of demands. The AKP's recent Kurdish policies have shown that the party has returned to the Republic's founding ideology, and it is determined to refuse to grant the Kurds their political status. The AKP's principal cooperation with the ultra-secular nationalist Doğu Perinçek's Vatan Party and its alliance with the ultra-nationalist MHP, and the intensifying pressure on the Kurds and Kurdish identity, both show that the party has closed its doors to addressing the Kurdish question through dialogue and talks. The party's harsh and humiliating stance against the KRG's independence referendum and its recent seizure of Afrin from the Kurdish forces (YPG) have further illustrated that they will not tolerate the Kurds' status achievements.

Turkey's mentioned stances have the potential to play a considerable role in the majority of the Kurds' mistrust of the state and in bringing them together around a common political agenda and model. Especially the Turkish state's taking of Afrin has brought various Kurds from diverse backgrounds together. This is because most of the Kurds consider Turkey's stance to be against the Kurds, not YPG forces.

The AKP's recent political stance, on the other hand, also has the potential to raise concerns within its Kurdish-origin followers to some extent. The AKP's flirtation with nationalism and even its attempts to nationalize society are likely to generate concerns within the party's Kurdish followers. These Kurds first of all are not happy with the AKP's harsh stance against the KRG's independence referendum, which has the potential to lead these Kurds to think that the AKP is against the Kurds. It is still difficult to measure the impact of the Afrin operation on the party's Kurdish supporters, but it would not be hard to say that most of the party's Kurdish voters are not happy with this as well, especially considering the Syrian Kurds' successful resistance against ISIS and like-minded groups. Taking the impact of Turkey's recent policies on its Kurdish followers in this sense, it still might be too early to say whether these Kurds will insist on the need for a common political agenda and ethnic territorial model within the Kurds. But it would not be wrong to say that the AKP's recent policies may potentially lead its Kurdish-origin supporters to be aware of their Kurdish ethnic identity, especially within the new generations.

Appendix 1

Table 2.1 List of Interviewees

	DEMAND	NAME	ORGANIZATION	POSITION	PLACE	DATE
1		Kudret GÜLÜN	BDP	Esenyurt Co-Chair	İstanbul	25.12.2012
2		Arif EROL	BDP	Esenyurt Co-Chair	İstanbul	25.12.2012
3		Edibe ŞAHİN	BDP	Tunceli Mayor	Tunceli	13.05.2013
4		Halis YURTSEVEN	BDP	Bingöl Provincial President	Bingöl	10.05.2013
5	DEMOCRATIC AUTONOMY	Emine AYNA	BDP	Diyarbakır MP	Diyarbakır	03.05.2013
6		Fırat ANLI	BDP	Diyarbakır Mayor	Diyarbakır	08.05.2013
7		Sako	BDP and DÖKH	Activist	İstanbul	28.04.2012
8		Zuhal	BDP	Academician	İstanbul	14.11.2012
9		Kadir KONUR	DBP	Cizre Co-Mayor		21.12.2015
10		Altan TAN	BDP	Diyarbakır MP	London	18.10.2013
11		Selim KURBANOĞLU	BDP	Yenişehir Mayor	Diyarbakır	07.05.2013
12		Rahime KANILGA	HDP	Çanakkale Provincial Executive	Çanakkale	15.11.2014
13		Mehmet Emin ADIYAMAN	HDP	Iğdır MP	Phone Interview	20.12.2015
14		Sdem GEVERİ (ÖZCANER)	HDP	Van MP	Phone Interview	23.12.2015
15		Hasan YILDIZ	HDP	Lawyer and Politician	İstanbul	16.12.2012

DEMAND	NAME	ORGANIZATION	POSITION	PLACE	DATE
16	Mustafa ÜNLÜ	HDP	Former Activist	Gaziantep	15.11.2014
17	Ahmet ŞEKER	HDP	Former Youth's Branch President	London	10.09.2014
18	İlhan ILBAY	EMEP	Central Executive Committee Member	Tunceli	12.05.2013
19	Mustafa TAŞKALE	EMEP	Tunceli Provincial President	Tunceli	12.05.2013
20	Baran	PKK/KCK	Politician	Makhmur /Iraq	25.11.2009
21	Sami TAN	İstanbul Kurdish Institute	President	İstanbul	27.04.2013
22	Seydi FIRAT	Peace Assembly	Spokesman	Diyarbakır	10.05.2013
23	Cafer SOLGUN	Yüzleşme Association	President	İstanbul	16.05.2013
24	Dorşin	Kurdish Diaspora	Women Activist	London	24.09.2014
25	Zübeyde TEKER	Wise People Com	East Anatolia Representative	Bingöl	11.05.2013
26	Hıdır ÇELİK	ZAZA-DER	President	İstanbul	19.12.2012
27	Jiyan	Roj Women Activist	Activist	London	23.09.2014
28	Şahan	Zehra Community		Diyarbakır	08.05.2013
29	Tahir	Zehra Community		İstanbul	24/25.07.2014
30	Halis	Zehra community		İstanbul	24.07.2014

DEMAND		NAME	ORGANIZATION	POSITION	PLACE	DATE
31	FEDERALIZM	Sıddık DURSUN-SEYHANZADE	Med-Zehra Community	Founder and Leader of the Community	İstanbul	27.04.2013
32		Nevzat EMİNOĞLU	Zehra Community		İstanbul	10.07.2012
33		Recep	Zehra Community		İstanbul	23/24.04.2013
34		Süleyman ÇEVİK	Nûbihar and Zehra Community	Follower	İstanbul	15.07.2012
35		Rauf ÇİÇEK	Nubihar Association	President	Diyarbakır	06.05.2013
36		Vedat TURGUT	Hüda-Par	Diyarbakır Provincial President	Diyarbakır	08.05.2013
37		Aydın GÖK	Hüda-Par	Batman Provincial President	Batman	10.05.2013
38		Necat ÖZDEMİR	Hüda-Par	General Vice President	Diyarbakır	07.05.2013
39		Orhan AÇIKBAŞ	Hüda-Par	Bingöl Provincial Executive	Bingöl	11.05.2013
40		Lokman YALÇIN	Hüda-Par	Şanlı Urfa Provincial Chairman	Phone Interview	
41		Hamdullah TASALI	Hüda-Par	Bingöl Provincial Executive	Phone Interview	21.12.2015
42		Mehmet Emin DOĞRU	Hüda-Par	Batman Provincial Executive	Phone Interview	22.12.2015

DEMAND	NAME	ORGANIZATION	POSITION	PLACE	DATE
43	Enes	Hezbollah	Activist	İstanbul	10.07.2012
44	Murat	Hezbollah	Activist	İstanbul	15.07.2012
45	Cemal	Hezbollah	Activist	İstanbul	11.07.2012
46	Ismail	Mustazaf-Der	Executive	İstanbul	10.01.2013
47	Mehmet Baki ASLANURGUN	Hak-Par	İstanbul Provincial Executive	İstanbul	02.07.2012
48	Mehmet Emin EREN	Hak-Par	Tev-Kurd Executive	İstanbul	25.07.2012
49	Semra ARCAN	Hak-Par	İstanbul Provincial President	İstanbul	02.07.2012
50	Kemal BURKAY	Hak-Par	Party Leader	İstanbul	15.06.2012
51	Burkay ASLAN	Kom-Kar	Executive	London	21.07.2013
52	Cudi DABAKOGLU	Kom-Kar	President	London	26.03.2013
53	Azad AYYILDIRIM	Kom-Kar	Executive	London	25.03.2013
54	Eşref ÇAKAN	Hak-PAR	Diyarbakır Provincial Executive	Diyarbakır	06.05.2013
55	Arif SEVİNÇ	Hak-Par	General Vice President		20.12.2015
56	Vasıf KAHRAMAN	Hak-Par	Diyarbakır Provincial President	Diyarbakır	06.05.2013
57	Ciwanroj CEYHAN	KADEP	Diyarbakır Provincial President	Diyarbakır	08.05.2013
58	Mesut TEK	PSK	Party Leader	London	25.02.2013
59	Halim IPEK	DDKD	Diyarbakır Executive	Diyarbakır	05.05.2013

DEMAND	NAME	ORGANIZATION	POSITION	PLACE	DATE
60	Aziz Mahmut AK	ÖSP	General Vice President	Diyarbakır	07.05.2013
61	Sinan ÇİFTYÜREK	ÖSP	Party Leader	İstanbul	15.05.2013
62	Mustafa PEKÖZ	Researcher		London	15/20.03.2013
63	Dersim	Kurdish Diaspora in London	Politician	London	08.11.2014
64	Mehmet Emin KARDAŞ	TKDP	General President	İstanbul	25.11.2014 and 25.12.2015
65	Mustafa ÖZÇELİK	PAK	Party Leader	Ankara	20.11.2014
66	Vahit ABA	PAK	Executive	Ankara	18.11.2014
67	Mahmut KOYUNCU	Azadî Initiative	İstanbul Representative	İstanbul	31.01.2012
68	Adnan FIRAT	Azadî Initiative	Press Secretary and Executive	Diyarbakır	07.05.2013
69	Zelal	DHF	Activist	İstanbul	02.11.2013
70	Fırat	DHF	Activist	Tunceli	12.05.2013
71	Ruşen ASLAN	Ismail Beşikçi Foundation	Executive and Politician	İstanbul	20.05.2013
72	Fuat ÖNEN	Tev-Kurd	Writer and Politician	İstanbul	20.09.2014
73	Devrim	Kurdish Diaspora in London	Activist	London	01.03.2013

FORMATION OF A KURDISH NATION-STATE (rows 64–73)

DEMAND		NAME	ORGANIZATION	POSITION	PLACE	DATE
	74	Kani YADO	Activist	Politician	Diyarbakır	27.09.2014
	75	Irak	Gik-Der	Activist	London	04.03.2013
	76	Ali	İşçi-Köylü (Kızılbayrak) group	Activist	İstanbul	03.05.2012
	77	Vahap	İşçi-Köylü (Kızılbayrak) Group	Activist	İstanbul	03.05.2012
	78	Ekber	Kurdish Diaspora in London	Activist	London	17.03.2013
CULTURAL RIGHT	79	Helin		Academician	Hakkari	23.11.2014
	80	Adnan NABİKOĞLU	AKP	Diyarbakır Provincial Executive	Diyarbakır	05.05.2013
	81	Muhammed Dara AKAR	AKP	AKP Diyarbakır Provincial President	Phone Interview	22.12.2015
	82	Adile GÜRBÜZ	AKP	Batman Provincial Executive	Batman	09.05.2013
	83	Aydın ALTAÇ	AKP	Diyarbakır Provincial President	Diyarbakır	04.05.2013
	84	Ahmet	AKP	Sur District Executive	Diyarbakır	03.05.2013
	85	Rıza TAŞKIN	AKP	Tunceli Provincial Executive	Tunceli	13.05.2013
	86	Candaş ÖZÇELİK	AKP	Tunceli Provincial Executive	Tunceli	13.05.2013

DEMAND	NAME	ORGANIZATION	POSITION	PLACE	DATE
87	Abdurrahman KURT	AKP	Diyarbakır MP	London	10.09.2013
88	Hasan	AKP	Diyarbakır Sur District Executive	Diyarbakır	03.05.2013
89	Sinan	AKP	AKP Bingöl Provincial Executive	Bingöl	11.05.2013
90	Düzgün AKYILDIZ	AKP	Central District President	Tunceli	13.05.2013
91	Kemal BOZKURT	CHP	Tunceli Provincial President	Tunceli	13.05.2013
92	Imam GÖÇER	CHP	Tunceli Central District President	Tunceli	13.05.2013
93	Muslim SARI	CHP	İstanbul MP	London	15.06.2014
94	Mustafa KURBAN	CHP	Bingöl Provincial President	Bingöl	10.05.2013
95	Mustafa ALABAT	CHP	Tunceli Provincial Executive	Tunceli	13.05.2013
96	Aydın KARATAŞ	CHP	Tunceli Provincial Executive	Tunceli	13.05.2013
97	Kemal Deniz BOZKURT	CHP	İstanbul Esenyurt District President	İstanbul	08.01.2013
98	Zülfü KULACI	CHP	Tunceli Provincial Executive	Tunceli	13.05.2013
99	Hıdır ARAT	CHP	Tunceli Provincial Executive	Tunceli	13.05.2013

DEMAND	NAME	ORGANIZATION	POSITION	PLACE	DATE
100	Hakan	CHP	Activist	İstanbul	24.04.2012
101	Ziya SÖZEN	Martyrs Family Associations	President	Bingöl	11.05.2013
102	Suat ÖZDEMİR	MASİAD	MASİAD Batman President	Batman	09.05.2013
103	Mirza GÜÇLÜ	MASİAD	MASİAD Executive	İstanbul	21.12.2011
104	Fahri ASLAN	TUMSİAD	Diyarbakır Executive	Diyarbakır	06.05.2013
105	Aynur DOĞAN	Glasgow Alevi Federation Association	President	London	15.06.2014
106	Yaşar DEMİRALAY	London Alevi Cultural Centre and Cem Evi	President	London	15.06.2014
107	İsrafil ERBİL	British Alevi Federation	President	London	15.06.2014
108	Zeynep	London Alevi Cultural Centre and Cem Evi	Activist	London	03.04.2014
NON-AFFILIATED TO ANY GROUPS					
109	Vahap Coşkun	Dicle University	Academician	Phone Interview	21.12.2015
110	Fehim IŞIK		Journalist	Phone Interview	20.12.2015
111	Nevzat ÇİÇEK	Time Türk	Journalist	İstanbul	14.03.2011
112	Serhat		Journalist	Phone Interview	26.12.2015

Notes

Introduction

1 The Kurds' political claims are represented through various social, religious and political organizations in Turkey, particularly political parties. However, not all of the organizations stem from a Kurdish origin, as will be discussed in greater detail in the analysis chapters to follow. A large number of the Kurds gather around political parties, which, despite acknowledging their Kurdish supporters' political demands, are in fact non-Kurdish in origin such as AKP and CHP.
2 There are close links between federalism and nation state, as both are considered ethnic territorial political units and federalism in a way is a pre-phase and/or transitional period for a nation state. This connection complicates the analysis of Kurds' independence demands because the Kurds who are in favour of it also acknowledge the ideologies of a federal model. Their intention is to establish their own state by accepting the federalism model because they see federalism as the system that will lead to their independence. However, this results in confusion when classifying them – are they federalism or independence supporters? To clarify the latter, their classification was decided based upon their ultimate aim. Taking this into account, Kurds who consider federalism only for a transitional period, and the creation of a Kurdish nation state as their primary aim, are grouped as Kurds who request a Kurdish nation state.
3 Federalism supporters agree on the model's main principles, yet differ and/or are flexible in certain principles. This is especially the case with Hüda-Par. The group does not openly call for federalism in its party programme, but the principles it highlights in its party programme and during the interviews allow us to classify its approach in dealing with the Kurdish question under federalism.
4 Please see the appendix for Table 2. The participants with name and surname reflect the real identity, the participants only with forename are pseudonyms.

Chapter 1

1 The idea of a state has been considered with considerable interest since the ancient period (for an extensive discussion on the modern state formation and its main components, see Cohen 1984; Deth and Newton 2005; Hall and Ikenberry 1989;

Poggi 1990; Spruyt 2007; Tilly 1975; Tilly 1985). Yet it is Max Weber's (1864–1920) elaborate understanding of the state that is currently the conceptualization that is most widely accepted in the literature. Prior to defining the state, Weber acknowledges territory and physical force to play a large part when considering a state. He specifically underlines that the 'ruling organization' may be classed as 'political' if the 'ruling organization's' existence and order are uninterruptedly 'safeguarded within a given territorial area by the threat and application of physical force on the part of administrative staff'. Therefore, for Weber, only the state (authorities) has legitimacy for using this type of force. Based on these stipulations, Weber concludes that the state is therefore a 'compulsory political organization', 'insofar as its administrative staff successfully upholds the claim to the monopoly of the legitimate use of physical force in the enforcement of its order' (Weber 1978, 54).

2 It was with the French Revolution that the discussions on state and sovereignty reached a new phase, and the term 'state' obtained a national character – national sovereignty (Tibi 1990, 145). In other words, 'with the French Revolution, nation and state merged' (Rejai and Enloe 1969, 145). The construction of nation could in one way be explained through the socio-cultural and economic conditions of the time, for instance in modernist terms (Anderson 2006; Breuilly 2005; Gellner 2006; Hobsbawm 1990); however, the nation's merging with the state led to the emergence of the idea that the primary goal of the modern state is 'to create a population with precisely those standardized characteristics which will be easier to monitor, count, assess, and manage' (Scott 1998, 81–82). The amalgamation of the nation with the state would allow the latter to run a nationalization process, creating a national identity through a (common) language, culture, myth, symbols and feeling of belonging among the citizens (Deth and Newton 2005, 14). This would in turn allow for the development of the modern state to be considered a national state, through the articulation that the 'characteristic features' of a modern state were equivalent to the main 'characteristic features' of a nation state (Cornelia 1981, 35–36; Pierson 2004, 47).

3 For instance, despite stating that there are group rights, the United Nations Universal Declaration of Human Rights (UNUDHR) regards cultural rights at the individual level. Article 27 (1 and 2) of UNUDHR neglects to make reference to the terms 'group' or 'collectivity', and instead stresses individual (everyone's) rights (United Nations Universal Declaration of Human Rights 1948, Article 27 (1–2)).

Chapter 2

1 Turkish History Thesis put forward that the Turks' ethnic roots come from Central Asia, and that they are the community who disseminated civilization to the rest of the world. The Turkish History Thesis in that sense claims that there is continuity

between the Turks in Anatolia and the Sumerians and Hittites of the ancient world (Kirişçi and Winrow 1997, 121).
2. The Sun Language Theory is based on the idea that only the Turkish language was previously spoken in Central Asia. And so, according to this theory, the Turkish language formed the main foundation for all other languages. Consequently, this theory claims that the present Anatolian Turkish language is the perpetuation of the Turkish that was spoken in Central Asia (Kirişçi and Winrow 1997, 121).
3. The name Qizilbaşh is given to some Alevi groups, such as 'Anşa Bacılıhar', as they put on a red hat (Selçuk 2012).

Chapter 3

1. Accordingly, in order to receive the full support of the Kurds when he started the War of Independence in Anatolia, M. Kemal drew on loyalty to the Caliphate, religion and the Armenian issue (Gawrych 2013, 88). He sent letters to numerous Kurdish Aghas and Sheikhs, who already had social influence over the masses, requesting their support in freeing Anatolia and the Caliph (Gawrych 2013, 88). For that purpose, he invited many of the Kurdish notables in preparation for the Congresses of Sivas (in 1919) (Akyol 2007, 79) and Erzurum (in 1919) (Gawrych 2013, 88).
2. Based on its agenda for securing the Kurds' national freedom, the Azadî movement organized attacks against the Turkish military in the Beytussebap region in 1924. In line with its nationalist purpose, the Azadi aimed to raise a rebellion with this attack. This failed, but it created the groundwork for the Sheikh Said rebellion in 1925 (Gündoğan 1994).
3. The basic principles of the Obligatory Settlement Law were briefly outlined under the following articles:
(Article 7-B); those who are not of Turkish race, albeit do not want support from the government, have to settle in the places that the government deems fit and to stay there as long as the state does not allow them to settle in other areas.... (Article 11-A); it is prohibited for those whose mother tongue is not Turkish to establish village, district and worker or artist unions, collectively. It is forbidden for the same to restrict a village, district, a profession or art to their own kin.
(Article 13/3); it is obligatory to settle those who are not of Turkish origin to villages, separate districts or into towns or cities on the condition that they will not constitute a mass (cited from Beşikçi 1977, 132–46).
In order to apply this plan, in other words to eliminate Kurdish identity, the Republic also issued the 'Law on Resettlement, no. 2510' (McDowal 2004, 207). To easily assimilate Kurdish identity into Turkish identity, Turkish territory was grouped into three zones in line with this resettlement:

- The First Zone: The first zone comprised the areas where the 'original' Turks lived; mostly in the western parts of the state. Settlers from this part of country were intended to be resettled in Kurdish populated areas as a part of the Turkification process.
- The Second Zone: The second zone was named as covering the 'receiver' areas, which were safely Turkish enough in culture and mentality to resettle Kurds from the East. The second zone was where the Kurds would gradually get assimilated and dissolved among the large Turkish populations.
- The Third Zone: 'Regions to be completely evacuated', where the Kurdish tribes mostly lived and the Kurdish language was the mother tongue. The third zone would be the refugee sender part of the country and its inhabitants would have to adopt the Turkish more gradually in the second zone. Resettled Kurds were banned from forming more than 5 per cent of the population in the localities where they were settled, and the laws prevented them from forming civil institutions, villages or groups (Kurdish Human Rights Project April 2003, 7 cited in Sagnıç 2010, 131).

4 For instance, while nearly all of the political prisoners were released after the coup d'état, the political Kurdish prisoners whom the Menderes government imprisoned (the '49s') and those arrested after the coup were kept imprisoned. All of this, as stated by Naci Kutlay, who was also among the '49s' arrested, clearly illustrates the state's determination to maintain restrictions on the Kurdish identity (Kutlay 2006b, 159–60). In parallel with the Kurds' political struggle in Iraq and the emergence of a Kurdish consciousness among some Kurdish students, the state even further intensified its pressure on the Kurdish identity. In order to carry out and tighten its authority over and assimilation of the Kurdish identity, the state renamed most of the Kurdish villages into Turkish (Beşikçi 1969b), and arrested and sent 380 Kurdish notables to the Sivas camp, just four days after coup d'état in 1960 (Kutlay 2012a, 32). Among them, fifty-five were then chosen and settled in western parts of Turkey on suspicion of supporting Kurdish national awareness (Aydın 2005, 238). Most of those who were sent to the camp had a level of influence on Kurdish society, for example Kurdish intellectuals, Sheikhs and Aghas. Against the expectations of the state, many of these individuals became proactive in Kurdish politics following their release (Kutlay 2012a, 31–32). As Nevzat Çiçek highlights, although most of those sent to the camp were of Kurdish origin, not all of them were aware of their Kurdish identity. He adds that sharing up to nine months detainment in the Sivas camp reinforced their Kurdish identity (Çiçek 2010, 20–21). Among the arrestees, for instance, Faik Bucak formed the Turkish Kurdistan Democrat Party (TKDP in 1965) and Kinyas Kartal's nephew of another arrestee from the Sivas camp, Remzi Kartal, became and is still head of the Kurdish National Congress (KNK). These are only two samples to illustrate how the state's punishment mechanism against the Kurds backfired, which is going to be covered in the coming sections.
5 For further discussions on TİP see (Aren 1993).

Chapter 4

1. In 2014, the number of temporary and volunteer village guards was more than 80,000 (Geerdink 2014).
2. To see the decision in the HEP's closing case, see (The Turkish Constitutional Court 1992/1 E, 1993/1 K, Date: 14 July 1993).
3. To see the decision of the DEP's closing case, see (The Turkish Constitutional Court 1993/3 E, 1994/2 K, Date: 30 June 1994).
4. For the votes that the RP obtained in the 1995 general election in total, and in the regions mostly dominated by the Kurds, see (Turkish Statistical Institute 2012).
5. To see the decision of the HADEP's closing case, see (The Turkish Constitutional Court 1999/1 E, 2003/1 K, Date: 13 March 2003).
6. The cities in which the DTP obtained seats were Batman (2), Bitlis (1), Diyarbakır (4), Hakkâri (1), Iğdır (1), İstanbul (2), Mardin (2), Muş (2), Siirt (1), Şanlıurfa (1), Şırnak (2), Tunceli (1) and Van'da (2).
7. For the 22 July 2007 General Election result also, visit the Supreme Committee of Elections (Yüksek Seçim Kurulu). Homepage available at (http://www.ysk.gov.tr/ysk/faces/Secimler?_adf.ctrl-state=9cgjmzhve_9&wcnav.model=YSKUstMenu&_afrLoop=22089026474476664 (Accessed 11 August 2014).
8. To see the decision of DTP's closing case, see (the Turkish Constitutional Court 2007/1 E, 2009/4 K, Date: 11 December 2009).
9. The HDP's party programme is available on the party's home page, available at http://www.hdp.org.tr/parti/parti-programi/8
10. Phone interview with Adem Geveri, 20 December 2015.
11. Concerning the Turkish state's brutal military operation in Cizre, which is one of the first places YDG-H dug ditches, the DBP Cizre co-mayor, Kadir Konur, stated that the state used the ditches as a pretext to destroy the Kurds: 'This is not just a basic military operation and about ditches. The state's aim is to eliminate the Kurds' (Phone interview with Kadir Konur, 21 December 2015). This view is also shared by Serhat, who is a Cizre-based independent journalist. Highlighting Cizre's high degree of support for the HDP and sympathy for the PKK, Serhat said that the state aims to punish Kurds, weaken their will and push them to migrate (Interview Serhat, 3 January 2016).
12. Highlighting the class-based character of the issue, academic Vahap Coşkun stated that the ditches were dug in areas with economically less well-developed settlements compared with other Kurdish areas, especially in Diyarbakır. Neither these people nor the Kurdish middle and upper classes support the PKK's strategy. Even those who do support the PKK preferred to leave their houses rather than pay attention to the PKK's call for resistance (Phone interview with Vahap Coşkun, 21 December 2015).
13. Interview with Kudret Gülün in İstanbul, 25 December 2012.

14   Interview with Arif Erol in İstanbul, 25 December 2012.
15   Interview with Hasan Yıldız in İstanbul, 16 December 2012.
16   To further clarify the interviewees' explanations or what they mean by some words I make quite short explanations in italics in some of the direct quotations. Hereafter, all of the parts in italics in the direct citations belong to me.
17   Phone Interview with Rahime Kanilga, 15 November 2014.
18   Nationalism has been one of the vital constructors of modern Turkey's ideology, and has been more influential in establishing the state's political stance against minority groups. It has been viewed as a leading medium in the construction of 'cohesion' in society (Dumont 1984, 29). The impact of Turkish nationalism on Turkey's internal politics has escalated in line with the development of the Kurdish issue. It is purposely employed against Kurdish ethnicity in order to create a homogeneous Turkish nation (Beller-Han and Hann 2001, 39–40; Yeğen 2007b).
19   Interview with Emine Ayna in Diyarbakır, 3 May 2013.
20   Interview conducted with Altan Tan (by Deniz Cifci, Zeynep Kösereisoglu, Serdar Sengul, Buket Bora and Jonathan Friedman, on behalf of the CEFTUS) in London, 18 October 2013, available at CEFTUS (Centre for Turkey Studies 2013) homepage, http://ceftus.org/2014/01/28/ceftus-insights-interview-with-altan-tan-peace-and-democracy-party-bdp-mp/#.VGELwvSUefM (Accessed 9 October 2014).
21   Interview conducted with Altan Tan (by Deniz Cifci, Zeynep Kösereisoglu, Serdar Sengul, Buket Bora and Jonathan Friedman, on Behalf of the Ceftus) in London, 18 October 2013.
22   In the 30 March 2014 Local Election BDP won 103 municipalities. For the 30 March Local Election results visit Supreme Committee of Election's (YSK) homepage, available at (Http://www.ysk.gov.tr/ysk/faces/Secimler?_adf.ctrl-state=9cgjmzhve_9&wcnav.model=YSKUstMenu&_afrLoop=22089026474476664 (Accessed 11 August 2014).
23   Interview with Fırat ANLI in Diyarbakır, 8 May 2013.
24   Fırat ANLI was arrested in October 2016. Soon after his and the other co-mayor Gülten Kışanak's arrest, a trustee was appointed to Diyarbakır municipality on the 1 November 2016.
25   For details about the peace process and its background, see research conducted by (Ankara Strateji Enstitüsü 2013).
26   Interview with Fırat ANLI in Diyarbakır, 8 May 2013.
27   According to Journalist Fehim Isik, who has been following the Kurdish issue for a long time, the Dolmabahce Declaration's aim was to sort out the Kurdish issue by granting Kurds their status. To Isik, Recep Tayyip Erdogan initially aimed to benefit from the peace talks, but when he realized that granting the Kurds their status might cost him in an election he made a U-turn and ignored the declaration (Phone interview with Fehim Isik, 20 December 2015).

28 Phone interview with Mehmet Emin Adiyaman, 20 December 2015, Phone interview with Adem Geveri (Özcaner), 23 December 2015.
29 Phone interview with Arif Sevinç, 20 December 2015; Phone interview with Lokman Yalçın, 22 December 2015.
30 Interview with Arif Erol in İstanbul, 25 December 2012.
31 Interview with Sako in İstanbul, 28 April 2012.
32 Interview with Seydi Fırat in Diyarbakır, 10 May 2013.
33 Interview with Sami Tan in İstanbul, 27 April 2013.
34 Interview with Cafer Solgun in İstanbul, 16 May 2013.
35 Skype Interview with Mustafa Ünlü, 15 November 2014.
36 Phone Interview with Mustafa Ünlü, 15 November 2014.
37 Interview with Selim Kurbanoğlu in Diyarbakır, 7 May 2013.
38 Interview with Jiyan in London, 23 September 2014.
39 Interview conducted with Altan Tan (by Deniz Cifci, Zeynep Kösereisoglu, Serdar Sengul, Buket Bora and Jonathan Friedman on behalf of the CEFTUS) in London, 18 October 2013, Available at CEFTUS' (Centre for Turkey Studies 2013) homepage, http://ceftus.org/2014/01/28/ceftus-insights-interview-with-altan-tan-peace-and-democracy-party-bdp-mp/#.VGELwvSUefM (Accessed 9 October 2014).
40 Interview with Seydi Fırat in Diyarbakır, 10 May 2013, and interview with Selim Kurbanoğlu in Diyarbakır, 7 May 2013.
41 Interview with Sako in İstanbul, 28 April 2012.
42 Interview with Emine Ayna in Diyarbakır, 3 May 2013.
43 Interview with Hasan Yıldız in İstanbul, 16 December 2012.
44 Interview with Sako in İstanbul, 28 April 2012.
45 Interview with Selim Kurbanoğlu in Diyarbakır, 7 May 2013.
46 Interview with Emine Ayna in Diyarbakır, 3 May 2013.
47 Ibid.
48 Interview with Hıdır Celik in İstanbul, 19 December 2012.
49 Interview with Zuhal in İstanbul, 14 November 2012.
50 Idris-i Bitlisi, who lived between second half of the fifteenth century and beginning of the sixteenth century, was a famous statesmen, religious scholar and philosopher of the Ottoman Empire (see Başaran 2002, 201; Bayraktar 2006; Imber 2002, 45).
51 Interview with Hasan Yildiz in İstanbul, 16 December 2012.
52 Interview with Edibe Sahin in Tunceli, 13 May 2013.
53 Interview with Zuhal in İstanbul, 14 November 2012.
54 Wise Man Committee's meeting in Bingöl, 11 May 2013.
55 Interview with Zubeyde Teker in Bingol, 11 May 2013.
56 Interview with Cafer Solgun in İstanbul, 16 May 2013.
57 Interview with Halis Yurtseven in Bingöl, 10 May 2013.
58 Interview with Emine Ayna in Diyarbakır, 3 May 2013.

59 Interview with Hasan Yildiz in İstanbul, 16 December 2012.
60 Interview with Halis Yurtseven in Bingöl, 10 May 2013.
61 Interview with Cafer Solgun in İstanbul, 16 May 2013.
62 Interview with Halis Yurtseven in Bingöl, 10 May 2013.
63 Interview with Ilhan Ilbay in Tunceli, 12 May 2013, Interview with Edibe Sahin in Tunceli, 13 May 2013 and Interview with Mustafa Taskale in Tunceli, 12 May 2013.
64 Interview with Edibe Sahin in Tunceli, 13 May 2013.
65 Interview with Mustafa Taskale in Tunceli, 12 May 2013.
66 Interview with Sami Tan in İstanbul, 27 April 2013.
67 Interview with Halis Yurtseven in Bingöl, 10 May 2013.
68 Interview with Emine Ayna in Diyarbakır, 3 May 2013.
69 Interview with Seydi Fırat in Diyarbakır, 10 May 2013.
70 Interview with Selim Kurbanoğlu in Diyarbakır, 7 May 2013.
71 Interview with Zuhal in İstanbul, 14 November 2012.
72 Interview with Sako in İstanbul, 28 April 2012.
73 Interview with Sami Tan in İstanbul, 27 April 2013.
74 Interview with Kudret Gülün in İstanbul, 25 December 2012.
75 Interview with Ahmet Şeker in London, 10 September 2014.
76 Interview with Dorsin in London, 24 September 2014.
77 Interview with Sami Tan in İstanbul, 27 April 2013.
78 Interview with Dorsin in London, 24 September 2014.
79 Interview with Emine Ayna in Diyarbakır, 3 May 2013.
80 Like his challenge to the state, Abdullah Öcalan also criticizes other forms of ethnic federalism. He recalls that the Kurds' previous autonomous status and state-aimed struggles were based on their feudal and tribal characters. He states: 'It is difficult to view these uprisings as movements based on the free will of the population.' To Öcalan, feudal and tribal structures and the prioritizing of tribal interests impeded the development of democratic values and the significance of the people's will. With reference to this, he says:
The concept of federation, which now being discussed in this context, would be dependent on a backward social structure; this would not really allow for the development of democratic values. It would do more to strengthen feudal and tribal remnants. The experience of southern Kurds largely proves this. Furthermore, this is the form most conducive to collaborationism and becoming a tool in the hands of whoever wants to use it the most and has the power to do so. Because they [the Kurds] have not evolved democratically, they are quite open to both traditional types of rebellion and destruction (Öcalan 1999, 78).
81 Interview with Seydi Fırat in Diyarbakır, 10 May 2013.
82 Interview with Kudret Gülün in İstanbul, 25 December 2012.
83 Interview with Sami Tan in İstanbul, 27 April 2013.
84 Interview with Baran in Iraq, 25 November 2009.

85 Interview with Seydi Fırat in Diyarbakır, 10 May 2013.
86 Interview with Arif Erol in İstanbul, 25 December 2012.

Chapter 5

1. For instance, for the General Election of Representatives Province and District Results 2011, 2007, 2002, 1999, 1995, 1991, see the booklet published by the Turkish Statistical Institute (2012).
2. To see the decision of RP closing case, see (The Turkish Constitutional Court 1997/1 E, 1998/1 K, Date: 16 January 1998).
3. For further details on the phrase 'conservative democrat', see (Akdogan 2006).
4. Along with secularism, nationalism is also a key component of the CHP's identity. Nationalism constitutes one of the six branches of the party. The party programme identifies nationalism as *Ataturk's nationalism*. According to the CHP, its nationalism therefore does not focus on an ethnic, religious, cultural or regional group, and it does not consider racial or blood ties. It considers all diverse groups equal, and respects their individual cultural rights in a union with Turkey (Cumhuriyet Halk Partis Programı 2013, 13–14).
5. The Alevis' interest in the CHP dates back to the formation of the Republic, which takes secularism (Laicism) as one of the main principles in its identification. The republicans' secular ideology was the main factor in ensuring Alevis' contentment. The Kemalist regime's secular character and guarantee of the separation of state from religious affairs, as well as the removal of religious power from the public sphere, made Alevis more accepting of secular republicanism because the majority of Alevis believed these steps would remove any risk posed to their identity (Kehl-Bodrogi 2003; Neyzi 2003, 113; Shakland 1999). Put more clearly, the Alevis perceived the Kemalist regime as the power which could protect them from oppression, mostly coming from the Sunni groups (Kehl-Bodrogi 2003). On the other hand, despite the Kemalist regime's negative stance towards ethnic and even religious identities to some extent (Geaves 2003), and their opposition to a homogeneous Turkish nation creation project, the Kurdish Alevis gladly welcomed the secular character of Kemalism (van Bruinessen 2000d, 35).
6. Interview with Riza Taşkın in Tunceli, 13 May 2013.
7. Interview with Candaş Özçelik in Tunceli, 13 May 2013.
8. Interview with Adnan Nabikoğlu in Diyarbakır, 5 May 2013.
9. Interview with Mustafa Kurban in Bingöl, 10 May 2013.
10. Ibid.
11. Interview with Suat Özdemir in Batman, 9 May 2013.
12. Interview with Kemal Deniz Bozkurt in İstanbul, 8 January 2013.

13   Interview with Mirza Güçlü in İstanbul, 21 December 2011.
14   Interview with Kemal Deniz Bozkurt in İstanbul, 8 January 2013.
15   Interview with Adnan Nabikoglu in Diyarbakır, 5 May 2013.
16   Interview with Aydin Karatas (Focus Group) in Tunceli, 13 May 2013.
17   Interview with Fahri Aslan in Diyarbakır, 6 May 2013.
18   Interview with Mirza Güçlü in İstanbul, 21 December 2011.
19   Interview with Aydin Altac in Diyarbakır, 4 May 2013.
20   Interview with Mustafa Kurban in Bingol, 10 May 2013.
21   Interview with Ahmet in Diyarbakır, 3 May 2013.
22   Interview with Hakan in İstanbul, 24 April 2012.
23   Interview with Kemal Deniz Bozkurt in İstanbul, 8 January 2013.
24   Interview with Adnan Nabikoğlu in Diyarbakır, 5 May 2013.
25   Interview with Mustafa Kurban in Bingöl, 10 May 2013.
26   Interview with Aydin Altac in Diyarbakır, 4 May 2013.
27   Interview with Mirza Güçlü in İstanbul, 21 December 2011.
28   Ibid.
29   Interview with Sinan in Bingöl, 11 May 2013.
30   Interview with Adnan Nabikoglu in Diyarbakır, 5 May 2013.
31   Interview with Mirza Güçlü in İstanbul, 21 December 2011.
32   Interview with Ahmet in Diyarbakır, 3 May 2013.
33   Ibid.
34   Interview with Adnan Nabikoglu in Diyarbakır, 5 May 2013.
35   Interview with Adile Gurbuz in Batman, 9 May 2013.
36   Interview with Mirza Güçlü in İstanbul, 21 December 2011.
37   Interview conducted with Abdurrahman Kurt (by Deniz Cifci, Buket Bora, Nazli Akyuz, Zeynep Kösereisoglu, Serdar Sengul and Josie Delves on behalf of CEFTUS) in London, 10 September 2013, available at the CEFTUS homepage (CEFTUS 2013) at http://ceftus.org/2014/02/07/ceftus-insights-interview-with-abdurrahman-kurt/#.VHN1s2SUci4 (Accessed 23 October 2014).
38   Interview with Mirza Güçlü in İstanbul, 21 December 2011.
39   Interview with Yasar Demiralay in London, 15 June 2014.
40   Interview with Kemal Bozkurt in Tunceli, 13 May 2013.
41   Ibid.
42   Interview with Nevzat Çiçek in İstanbul, 14 March 2011.
43   Interview with Muslim Sari in London, 15 June 2014.
44   Interview with Mustafa Kurban in Bingöl, 10 May 2013.
45   Interview with Muslim Sari in London, 15 June 2014.
46   Interview with Zeynep (Focus group discussion) in London, 3 April 2014.
47   Interview with İsrafil ERBİL in London, 15 June 2014.
48   Interview with Aydin Karatas (Focus group) in Tunceli, 13 May 2013.
49   Ibid.

50 Interview with Muslim Sari in London, 15 June 2014.
51 As a part of peace process continued between the state and PKK, Abdullah Öcalan's letter written in Imrali prison was declared to the public at the Newroz festival in Diyarbakır on 21 March 2013.
52 Interview with Muslim Sari in London, 15 June 2014.
53 Interview with Yaşar Demiralay in London, 15 June 2014.
54 Interview with Mustafa Alabat (Focus group) in Tunceli, 13 May 2013.
55 Interview with Mustafa Kurban in Bingöl, 10 May 2013; interview with Imam Gucer (Focus group) in Tunceli, 13 May 2013; and interview with Mustafa Alabat (Focus group) in Tunceli, 13 May 2013.
56 Interview with Mustafa Kurban in Bingöl, 10 May 2013.
57 Interview with İsrafil ERBİL in London, 15 June 2014.
58 Interview with Muslim Sari in London, 15 June 2014.
    The fear of Sunni identity is not only common among the Alevis in Turkey. For instance, born in Turkey and an Arab Alevi, the president of the Glasgow Alevi Federation, Aynur Doğan, highlighted that Alevism has to be a supra-identity for all Alevism. In response to the question, *'what do you consider Sunni identity?'* Aynur responded:
    I'm Arab Alevi… But my ethnic origin does not matter at all; I am totally Alevi. […] I am against the structure you mentioned (*Sunni identity*), Alevi identity… Look, we have never been accepted… Since Karbala, we have been exposed to massacres. […] I am opposed to the system that does not accept us, does not recognize us. […] This is our reaction. We have to protect our identity […]. Alevism is the supra-identity for me. Our concern is Alevism; protecting Alevism and its unity. (Interview with Aynur Dogan in London, 15 June 2014).
59 Interview with Düzgün Akyildiz in Tunceli, 13 May 2013.
60 Interview with Aydin Altaç in Diyarbakır, 4 May 2013.
61 Interview with Düzgün Akyildiz in Tunceli, 13 May 2013.
62 Interview with Kemal Bozkurt in Tunceli, 13 May 2013.
63 Ibid.
64 Interview with Ahmet in Diyarbakır, 3 May 2013.
65 Interview with Ziya Sözen in Bingöl, 11 May 2013.
66 Interview with Hasan in Diyarbakır, 3 May 2013.
67 Phone interview with Muhammed Dara Akar, 22 December 2015.

Chapter 6

1 Said-i Nursi used the surname 'Kurdi' until the adoption of the Surname Act in 1934. Under this law, the state gave him the surname 'Okur', but he never used it. He used Nursi – the name of the place where he was born (Zınar 2011, 156).

2   The name Med-Zehra derives from the name of a university, 'Medresetul Zehra', which Said-Nursi proposed should be formed in the city of Van, providing education in three languages, Kurdish, Turkish and Arabic (Atacan 2001, 112).
3   Kurdish Islamists' emphasis on Said-i Nursi's Kurdish identity, on the other hand, led many to criticize them. This is because the Kurdish Nurcus were accused of being in close interaction with Kurdish nationalism. It is, without a doubt, incredibly difficult to define the borders between religion and nationality; however, it is safe to say that Turkish Islamists' attempts to ignore the Nursi's Kurdish identity and interactions with Turkish nationalism generated a counter-reaction from Kurdish Islamists. This was seen primarily in an increase in focus on Saidi'i Nursi's Kurdish identity. Considering this discussion on Nursi's ethnic identity, as Yavuz (2003,176) suggests, Kurdish Islamists' counter-reaction to the approach taken by Turkish Islamists to Said Nursi's Kurdish identity was their way of placing emphasis on 'a Kurdish Nursi'.
4   The leader of the Zehra community, Izzettin Yildirim (killed in 2000), was well respected among the Kurds. Yildirim was born in the city of Agri in 1946. In order to spread the teachings of Nursi, he actively took part in Nurcu communities from the outset. Along with his focus on religion, Yıldırım also concentrated on the Kurdish issue, and often mentioned Kurdish identity and the suffering they experienced. He made great practical and intellectual efforts to solve the Kurdish question (Çakır 2011a, 281; Tekin 2013).
5   Interview with Şahan in Diyarbakır, 8 May 2013.
6   The name Nûbihar comes from the Kurdish philosopher Ahemd-i Xani's book (*Nûbihara Piçûkan*). Nûbihar started its publication in 1992, and it mostly focuses on the Kurdish language and Kurdish issue through Said-i Nursi's approach from an Islamic perspective.
7   Interview with Vedat Turgut in Diyarbakır, 8 May 2013.
8   This book is almost the first to be published by Hezbollah. Hezbollah in this regard was one of the most mysterious organizations until the group's release of the book and other publications following the killing of its leader, Huseyin Veligoglu.
9   The Hezbollah members who gathered around the 'Menzil' bookstore were named the Hezbollah Menzil group, while others who gathered around the 'Ilim' bookstore were called the Hezbollah Ilim group. The Ilim group, under the leadership of Huseyin Velioglu, harshly attacked Menzil members and killed many of them, including its leadership cadres. The Hezbollah Menzil group, therefore, does not currently have any power over the Kurds (Aydıntaşbaş 2000), and so the current Hezbollah is known as the Hezbollah Ilim group.
10 The competition and tension between both parties sometimes turned into clashes between their followers in the city centres. During the Kobani protests, which began over Turkey's prevention of aid support across its borders to the YPG fighters resisting against the ISIS, the Kurds came onto the streets to protest the Turkish

government's stance. Because of Hezbollah's ideological connections with the extremist Islamist groups and its extremely violent methods in the past, the Kobani protests soon turned into clashes between the HDP and Hüda-Par followers in Diyarbakır, Batman, Mardin, Van and Muş and some other areas, resulting in more than fifty deaths and many wounded (Hürriyet 2014).

11 Despite laying down its arms, Hezbollah never declared that it had buried them completely. The Hezbollah-affiliated Huseyni Sevdam webpages, for instance, regard the armed *Şeyh Said Seriyyeleri* (Sheikh Said Brigades) as Hezbollah's armed wing (Huseyni Sevdam n.d.); it is also believed that the group is responsible for killing some HDP members, including Bayram Özelçin, Emin Ensen and Bayram Dağtan, killed on 15 June 2015 in reprisal for the killing of the Hezbollah-affiliated Ihya-Der organization's leader Aytaç Baran.

12 For the votes Hûda-Par obtained on 30 March 2014 local election, visit the Supreme Election Committee (Yüksek Seçim Kurulu-YSK) homepage: (http://www.ysk.gov.tr/ysk/faces/Secimler?_adf.ctrl-state=9cgjmzhve_9&wcnav.model=YSKUstMenu&_afrLoop=22089026474476664 (Accessed 11 August 2014).

13 For the judicial decision about to close Hak-Par, see (the Turkish Constitutional Court 2002/1 E, 2008/1 K, Date. 29.01.2008).

14 Phone Interview with Mehmet Emin Kardaş, 25 December 2015.

15 Interview with Halis in İstanbul, 24 July 2015.

16 Interview with Tahir in İstanbul, 24 and 25 July 2014.

17 Interview with Şahan in Diyarbakır, 8 May 2013.

18 Interview with Recep in İstanbul, 23 and 24 April 2013.

19 Interview with Şahan in Diyarbakır, 8 May 2013.

20 Interview with Mustafa Peköz in London, 20 March 2013.

21 Interview with Murat in İstanbul 15 July 2012.

22 Interview with Şahan in Diyarbakır, 8 May 2013.

23 Interview with Aydin Gök in Batman, 10 May 2013.

24 Interview with Tahir in İstanbul, 24 and 25 July 2014.

25 Interview with Enes in İstanbul, 10 July 2012.

26 Interview with Recep in İstanbul, 24 April 2013.

27 Interview with Aydin Gök in Batman, 10 May 2013.

28 Interview with Rauf Çiçek in Diyarbakır, 6 May 2013.

29 Interview with Aydin Gök in Batman, 10 May 2013.

30 Interview with Recep in İstanbul, 24 April 2013, and interview with Sıddık Dursun Seyhanzade in İstanbul, 27 April 2013.

31 Interview with Nevzat Eminoğlu in İstanbul, 10 July 2012.

32 Interview with Azad Ayyildirim in London, 25 March 2013, and interview with Burkay Aslan in London, 21 March 2013.

33 Interview with Azad Ayyildirim in London, 25 March 2013. Interview with Cudi Dabakoglu in London, 26 March 2013. Interview with Tahir in İstanbul, 24 and 25

July 2014. Interview with Mesut Tek in London, 25 February 2013. Interview with Cemal in İstanbul, 11 July 2012.
34 Medine Vesikasi (Medina Constitution) 'establishe[d] a kind of alliance or federation between nine different groups' during the period of the Prophet (Muhammad) (Watt 1970, 41).
35 Interview with İsmail in İstanbul, 10 January 2013.
36 Interview with Ciwanroj Ceyhan in Diyarbakır, 8 May 2013.
37 Interview with Mesut Tek in London, 25 February 2013.
38 Interview with Halim Ipek in Diyarbakır, 5 May 2013.
39 Ibid.
40 Interview with Kemal Burkay, in İstanbul, 15 June 2012, and his talk at Hak-Par İstanbul Provincial.
41 Interview with Süleyman Çevik in İstanbul, 15 July 2013.
42 Interview with İbrahim Güçlü in Diyarbakır, 8 May 2012.
43 Interview with Vedat Turgut in Diyarbakır, 8 May 2013.
44 Interview with Halim İpek in Diyarbakır, 5 May 2013.
45 Interview with Semra Arcan in İstanbul, 2 July 2012.
46 Interview with Kemal Burkay in İstanbul, 15 June 2012, and his talk at the Hak-Par İstanbul provincial.
47 Interview with Cudi Dabakoglu in London, 26 March 2013.
48 Interview with İbrahim Güçlü in Diyarbakır, 8 May 2013.
49 Interview with Azad Ayyildirim in London, 25 March 2013.
50 Interview with Necat Özdemir in Diyarbakır, 7 May 2013.
51 Interview with Halim İpek in Diyarbakır, 5 May 2013.
52 Interview with İbrahim Güçlü in Diyarbakır, 8 May 2013.
53 Interview with Orhan Açikbaş in Bingöl, 11 May 2013.
54 Interview with İbrahim Güçlü in Diyarbakır, 8 May 2012.
55 Interview with Aziz Mahmut AK in Diyarbakır, 7 May 2013.
56 Interview with Vasıf Kaharaman in Diyarbakır, 6 May 2013.
57 Interview with İbrahim Güçlü in Diyarbakır, 8 May 2013.
58 Interview with Eşref Çakan in Diyarbakır, 6 May 2013.
59 Interview with Aziz Mahmut AK in Diyarbakır, 7 May 2013.
60 Interview with Burkay Aslan in London, 21 July 2013.
61 Interview with Cudi Dabakoglu in London, 25 July 2013.
62 Interview with Aziz Mahmut Ak in Diyarbakır, 7 May 2013.
63 Interview with Sinan Çiftyürek in İstanbul, 15 May 2013.
64 Interview with Vasıf Kaharaman in Diyarbakır, 6 May 2013.
65 Ibid.
66 Interview with İbrahim Güçlü in Diyarbakır, 8 May 2013.
67 Interview with Mehmet Emin Eren in İstanbul, 25 July 2012.
68 Interview with Necat Özdemiz in Diyarbakır, 7 May 2013.

69 Interview with Murat in İstanbul, 15 July 2012.
70 Interview with Nevzat Eminoğlu in İstanbul, 10 July 2012.
71 Interview with Enes in İstanbul, 10 July 2012.
72 Interview with Azad Ayyildirim in London, 25 March 2013.
73 Interview with İbrahim Güçlü in Diyarbakır, 8 May 2012.
74 Interview with Mesut Tek in London, 25 February 2013.
75 Interview with Burkay Aslan in London, 21 July 2013.
76 Interview with Kemal Burkay in İstanbul, 15 June 2012, and his talk at Hak-Par İstanbul provincial.
77 Phone Interview with Hamdullah Tasali, 21 December 2015.
78 Phone Interview with Mehmet Emin Doğru, 22 December 2015.
79 Phone Interview with Mehmet Emin Kardaş, 25 December 2015.
80 Interview with Azad Ayyildirim in London, 25 March 2013, and interview with Tahir in İstanbul, 24 and 25 July 2014.
81 Interview with Cudi Dabakoğlu in London, 25 July 2013.
82 Interview with Mustafa Peköz in London, 15 March 2013.
83 Interview with Ciwanroj Ceyhan in Diyarbakır, 8 May 2013
    Interview with Mehmet Baki Aslanurgun in İstanbul, 2 July 2012.

Chapter 7

1 For further details on Ismail Besikci Vakfi (Foundation), visit their homepage (http://www.ismailbesikcivakfi.org/Default.asp?)
2 For further details on DHF, visit their homepage (http://www.demokratikhaklarfederasyonu.org/demokratik-haklar-dernekleri-federasyonu-tuzugu.html).
3 For further details on Isci-Koylu (Kizilbayrak) group, visit homepage (http://www.kizilbayrak.net/ana-sayfa/).
4 Interview with Mahmut Koyunci in İstanbul, 31 January 2012.
5 Interview with Adnan Firat in Diyarbakır, 7 May 2013.
6 Phone Interview with Fuat Önen in İstanbul, 20 September 2014.
7 Interview with Adnan Firat in Diyarbakır, 7 May 2013.
8 Interview with Zelal in İstanbul, 2 December 2013.
9 Interview with Rusen Aslan in İstanbul, 20 May 2013.
10 Interview with Adnan Firat in Diyarbakır, 7 May 2013.
11 Interview with Irak in Londra, 4 March 2013.
12 Phone interview with Vahit Aba in Ankara, 19 November 2014.
13 Interview with Dersim in London, 8 November 2014.
14 Phone interview with Mustafa Özçelik in Ankara, 20 November 2014.

15 Interview with Ruşen Aslan in İstanbul, 20 May 2013.
16 Written interview with Kani Yado in Diyarbakır, 27 September 2014.
17 Phone interview with Fuat Önen in İstanbul, 20 September 2014. On this point, these Kurds even go one step further, and consider the predominantly Kurdish-settled region as an occupied region and claim they live within Turkey because of the force of guns, not through free will. For example, the Kurdish Communist Party, which demands the creation of a united Kurdish nation state (with the merging of all the regions mostly populated by the Kurds) describes the Kurdish area as an occupied region, and label Turkey's Kurdish policy as a type of colonial policy. In other words, this party considers Turkey as a country that has annexed the Kurdish region (Kurdistan Kominist Partisi 1990, 8) which has been responsible for 'enforcing captivity on the Kurdish nation' (Written interview with Kani Yado in Diyarbakır, 27 September 2014). With reference to this, Adnan Firat highlighted that their nation has been taken under control and dominated by other powers against their will. Therefore, he said, Kurds' right to self-determination cannot be rejected or denied. On what grounds can it be rejected? By which right and law can it be rejected? If they reject it, it will be fascism… colonialism. Look at it from another view. Look at Turkey, which rules Kurdistan… I am a nation that is oppressed and placed under control by force of arms. All my rights were taken away from me through that. Even this shows us that the solution is the right to govern, right to govern by arms, so that you can protect yourself (Interview with Adnan Firat in Diyarbakır, 7 May 2013).
18 Phone interview with Fuat Önen in İstanbul, 20 September 2014.
19 Written interview with Kani Yado in Diyarbakır, 27 September 2014.
20 Ibid.
21 Interview with Vahap in İstanbul, 3 May 2012.
22 Interview with Firat in Tunceli, in 12 May 2013.
23 Written interview with Kani Yado in Diyarbakır, 27 September 2014.
24 Phone interview with Vahit Aba in Ankara, 19 November 2014.
25 Written interview with Kani Yado in Diyarbakır, 27 September 2014.
26 Phone interview with Mustafa Özçelik in Ankara, 20 November 2014.
27 Ismail Besikci's talk at the SOAS University London, 8 April 2014.
28 Phone interview with Mehmet Emin Kardaş in İstanbul, 25 November 2014.
29 Phone interview with Mustafa Özçelik in Ankara, 20 November 2014, and phone interview with Vahit Aba in Ankara 19 November 2014.
30 Interview with Rusen Aslan in İstanbul, 20 May 2013.
31 Phone interview with Helin in Hakkari, 23 November 2014.
32 Phone interview with Fuat Önen in İstanbul, 20 September 2014.
33 Interview with Dersim in London, 08 November 2014.
34 Interview with Ekber in London, 17 March 2013.
35 Interview with Mahmut Koyuncu in İstanbul, 31 January 2012.

36 Phone interview with Mustafa Özçelik in Ankara, 20 November 2014.
37 Interview with Mahmut Koyuncu in İstanbul, 31 January 2012.
38 Written interview with Kani Yado in Diyarbakır, 27 September 2014, and interview with Devrim in London, 1 March 2013.
39 Interview with Mahmut Koyuncu in İstanbul, 31 January 2012.
40 Written interview with Kani Yado in Diyarbakır, 27 September 2014.
41 Phone Mustafa Özçelik in Ankara, 20 November 2014.
42 Phone interview with Helin in Hakkari, 23 November 2014.
43 Democratic autonomy model was formed in Rojava by the PKK-affiliated organization PYD in 2012–13 (Kurdistan National Congress 2014).
44 Phone interview with Mehmet Emin Kardaş in İstanbul, 25 November 2014.
45 Phone interview with Fuat Önen in İstanbul, 20 September 2014.
46 Interview with Mahmut Koyuncu in İstanbul, 31 January 2012.
47 Written interview with Kani Yado in Diyarbakır, 27 September 2014.
48 Interview with Ali in İstanbul, 3 May 2012.
49 Phone interview with Mehmet Emin Kardaş in İstanbul, 25 November 2014.
50 Interview with Mahmut Koyuncu in İstanbul, 31 January 2012.
51 Interview with Adnan Firat in Diyarbakır, 7 May 2013.

Chapter 8

1 For further information on the contribution of 'dispersed settlements' to integration and the assimilation of minorities, see: Van der Laan Bouma-Doff (2007).
2 See the Socio-Economic Development of the Provinces and Regions' Research (SEGE (2011) Results 2013, 67–84).

Bibliography

Abdulla, Nejat. 2009. *İmparatorluk Sınır ve Aşiret: Kürdistan ve 1843-1932 Türk-Fars Sınır Çatışması*. Translated by Mustafa Aslan. İstanbul: Avesta.

Abercrombie, Nicholas, Stephan Hill, and Bryan S. Turner. 2006. 'Culture'. In *Dictionary of Sociology*. London and New Jersey: Penguin Books.

Aboona, Hirmis. 2008. *Assyrians, Kurds, and Ottomans*. Amherst, NY: Cambria press.

Açıkyıldız, Birgül. 2010. *The Yezidis: The History of a Community, Culture and Religion*. New York: I.B.Tauris.

Acker, Vanessa G. 2004. 'Religion among the Kurds: Internal Tolerance, External Conflict'. *Kennedy School Review* 5: 99-109.

Adegbite, Lateef. 1979. 'The Organisation and Role of the Judiciary under a Federal Constitution'. In *Readings on Federalism*, edited by A.B. Akinyemi, P.D. Cole, and Walter Ofonagoro, 44-51. Lagos: Nigerian Institute of International Affairs.

Ahmad, Feroz. 2003. *Turkey: The Quest for Identity*. Oxford: Oneworld.

Ahmed, Kemal Mazhar. 1992. *Birinci Dünya Savaşı Yıllarında Kürdistan*. Translated by Mustafa Düzgün. 2nd ed. Ankara: Berhem.

Ak, Aziz Mahmut. 2010. 'Niiçin Federasyon?' *Sosyalist Mezopotamya* (27), *Mart*: 14-18.

Akat Ata, Ayla. 2012. 'Anayasa Çalışmaları ve Demokratik Özerklik'. In *Kürt Sorununun çözümü için Demokratik Özerklik*, 52-72. İstanbul: Aram Yayınları.

Akçam, Taner. 2004. *From Empire to Republic: Turkish Nationalism and the Armenian Genocide*. London: Zed Books.

Akdogan, Yalcin. 2006. 'The Meaning of Conservative Democratic Political Identity'. In *The Emergence of a New Turkey*, edited by M. Hakan Yavuz, 49-65. Utah: University of Utah Press.

Akdogan, Yalcin. 2011. 'Kurt Meselesin'de Paradigma Degisimi: Demokratik Acilim'. In *Turkiye'de Acilim Politikalari*, edited by Huseyin Yayman, 19-46. İstanbul: Meydan Yayincilik.

Akkaya, Ahmet Hamdi, and Joost Jongerden. 2013. 'Doğuştan Solcu; PKK'nin Ortaya Çıkışı'. In *Türkiye'de Milliyetçilik ve Politika: Politik İslam, Kemalizm ve Kürt Sorunu*, edited by Marlies Casier and Joost Jongerden, translated by Pınar Uygun, Batu Boran, Muhtesim Güvenç, and Metin Çulhaoğlu, 201-32. İstanbul: Vate.

Akkaya, Ahmet Hamdi, and Joost Jongerden. 2013. '2000'lerde PKK: Kirilmalara Rağmen Süreklilik?' In *Türkiye'de Milliyetçilik ve Politika: Politik İslam, Kemalizm ve Kürt Sorunu*, edited by Marlies Casier and Joost Jongerden, translated by Pınar Uygun, Batu Boran, Muhtesim Güvenç, and Metin Çulhaoğlu, 233-62. İstanbul: Vate.

Akkaya, Ahmet Hamdi, and Joost Jongerden. 2012. 'Reassembling the Political: The PKK and the Project of Radical Democracy'. *European Journal of Turkish Studies. Social Sciences on Contemporary Turkey* 14 (June): 1–18. https://ejts.revues.org/4615.

AKP Booklet; Demokratikleşme Adımlarının Bölgeye Yansımaları (2002–12). 2013.

Akpınar, Alişan, and Eugene L. Rogan. 2001. *Aşiret Mektep Devlet: Osmanlı Devletinde Aşiret Mektebi*. İstanbul: Aram.

Akşam Newspaper. 2013. 'İşte Öcalan'ın Mektubu'. 30 August. 21 Mart, http://www.aksam.com.tr/siyaset/iste-ocalanin-mektubu/haber-179573.

Aksoy, Gürdal. 1996. *Tarihi Yazılmayan Halk Kürtler*. İstanbul: Avesta.

Aktoprak, Elçin. 2010. *Devletler ve Ulusları: Bati Avrupa'da Milliyetçilik ve Ulusal Azınlık Sorunları*. Ankara: Tan.

Akyol, Mustafa. 2007. *Kürt Sorununu Yeniden Düşünmek; Yanlış Giden Neydi? Bundan Sonra Nereye Gider?* 5th ed. İstanbul: Dogan Kitap.

Alakom, Rohat. 1998. *Hoybun Örgütü ve Ağrı Ayaklanması*. İstanbul: Avesta.

Alba, Richard, and Victor Nee. 1997. 'Rethinking Assimilation Theory for a New Era of Immigration'. *International Migration Review; Special Issue: Immigrant Adaptation and Native-Born Responses in Making of Americans* 31 (4): 826–74.

Alınak, Mahmut. 1996. *HEP, DEP ve Devlet: Parlamento'dan 9. Koğuşa*. İstanbul: Kaynak Yayınları.

Ambrosius, Lloyde E. 1987. *Woodrow Wilson and the American Diplomatic Tradition*. Cambridge, New York, Port Chester, Melbourne, and Sydney: Cambridge University Press.

Amoretti, Ugo M. 2004. 'Introduction: Federalism and Territorial Cleavages'. In *Federalism and Territorial Cleavages*, edited by Nancy Bermeo and Ugo M. Amoretti, 1–23. Baltimore, MD and London: The Johns Hopkins University Press.

Anderson, Benedict. 1997. 'The Nation and the Origins of National Consciousness'. In *The Ethnicity Reader: Nationalism, Multiculturalism and Migration*, edited by Montserrat Guibernau and John Rex, 43–51. Cambridge: Polity Press.

Anderson, Benedict. 2006. *Imagined Communities*. Revised. London and New York: Verso.

Anderson, Lisa. 1987. 'The State in the Middle East and North Africa'. *Comparative Politics* 20 (1): 1–18.

Andrews, Peter A. 1992. *Türkiye'de Etnik Guruplar*. Translated by Mustafa Küpüşoğlu. İstanbul: ANT Yayınları.

Ankara Strateji Enstitüsü. 2013. *Çözüm Süreci*. 2013–2. Ankara.

ANF News. 2010. 'Ocalan Unveils Pillars of Democratic Autonomy'. 20 August 2010. https://anfenglish.com/news/ocalan-unveils-pillars-of-democratic-autonomy-1814.

Arakelova, Victoria. 1999. 'The Zaza People as a New Ethno-Political Factor in the Region'. *Iran and Caucasus* 3 (4): 397–408.

Aras, Ramazan. 2014. *The Formation of Kurdishness in Turkey: Political Violence, Fear and Pain*. New York: Routledge.

Arendt, Hannah. 1973. *The Origins of Totalitarianism*. San Diego, CA, New York and London: Harcourt Brace.

Aren, Sadun. 1993. *TİP Olayı (1961–71)*. İstanbul: Cem.

Arik, Selahattin Ali. 2011. *Dr. Şivan, Sait Elçi-Suleyman Muînî ve Kürt Trajedisi (1960–75)*. İstanbul: Pêrî.

Aristova, T.F. 2002. *Kürtlerin Maddi Kültürü*. Translated by İbrahim Kale and Arif Karabağ. İstanbul: Avesta.

Arnason, Johann P. 2006. 'Nations and Nationalisms: Between General Theory and Comparative History'. In *Nations and Nationalism*, edited by Gerard Delanty and Krishan Kumar, 44–56. London, Thousand Oaks, CA and New Delhi: Sage.

Arokan, Maya. 2014. 'Kurds at the Transition from the Ottoman Empire to the Turkish Republic'. *Turkish Policy Quarterly* 13 (1): 139–48.

Aroney, Nicholas. 2009. 'Before Federalism? Thomas Aquinas, Jena Quidort and Nicolas Cusanus'. In *The Ashgate Research Companion Federalism*, edited by Ann Ward and Lee Ward, 31–48. Surrey: Ashgate.

Arti Gercek. 2018. '3 yılda 11 bin 631 HDP'li gozaltına alındı, 3 bin 382'si ….' Arti Gercek. 3 September 2018. http://www.artigercek.com/3-yilda-11-bin-631-hdp-ligozaltina-alindi-3-bin-382-i-tutuklandi.

Asatrian, Garnik. 2009. 'Prolegomena to the Study of the Kurd: Research Papers from the Caucasian Centre for Iranian Studies, Yerevan'. In *Iran and the Caucasus*, 1–58. Leiden and Boston, MA: Brill.

Atacan, Fulya. 2001. 'A Kurdish Islamist Group in Modern Turkey: Shifting Identities'. *Middle Eastern Studies* 37 (3): 111–44.

Attar, Ali Rıza Ş. 2004. *Kürtler ve Bölgesel ve Bölge Dışı Güçler*. Translated by Alptekin Dursunoğlu. İstanbul: Anka.

Avery, Peter. 1965. *Modern Iran*. London: Ernest Benn Limited.

Avineri, Shlomo. 1987. 'Hegel, Georg Wilhelm Friedrich (1770–1831)'. In *The Blackwell Encyclopedia of Political Thought*, edited by David Miller, Janet Coleman, William Connolly, and Alan Ryan. Victoria: Blackwell Publishing.

Avyarov. 1995. *Osmanlı-Rus ve İran Savaşlar'ında Kürtler*. Translated by Muhammed Varlı. Ankara: Sipan.

Ayata, Ayşe-Güneş. 1992. *CHP (Örgüt ve İdeoloji)*. Translated by Belkıs Tarhan and Nüvit Tarhan. Ankara: Gündoğan.

Ayata, Sencer, and Ayşe-Güneş Ayata. 2007. 'The Center-Left Parties in Turkey'. *Turkish Studies* 8 (2): 211–32.

Aybar, Mehmet Ali. 1988. *TİP (Türkiye İşçi Partisi) Tarihi-3*. İstanbul: BDS.

Aydinkaya, Firat. 2012. 'Dördüncü Sait Dönemi: Nur Hareketlerinin Kürt Meselesine Bakışı'. *Dipnot* (11–12) (Ekim-Kasim-Aralik): 125–49.

Aydın, Osman. 2006. *1925 Kürt Ulusal Hareketi*. İkinci. İstanbul: Doz.

Aydıntaşbaş, Aslı. 2000. 'Murder on the Bosporus'. *Middle East Quarterly* VII (2): 15–22.

Aydın, Zülküf. 2005. *The Political Economy of Turkey*. London and Ann Arbor, MI: Pluto Press.

Aziz, Mahir. 2011. *The Kurds of Iraq: Ethnonationalism and National Identity in Iraqi Kurdistan*. New York: I.B.Tauris.

Bachtiger, Andre, and Jurg Steiner. 2004. 'Territorial Cleavage Management as Paragon and Paradox'. In *Federalism and Territorial Cleavages*, edited by Ugo M. Amoretti and Nancy Bermeo, 27–54. Baltimore, MD and London: The Johns Hopkins University Press.

Bahçeli, Tözün, and Said Noel. 2013. 'Adalet ve Kalkınma Paetisi ve Kürt Meselesi'. In *Türkiye'de Milliyetçilik ve Politika: Politik İslam, Kemalizm ve Kürt Sorunu*, edited by Marlies Casier and Joost Jongerden, translated by Pınar Uygun, Batu Boran, Muhtesim Güvenç, and Metin Çulhaoğlu, 163–98. İstanbul: Vate.

Bajalan, Djene Rhys. 2010. *Jön Kürtler: Birinci Dünya Savaþý'ndan Önce Kürt Harekaeti (1898–1914)*. Translated by Burcu Yalçınkaya. İstanbul: Avesta.

Bali, Rifat N. 2006. 'The Politics of Turkification during the Single Party Period'. In *Turkey beyond Nationalism: Towards Post-Nationalist Identities*, edited by Hans-Lukas Keiser, 43–49. London and New York: I.B.Tauris.

Ballı, Rafet. 1991. *Kürt Dosyası*. İstanbul: cem yayınevi.

Barış ve Demokrasi Partisi Tüzüğü. 2008. https://bdpblog.wordpress.com/parti-tuzugumuz/.

Barkey, Henri J. 2000. 'The Struggles of a "Strong State"'. *Journal of International Affairs* 51 (1): 87–105.

Barkey, Henri J. 2009. *Preventing Conflict over Kurdistan*. Washington, DC: Carnegıe Endowment. www.CarnegieEndowment.org/pubs.

Barkey, Henri J., and Graham E. Fuller. 1998. *Turkey's Kurdish Question*. Lanham, MD, New York and Oxford: Rowman & Littlefield Publishers.

Barkey, Karen, and Sunita Parikh. 1991. 'Comparative Perspectives on the State'. *Annual Review of Sociology* 17: 523–49.

Barth, Fredrik. 1953. *Principles of Social Organization in South Kurdistan*. Oslo: Brødrene Jørgensen.

Başaran, Orhan. 2002. 'İdris-I Bitlisi Hakkında Bazı Yeni Bilgiler'. Akademik Araştırmalar Dergisi (14): 201–8.

Bayrak, Mehmet. 2009. *Kürtler'e Vurulan Kelepçe: Şark Islahat Planı*. Ankara: Özge.

Bayrak, Mehmet. 2010. *Dersim-Koçgiri: Te'dib-Tenkil-Taqtil-Tehcir-Temsil-Temdin-Tasfiye*. Ankara: Özge.

Bayrak, Mehmet. 2011. *Bir Siyaset Tarzı Olarak Alevi Katliamları*. Ankara: Özge.

Bayraktar, Mehmet. 2006. *Kutlu Müderris İdris-î Bitlisî*. İstanbul: Biyografi net.

BBC News. 2000. 'More Bodies in Hezbollah Probe'. 23 January 2000. http://news.bbc.co.uk/1/hi/world/europe/615070.stm.

BBC News. 2013. 'Turkey Kurds: PKK Chief Ocalan Calls for Ceasefire'. *BBC News*, 21 March 2013, sec. Europe. http://www.bbc.co.uk/news/world-europe-21874427.

BBC Türkçe. 2012. 'Oslo süreci neden tıkandı?' 24 September 2012. http://www.bbc.com/turkce/haberler/2012/09/120924_oslo_pkk.shtml.

BBC Türkçe. 2017. 'BM Raporu: Güneydoğu'da 18 Ayda Yaşanan Ölüm ve Yıkımlar Soruşturulsun'. *BBC Türkçe*, 10 March 2017, sec. Türkiye. http://www.bbc.com/turkce/haberler-turkiye-39230287.

Beck, Lois. 1990. 'Tribe and State in Nineteenth-and Twentieth-Century Iran'. In *Tribes and State Formation in the Middle East*, edited by Philip S. Khoury and Joseph Kostiner, 185–225. Berkeley: University of California Press.

Bedirhan, Süreyya. 1994. *Kürt Dosyası ve Hoybun*. Translated by Zîrek Dîlara. İstanbul: Med.

Beland, Daniel, and Andre Lecours. 2007. 'Federalism, Nationalism, and Social Policy Decentralisation in Canada and Belgium'. *Regional and Federal Studies* 17 (4): 405–19.

Bell, Daniell. 1975. 'Ethnicity and Social Change'. In *Ethnicity: Theory and Experience*, edited by Nathan Glazer and Daniel P. Moynihan, 141–74. Cambridge, MA: Harvard University Press.

Beller-Han, Ildiko, and Chris Hann. 2001. *Turkish Region*. Oxford: James Currey.

Bender, Cemşid. 1991. *Kürt Tarihi ve Uygarlığı*. İstanbul: Kaynak.

Ben-Dor, Gabriel. 2004. 'Etno-Politiakalar ve Ortadoğu Devleti'. In *Ortadoğu'da Etnisite, Çoğulculuk ve Devlet*, edited by Milton J. Esman and İtamar Rabinoviç, translated by Zafer Avşar, 109–38. İstanbul: Avesta.

Beramendi, Pablo, and Ramon Maiz. 2004. 'Spain: Unfulfilled Federalism (1978–96)'. In *Federalism and Territorial Cleavages*, edited by Ugo M. Amoretti and Nancy Bermeo, 123–54. Baltimore, MD and London: The Johns Hopkins University Press.

Beşikçi, İsmail. 1969a. *Doğuda Değişim ve Yapısal Sorunlar: Göçebe Alikan Aşireti*. Ankara: Doğan Yayınevi.

Beşikçi, İsmail. 1969b. *Doğu Anadolu'nun Düzeni: Sosyo-Ekonomik ve Etnik Temeller*. Ankara: e.yayınları.

Beşikçi, İsmail. 1977. *Bilim Yöntemi Türkiyede'ki Uygulamaları-1: Kürtlerin Mecburi Iskanı*. İstanbul: Komal.

Beşikçi, İsmail. 1990. *Devletlerarası Sömürge, Kürdistan*. 1st ed. İstanbul: Alan Yayıncılık.

Beşikçi, İsmail. 1991. *Türk Tarih Tezi Güneş Dil-Dil Teorisi*. Ankara: Yurt Kitap Yayın.

Beşikçi, İsmail. 1992. *PKK Üzerine Düşünceler;özgrlüğün Bedeli*. İstanbul: Melsa.

Beşikçi, İsmail. 1993. *Kendini Keşfeden Ulus Kürtler*. Ankara: Yurt Yayınları.

Beşikçi, İsmail. 2008. *Ziman-Nasname-Netewe Û Netewperwerî*. Translated by Roşan Lezîn. İstanbul: Pêrî.

Beşikçi, İsmail. 2013. *Develt ve Kürtler: Dil, Kimlik, Millet, Milliyetçilik (Makaleler 2005–13)*. İstanbul: İsmail Beşikçi Vakfı Yayınları.

Biersteker, Thomas. 2013. 'State, Sovereignty and Territory'. In *Handbook of International Relations*, edited by Walter Carlsnaes, Thomas Risse, and Beth

A. Simmons, 245–72. Los Angeles, CA, London, New Delhi, Singapore and Washington, DC: Sage.

Bilim Aydınlanma Komitesi. 2009. *Kürt Sorununda Çözüme Doğru: Demokratik Özerklik*. Cologne, Germany: Weşanên Serxwebûn, 146.

Blaike, Norman. 2000. *Designing Social Research: The Logic of Anticipation*. Cambridge: Polity.

Blau, Joyce. 1996. 'Kurdish Written Language'. In *Kurdish Culture and Identity*, edited by Philip G. Kreyenbroek and Christine Allison, 20–28. London and New Jersey: Zed Books.

Blau, Joyce. 2006. 'Refinement and Oppression of Kurdish Language'. In *The Kurds: Nationalism and Politics*, edited by Faleh A. Jabar and Hosham Dawod, 103–12. London, San Francisco, CA and Beirut: Saqi.

Blondel, Jean. 2004. *Comparative Government: An Introduction*. 6th ed. London: Palgrave Macmillan.

Bois, Thomas. 1966. *The Kurds*. Translated by M.W. M Welland. Beirut: Khayats.

Borchgrevink, Tordis, and Grete Brochmann. 2003. 'Comparing Minority and Majority Rights: Multicultural Integration in a Power Perspective'. In *The Multicultural Challenge*, edited by Grete Brochmann, 69–99. Amsterdam, Boston, MA, Heidelberg, London and New York: Elsevier.

Bozarslan, Hamit. 2002. 'Kürd Miilliyetçiliği ve Kürd Hareketi (1898–2000)'. In *Modern Türkiye'de Siyasi Düşünce: Milliyetçilik*, edited by Tanıl Bora and Murat Gültekingil, 4: 841–70. İstanbul: İletişim.

Bozarslan, Hamit. 2004a. *Türkiye'nin Modern Tarihi*. Translated by Heval Bucak. İstanbul: Avesta.

Bozarslan, Hamit. 2004b. 'The Kurdish Question: Can It Be Solved within Europe'. In *Turkey Today a European Country?* edited by Olivier Roy, translated by Monica Sandor, 72–89. London: Anthem Press.

Bozarslan, Hamit. 2005. 'Türkiye'de Kürt Milliyetçiliği: Zımni Sözleşmeden İsyana (1919–25)'. In *Kürt Milliyetçiliğinin Kökenleri*, edited by Abbas Vali, translated by Fahriye Adsay, Ümit Aydoğmuş, and Sema Kılıç, 199–230. İstanbul: Avesta.

Bozarslan, Hamit. 2007. 'Türkiye'de Kürt Sol Hareketi'. In *Modern Türkiye'de Siyasi Düşünce: Sol*, edited by Tanıl Bora and Murat Gültekingil, 1169–1206. İstanbul: İletişim Yayınları.

Bozarslan, M. Emin, trans. 1988. 'Kürt Talebe Hêvî Cemiyeti Beyannamesi'. *Jîn* (1918–19).

Bozyel, Bayram. 2012. 'Kürt Halkı Mutlaka Kazanacaktır'. *Deng* (89), November: 24–34.

Brass, Paul R. 1996. 'Ethnic Groups and Ethnic Identity Formation'. In *Ethnicity*, edited by John Hutchinson and Anthony D. Smith, 85–90. Oxford and New York: Oxford University Press.

Breuilly, John. 2005. 'Dating the Nation: How Old Is an Old Nation?' In *When Is the Nation? Towards an Understanding of Theories of Nationalism*, edited by Atsuko Ichijo and Gordana Uzelac, 13–39. New York: Routledge.

Brochmann, Grete. 2003. 'Citizenship of Multicultural States: Power and Legitimacy'. In *The Multicultural Challenge*, edited by Grete Brochmann, 1-11. Amsterdam, Boston, MA, Heidelberg, London and New York: Elsevier.

Brown, Bernard E. 2006. *Comparative Politics*. Tent. Belmont: Thomson Wadsorth.

Brown, David L., and Kai A. Schafft. 2011. *Rural People and Communities in the 21st Century Resilience and Transformation*. Cambridge: Polity.

Brubaker, Rogers, and David L. Laitin. 1998. 'Ethnic and Nationalist Violence'. *Annual Review of Sociology* 24: 423-52.

Bruer, Stefan. 2010. *Milliyetçilikler ve Faşizmler; Fransa, İtalya ve Fransa Örnekleri*. Translated by Çiğdem Canan Dikmen. İstanbul: İletişim.

Buchanan, Allen. 1991. *Secession: The Morality of Political Divorce from Fort Sumter to Lithuania and Quebec*. Boulder, CO, San Francisco, CA and Oxford: Westview Press.

Budeiri, Musa. 1997. 'The Palestinians: Tensions between Nationalist and Religious Identities'. In *Rethinking Nationalism in the Arab Middle East*, edited by İsrael Gershoni and James Jankowski, 191-206. New York: Colombia University.

Bulut, Faik. 2005. *Kürdistan'da Etnik Çatışmalar: Dar Üçgende Üç İsyan*. 2nd ed. İstanbul: Everest Yayınları.

Bulut, Faik. 2009. *İslamcı Örgütler 3*. 4th ed. İstanbul: Cumhuriyet Kitapları.

Buran, Ali. 2011. *Bir DDKO'lunun Kürt Yaşamı*. İstanbul: Pêrî.

Burgess, Michael. 1993. 'Federalism and Federation: A Reappraisal'. In *Comparative Federalism and Federation; Competing Traditions and Future Directions*, edited by Michael Burgess and Alain G. Gagnon, 3-14. New York, London and Toronto: Harvester Wheatsheaf.

Burkay, Kemal. 1992. *Geçmişten Günümüze Kürtler ve Kürdistan*. Cilt 1. İstanbul: Deng Yayınları.

Burkay, Kemal. 2002. *Anılar Belgeler Cilt 1*. Vol. 1. İstanbul: Deng Yayınları.

Burkay, Kemal. 2004. *Kurdish Question and Socialist Party of Kurdistan*. Bromma: Roja nû publications.

Burkay, Kemal. 2010. *Anılar Belgeler Cilt 2*. 2nd ed. İstanbul: Deng Yayınları.

Burkay, Kemal. 2012a. 'Eşitlik Temelinde Bir Çözüm Istiyoruz. Bunun Biçimi Federasyondur'. *Deng* (89), *November*: 11-23.

Burkay, Kemal. 2012b. 'Hak-Par 5. Olağan Kongresi (4 Kasım 2012)'. (Kemal Burkay 5. Olağan Kongre Konuşması)

Burulday, Irfan. 2013. 'Siyasal Değişim-Dönüşüm Ekseninde Kürdler ve Kürdistan'. *Bağımsız ve Özgür Kürdistan*. Agustos. http://irfanburulday.blogspot.co.uk/2013_08_01_archive.html (Accessed 20 February 2014, 13:49).

Büyükkaya, Necmettin. 2008. *Kalemimden Sayfalar*. İstanbul: Vate.

Cağatay, Soner. 2014. *Turkey's Presidential Prospects, Assessing Recent Trends*. 18. The Washington Institute for Near East Policy. http://www.washingtoninstitute.org/uploads/Documents/pubs/ResearchNote18_Cagaptay.pdf.

Cağlıyan-İcener, Zeyneb. 2009. 'The Justice and Development Party's Conception of "Conservative Democracy": Invention or Reinterpretation?' *Turkish Studies* 10 (4): 595-612.

Caha, Omer, Metin Toprak, and Nasuh Uslu. 2010. 'Religion and Ethnicity in the Construction of Official Ideology in Republican Turkey'. *The Muslim World* 100 (January): 33–44.

Cairns, Ed, and Mícheál Roe. 2003. 'Introduction: Why Memories in Conflict?' In *The Role of Memory in Ethnic Conflict*, edited by Ed Cairns and Mícheál Roe, 3–8. New York: Palgrave Macmillan.

Cairns, Ed, and Mícheál Roe. 2011. *12 Eylül'den 12 Haziran'a Siyasi Partiler-Barış ve Demokrasi Partisi (BDP)*. İstanbul: SETA Analiz.

Cakır, Ruşen. 2011a. *Derin Hizbulah: İslamcı Şiddetin Gelceği*. İkinci. İstanbul: Metis.

Calışlar, Oral. 2013. 'The Kurdısh Issue in Turkey: Its Social, Political, and Cultural Dimensions'. In *Understanding Turkey's Kurdish Question*, 29–46. Lanham, MD, Boulder, CO, New York, Toronto and Plymouth: Lexington Books.

Calhoun, Craig. 1993. 'Nationalism and Ethnicity'. *Annual Review of Sociology* 19: 211–39.

Calmuk, Fehmi. 2001. *Erbakan'in Kurtleri: Milli Gorus'un Guneydogu Politikasi*. İstanbul: Siyah beyaz.

Camlıbel, Yılmaz. 2007. *49'lar Davası: Bir Garip Davanın Idamlık Kurtleri*. Ankara: algıyayın.

Candar, Cengiz. 2011. *Dağdan İniş – PKK Nasıl Silah Bırakır? Kurt Sorunu'nun Şiddetten Arındırılması*. İstanbul: TESEV.

Candar, Cengiz. 2013. 'On Turkey's Kurdish Question: Its Roots, Present State, Prospects'. In *Understanding Turkey's Kurdish Question*, edited by Fevzi Bilgin and Ali Sarihan, 59–72. Lanham, MD, Boulder, CO, New York, Toronto and Plymouth: Lexington Books.

Canefe, Nergis. 2007. *Anavatandan Yavruvatana: Milliyetçilik, Bellek ve Aidiyet*. Translated by Deniz Boyraz. İstanbul: İstanbul Bilgi üniversitesi yayınları.

Canlı, Cemalettin, and Yusuf Kenan Beysülen. 2010. *Zaman Içinde Bediüzaman*. İstanbul: İletişim.

Carley, Patricia. 1995. *Self-Determination Sovereignty, Territorial Integrity, and the Right to Secession*. Self-Determination; Sovereignty, Territorial Integrity, and the Right to Secession. United States Institute of Peace. http://www.usip.org/sites/default/files/pwks7.pdf.

Casals, Neus Torbisco. 2006. *Group Rights as Human Rights: A Liberal Approach to Multiculturalism*. Dordrecht: Springer.

Castless, Steven, Bill Cope, Mary Kalantzis, and Michael Morrissey. 1996. 'Australia: Multi-Ethnic Community without Nationalism?' In *Ethnicity*, edited by John Hutchinson and Anthony D. Smith, 358–67. Oxford and New York: Oxford University Press.

Cay, Abdulhaluk. M. 2010. *Kurt Dosyası*. 8 Baskı. İstanbul: İlgi Kultur Sanat Yayıncılık.

Cederman, Lars-Erik, Andreas Wimmer, and Brian Min. 2010. 'Why Do Ethnic Groups Rebel?: New Data and Analysis'. *World Politics* 62 (1): 87–119.

CEFTUS. 2013. 'CEFTUS Insights: Interview with Altan Tan, Peace and Democracy Party (BDP) MP, by Deniz Çifçi, Zeynep Kösereisoglu, Serdar Sengul, Buket Bora,

Deniz Çifçi and Jonathan Friedman'. 28 January 2014. http://ceftus.org/2014/01/28/ceftus-insights-interview-with-altan-tan-peace-and-democracy-party-bdp-mp/#.VGELwvSUefM.

CEFTUS. 2013. 'CEFTUS Insights: Interview with Abdulrahman Kurds by Deniz Çifçi, Buket Bora, Nazli Akyuz, Zeynep Kösereisoglu, Serdar Sengul, and Josie Delves'. 9 October. http://ceftus.org/2014/02/07/ceftus-insights-interview-with-abdurrahman-kurt/#.VHN1s2SUci4.

Celik, Ayşe Betul. 2012. 'Ethnopolitical Conflict in Turkey: From the Denial of the Kurds to Peaceful Co-existence'. In *Handbook of Ethnic Conflict: International Perspectives*, 241–61. New York, Heidelberg and London: Springer.

Celik, Demir. 2012a. 'Cozum Modeli Icin Demokratik Ozerklik'. In *Kurt Sorununun Cozulmesi Icin Demokratik Ozerklik*, 25–35. İstanbul: Aram Yayınları.

Celik, Demir. 2012b. 'Demokratik Ozerkliğin Siyasi Boyutu in "Kurt Sorununun Cozumu Icin Demokratik Ozerklik"', 107–44. İstanbul: Aram Yayınları.

Celil, Celilé. 1992. *XIX. Yüzyıl Osmanlı İmparatorluğu'nda Kürtler*. Translated by Mehmet Demir. Ankara: Özge.

Celil, Celilé, M.S. Lazarev, O.İ. Jagalina, M.A. Gasaratyan, and M.A Mıhoyan. 1998. *Yeni ve Yakın Çağda Kürt Siyaset Tarihi*. Translated by M. Aras. İstanbul: Pérî.

Cevdet, Abdullah. 1913. 'Bir Hitab'. *Rojî Kurd* (1): 17–18.

Chaliand, Gerard. 1994. *The Kurdish Tragedy*. Translated by Philip Black. London and New Jersey: Zed Books.

Charter of United Nations and Statute of the International Court of Justice. 1945. https://treaties.un.org/doc/publication/ctc/uncharter.pdf.

Chomsky, Noam, and Samir Amin. 1995. *Düşük Yoğunlulu Demokrasi, Yeni Dünya Düzeni ve Politik Güçler*. Translated by Ahmet Fethi. İstanbul: Alan.

Christiano, Kevin J., William H. Swatos JR, and Peter Kivisto. 2008. *Sociology of Religion: Contemporary Developments*. Second. Lanham, MD, Boulder, CO, New York, Toronto and Plymouth: Rowman& Littlefield Publishers.

Cicek, Cuma. 2011. 'Elimination or Integration of Pro-Kurdish Politics: Limits of the AKP's Democratic Initiative'. *Turkish Studies* 12 (1): 15–26.

Cicek, Nevzat. 2010. *27 Mayıs'ın Oteki Yuzu*. İstanbul: Lagin.

Çifçi, Deniz. 2014. 'HÜDA-PAR: Kaybeden Mi Kazanan Mı?' Radikal. 15 April 2014. http://www.radikal.com.tr/yenisoz/huda_par_kaybeden_mi_kazanan_mi-1186839/.

Çıla. 2013. 'FDG: İslam Temelli Barış Bizi Endişelendiriyor,' 24 March. http://www.cilagazete.com/fdg-islam-temelli-baris-bizi-endiselendiriyor-3/, accessed at 17;13.

Ciment, James. 1996. *The Kurds: State and Minority in Turkey, Iraq and Iran*. New York: Facts On File, Inc.

Clark, Gordon L. 1984. 'A Theory of Local Autonomy'. *Annals of the Association of American Geographers* 74 (2): 195–208.

Clark, William Roberts, Mark Golder, and Sona Nadenichek-Golder. 2009. *Principles of Comparative Politics*. Washington, DC: CQ Press.

Cleveland, William L. 2008. *Modern Ortadoğu Tarihi*. Translated by M. Harmanı. İstanbul: Agora Kitaplığı.

Coakley, John. 2003. 'Introduction: The Challenge'. In *The Territorial Management of Ethnic Conflict*, edited by John Coakley, Second revised and expanded edition, 1–22. London and Portland, OR: Frank Cass.

Coakley, John. 2004. 'Religion and Nationalism in the First World'. In *Ethnonationalism in the Contemporary World*, edited by Daniele Conversi, 206–25. New York: Routledge.

Cockburn, Patrick. 2017. 'Kurds Face Transformation of Iraq's Political Map as They Lose Territory in Face of Government Advance'. *The Independent*. 17 October 2017. http://www.independent.co.uk/news/world/middle-east/iraq-kirkuk-battle-withdrawal-peshmerga-baghdad-latest-advance-disaster-a8006036.html.

Cohen, Erik H. 2004. 'Components and Symbols of Ethnic Identity: A Case Study in Informal Education and Identity Formation in Diaspora'. *International Association for Applied Psychology* 53 (1): 87–112.

Cohen, Ronald. 1984. 'Warfare and State Formation: War Makes States and States Make War'. In *Warfare, Culture, and Environment*, edited by Brain R. Ferguson, 329–58. Orlando, FL: Academic Press.

Cole, James. 2014. 'The Identity Model; A Theory to Access Visual Display and Hominin Cognition within the Palaeolithic'. In *Lucy to Language: The Benchmark Papers*, edited by R.I. Dubar, Clive Gamle, and A.J. Gowlett, 90–107. Oxford: Oxford University Press.

Cole, Juan R.L., and Deniz Kandiyoti. 2002. 'Nationalism and Colonial Legacy in the Middle East and Central Asia: Introduction'. *J. Middle East Studies* 34 (2): 189–203.

Connor, Walker. 2004. 'Nationalism and Political Illegitimacy'. In *Ethnonationalism in the Contemporary World*, edited by Daniele Conversi, 24–49. New York: Routledge.

Conversi, Daniele. 2000. 'From Centralist Dictatorship to Federal Democracy: The Case of Spain'. In *Redefining the Nation, State and Citizen*, by Günay Göksu Özdoğan and Gül Tokay, 151–75. İstanbul: Eren.

Conversi, Daniele. 2004. 'Conceptualizing Nationalism: An Introduction to Walker Connor's Work'. In *Ethnonationalism in the Contemporary World*, edited by Daniele Conversi, 1–23. New York: Routledge.

Cook, Terrence E. 2003. *Separation, Assimilation, or Accommodation*. Westport, CT: Greenwood (Prager).

Coontz, Phyllis D. 1986. 'The Etymology of Minority and Women in International Law'. In *International Protection of Minorities*, edited by Satist Chandra, 154–67. Delhi: Mittal Publications.

Corbin, Henry. 1993. *History of Islamic Philosophy*. Translated by Liadain with the assistance of Philip Sherrard. Reprint ed. London and New York: Kegan Paul International.

Cornelia, Navari. 1981. 'The Origins of the Nation-State'. In *The Nation-State: The Formation of Modern Politics*, edited by Leonard Tivey, 13–38. Oxford: Martin Robertson.

Cowan, Jane K., Marie-Bènèdicte Dembour, and Rochard A. Wilson. 2001. 'Introduction'. In *Culture and Rights*, edited by Jane K. Cowan, Marie-Bènèdicte Dembour, and Rochard A. Wilson, 1–26. Cambridge: Cambria press.

Crawford, James. 2006. *The Creation of States in International Law*. Second. Oxford: Clarendon Press.

Creswell, John W. 2009. *Research Design: Qualitative, Quantitative, and Mixed Methods Approaches*. Third. Los Angeles, London, New Delhi and Singapore: Sage Publication.

Cumhurriyet. 2016. 'Arınç Canlı Yayında Erdoğan'ı Yalanladı: Görüşmelerden Haberi Vardı'. 29 January 2016. http://www.cumhuriyet.com.tr/haber/siyaset/472408/Arinc_canli_yayinda_Erdogan_i_yalanladi__Gorusmelerden_haberi_vardi.html.

Cumhurriyet Halk Partisi Tüzük. 2012. The PDF draft of the party's rules and regulations is available on the party's official website; http://content.chp.org.tr/file/chp_tuzuk_10_03_2018.pdf.

Cumhurriyet Halk Partis Programı. 2013. The PDF draft of the party's program is available on the party's official website; https://chp.azureedge.net/1d48b01630ef43d9b2edf45d55842cae.pdf.

Dahlman, Carl. 2002. 'The Political Geography of Kurdistan'. *Eurasian Geography and Economics*, 4 (43): 271–99.

Daily Sabah. 2014. 'More Police Officers behind Bars over Espionage, Prosecutor Seeks Arrest of 13 Others'. DailySabah. 8 July 2014. https://www.dailysabah.com/politics/2014/08/08/more-police-officers-behind-bars-over-espionage-prosecutor-seeks-arrest-of-13-others.

Daily Sabah. 2015. 'Erdoğan Renounces Dolmabahçe Declaration, Says HDP Should Try Its Best for PKK's Disarmament'. 17 July 2015. https://www.dailysabah.com/politics/2015/07/17/erdogan-renounces-dolmabahce-declaration-says-hdp-should-try-its-best-for-pkks-disarmament.

Dare, L.O. 1979. 'Perspectives on Federalism'. In *Readings on Federalism*, edited by A.B. Akinyemi, P.D. Cole, and Walter Ofonagoro, 26–35. Lagos: Nigerian Institute of International Affairs.

Das, Arvind N. 1975. 'Theories of State: Aristotle to Marx'. *Social Scientist* 3 (8): 63–69.

DAVA Dergisi. 1993. 'Bediüzzamanın Ölümünden Sonra Gelişen Nur Ekolü'. *DAVA* (36) (March): 12–14.

Davison, Roderic H. 1998. *Turkey: A Short History*. Third (Updated by Clement H. Dodd). Huntingdon: The Eothen Press.

Demokratik Bolgeler Partisi Tuzuğu. 2016. 'Demokratik Bölgeler Partisi Programı'. *Demokratik Bölgeler Partisi* (blog). 2016. http://www.dbp.org.tr/index/partidetay/demokratik-bolgeler-partisi-tuzugu-12476027/.

Deth, Jan W. Van, and Kenneth Newton. 2005. *Foundation of Comparative Politics*. Cambridge: Cambridge University Press.

Dinçşahin, Şakir. 2012. 'A Symptomatic Analysis of the Justice and Development Party's Populism in Turkey, 2007–10'. *An International Journal of Comperative Politics* 47 (4): 618–40.

Dodd, C.H. 1992. 'The Development of Turkish Democracy'. *British Journal of Middle Eastern Studies* 19 (1): 16–30.

Doğan, Tuğba. 2012. 'Arşiv Belgelerine Göre 1937–38 Dersim İsyani'. *History Studies International Journal of History* 4 (1): 157–69.

Draft Submission for a Democratic Autonomous Kurdistan. 2011. Drafted by Democracy Society Congress (Hand book).

Drucker, Peter F. 1997. 'The Global Economy and the Nation-State'. *Foreign Affairs* 76 (5): 159–71.

Dumont, Paul. 1984. 'The Origins of Kemalist Ideology'. In *Atatürk and the Modernization of Turkey*, edited by Jacob M. Landau, 25–44. Boulder, CO: Westview Press.

Duncan, Raymond, Barbara Jancar-Webster, and Bob Switky. 2009. *World Politics in the 21st Century: Student Choice.* Boston, MA: Houghton Mifflin Harcourt.

Dündar, Fuat. 2006. 'The Settlement Policy of the Committee of Union and Progress Party'. In *Turkey beyond Nationalism: Towards Post-Nationalist Identities*, edited by Hans-Lukas Kieser, 37–42. London and New York: I.B.Tauris.

Dunleavy, Patrick, and Brendan O'leary. 1987. *Theories of the State: The Politics of Liberal Democracy.* London: Macmillan.

Duran, Burhanettin. 1998. 'Approaching the Kurdish Question via Adil Düzen: An Islamist Formula of the Welfare Party for Ethnic Coexistence'. *Journal of Muslim Minority Affairs* 18 (1): 111–28.

Dursun (Seyhanzade), M.Sıddık. 1993. 'Hutbe-I Şamiye Üzerine'. *DAVA*, (43–44) (Ekim Kasım): 27–47.

Dursun (Seyhanzade), M.Sıddık.1998. 'Nurani Mudafa'. *DAVA* (86) (Temmuz-Agustos-Eylul): 5–12.

Düzgit Aydın, Senem, and Ruşen Çakır. 2009. 'Turkey: A Sustainable Case of De-radicalisation?' In *Islamic Radicalisation the Challenge for Euro-Mediterranean Relations*, edited by Michael Emerson, Kristina Kausch, and Richards Youngs, 87–107. Brussel: Center for European Policy Studies.

Efegil, Ertan. 2011. 'Analysis of the AKP Government's Policy toward the Kurdish Issue'. *Turkish Studies* 12 (1): 27–40.

Ehmedê Xanî (1695). 1990. *Mem û Zîn*. Translated by Mehmet Emin Bozarslan. 3rd ed. İstanbul: Hasat Yayınları.

Eide, Asbørn. 1998. 'Cultural Autonomy: The Concept, Content, History and Role in the World Order'. In *Autonomy: Applications and Implications*, edited by Markku Suksi, 251–76. The Hague, London and Boston, MA: Kluwer Law.

Eisenhardt, Kathleen M. 1989. 'Building Theories from Case Study Research'. *The Academy of Management Review*, 14 (4): 532–50.

Ekinci, Tarık Ziya. 2010. *Lice'den Paris'e Anılarım*. İstanbul: İletişim.

Ekinci, Tarık Ziya. 2011. *Kürt Siyasal Hareketlerinin Sınıfsal Analizi*. İstanbul: Sosyal Tarih Yayınları.

Ekrem Cemil Paşa. 1995. *Dîroka Kurdîstan Bi Kurteberî*. Brukselê: Enstituya Kurdî Ya Brukselê.

Elazar, Daniel J. 2006. *Exploring Federalism*. Alabama: The University of Alabama Press.
Enloe, Cynthia. 1996. 'Religion and Ethnicity'. In *Ethnicity*, edited by John Hutchinson and Anthony D. Smith, 197–202. Oxford and New York: Oxford University Press.
Epözdemir, Şakir. 2005. *Türkiye Kürdistan Demokrat Partisi 1968/235 Antalya Savunma Davası*. İstanbul: Pêrî.
Eppel, Michael. 2014. 'Historical Settings: The Roots of Modern Kurdish Nationalism'. In *Kurdish Awakening: Nation Building in a Fragmented Homeland*, edited by Ofra Bengio, 37–62. Austin: University of Texas Press.
Erdoğan, Mustafa. 2009. 'Türkiye'nin Kürt Sorunu'. In *Güneydoğu Sorunu: Tarihi-Kaynağı-Çözümü*, edited by Risale-i Nur Enstitüsü, 61–74. İstanbul: Yeni Asya Yayınları.
Eriksen, Thomas Hylland. 1992. 'Linguistic Hegemony and Minority Resistance'. *Journal of Peace Research* 29 (3): 313–32.
Eriksen, Thomas Hylland. 1997. 'Ethnicity, Race and Nation'. In *The Ethnicity Reader: Nationalism, Multiculturalism and Migration*, edited by Montserrat Guibernau and John Rex, 33–42. Cambridge: Polity Press.
Eriksen, Thomas Hylland. 2002. *Etnisite ve Milliyetcilik: Antropolojik Bir Bakış*. Translated by Ekin Usakli. İstanbul: Avesta.
Ersanlı, Büşra, and Halil Bayhan. 2012. 'Demokratik Özerklik: Statü Talebi ve Demokratikleşme Arzusu'. In *Türkiye Siyasetinde Kürtler: Direniş, Hak Arayışı, Katılım*, edited by Büşra Ersanlı, Nesrin Göksu Özdoğan, and Nesrin Uçarlar, 203–50. İstanbul: İletişim.
Eryıldız, Semih. 2012. *Yerinde Yönetişim Özerklik: Basklar Kürtler Katalanlar*. İstanbul: Algı.
Esman, Milton J., and Itamar Rabinovic. 2004. 'Ortadoğuda Etno-Politika Çalışamaları'. In *Ortadoğu'da Etnisite, Çoğulculuk ve Devlet*, edited by Milton J. Esman and Itamar Rabinoviç, translated by Zafer Avşar, 17–46. İstanbul: Avesta.
European Charter of Local Self-Government. 1985. *European Charter of Local Self-Government*. 122. Council of Europe. http://unipd-centrodirittiumani.it/public/docs/self_government_coe.pdf (Accessed 11 May 2014; 15;03).
Fenton, Steve. 2003. *Ethnicity*. Cambridge: Polity Press.
Findley, Carter Vaughn. 2010. *Turkey, Islam, Nationalism, and Modernity*. New Haven, CT and London: Yale University Press.
Fırat, Mehmet Ş. 1970. *Doğu İlleri ve Varto Tarihi*. Üçüncü. Ankara: Kardeş.
Flyvbjerg, Bent. 2006. 'Five Misunderstandings about Case-Study Research'. *Qualitative Inquiry* 12 (2): 219–45.
Friedman, Jonathan. 1994. *Cultural Identity and Global Process*. London, Thousand Oaks, CA and New Delhi: Sage.
Friendly Relations Declaration (FRD) 1970. 'Declaration on Principles of International Law Concerning Friendly Relations and Co-operation among States in Accordance with the Charter of the United Nations (GAR 2625)'. UN General Assembly Resolution 2625 (XXV) of 24 October 1970.

Fuccaro, Nelida. 1999. *The Other Kurds: Yazidis in Colonial Iraq*. New York: I.B.Tauris.
Fuccaro, Nelida. 2012. 'Sömürge Yönetimi Altındaki Suriye'de Kürtler ve Kürt Milliyetçiliği: Siyaset, Kültür ve Kimlik'. In *Geşepèdanèn Rojhelatanavîn, Sûrye Û Kurdistana Rojava (Ortadoğu, Suriye ve Batı Kürdistandaki Gelişmeler)*, edited by Seid Veroj, 87–118. İstanbul: Doz.
Fuller, Graham E. 2008. *The New Turkish Republic: Turkey as a Pivotal State in the Muslim World*. Washington, DC: United States Institute of Peace Press.
Gagnon, Alain G. 1993. 'The Political Uses of Federalism'. In *Comparative Federalism and Federation; Competing Traditions and Future Directions*, edited by Michael Burgess and Alain G. Gagnon, 15–44. New York, London and Toronto: Harvester Wheatsheaf.
Galnoor, Itzhak. 1995. *The Partition of Palestine: Decision Crossroads in the Zionist Movement*. Albany, NY: State University of New York Press.
Gambetti, Zeynep. 2007. 'Linç Girişimleri, Neoliberalizm ve Güvenlik Devleti'. *Toplum ve Bilim*, (109) (Yaz): 7–34.
The Guardian. 2017. 'More than 92% of Voters in Iraqi Kurdistan Back Independence | World News | The Guardian'. 28 September 2017. https://www.theguardian.com/world/2017/sep/27/over-92-of-iraqs-kurds-vote-for-independence.
Gawrych, George W. 2013. *The Young Atatürk: From Ottoman Soldier to Statesman of Turkey*. London and New York: I.B.Tauris.
Geaves, Ron. 2003. 'Religion and Ethnicity: Community Formation in the British Alevi Community'. *Numen* 50 (1): 52–70.
Geerdink, Frederike. 2014. 'Kurds Who Became "Village Guards" and Fought PKK Rebels in Turkey to Be Disbanded'. *The Independent*. 16 February 2014. http://www.independent.co.uk/news/world/europe/kurds-who-became-village-guards-and-fought-pkk-rebels-in-turkey-to-be-disbanded-but-they-fear-a-9131095.html.
Geertz, Clifford. 1963. *Old Societies and New States-The Quest for Modernity in Asia and Africa*. Illinois: Free Press of Glencoe.
Geertz, Clifford. 1996. 'Primordial Ties'. In *Ethnicity*, edited by John Hutchinson and Anthony D. Smith, 40–45. Oxford and New York: Oxford University Press.
Gellner, David N. 2001. 'From Group Rights to Individual Rights and Back: Nepalese Struggles over Culture and Equality'. In *Culture and Rights*, edited by Jane K. Cowan, Marie-Bènèdicte Dembour, and Rochard A. Wilson, 177–200. Cambridge: Cambridge University Press.
Gellner, Ernest. 1997. 'Nationalism as a Product of Industrial Society'. In *The Ethnicity Reader: Nationalism, Multiculturalism and Migration*, edited by Montserrat Guibernau and John Rex, 52–69. Cambridge: Pluto Press.
Gellner, Ernest. 2006. *Uluslar ve Ulusçuluk*. Translated by Günay Göksu Özdoğan. İstanbul: Hil Yayınları.
George, Alexander L., and Andrew Bennet. 2005. *Case Studies and Theory Development in the Social Sciences*. Cambridge, MA and London: MIT Press.

Gerring, John. 2004. 'What Is a Case Study and What Is It Good For?' *The American Political Science Review* 98 (2): 341–54.

Gezik, Erdal. 2012. *Dinsel, Ethnik ve Politik Sorunlar Baglaminda; Alevi Kürtler.* İstanbul: İletişim.

Ghanem, As'ad. 2012. 'Understanding Ethnic Minority Demands: A New Typology'. *Nationalism and Ethnic Politics* 18 (3): 358–79.

Giddens, Anthony. 1987. *The Nation-State and Violance; Volume Two of a Contemprary Critique of Historical Materialism.* Berkeley and Los Angeles: University of California Press.

Gijsberts, Mérove, and Jaco Dagevos. 2007. 'The Socio-Cultural Integration of Ethnic Minorities in the Netherlands: Identifying Neighbourhood Effects on Multiple Integration Outcomes'. *Housing Studies* 22 (5): 805–31.

Glazer, Nathan, and Daniel P. Moynihan, eds. 1975. 'Ethnicity: Theory and Experience (Introduction)'. In *Ethnicity: Theory and Experience*, 1–26. Cambridge, MA: Harvard University Press.

Gökhalp, Ziya. 2011. *Kürt Aşiretleri Hakkında Sosyolojik Tetkikler*. 3rd ed. İstanbul: Kaynak Yayınları.

Göktaş, Hıdır. 1991. *Kürtler İsyan-Tenkil-1*. İstanbul: Alan Yayıncılık.

Göldaş, İsmail. 1991. *Kürdistan Teali Cemiyeti*. İstanbul: Doz.

Gomm, Roger, Martyn Hammersly, and Peter Foster. 2000. 'Case Study and Generalization'. In *Case Study Method*, edited by Roger Gomm, Martyn Hammersly, and Peter Foster, 98–116. London: Sage Publication.

Gordon, M. 1964. *Assimilation in American Life. The Role of Race, Religion and National Origins*. New York: Oxford University Press.

Gray, David H. 2009. *Doing Research in the Real World*. Second. Los Angeles, CA, London, New Delhi, Singapore and Washington, DC: Sage Publication.

Grigoriadis, Ioannis N. 2006. 'Political Participation of Turkey's Kurds and Alevis: A Challenge for Turkey's Democratic Consolidation'. *Southeast European and Black Sea Studies* 6 (4): 445–61.

Grimshaw, Tammy. 2006. 'The Gay "Community": Stabilising Political Construct or Oppressive Regulatory Regime?' In *Returning (to) Communities Theory Culture and Political Practice of the Communal*, edited by Stefan Herbrechter and Michael Higgins, 315–30. New York: Rodophi.

Grosby, Steven. 2005. 'The Primordial, Kinship and Nationality'. In *When Is the Nation? Towards an Understanding of Theories of Nationalism*, edited by Atsuko Ichijo and Gordana Uzelac, 56–78. London and New York: Routledge.

Gstrein, Heinz. 2009. *Avukatsız Halk Kürtler*. Translated by Kemal Yalım. İstanbul: Parşömen.

Guibernau, Montserrat. 2007. *The Identity of Nations*. Cambridge: Polity.

Guibernau, Montserrat. 2010. 'Devletsiz Uluslar-Ulussuz Devletler'. In *Ulusal Kimlik ve Etnik Açılım*, edited by Vasıf Eranus, translated by Neşe Nur Domaniç, 95–138. İstanbul: Sarmal.

Gunaratna, Rohan, Arabinda Acharya, and Wang Pengxin. 2010. *Ethnic Identity and National Conflict in China*. New York: Palgrave Macmillan.

Gunter, Michael M. 1990. *The Kurds in Turkey: A Political Dilemma*. Boulder, CO, San Francisco, CA and oxford: Westview Press.

Gunter, Michael M. 2004. 'The Kurdish Question in Perspective'. *World Affairs* 166 (4): 197–205.

Gunter, Michael M. 2005. 'Turkey's New Neighbour, Kurdistan'. In *The Future of Kurdistan in Iraq*, edited by Brendan O'leary, John McGray, and Khaled Salih, 219–34. Philadelphia: University of Pennsylvania Press.

Gunter, Michael M. 2009. *The A to Z of the Kurds*. 35. Lanham, MD, Toronto, and Plymouth: The Scarecrow Press, Inc.

Gunter, Michael M. 2013. 'The Multifaceted Kurdish Movement in Turkey'. In *Understanding Turkey's Kurdish Question*, edited by Fevzi Bilgin and Ali Sarihan, 73–87. Lanham, MD: Lexington Books.

Güçlü, İbrahim. 2005. *Hepimizin Sevgili Ağabeyi Edip Karahan*. İstanbul: elma.

Güçlü, İbrahim. 2006. 'DDKO: Bingeha Pêvajoya Yekemîn Bihara Tevgera Bakûrê Kurdêstanê'. *Bîr* (5) (Havîn-Payîz): 23–70.

Gülalp, Haldun. 2006a. 'Introduction: Citizenship vs. Nationality?' In *Citizenship and Ethnic Conflict Challenging the Nation-State*, edited by Haldun Gülalp, 1–18. London and New York: Routledge.

Gülalp, Haldun. 2006b. 'Concluding Thoughts: Transcending the Nation-State?' In *Citizenship and Ethnic Conflict Challenging the Nation-State*, edited by Haldun Gülalp, 133–39. London and New York: Routledge.

Gündoğan, Cemil. 1994. *1924 Beytüşşebap İsyanı*. İstanbul: Komal.

Güneş-Ayata, Ayşe, and Sencer Ayata. 2002. 'Ethnic and Religious Bases of Voting'. In *Politics, Parties and Elections in Turkey*, edited by Sabri Sayarı and Yılmaz Esmer, 137–56. Boulder, CO and London: Lynne Rienner Publishers.

Güneş, Cengiz. 2012. *The Kurdish National Movement in Turkey: From Protest to Resistance*. London and New York: Routledge.

Güney, Aylin. 2002. 'People's Democracy Party'. In *Political Parties in Turkey*, edited by Barry Rubin and Metin Heper, 122–37. London and Portland, OR: Frank Cass.

Gürer, Çetin. 2015. *Demokratil Özerklik: Bir Yurttaşlık Heterotopyası*. Ankara: NotaBene Yayınları. https://www.amazon.com/Demokratik-Ozerklik-Cetin-Gurer/dp/6059020569.

Gürbey, Gülistan. 1996. 'The Kurdish Nationalist Movement in Turkey since the 1980s'. In *The Kurdish Nationalist Movement in the 1990s: Its Impact on Turkey and the Middle East*, edited by Robert Olson, 9–37. Kentucky: The University press of Kentucky.

Gürbey, Gülistan. 2006. 'The Urgency of Post-Nationalist Perspectives: "Turkey for the Turks" or An Open Society on the Kurdish Conflict'. In *Turkey beyond Nationalism: Towards Post-Nationalist Identities*, edited by Hans-Lukas Keiser, 155–63. London and New York: I.B.Tauris.

Gurr, Ted Roberts. 1993. *Minorities at Risk*. Washington, DC: United States Institute of Peace Press.
Gurr, Ted Roberts. 1994. 'Peoples against States: Ethnopolitical Conflict and the Changing World System'. *International Studies Quarterly* 38 (3): 347–77.
Güzel, M.Şehmus. 1995. *Devlet-Ulus*. Birinci. İstanbul: Alan Yayıncılık.
Hadden, Tom. 2010. 'Uluslararası Hukukta Azınlıkların ve Halkların Hakları'. In *Ulusal Kimlik ve Etnik Açılım*, edited by Vasıf Eranus, translated by Işıtan Gündüz, 79–94. İstanbul: Sarmal.
Hague, Rod, and Martin Harrop. 2004. *Comparative Government and Politics: An Introduction*. 6th ed. London: Palgrave Macmillan.
Hak-Par Açılım ve Kürt Sorunu İçin Federal Çözüm Önerisi (Kitapcığı). 2009.
Hak-Par Parti Tüzüğü. 2002. The PDF draft of the party's rules and regulations is available on the party's official website; https://www.hakpar.org.tr/root/images/tuzuk.pdf.
Hak-Par Programi. 2002. The PDF draft of the party's program is available on the party's official website; https://www.hakpar.org.tr/root/index.php?option=com_cont ent&view=article&id=60&Itemid=86&lang=en.
Halbwachs, Maurice. 1992. *On Collective Memory*. Edited and translated by Lewis A. Coser. Chicago, IL and London: The University of Chicago Press.
Hale, William. 1994. *Türkiye'de Ordu ve Siyaset: 1789'dan Günümüze*. Translated by Ahmet Fethi. İstanbul: Hil Yayın.
Halfin. 1992. *XIX. Yuzyilda Kurdistan Uzerine Mucadeleler*. İstanbul: Komal.
Halliday, Fred. 2006. 'Can We Write a Modernist History of Kurdish Nationalism?' In *The Kurds: Nationalism and Politics*, edited by Faleh A. Jabar and Hosham Dawod, 9–20. London, San Francisco, CA and Beirut: Saqi.
Hall, John A., and G. John Ikenberry. 1989. *The State*. Stratford: Open University Press.
Halkların Demokratik Partisi Tüzüğü. 2014. *Halkların Demokratik Partisi Tüzüğü*. http://www.hdp.org.tr/tr/parti/parti-tuzugu/10.
Hamelink, Cees J. 2003. 'Cultural Rights in the Global Village'. In *Cultural Rights in Global World*, edited by Anura Goonasekera, Cees J. Hamelink, and Venkat Iyer, 7–25. Singapore: Eastern Universities Press.
Hamid, Ahmed Fauzi Abdul. 1999. 'The Making of Nation-State in the Arab World: The Roles for Oil, Islam and Arab Nationalism'. *IKIM Journal* 7 (2): 19–45.
Hammond, Phillip E., and Kee Warner. 1993. 'Religion and Ethnicity in Late-Twentieth-Century America'. *Annals of the American Academy of Political and Social Science* 527: 55–66.
Hamut, Ali Hasan. 2011. *Kürt Sorununa İslami Bakış*. Ankara: ARGE Analiz, 15–17.
Hannum, Hurst. 1990. *Autonomy, Sovereignty, and Self-Determination: The Accommodation of Conflicting Rights*. Philadelphia: University of Pennsylvania Press.
Harik, Illiya. 1972. 'The Ethnic Revolution and Political Integration in the Middle East'. *International Journal of Middle East Studies* 3 (3): 303–23.
Hassanpour, Amir. 1997. *Kurdistan'da Milliyetcilik ve Dil 1918–85*. Translated by İbrahim Bingol and Cemil Gundogan. İstanbul: Avesta.

Hassanpour, Amir. 2005. 'Kürt Kimliğinin İnşası: Yirminci Yüzyıl Öncesi Tarihsel ve Edebi Kaynaklar'. In *Kürt Milliyetçiliğinin Kökenleri*, edited by Abbas Vali, translated by Fahriye Adsay, Ümit Aydoğmuş, and Suat Kılıç, 135–98. İstanbul: Avesta.

Hassanpour, Amir, Tove Skutnabb-Kangas, and Michael Chyet. 1996. 'The Non-Education of Kurds: A Kurdish Perspective'. *International Review of Education* 42 (4): 367–79.

Hay, W.R. 2005. *Kürdistan'da İki Yıl (1918–20)*. Translated by Fahriye Adsay. İstanbul: Avesta.

HDP Parti Programı. 2014. 'Halkların Demokratik Partisi Programı'. Halklarin Demokratik Partisi. 2014. http://www.hdp.org.tr/tr/parti/parti-programi/8.

Hechter, Michael. 1986. 'A Rational Choice Approach to Race and Ethnic Relations'. In *Theories of Race and Ethnic Relations*, edited by David Mason and John Rex, 264–79 Cambridge: Cambridge University Press.

Heckmann, Friedrich. 1983. 'Towards the Development of a Typology of Minorities'. In *Minorities: Community and Identity*, edited by C. Fried, 9–23. Berlin, Heidelberg, New York and Tokyo: Springer-Verlag.

Heckmann, Friedrich. 1998. 'Typology of Racially Discriminated and Ethnic Minorities in Europe? or On the Relations between Ethnic Minorities, Racism and Affirmative Action'. In, 1–6. University of Innsbruck and Commission of the European Community, Directorate General V Innsbruck, efms Paper Nr. 22.

Heintze, Hans-Joachim. 1998. 'On the Legal Understanding of Autonomy'. In *Autonomy: Applications and Implications*, edited by Markku Suksi, 7–32. Hague and Cambridge: Kluwer Law International.

Held, David. 1992. 'The Development of Modern State'. In *Formations of Modernity*, edited by Stuart Hall and Bram Gieben, 71–125. Cambridge: Polity Press.

Heraclides, Alexis. 1991. *The Self-Determination of Minorities in International Politics*. London: Frank Cass.

Hilmi, Refik. 1995. *Anılar / Şeyh Mahmud Berzenci Hareketi*. İstanbul: Peri Yayınları.

Hirschler, Konrad. 2001. 'Defining the Nation: Kurdish Historiography in Turkey in the 1990s'. *Middle Eastern Studies* 37 (3): 145–66.

Hizbullah manifestosu. 2012. Available at http://huseynisevda.biz/Dokumanlar/Hizbullah-Manifestosu.pdf

Hobsbawm, E.J. 1990. *Nations and Nationalism since 1780: Programme, Myth, Reality*. Second. Cambridge: Cambridge University Press.

Hooghe, Liesbet. 2004. 'Belgium; Hollowing Center'. In *Federalism and Territorial Cleavages*, edited by Ugo M. Amoretti and Nancy Bermeo, 55–92. Baltimore, MD and London: The Johns Hopkins University Press.

Hooglund, Eric. 1996. 'The Society and Its Environment'. In *Turkey: A Country Study*, edited by Helen Chapin Metz, Fifth, 71–145. Lanham, MD: Bernan.

Horowitz, Donald. L. 2008. 'The Many Uses of Federalism'. *Duke Law School Faculty Scholarship Series*, 134, March, 101–13. http://lsr.nellco.org/cgi/viewcontent.cgi?article=1134&context=duke_fs.

Horowitz, Donald.L. 2004. 'The Primordialists'. In *Ethnonationalism in the Contemporary World*, edited by Daniele Conversi, 72–82. London and New York: Routledge.

Hourani, Albert. 1997. *Arap Halkları Tarihi*. Translated by Yavuz Alogan. İstanbul: İletişim.

Houston, Christopher. 2001. *Islam, Kurds and the Turkish Nation State*. Oxford and New York: Berg.

Hroch, Miroslav. 1996. 'From National Movement to the Fully Formed Nation: The Nation-Building Process in Europe'. In *Becoming National*, edited by Geoff Eley and Ronal Grigor Suny, 61–77. Oxford and New York: Oxford University Press.

http://www.demokratikhaklarfederasyonu.org/demokratik-haklar-dernekleri-federasyonu-tuzugu.html.

http://www.demokratiktoplumkongresi.com/tr/index (Accessed 29 November 2014).

http://www.ismailbesikcivakfi.org/Default.asp?

http://www.kizilbayrak.net/ana-sayfa/.

http://www.risale-inur.org/risaleinur.php.

Http://www.ysk.gov.tr/ysk/faces/Secimler?_adf.ctrl-state=9cgjmzhve_9&wcnav.model=YSKUstMenu&_afrLoop=22089026474476664 (Accessed 11 August 2014).

Hutchinson, John. 1996. 'Ethnicity (in Introduction)'. In *Ethnicity*, edited by John Hutchinson and Anthony D. Smith, 3–14. Oxford and New York: Oxford University Press.

Huseyni Sevdam. n.d. 'Şeyh Said Serriyeleri Görevde'. https://huseyni-sevdam.tr.gg/Seyh-Said-Seriyyelerinden-flas-aciklama.htm (Accessed 20 November 2017).

Hür Dava Partisi Programı. 2012. The PDF draft of the party's programme is available on the party's official website; https://hudapar.org/parti/parti-programi-3/genel-merkez/.

Hürriyet. 2014. '6-7 Ekim'in Acı Bilançosu 50 Ölü'. 11 June 2014. http://www.hurriyet.com.tr/6-7-ekim-in-aci-bilancosu-50-olu-27525777.

Hürriyet Daily News. 2016. 'There's No Kurdish Issue in Turkey, Just Terrorism: Erdoğan'. January 2016. http://www.hurriyetdailynews.com/theres-no-kurdish-issue-in-turkey-just-terrorism-erdogan.aspx?pageID=238&nID=93511&NewsCatID=338.

Iadicola, Peter. 1981. 'Desegregation: The Assimilation of a Minority Population'. *Sociological Focus* 14 (3): 193–206.

I. Baggasi 2004. *Kendi Dilinden Hizbullah ve Mücadele Tarihinden Önemli Kesitler*. Unknown Publisher.

İçduygu, Ahmet, David Romano, and İbrahim Sirkeci. 1999. 'The Ethnic Question in an Environment of Insecurity: The Kurds in Turkey'. *Ethnic and Racial Studies* 22 (6): 991–1010.

IHD Araştırma Raporu. 2010. 'Bursa İnegöl Linç Girişimleri İnceleme ve Araştrma Raporu'. *İnsan Hakları Derneği (IHD)*. Ağustos. http://www.ihd.org.tr/index.php/raporlar-mainmenu-86/el-raporlar-mainmenu-90/2119-bursa-inegol-linc-girisimleri-inceleme-ve-arastirma-raporu.html (Accessed 23 April 2014; 0:42).

İhsan Nuri Paşa. 1992. *Ağrı Dağı İsyanı*. İstanbul: Med Yayıncılık.
Imber, Colin. 2002. *The Ottoman Empire, 1300–1650 : The Structure of Power*. New York: Palgrave Macmillan.
Imset, Ismet G. 1992. *The PKK: A Report on Separatist Violence in Turkey*. Ankara: Turkish Daily News Publications.
Înîsiyatîfa Azadî (Metnèn Declerasyone û Mutabeqetè Ji Bo Dad Û Azdîyè Însîyatîfa Îslamî Ya Kurdistanè). 2012.
International Covenant on Civil and Political Rights (ICCPR). 1966. United Nations Treaty Series. https://treaties.un.org/doc/Publication/UNTS/Volume%20999/volume-999-I-14668-English.pdf.
International Covenant on Economic, Social and Cultural Rights (ICESCR). 1966. http://www.ohchr.org/Documents/ProfessionalInterest/cescr.pdf.
International Crisis Group. 2012. *Turkey's Kurdish Impasse: The View from Diyarbakır*. Europe Report No; 222. http://www.crisisgroup.org/~/media/Files/europe/turkey-cyprus/turkey/222-turkeys-kurdish-impasse-the-view-from-diyarbaDiyarbakır.pdf (Accessed 27 February 2014, 00;23).
Isaacs, Harold. 1975. 'Basic Group Identity: The Idols of the Tribe'. In *Ethnicity: Theory and Experience*, edited by Nathan Glazer and Daniel P. Moynihan, 29–52. Cambridge, MA, and London: Harvard University Press.
Ishay, Micheline R. 2007. *The Human Rights Reader: Major Political Essays, Speeches, and Documentaries from Ancient Times to the President*. Second. New York and Oxon: Routledge.
Ishiyama, John T. 2012. *Comparative Politics: Principles of Democracy and Democratization*. Sussex: Blackwell Publishing.
Işık, İbrahim S. 2013. *A'dan Z'ye Kürtler*. İkinci. İstanbul: Nûbihar.
Izady, Mehrdad R. 2004. *Kürtler*. Translated by Cemal Atilla. İstanbul: Doz.
Jaffrelot, Christophe. 1996. 'Bazi Ulus Teorileri'. In *Uluslar ve Milliterçilikler*, edited by Jean Leca, translated by Siren Idemen, 54–65. İstanbul: Metis.
James, Boris. 2011. *Selahaddin ve Kürtler: Haçlılar Döneminde Bir Topluluğun Kavranması*. Translated by Nazlı Bilgiç. İstanbul: Avesta.
Jenkins, Gareth. 2006. *Symbols and Shadow Play: Military-JDP Relations, 2002–04*. Edited by M. Hakan Yavuz. Utah: University of Utah Press.
Jenkins, Gareth. 2012. 'Values and Identity: The Resurgence of the Kurdish Identity'. *Turkey Analyst* 5 (9). http://www.silkroadstudies.org/new/inside/turkey/2012/120430a.html.
Jesse, Neal G., and Kristen P. Williams. 2011. *Ethnic Conflict: A Systematic Approach to Cases of Conflict*. Washington, DC: CQ Press.
Jinadu, L. Adele. 1979. 'A Note on the Theory of Federalism'. In *Readings on Federalism*, edited by A.B. Akinyemi, P.D. Cole, and Walter Ofonagoro, 13–25. Lagos: Nigerian Institute of International Affairs.
Jongerden, Joost. 2017. 'The Kurdistan Workers' Party (PKK): Radical Democracy and the Right to Self-Determination beyond the Nation-State'. In *The Kurdish Question*

Revisited, edited by Gareth Stansfield and Muhammed Shareef, 245-94. London: Hurst Company.

Jwaideh, Wadie. 1999. *Kürt Milliyetçiliğinin Tarhi Kökenleri ve Gelişimi*. Translated by İsmail Çekem and Alper Duman. 2nd ed. İstanbul: İletişim.

Kadep Parti Programi. 2006. The PDF draft of the party's proramme is available on; http://www.arsivakurd.org/images/arsiva_kurd/belge/rexistin/kadep/parti_programi.pdf.

Kaiser, Robert Z. 2004. 'Homeland Making and the Territorialization of National Identity'. In *Ethnonationalism in the Contemporary World*, edited by Daniele Conversi, 229-47. London and New York: Routledge.

Kalaycı, Hüseyin. 2008. 'Etnisite ve Ulus Karşılaştırılması'. *Doğu-Batı* (44) (March): 91-113.

Kalkan, Duran. 2012. 'Demokratik Özerklik İnşa Edilmiş Toplumsal Sorunların Çöküş Sistemidir'. In *Yerel Bölgesel Sorunlar ve Demokratik Ulus Çözümü*, edited by Serxwebûn, 41-70. Cologne, Germany: Weşanen Serxwebûn 154.

Kalkınma Bakanlığı. 2013. *İllerin ve Bölgelerin Sosyo-Ekonomik Gelişmişlik Sıralaması Araştırması (SEGE 2011)*. Ankara: T.C.Kalkınma Bakanlığı.

Kalman, M. 1997. *Belge, Tanık ve Yasayanları Ile Ağrı Direnişi 1926,1930*. İstanbul: Peri.

Kalmijn, Matthjs. 1998. 'Intermarriage and Homogamy: Causes, Patterns, Trends'. *Annual Review of Sociology* 24: 395-421.

Kamal, Muhammed. 2001. 'Religion and Faith in Kurdistan: Voices from Kurdistan'. In *Fire, Snow & Honey*, edited by Gina Lennox, 35-45. New South Wales: Halstead Press.

Kapmaz, Cengiz. 2010. *Öcalan'in İmralı Günleri*. İstanbul: ithaki.

Karadoğan, Yaşar. 2006. 'Kürd Demokratik Mücadelesinde Bir Kilometre Taşi : 1967-69 Doğu Mitingleri ve Kürd Uyanışı'. *Bîr* (5) (Havîn-Payîz): 254-83.

Karasu, Mustafa. 2009. *Radikal Demokrasi*. Neuss: Mezopotamya Yayınları.

Karasu, Mustafa. 2012. 'Türkiye'yi Demokratikleştirme Projesi'. In *Yerel Bölgesel Sorunlar ve Demokratik Ulus Çözümü*, edited by Serxwebûn, 71-88. Cologne, Germany: Weşanen Serxwebûn 154.

Karayılan, Murat. 2012. *Bir Savaşın Anatomisi: Kürdistanda Askeri Çizgi*. IV. Neuss: Mezopotamya Yayınları.

Karlsson, Ingmar. 2008. *Bir Diplomatın Gözüyle Kürt Sorunu*. İstanbul: Homer Kitabevi.

Karpat, Kemal H. 2004. 'Orta Doğu'da Osmanlı Etnik ve Dini Mirası'. In *Ortadoğu'da Etnisite, Çoğulculuk ve Devlet*, edited by Milton J. Esman and Itamar Rabinovic, translated by Zafer Avşar, 59-83. İstanbul: Avesta.

Karpat, Kemal H. 2010. *Türk Demokrasi Tarihi*. İstanbul: Timaş Yayınları.

Kasaba, Reþat. 1997. 'Kemalist Certainties and Modern Ambiguities'. In *Rethinking Modernity and National Identity in Turkey*, by Sibel Bozdoðan and Reþat Kasaba, 15-37. Seattle and London: University of Washington Press.

Kaya, Mehmet S. 2011. *The Zaza Kurds of Turkey*. London and New York: I.B.Tauris.

Keating, Michael. 1997. 'Stateless Nation-Building: Quebec, Catalonia and Scotland in the Changing State System'. *Nations and Nationalism* 3 (4): 689-717.

Keating, Michael. 2001. 'Nation without States: The Accommodation of Nationalism in the New State Order'. In *Minority Nationalisms and the Changing International Order*, edited by Michael Keating and John McGray, 19–43. Oxford and New York: Oxford University Press.

Keating, Michael. 2004. 'The United Kingdom: Political Institutions and Territorial Cleavages'. In *Federalism and Territorial Cleavages*, edited by Ugo M. Amoretti and Nancy Bermeo, 155–79. Baltimore, MD and London: The Johns Hopkins University Press.

Keddie, Nikki R. 2003. *Modern Iran: Roots and Results of Revolution*. New Haven, CT and London: Yale University Press.

Kedourie, Elie. 2004a. 'National Self-Determination'. In *Nationality and Nationalism*, edited by Athena S. Leoussi and Steven Grosby, 102–18. London and New York: I.B.Tauris.

Kedourie, Elie. 2004b. 'Orta Doğu'da Etniste, Çoğunluk ve Azınlık'. In *Ortadoğu'da Etnisite, Çoğulculuk ve Devlet*, edited by Milton J. Esman and İtamar Rabinoviç, translated by Zafer Avşar, 47–56. İstanbul: Avesta.

Kehl-Bodrogi, Krisztina. 2003. 'Atatürk and the Alevis: A Holy Alliance'. In *Turkey's Alevi Enigma; A Comprehensive Overview*, edited by Paul J. White and Joost Jongerden, 88: 53–69. Leiden-Boston: Brill.

Keiser, Hans-Lukas. 2003. 'Alevis, Armenians and Kurds in Unionist-Kemalist Turkey'. In *Turkey's Alevi Enigma; A Comprehensive Overview*, edited by Joost Jongerden and Paul J. White, 177–96. 88. Leiden-Boston: Brill.

Kelidar, Abbas. 1993. 'States without Foundations: The Political Evolution of State and Society in the Arab East'. *Journal of Contemporary History* 28 (2): 315–39.

Kelman, Herbert C. 1997. 'Negotiating National Identity and Self-Determination in Ethnic Conflicts: The Choice between Pluralism and Ethnic Cleansing'. *Negotiation Journal* 13 (4): 327–40.

Kendal. 1993. 'The Kurds under the Ottoman Empire'. In *A People without a Country: The Kurds and Kurdistan*, edited by Gerard Chaliand, translated by Michael Pallis, 11–37. London: Zed Books.

Kentel, Ferhat. 2014. 'Kaybolan Sinirlarin Işığında 'Milliyetçi' Yeniden İnşa'. In *Türkiye'de Milliyetçilik ve Politika: Politik İslam, Kemalizm ve Kürt Sorunu*, edited by Marlies Casier and Joost Jongerden, translated by Pınar Uygun, Batu Boran, Muhtesim Güvenç, and Metin Çulhaoğlu, 79–105. İstanbul: Vate.

Keyman, E. Fuat, and Umut Özkırımlı. 2013. 'The Kurdish Question' Revisited: Modernity, Nationalism, and Citizenship in Turkey'. In *Understanding Turkey's Kurdish Question*, edited by Fevzi Bilgin and Ali Sarihan, 47–56. Lanham, MD, Boulder, CO, New York, Toronto and Plymouth: Lexington Books.

Khalil, Aldar. 2017. 'Syria's Kurds Are Not the PKK'. *Foreign Policy* (blog). 15 May 2017. https://foreignpolicy.com/2017/05/15/syrias-kurds-are-not-the-pkk-erdogan-pyd-ypg/.

Khoury, Philip S., and Joseph Kostiner. 1990. 'Introduction: Tribes and the Complexities of State Formation in the Middle East'. In *Tribes and State Formation in the Middle*

East, edited by Philip S. Khoury and Joseph Kostiner, 1–22. Berkeley, Los Angeles, and Oxford: University of California Press.

Kieser, Hans-Lukas. 2001. 'Muslim Heterodoxy and Protestant Utopia. The Interactions between Alevis and Missionaries in Ottoman Anatolia'. *Die Welt Des Islams, New Series* 41 (1): 89–111.

King, Preston. 1993. 'Federation and Representation'. In *Comparative Federalism and Federation: Competing Traditions and Future Directions*, edited by Michael Burgess and Alain G. Gagnon, 94–101. New York, London and Toronto: Harvester Wheatsheaf.

King, Roger, and Gavin Kendall. 2004. *The State, Democracy and Globalization*. London: Palgrave Macmillan.

Kirişçi, Kemal. 1998. 'Minority/Majority Discourse: The Case of the Kurds in Turkey'. In *Making Majorities: Constituting the Nation in Japan, Korea, China, Malaysia, Fiji, Turkey, and the United States (Contemporary Issues in Asia and Pacific)*, 227–48. Stanford, CA: Stanford University Press.

Kirişçi, Kemal. 2004. 'The Kurdish Question and Turkish Foreign Policy'. In *The Future of Turkish Foreign Policy*, edited by Lenore G. Martin and Dimitris Keridis, 273–315. Cambridge, MA: The MIT Press.

Kirişçi, Kemal. 2007. 'The Kurdish Question and Turkey: Future Challenges and Prospects for a Solution'. Working Paper. *Instituto Per Gli Studi Di Politica Internazionale (ISPI)* (24): 1–36. https://www.ispionline.it/it/documents/wp_24_2007.pdf.

Kirişçi, Kemal, and Gareth M. Winrow. 1997. *Kürt Sorunu Kökeni ve Gelişimi*. Translated by Ahmet Fethi. İstanbul: Tarih Vakfı Yurt Yayınları.

Kırmızı, Abdulhamit, and Selin Bölme. 2009. 'Kürt Hareketlerinde Dindarlığın Yeni Tezahürü'. In *Güneydoğu Sorunu: Tarihi-Kaynağı- Çözümü*, edited by Risale-i Nur Enstitüsü, 115–28. İstanbul: Yeni Asya Yayınları.

Kısacık, Raşit. 2012. *Kürt Sorunu ve Etnik Örgütlenmeler-3; Minareden Kandil'e*. İstanbul: Ozan Yayıncılık.

Kıvanç, Ümit. 2015. 'Şeyh Said Seriyyeleri'. *Radikal*. 18 June 2015.

Klein. 2011. *The Margins of Empire: Kurdish Militias in the Ottoman Tribal Zone*. Stanford, CA: Stan.

Klein, Janet. 2007. 'Kurdish Nationalists and Non-Nationalist Kurdists: Rethinking Minority Nationalism and the Dissolution of the Ottoman Empire, 1908–09'. *Nations and Nationalism* 13 (1): 135–53.

Koğacioğlu, Dicle. 2004. 'Progress, Unity, and Democracy: Dissolving Political Parties in Turkey'. *Law & Society Review* 38 (3): 433–62.

Kohli, Atul. 2004. 'India: Federalism and Accommodation of Ethnic Nationalism'. In *Federalism and Territorial Cleavages*, edited by Ugo M. Amoretti and Nancy Bermeo, 281–99. Baltimore, MD and London: The Johns Hopkins University Press.

Kohn, Hans. 1944. *The Idea of Nationalism: A Study in Its Origin and Background*. New York: The Macmillan Company.

Koker, Levent. 2010. 'A Key to the "Democratic Opening": Rethinking Citizenship, Ethnicity and Turkish Nation-State'. *Insight Turkey* 12 (2): 49–69.

KONDA. 2006. *Toplumsal Yapı Araştırması: Biz Kimiz?* İstanbul: KONDA.

KONDA. 2011. *Kürt Meselesi'nde Algı ve Beklentiler*. İstanbul: İletişim.

Kónya, István. 2005. 'Minorities and Majorities: A Dynamic Model of Assimilation'. *The Canadian Journal of Economics / Revue Canadienne d'Economique* 38 (4): 1431–52.

Kreyenbroek, Philip G. 1996. 'Religion and Religions in Kurdistan'. In *Kurdish Culture and Identity*, edited by Philip G. Kreyenbroek and Christine Allison, 85–110. London and New York: Zed Books.

Kumar, Rajan. 2007. *Ethnicity, Nationalism and Conflict Resolution*. Gurgaon: Hope India Publication.

Kupper, Adam. 1999. *Culture: The Anthropologists Account*. Cambridge, MA and London: Harvard University Press.

Kurdish Human Rights Project. 2003. *This Is the Only Valley Where We Live: The Impact of the Munzur Dams: The Report of the KHRP Fact-Finding Missionto Dersim/Tunceli*. London: KHRP/The Cornerhouse.

Kurdistan Kominist Partisi. 1990. 'III.Kongre'ye Giderken KKP'de Acık Tartısma'. Denge Kurdistan. http://netewe.com/PDF/kovar/DengeKurdistan/ek1.pdf.

Kurdistan National Congress. 2014. https://peaceinkurdistancampaign.files.wordpress.com/2011/11/rojava-info-may-2014.pdf, Accessed 29/11/2014.

Kurdistan Ozgurluk Partisi Programı. 2014. The party's programme is available on the part's official website; http://www.partiyaazadiyakurdistane-pak.org/page9.php.

Kurdoloji Calışmaları Gurubu. 2011. *Osmanlı Kurdistanı-1(Lekolinnen Diroka Kurds*1)*. İstanbul: bgst yayınları.

Kurt, Mehmet. 2015. *Din, Şiddet ve Aidiyet: Türkiye'de Hizbullah*. İstanbul: İletişim Yayınları.

Kuru, Ahmet. 2007. 'Passive and Assertive Secularism: Historical Conditions, Ideological Struggles, and State Policies toward Religion'. *World Politics* 59 (4) (July): 568–94.

Kurubaş, Erol. 1997. *Başlangıçtan 1960' Değin Kürt Sorununun Uluslararası Boyutu*. Ankara: Ümit Yayıncılık.

Kurubaş, Erol. 2008. 'Etnik Grup-Devlet İlişkilerinin Sorunsallaşması ve Aktör Tutumlarındaki Açmazlar: Türkiye'deki Kürt Sorunu Örneği'. *Liberal Düşünce* (50) (lkbahar): 19–53.

Kutlay, Naci. 2002. *21. Yüzyıla Girerken Kürtler*. İstanbul: Pêrî.

Kutlay, Naci. 2006a. *Kürtlerde Değişim ve Milliyetçilik*. Ankara: Dipnot Yayınları.

Kutlay, Naci. 2006b. 'Devrimc Doğru Kültür Ocakları ve Öncesi'. *Bîr* (5): 157–72.

Kutlay, Naci. 2012a. *Kürt Kimliğinin Oluşum Süreci*. İstanbul: Dipnot yayınları.

Kutlay, Naci. 2012b. *İslamiyet-Osmanlı-Cumhurriyet;Kürt Tarihini Yeniden Okumak*. İstanbul: Peri Yayınları.

Kutschera, Chris. 2001. *Kürt Ulusal Hareketi*. Translated by Fikret Başkaya. İstanbul: Avesta.

Kymlicka, Will. 1995. *Multicultural Citizenship: A Liberal Theory of Minority Rights*. Oxford: Oxford University Press.
Kymlicka, Will. 2008. 'Sonuç: Milliyetçiliğin Geleceği'. In *21. Yüzyılda Milliyetçilik*, edited by Umut Özkırımlı, translated by Yetkin Başkavak, 159–66. İstanbul: İstanbul Bilgi üniversitesi Yayınları.
Laçiner, Sedat, and İhsan Bal. 2004. 'The Ideologicial and Historical Roots of the Kurdish Movements in Turkey: Ethnicity, Demography, and Politics'. *Nationalism and Ethnic Politics* 10 (3): 473–504.
Lake, David A., and Donald Rotchild. 1996. 'Containing Fear: The Origins and Management of Ethnic Conflict'. *International Security* 21 (2): 41–75.
Landman, Todd. 2003. *Issues and Methods in Comparative Politics: An Introduction*. Second. New York: Routledge.
Lapidus, Ira M. 1990. 'Tribe and State Formation in Islamic History'. In *Tribes and State Formation in the Middle East*, edited by Philip S. Khoury and Joseph Kostiner, 25–47. Berkeley, Los Angeles and Oxford: University of California Press.
Laselva, Samuel V. 1996. *The Moral Foundations of Canadian Federalism: Paradoxes, Achievements, and Tragedies of Nationhood*. Montreal: McGill-Queen's University Press.
Lazarev, M.S., Ş.X. Mıhoyan, E.İ. Vasilyeva, M.A. Gastratyan, and O.İ. Jigalina. 2001. *Kürdistan Tarihi*. Edited by M.S. Lazarev and Ş.X Mıhoyan. Translated by İbrahim Kale. İstanbul: Avesta.
Leezenberg, Michiel. 2003. 'Kurdish Alevis and the Kurdish Nationalist Movement in the 1990s'. In *Turkey's Alevi Enigma: A Comprehensive Overview*, edited by Paul J. White and Joost Jongerden, 197–212. 88. Leiden and Boston, MA: Brill.
Lenin, Vilademir I. 1998. *Uluslarin Kendi Kaderini Tayin Hakki*. Altinci. Ankara: Sol Yayinlari.
Leopold, Patricia M. 2009. 'Autonomy and the British Constitution'. In *The Ashgate Research Companion Federalism*, edited by Ann Ward and Lee Ward, 223–50. Surrey: Ashgate.
Levey, Geoffrey. 1997. 'Equality, Autonomy, and Cultural Rights'. *Political Theory* 25 (2): 215–48.
Lewellen, Ted. C. 2011. *Siyasal Antropoloji*. Edited by Erkan Koca. Ankara: Birleşik.
Lewis, Bernard. 1968. *The Emergence of Modern Turkey*. 2nd ed. London and New York: Oxford University Press.
Lijphart, Arend. 1999. *Patterns of Democracy: Government Forms and Performance in Thirty-Six Countries*. New Haven, CT: Yale University Press.
Llera, Francisco J. 2000. 'Basque Polarization: Between Autonomy and Independency'. In *Identity and Territorial Autonomy in Plural Societies*, edited by William Safran and Ramon Maiz, 101–20. London and Portland, OR: Frank Cass.
Llobera, Josep R. 2007. *Modernliğin Tanrısı Batı Avrupa'da Milliyetçiliin Gelişmesi*. Translated by Emek Akman and Ebru Akman. Ankara: Poenix.
Locke, John. 1967. *Two Treatises of Government*. Edited by Peter Laslett. Cambridge: Cambridge University Press.

Lundgren, Asa. 2007. 'Kurdish Identity in the Turkish Republic'. In *The Unwelcome Neighbour: Turkey's Kurdish Policy*, 41-57. London: I.B.Tauris.
Magnet, Joseph Eliot. 2001. 'National Minorities and the Multinational State'. *Queen's Law Journal* (26): 397-450.
Maiz, Ramon. 2000. 'Democracy, Federalism and Nationalism in Multinational States'. In *Identity and Territorial Autonomy in Plural Societies*, edited by William Safran and Roman Maiz, 35-61. London and Portland, OR: Frank Cass.
Majeed, Akhtar. 2009. 'India: A Model of Cooperative Federalism'. In *The Ashgate Research Companion Federalism*, edited by Ann Ward and Lee Ward, 503-16. Surrey: Ashgate.
Majocchi, Alberto. 2009. 'Theories of Fiscal Federalism and the European Experience'. In *The Ashgate Research Companion Federalism*, edited by Ann Ward and Lee Ward, 425-40. Surrey: Ashgate.
Malesevic, Sinisa. 2006. *Identity as Ideology: Understanding Ethnicity and Nationalism*. New York: Palgrave Macmillan.
Maliepaard, Mieke, Marcel Lubbers, and Me´rove Gijsberts. 2010. 'Generational Differences in Ethnic and Religious Attachment and Their Interrelation. A Study among Muslim Minorities in the Netherlands'. *Ethnic and Racial Studies* 33 (3): 451-72.
Malmîsanij. 1986. *Kürt Milliyetçiliği ve Dr. Abdullah Cevdet*. Uppsala: Jina Nu Yayınları.
Malmîsanij. 1991. *Said-I Nursi ve Kürt Sorunu*. Uppsala: Jina Nu Yayınları.
Malmîsanij. 1999. *Kürt Teavün ve Terakki Cemiyeti ve Gazetesi*. İkinci. İstanbul: Avesta.
Malmîsanij. 2004. *Diyarbekirli Cemilpaşazadeler ve Kürt Milliyetçiliği*. İstanbul: Avesta.
Malmîsanij. 2010. *Yirminci Yüzyılın Başında Diyarbekir'de Kürt Ulusçuluğu (1900-20)*. İstanbul: Vate.
Maraşlı, Recep. 2010. 'Rizgari'nin Sosyalist Hareket ve Kürdistan Ulusal Kurtuluş Mücadelesindeki Yeri Üzerine Bir Deneme -I-'. *Mesafe* (4) (Bahar): 68-93.
Marchildon, Greg. 2009. 'Postmodern Federation and Sub-State Nationalism'. In *The Ashgate Research Companion Federalism*, edited by Ann Ward and Lee Ward, 441-55. Surrey: Ashgate.
Marcus, Aliza. 1993. 'Turkey's Kurds after Gulf War: A Report from the Southeast'. In *A People without a Country: The Kurds and Kurdistan*, edited by Gerard Chaliand, translated by Michael Pallis and David McDowal, 238-47. London: Zed Books.
Marcus, Aliza. 2007. *Blood and Belief: The PKK and the Kurdish Fight for Independence*. New York and London: New York University Press.
Mardin, Şerif. 1991. *Türk Modernleşmesi*. İstanbul: İletişim.
Margulies, Roni, and Ramazan Yildizoğlu. 1997. 'The Resurgence of Islam and the Welfare Party in Turkey'. In *Political Islam*, edited by Joel Beinin and Joe Stork, 144-53. London and New York: I.B.Tauris.
Marshall, Gordon. 1999. *Sosyoloji Sözlüğü*. Translated by Osman Akınhay and Derya Kömürcü. Ankara: Bilim ve Sanat.

Martinez-Vazquez, Jorge, and Jameson Boex. 2001. *Russia's Transition to a New Federalism*. Washington, DC: World Bank Institute (WBI).

Marx, Anthony W. 2002. 'The Nation-State and Its Exclusions'. *Political Science Quarterly* 117 (1): 103–26.

Marx, Emanuel. 1977. 'The Tribe as a Unit of Subsistence: Nomadic Pastoralism in the Middle East'. *American Anthropologist, New Series* 79 (2): 343–63.

Marx, Karl, and Frederick (1848) Engels. 2007. *The Communist Manifesto*. New York: International Publishers.

MAZLUM-DER. 2008. *Türkiye de Etnik Ayrımcılık Raporu*. http://istanbul.mazlumder.org/fotograf/yayinresimleri/dokuman/etnik_ayrimcilik_raporu_2011.pdf.

McDowall, David. 1992. 'The Kurdish Question: A Historical Review'. In *The Kurds: A Contemporary Overview*, edited by Philip G. Kreyenbroek and Stefan Sperl, 8–25. London and New York: Routledge.

McDowall, David. 2004. *A Modern History of the Kurds*. Revised ed. London and New York: I.B.Tauris.

McGarry, John, and Margaret Moore. 2005. 'Karl Renner, Power Sharing and Nonterritorial Autonomy'. In *National Cultural Autonomy and Its Contemporary Critics*, edited by Ephraim Nimni, 64–81. London and New York: Routledge.

McGray, John, and Brendan O'leary. 1996. 'Eliminating and Managing Ethnic Difference'. In *Ethnicity*, edited by John Hutchinson and Anthony D. Smith, 333–41. Oxford and New York: Oxford University Press.

Meho, Lokman I. 1997. *The Kurds and Kurdistan: A Selective and Annotated Bibliography*. Westport, CT, London: Greenwood Press.

Meho, Lokman I., and Kelly L. Maglaughlin. 2001. *Kurdish Culture and Society*. Westport, CT and London: Greenwood Press.

Meinecke, Friedrich. 2004. 'General Remarks on the Nation, the National State, and Cosmopolitanism'. In *Nationality and Nationalism*, edited by Athena S. Leoussi and Steven Grosby, 1:59–69. London and New York: I.B.Tauris.

Melucci, Alberto. 1996. 'The Post-Modern Revival of Ethnicity'. In *Ethnicity*, edited by John Hutchinson and Anthony D. Smith, 367–70. Oxford and New York: Oxford University Press.

Miller, Benjamin. 2007. *States, Nations, and the Great Powers: The Sources of Regional War and Peace*. Cambridge: Cambridge University Press.

Miller, David. 1995. *On Nationality*. Oxford: Clarendon Press.

Miller, David. 1998. 'Secession and the Principle of Nationality'. In *National Self-Determination and Secession*, edited by Margaret Moore, 62–78. Oxford and New York: Oxford University Press.

Milliyet. 2013. '"Cami Cemevi" Projesine Alevilerden Sert Tepki'. Milliyet Haber. 9 April 2013. http://www.milliyet.com.tr/-cami-cemevi-projesine/gundem/detay/1758734/default.htm.

Milliyet. 2015. 'Dolmabahçe'de Tarihi Açıklama'. Milliyet Haber. 13 March 2015. http://www.milliyet.com.tr/dolmabahce-de-tarihi-aciklama-siyaset-2021055/.

Minorsky. 1988. *Kürtler*. Köln: Weşanen Halepçe.
Minorsky, V., T. H Bois, and D.N Mac Kenzie. 2004. *Kürtler ve Kürdistan*. Translated by Kamuran Fıratlı. İstanbul: Doz.
Mir-Hosseini, Ziba. 1994. 'Inner Truth and Outer History: The Two Worlds of the Ahl-I Haqq of Kurdistan'. *International Journal of Middle East Studies* 26 (2): 267–85.
Miroğlu, Orhan. 2012. *Silahları Gömmek*. İstanbul: Everest Yayınları.
MLKP. 2017. 'İbrahim Kaypakkaya'. 2017. http://mlkp-info.org/index. php?kategori=1115&icerik_id=6857&%C4%B0brahim_Kaypakkaya.
Mojuetan, B.A. 2005. 'Abu Madian, Al-Shadhili, and the Spread of Sufism in the Magrib'. Edited by Kevin Shillington. *Encyclopedia of African History*. New York: Fitzroy Dearborn.
Moltchanova, Anna. 2009. *National Self-Determination and Justice in Multinational States*. London and New York: Springer.
Moore, Margaret. 1998. 'The Territorial Dimension of Self-Determination'. In *National Self-Determination and Secession*, edited by Margaret Moore, 134–57. Oxford and New York: Oxford University Press.
Moore, Margaret. 2005. 'Internal Minorities and Indigenous Self-Determination'. In *Minorities within Minorities: Equality, Rights and Diversity*, edited by Avigail Eisenberg and Jeff Spinner-Halev, 271–93. Cambridge: Cambridge University Press.
Moots, Glenn A. 2009. 'The Covenant Tradition of Federalism: The Pioneering Studies of Daniel J. Elazar'. In *The Ashgate Research Companion Federalism*, edited by Ann Ward and Lee Ward, 391–412. Surrey: Ashgate.
Morde, Alexander Porter. 1900. 'The Civil and Political Status of Inhabitants of Ceded Territories'. *Harvard Law Review* 14 (4): 262–72.
Muhammed Emin Zeki Beg. 2010. *Kürtler ve Kürdistan Tarihi*. İstanbul: Nûbihar.
Mutlu, Servet. 1996. 'Ethnic Kurds in Turkey: A Demographic Study'. *International Journal of Middle East Studies* 28 (4): 517–41.
Mybury-Lewis, David. 2002. *Indigenous Peoples, Ethnic Groups, and the State*. Second. Boston, MA: Allyn and Bacon.
Natali, Denise. 2009. *Kürtler ve Devlet: Irak, Türkiye ve İran'da Ulusal Kimliğin Gelişmesi*. Translated by Ibrahim Bingol. Birinci. İstanbul: Avesta.
Nereid, Camilla T. 1997. *In the Light of Said-I Nursi*. Bergen: Centre for Middle Easter and Islamic Studies.
Nester, William R. 2010. *Globalization, Wealth, and Power in the Twenty-First Century*. New York: Palgrave Macmillan.
Neyzi, Leyla. 2003. 'The Alevi Renaissance, Media and Music in the Nineties'. In *Turkey's Alevi Enigma: A Comprehensive Overview*, edited by Paul J. White and Joost Jongerden, 88: 111–24. Leiden and Boston, MA: Brill.
Nezan, Kendal. 1996. 'The Kurds: Current Position and Historical Background'. In *Kurdish Culture and Identity*, edited by Philip G. Kreyenbroek and Christine Allison, 7–19. London and New Jersey: Zed Books.

Nikitin, Bazil. 1994. *Kürtler; Sosyolojik ve Tarihi İnceleme*. Translated by Hüseyin Demirhan and Cemal Süreyya. Dördüncü. Cilt 1-2. İstanbul: Deng Yayınları.

Nimni, Ephraim. 2009. 'Nationalism, Ethnicity and Self-Determination: A Paradigm Shift?' *Studies in Ethnicity and Nationalism* 9 (2): 319-32.

Norman, Wayne. 1998. 'The Ethics of Secession as the Regulation of Secessionist Politics'. In *National Self-Determination and Secession*, edited by Margaret Moore, 34-61. Oxford and New York: Oxford University Press.

NTV Haber. 2011. 'MİT-PKK Görüşmeleri Sızdı'. NTV. 14 September 2011. https://www.ntv.com.tr/turkiye/mit-pkk-gorusmeleri-sizdi,a87SUp4ta0akgKLpkhb5-w.

Nugent, John T. 2004. 'The Defeat of Turkish Hezbollah as Model for Counter-Terrorism Strategy'. *Middle East Review of International Affairs* 8 (1): 69-76.

Öcalan, Abdullah. 1993. *Kürdistan Devriminin Yolu (Manifesto)*. 6th ed. Köln: Weşanên Serxwebûn 24.

Öcalan, Abdullah. 1999. *Decleration on the Democratic Solution of the Kurdish Question*. Translated by Kurdistan Information Centre. London: Mesopotamia Publishers.

Öcalan, Abdullah. 2009. *Özgürlük Sosyolojisi*. Neuss: Mezopotamya Yayınları.

Öcalan, Abdullah. 2010a. *Demokratik Konfederalizm*. http://komunar.net/tr/pirtuk/Konfederalizm.pdf: Abdullah Öcalan Sosyal Bilimler Akademisi Yayınları.

Öcalan, Abdullah. 2010b. 'Demokratik Özerklik'. *Komunar* (47) (Agustos.Eylül. Ekim)

Öcalan, Abdullah. 2011a. *Democratic Confederalism*. Second. London: Transmedia Publishing.

Öcalan, Abdullah. 2011b. *Prison Writings: The PKK and the Kurdish Question in the 21st Century*. Translated by Klaus Happel. International Initiative Edition. London: Transmedia Publishing.

Öcalan, Abdullah. 2012a. 'Yerel Bölgesel Sorunlar ve Demokratik Ulus Çözümü'. In *Yerel Bölgesel Sorunlar ve Demokratik Ulus Çözümü*, edited by Serxwebûn, 9-28. Weşanen Serxwebûn 154.

Öcalan, Abdullah. 2012b. 'Demokratik Konfederal Örgütlenme ve Demokratik Özerklik'. In *Yerel Bölgesel Sorunlar ve Demokratik Ulus Çözümü*, edited by Serxwebun, 29-40. Weşanen Serxwebûn 154.

Öcalan, Abdullah. 2012c. *Prison Writings III: The Road Map to Negotiations*. Translated by Havin Güneser. Cologne: International Initiative Edition.

Öcalan, Abdullah. 2013a. *Demokratik Uygarlik Manifestosu: Kapitalist Uygarlik-Kitap II*. Abdullah Öcalan Sosyal Bilimler Akademisi Yayınları.

Öcalan, Abdullah. 2013b. *Demokratik Uygarlık Manifestosu: Kürt Sorunu ve Demokratik Ulus Çözümü*. Vol. 5. Abdullah Öcalan Sosyal Bilimler Akademisi Yayınları.

Öcalan, Abdullah. 2013c. *Demokratik Uygarlık Manifestosu: Özgürlük Sosyolojisi Üzerine Denemeler-III Kitap*. Abdullah Öcalan Sosyal Bilimler Akademisi Yayınları.

Öcalan, Abdullah. 2016. *Democratic Nation*. Translated by International Initiative. Neuss: International Initiative Edition in cooperation with Mesopotamian Publishers.

Öcalan, Abdullah. 2017. *Democratic Confederalism*. Fourth. Neuss: International Initiative Edition in cooperation with Mesopotamian Publishers.

O'Duffy, Brendan. 2009. 'The Territorial Dimension'. In *Comparative Politics: Explaining Democratic System*, edited by Judith Bara and Mark Pennington, 201–26. Los Angeles and London: Sage.

O'leary, Brendan. 2004. 'Federations and the Management of Nations'. In *Ethnonationalism in the Contemprary World*, edited by Daniele Conversi. London and New York: Routledge.

Olmez, A. Osman. 1995. *Turkiye Siyasetinde DEP Depremi*. Ankara: Doruk Yayınları.

Olson, Robert. 1991. 'Five Stages of Kurdish Nationalism: 1880–1980'. *Journal of Institute of Muslim Minority Affairs* 12 (2): 391–409.

Olson, Robert. 1992. *Kürt Milliyetçiliğinin Kaynakları ve Şeyh Said İsyanı 1880–1925*. Translated by Bülent Peker and Nevzat Kıraç. Ankara: Özge.

Olson, Robert. 2009. *Kan İnanç ve Oy Pusulaları: Türkiye'de Kürt Milliyetçiliğinin Yönetimi 2007–09*. İstanbul: Avesta.

Olson, Robert. 2011. *The Kurdish National Movements in Turkey: 1980 to 2011*. Costa Mesa, CA: Mazda Publishers.

Olzak, Susan. 1983. 'Contemporary Ethnic Mobilization'. *Annual Review of Sociology* 9: 355–74.

O'Neil, Patrick H. 2013. *Essential of Comparative Politics*. Fourth. New York and London: W. W. Norton & Company.

Oran, Baskın. 2002. 'Kürt Milliyetçiliğinin Diyalektiği'. In *Milliyetçilik*, edited by Tanıl Bora and Murat Gültekingil, 4: 871–80. İstanbul: İletişim.

Oran, Baskın. 2004. *Türkiye'de Azınlıklar, Kavramlar, Teori, Lozan, Mevzuat, İçtihat, Uygulama*. Birinci. İstanbul: iletisim.

O'Shea, Maria T. 2004. *Trapped between the Map and Reality: Geography and Perceptions of Kurdistan*. New York and London: Routledge.

ÖSP Programı ve Tüzük. 2011. The party's rules and regulations are available on the party's official website; http://osp.org.tr/tuzuk.

Østergaard-Nielsen, Eva. 2003. *Transnational Politics: The Case of Turks and Kurds in Germany*. Routledg. London-New York.

Özcan, Ali Kemal. 2011. '"Mağdur" Miiliyetçilik: KürtSiyasetinin "Demokratik" Zaafiyet Ulus Açmazı'. *Ekonomik Yaklaşım* 22 (80): 79–120.

Özer, Ahmet. 2003. *Doğu'da Aşiret Düzeni ve Brukanlar*. Ankara: Elips.

Özer, Ahmet. 2009. *Beş Büyük Tarihi Kavşakta Kürtler ve Türkler*. İstanbul: Hemen Kitap.

Özoğlu, Hakan. 1996. 'State-Tribe Relations: Kurdish Tribalism in the 16th- and 17th-Century Ottoman Empire'. *British Journal of Middle Eastern Studies* 23 (1): 5–27.

Özoğlu, Hakan. 2004. *Kurdish Notables and the Ottoman State: Evolving Identities, Competing Loyalties, and Shifting Boundaries*. Albany: State University of New York Press.

Pamak, Mehmet. 2005. *İslami Açıdan Kürt Sorunu*. İkinci. Ankara: İlim ve Kültür Yayınları.

Parlar, Suat. 2005. *Türkler ve Kürtler*. İstanbul: Bağdat yayınları.

Parla, Taha. 1993. *Türkiye'nin Siyasal Rejimi: 1980–89*. İstanbul: İletişim Yayınları.
Parsons, Talcott. 1975. 'Some Theoretical Considerations on the Nature and Change of Ethnicity'. In *Ethnicity: Theory and Experience*, edited by Nathan Glazer and Daniel P. Moynihan, 53–83. Cambridge, MA and London: Harvard University Press.
Partiya Azadiya Kurdistane Program. 2014. http://www.partiyaazadiyakurdistane-pak.org/page9.php.
Partiya Serbestiya Dersim (PSD) Program Taslagi. 2009. http://desmalasure.com/psd-programi-dersim-manifestosu (Accessed 2 April 2014).
Patten, Alan. 2005. 'The Rights of Internal Linguistic Minorities'. In *Minorities within Minorities: Equality, Rights and Diversity*, edited by Avigail Eisenberg and Jeff Spinner-Halev, 135–56. Cambridge: Cambridge University Press.
Pekoz, Mustafa. 2009. *Islami Cumhurriyete Dogru*. İstanbul: Kalkedon.
Philpott, Daniel. 1998. 'Self-Determination in Practice'. In *National Self-Determination and Secession*, edited by Margaret Moore, 79–102. Oxford and New York: Oxford University Press.
Pierson, Christopher. 2004. *Modern State*. Second. London and New York: Routledge.
PKK II. Kongresine Sunulan PKK-MK Çalışma Raporu. 1984. Birinci Baskı. Köln: Weşanen Serxwebun 20.
PKK (Partiya Karkerên Kurdistan) Kuruluş Bildirgesi. 1984. 3rd ed. Köln: Weşanên Serxwebûn 25.
PKK (Partiya Karkerên Kurdistan) Program ve Tüzüğü. 1995. Köln: Weşanên Serxwebûn 71.
Poggi, Gianfranco. 1990. *The State: Its Nature, Development and Prospects*. Cambridge: Polity Press.
Poggi, Gianfranco. 2006. *Weber: A Short Introduction*. Cambridge: Polity.
Poladyan, Arşak. 1991. *VII-X Yüzyıllarda Kürtler*. Translated by Mehmet Demir. Ankara: Öz-ge.
Pratchett, Lawrence. 2004. 'Local Autonomy, Local Democracy and the "New Localism"'. *Political Studies* 52: 358–75.
Preece, J. Jackson. 2008. 'Minority/Majority'. Edited by Richard Schaefer. *Encyclopedia of Race, Ethnicity and Society*. London: Sage.
Proudhon, P.-J. 2014. *Federasyon İlkesi*. Translated by Merve Özaslan. İstanbul: Öteki Yayınevi.
Provence, Michael. 2005. *The Great Syrian Revolt and the Rise of Arab Nationalism, Modern Middle East Series*. 22. Austin: University of Texas Press.
Rafaat, Aram. 2007. 'An Independent Kurdish State: Achievable or Merely a Kurdish Dream?' *The Journal of Social, Political and Economic Studies* 32 (3): 267–304.
Rasler, Karen A., and William R. Thompson. 1985. 'War Making and State Making: Governmental Expenditures, Tax Revenues, and Global Wars'. *The American Political Science Review* 79 (2): 491–507.
Rejai, Mostafa, and Cynthia Enloe. 1969. 'Nation-States and State-Nations'. *International Studies Quarterly* 13 (2): 140–58.

Renan, Ernest. 2004. 'What Is a Nation?' In *Nationality and Nationalism\Volume 1*, edited by Athena S. Leoussi and Steven Grosby, 1:27–39.London and New York: I.B.Tauris.
Resulalan, Osman. 1991. 'Kurtlerin Trajedisi'. *DAVA* (15) (Haziran): 13–15.
Rex, John. 1993. 'Religion and Ethnicity in the Metropolis'. In *Religion and Ethnicity: Minorities and Social Change in the Metropolis*, edited by Rohit Barot, 17–26. Kampen: Pharos.
Richter, Melvin. 1987. 'Absolutism'. Edited by David Miller, Janet Coleman, William Connolly, and Alan Ryan. *The Blackwell Encyclopedia of Political Thought*. Hoboken, New Jersey, US: Blackwell Publishing.
Robbins, Bruce, and Elsa Stamatopoulou. 2004. 'Reflections on Culture and Cultural Rights'. *The South Atlantic Quarterly* 103 (2/3): 419–34.
Robins, Philip. 1993. 'The Overlord State: Turkish Policy and the Kurdish Issue'. *International Affairs (Royal Institute of International Affairs 1944–69* (4): 657–76.
Romano, David. 2010. *Kürt Dirilişi, Mobilizasyon ve Kimlik*. Translated by Mustafa Topal and Erdoğan Gedik. İstanbul: Vate.
Rothchild, Donald, and Caroline A. Hartzell. 2000. 'Security in Deeply Divided Societies: The Role of Territorial Autonomy'. In *Identity and Territorial Autonomy in Plural Societies*, edited by William Safran and Ramon Maiz, 254–71. London and Portland, OR: Frank Cass.
Rudaw. 2015. 'HDP Azadi'yi Böldü'. Rudaw. 15 June 2015. http://www.rudaw.net/turkish/kurdistan/150620157.
Rubin, Michael. 2003. 'Are Kurds a Pariah Minority?' *Social Research* 70 (1): 295–330.
Ryan, Stephan. 1990. *Ethnic Conflict and International Relations*. Aldershot: Dartmouth.
Safran, William. 2000. 'Spatial and Functional Dimension of Autonomy: Cross-National and Theoretical Perspectives'. In *Identity and Territorial and Autonomy in Plural Societies*, edited by William Safran and Ramon Maiz, 11–34. London and Portland, OR: Frank Cass.
Safran, William, and Amy H. Liu. 2012. 'Nation-Building, Collective Identity, and Language Choices: Between Instrumental and Value Rationalities'. *Nationalism and Ethnic Politics* 18 (3): 269–92.
Safrastian, Arshak. 2007. *Kurd Û Kurdistan*. Translated by Ergin Opengîn. İstanbul: Avesta.
Sagnıç, Cenk. 2010. 'Mountain Turks: State Ideology and the Kurds in Turkey'. *Information, Society and Justice*, 3 (2): 127–34.
Samer, Mart. 2012. *Toplumsal Sorunlar & Yeni Anayasa; Algi, Beklenti ve Talepler*. Diyarbakır.
Sançar, Mithat. 2011. 'Barış ve Çözüm Sürecinin Dinamikleri Bölüm 1'. In *Barış ve Çözüm Sürecinin Dinamikleri*, edited by Priscilla Hayner, Kerim Yıldız, and Mithat Sançar, 11–28. London: Democratic Progress Institute.
Saraçoğlu, Cenk. 2010. 'The Changing Image of the Kurds in Turkish Cities: Middle-Class Perceptions of Kurdish Migrants in İzmir'. *Patterns of Prejudice* 44 (3): 239–69.

Sarıgöl, Zeki. 2010. 'Curbing Kurdish Ethnonationalism in Turkey: An Empirical Assessment of Pro-Islamic and Socio-Economic Approaches'. *Ethnic and Racial Studies* 33 (3): 533–53.

Sasoni, Garo. 1986. *Kürt Ulusal Haerketleri ve Ermeni Kürt İlişkileri (15. yy'dan Günümüze)*. Translated by Bedros Zartaryan and Memo Yetkin. Stockholm: Orfeus.

Schermerhon, Richard. 1996. 'Ethnicity and Minority Groups'. In *Ethnicity*, edited by John Hutchinson and Anthony D. Smith, 17–18. Oxford and New York: Oxford University Press.

Schulze, Hagen. 2005. *Avrupa'da Ulus ve Devletler*. Translated by Timuçin Binder. İstanbul: Literatür Yayınları.

Scott, James C. 2006. 'State Simplification'. In *Contemporary Political Philosophy*, edited by Robert E. Goodin and Philip Pettit, Second, 26–54. Victoria: Blackwell Publishing.

Scott, James C. 1998. *Seeing Like a State: How Certain Schemes to Improve the Human Condition Have Failed*. New Haven, CT: Yale University Press.

Seferoğlu, Şükrü Kaya, and Halil Kemal Türközü. 1982. *101 Soruda Türkler'in Kürt Boyu*. Ankara: Türk Kültürünü Araştırma Enstitüsü.

SEGE (2011) Sonuçları. 2013. *İllerin ve Bölgelerin Sosyo-Ekonomik Gelişmişlik Sıralaması Araştırması (SEGE–2011)*. T.C. Kalkınma Bakanlığı.

Selçuk, Ali. 2012. '.Merkezi Kurumsal Otoritenin Ötekileştirdiği Bir Topluluk; Anşa Bacılılar'. *Türk Kültürü ve Hacı Bektaşi ve Araştırma Dergisi* (61): 169–86.

Şener, Mustafa. 2007. 'Türkiye İşçi Partisi'. In *Modern Türkiye'de Siyasi Düşünce: Sol*, edited by Tanıl Bora and Murat Gültekingil, 356–417. İstanbul: İletişim.

Şengül, Serdar. 2004. 'İslamcılık, Kürtler ve Kürt Sorunu'. In *Modern Türkiye'de Siyasi Düşünce: İslamcılık*, 6: 525–43. İstanbul: İletişim.

Şenturk, Hulusi. 2011. *Turkiye'de Islami Olusum ve Siyaset: Islamcilik*. 2nd ed. İstanbul: Cira.

Şeref Han. 2006. *Şerefname (1597)*. Translated by M. Emin Bozarslan. İstanbul.

Serxwebûn. 1995. 'Kürdistan Sosyalizmi Sınırları Aşıyor', no. 166. Ekim.

Serxwebûn. 2000. 'Uusal Gelişimi Yaratacak Olan Demokratik Gelişimdir', no. 224. Agustos.

Serxwebûn. 2010. 'Demokratik Özerklik ve Siyaset Gerçeği', no. 346. Ekim.

Serxwebûn. 2011. 'Xweseriya Demokratik Pirozbe-Hejmar', no. 355.

Serxwebûn. 2012a. 'Demokratik Özerklikte Hukuki Boyut'. In *Yerel Bölgesel Sorunlar ve Demokratik Ulus Çözümü*, edited by Serxwebûn, 137–64. Köln/Cologne, Germany: Weşanen Serxwebûn 154.

Serxwebûn. 2012b. 'Demokratik Özerklik ve Siyaset Gerçeği'. In *Yerel Bölgesel Sorunlar ve Demokratik Ulus Çözümü*, edited by Serxwebûn, 125–36. Köln/Cologne, Germany: Weşanen Serxwebûn 154.

Serxwebûn. 2012c. 'Demokratik Ulus'. In *Yerel Bölgesel Sorunlar ve Demokratik Ulus Çözümü*, edited by Serxwebûn, 89–102. Köln/Cologne, Germany: Weşanen Serxwebûn 154.

SETA and POLLMARK. 2009. *Public Perception of the Kurdish Question in Turkey*. Ankara.

Seufer, Gunter. 1997. 'Between Religion and Ethnicty: A Kurdish-Alevi Tribe in Globalizing İstanbul'. In *Space Culture and Power*, edited by Ayşe Öncü and Petra Weyland, 157–76. London: Zed Books.
Sever, Tahsin. 2010. *Unutturulmaya Çalışılan Bir Örgüt ve Çarpıtılan Bir Tarih: 1925 Hareketi Azad Örgütü*. İstanbul: Doz.
Shakland, David. 1999. *Islam and Society in Turkey*. Cambridgeshire: The Eothen Press.
Shakland, David. 2003. *The Alevis in Turkey; The Emergence of a Secular Islamic Tradition*. London and New York: RoutledgeCurzon.
Sharma, P.K. 1979. *Federalism and Political Development (Developed and Developing Areas)*. Delhi: Pragati Publications.
Shaw, Standford J., and Ezel Kural Shaw. 1977. *History of the Ottoman Empire and Modern Turkey*. Cambridge: Cambridge University Press.
Sheyholislami, Jaffer. 2010. 'Identity, Language, and New Media: The Kurdish Case'. *Language Policy* 9 (4): 289–312.
Shorten, Andrew. 2008. 'Nation and State'. In *Issues in Political Theory*, edited by Catriona McKinnon, 31–55. Oxford and New York: Oxford University Press.
SHP *Doğu ve Guneydoğu Sorununa Bakışı ve Cozum Onerileri Raporu*. 1989. (SHPSosyal Demokrat Halkci Parti).
Silopi, Zınar. 1969. *Doza Kürdüstan: KürtMilletinin 60 Senedenberi Esaretten Kurtuluş Savaşı Hatıratı*. Paris: Stewr.
Simeon, Richard. 2004. 'Canada : Federalism, Language, and Regional Conflict'. In *Federalism and Territorial Cleavages*, edited by Ugo M. Amoretti and Nancy Bermeo, 93–122. Baltimore, MD and London: The Johns Hopkins University Press.
Şimşek, Sefa. 2004. 'New Social Movements in Turkey since 1980'. *Turkish Studies* 5 (2): 111–39.
Sirkeci, İbrahim. 2000. 'Exploring the Kurdish Population in the Turkish Context'. *Genus* 56 (1–2): 149–75.
Siverekli, İsmet. 2008. *Kürdistan'da Siyasal İslam*. İstanbul: Pêrî.
Skinners, Quention. 2006. 'The State'. In *Contemporary Political Philosophy*, edited by Robert E. Goodin and Philip Pettit, Second, 3–25. Victoria: Blackwell Publishing.
Smith, Anthony D. 1991. *National Identity*. London: Penguin Books.
Smith, Anthony D. 1993. 'The Ethnic Sources of Nationalism'. *Survival: Global Politics and Strategy* 35 (1): 48–62.
Smith, Anthony D. 1996. 'The Origin of Nation'. In *Becoming National*, edited by Geoff Eley and Ronald Grigor Suny, 106–30. Oxford and New York: Oxford University Press.
Smith, Anthony D. 2005. 'The Genealogy of Nations: An Ethno-Symbolic Approach'. In *When Is the Nation? Towards an Understanding of Theories of Nationalism*, edited by Atsuko Ichijo and Uzelac Gordona, 94–112. London and New York: Routledge.
Smith, Anthony D. 2009. *Ethno-Symbolism and Nationalism: A Cultural Approach*. London and New York: Routledge.
Smooha, Sammy, and Theodor Hanf. 1996. 'Conflict-Regulation in Deeply Divided Societies'. In *Ethnicity*, edited by John Hutchinson and Anthony D. Smith, 326–33. Oxford and New York: Oxford University Press.

Solgun, Cafer. 2008. *Alevilerin Kemalizm'le Imtihanı*. 1st ed. İstanbul: hayy.
Sol Portal. 2013. 'Türk Ulusuyla Kürt Milliyetini Eşit, Eş Değerde Gördüremezsiniz', 11 January. http://haber.sol.org.tr/devlet-ve-siyaset/birgul-ayman-guler-turk-ulusuyla-kurt-milliyetini-esit-es-degerde-gorduremezsiniz.
Somer, Murat. 2002. 'Ethnic Kurds, Endogenous Identities, and Turkey's Democratization and Integration with Europe'. *Global Review of Ethnopolitics* 1 (4): 74–93.
Somer, Murat, and Evangelos G. Liaras. 2010. 'Turkey's New Kurdish Opening: Religious Versus Secular Values'. *Middle East Policy* XVII (2): 152–65.
Somersan, Semra. 2008. 'Babil Kulesi'nde Etnilerden Ulus-Devletlere'. *Doğu-Batı Düşünce Dergisi* (44) (March): 75–90.
Song, Sarah. 2007. *Justice, Gender, and the Politics of Multiculturalism*. Cambridge: Cambridge University Press.
Sönmez, Mustafa. 2013. 'Kurds still Migrating to Western Turkish Cities'. *Hürriyet Daily News*. 5 April 2013. http://www.hurriyetdailynews.com/kurds-still-migrating-to-western-turkish-cities-46198.
Spanish Constitution. 1978. http://www.congreso.es/portal/page/portal/Congreso/Congreso/Hist_Normas/Norm/const_espa_texto_ingles_0.pdf.
Spira, Thomas. 2004. 'Ethnicity and Nationality: The Twin Matrices of Nationalism'. In *Ethnonationalism in the Contemporary World*, edited by Daniele Conversi, 248–68. London and New York: Routledge.
Spruyt, Hendrik. 2002. 'The Origins, Development, and Possible Decline of the Modern State'. *Annual Review of Political Science* 5: 127–49.
Spruyt, Hendrik. 2007. 'War, Trade, and State Formation'. In *The Oxford Handbook of Comparative Politics*, edited by Carles Boix and Susan Stokes, 211–35. Oxford and New York: Oxford University Press.
Stake, Robert E. 2000. 'Case Study'. In *Handbook of Qualitative Research*, edited by Norman K. Denzin and Yvonna S. Lincoln, Second, 435–54. Thousand Oaks, CA, London and New Delhi: Sage Publication.
Stavenhagen, Rodolfo. 2013. *Peasants, Culture and Indigenous Peoples: Critical Issues*. Vol. 4. Mexico: Springer.
Steen, Eveline Van Der. 2009. 'Tribal Societies in the Nineteenth Century: A Model'. In *Nomads, Tribes, and the State in the Ancient Near East Cross-Disciplinary Perspectives*, edited by Jeffrey Szuchman and Hans and other. Bernard, 105–17. The University of Chicago Oriental Institute Seminars, Number 5.
Steiner, Henri J. 1991. 'Ideals and Counter-Ideals in the Struggle over Autonomy Regimes for Minorities'. *Notre Dame Law Review* 66: 1539–60.
Stepan, Alfred. 2004. 'Federalism and Democracy'. In *Federalism and Territorial Cleavages*, edited by Ugo M. Amoretti and Nancy Bermeo, 441–56. Baltimore, MD and London: The Johns Hopkins University Press.
Storey, David. 2002. 'Territory and National Identity: Examples from the Former Yugoslavia'. *Geography* 87 (2): 108–15.
Strohmeier, Martin. 2003. *Crucial Images in the Presentation of a Kurdish National Identity: Heroes and Patriots, Traitors and Foes*. Leiden and Boston, MA: Brill.

Süreyya Bedirhan. 1994. *Kürt Davası ve Hoybun*. Translated by Dilara Zirek. İstanbul: Med Yayınları.

Symonides, Janusz. 1998. 'Cultural Rights: A Neglected Category of Human Rights'. *International Social Science Journal* 50 (158): 559–72.

Szyliowicz, Joseph S. 1966. 'Political Participation and Modernization in Turkey'. *The Western Political Quarterly* 19 (2): 266–84.

Tan, Altan. 2009. *Kürt Sorunu: Ya Tam Kardeşlik Ya Hep Birliket Kölelil*. 4th ed. İstanbul: Timaş.

Tannenbaum, Donald, and David Schultz. 2008. *Siyasi Düşünce Tarihi: Filozoflar ve Fikirleri*. Translated by Fatih Demirci. Ankara: Adress.

Tapper, Richard. 1990. 'Anthropologists, Historians, and Tribespeople: On Tribe and State Formation in the Middle East'. In *Tribes and State Formation in the Middle East*, edited by Philip S. Khoury and Joseph Kostiner, 48–73. Berkeley, Los Angeles and Oxford: University of California Press.

Taskin, Yuksel. 2008. 'AKP's Move to "Conquer" the Center-Right: Its Prospects and Possible Impacts on the Democratization Process'. *Turkish Studies* 9 (1): 53–72.

Taşpınar, Ömer. 2005. *Kurdish Nationalism and Political Islam in Turkey*. London and New York: Routledge.

Taşpınar, Ömer, and Gönül Tol. 2014. 'Turkey and the Kurds: From Predicament to Opportunity'. *US-Europe Analysis Series*. Center on the United States and Europe at Brookings (54) (January): 1–12. https://www.brookings.edu/wp-content/uploads/2016/06/Turkey-and-the-Kurds_Predicament-to-Opportunity.pdf

Tayiz, Kurtuluş. 2014. *30 Mart'a Doğru Barış ve Demokrasi Partisi*. 83. İstanbul: SETA.

Taylor, Brain D., and Roxana Botea. 2008. 'War-Making and State-Making in the Contemporary Third World'. *International Studies Review* 10 (1): 27–56.

T.C. Yüksek Seçim Kurulu. 2014. '2009 ve 2014 Mahalli İdareler Genel Seçimlerini Kazanan Kadın ve Erkek Adayların Siyasi Partilere Dağılımı'. *YSK (T.C. Yüksek Seçim Kurulu)*. http://www.ysk.gov.tr/ysk/faces/Secimler?_adf.ctrl-state=16dmhy0wlb_80&wcnav.model=YSKUstMenu&_afrLoop=15720928759270530. (Accessed 22 August).

Tekin, Osman. 2013. *İzzettin Yıldırım Mazlum Bir Şehidin Adanmışlık Öyküsü*. İstanbul: Gündönümü Yayınları.

Tezcür, Güneş Murat. 2009. 'Kurdish Nationalism and Identity in Turkey: A Conceptual Reinterpretation'. *European Journal of Turkish Studies* (10): 1–19. https://journals.openedition.org/ejts/4008

The Turkish Constitutional Court 1992/1 E, 1993/1 K, Date: 14 July 1993. http://www.kararlar.anayasa.gov.tr/karar.php?l=manage_karar&ref=show&action=karar&id=2154&content=HEP] (Accessed 31 March 2014).

The Turkish Constitutional Court 1993/3 E, 1994/2 K, Date: 30 June 1994. http://www.kararlaryeni.anayasa.gov.tr/Karar/Content/68992747-a31d-4797-bc8a-88277e2fbf58?excludeGerekce=False&wordsOnly=False.

The Turkish Constitutional Court 1997/1 E, 1998/1 K, Date: 16 January 1998. http://www.kararlaryeni.anayasa.gov.tr/Karar/Content/0acac7b9-4875-4c09-a89d-16336ed73728?excludeGerekce=False&wordsOnly=False.

The Turkish Constitutional Court 1999/1 E, 2003/1 K, Date: 13 March 2003. http://www.kararlaryeni.anayasa.gov.tr/Karar/Content/edb5ab7a-0fd0-45ee-b448-d8d6c6795f8c?excludeGerekce=False&wordsOnly=False, (Accessed 31 March 2014).

The Turkish Constitutional Court 2002/1 E, 2008/1 K, Date: 29 January 2008.

The Turkish Constitutional Court 2007/1 E, 2009/4 K, Date: 11 December 2009. http://www.kararlaryeni.anayasa.gov.tr/Karar/Content/bcc31b06-16c4-46cf-8c82-e293fbfce13e?excludeGerekce=False&wordsOnly=False (Accessed 31 March 2014).

The United Nations Educational, Scientific and Cultural Organization (UNESCO). 2002. *Records of the General Conference*. 31st. Paris: UNESCO.

Thompson, Simon. 2006. *The Political Theory of Recognition: A Critical Introduction*. Cambridge: Polity.

Tibi, Bessim. 1990. 'The Simultaneity of the Unsimultaneous: Old Tribes and Imposed Nation-States in the Modern Middle East'. In *Tribes and State Formation in the Middle East*, edited by Philip S. Khoury and Joseph Kostiner, 127–52. Berkeley, Los Angeles and Oxford: University of California Press.

Tilly, Charles. 1975. 'Reflections on the History of European State-Making'. In *The State Formation of National States in Western Europe*, edited by Charles Tilly, 3–83. Princeton, NJ and New Jersey: Princeton University Press.

Tilly, Charles. 1985. 'War Making and State Making as Organized Crime'. In *Bringing the State Back In*, edited by Peter B. Evans, Dietrich Rueschemeyer, and Theda Skocpol, 169–91. Cambridge: Cambridge University Press.

Tivey, Leonard James. 1981. 'Introduction'. In *The Nation-State the Formation of Modern Politics*, edited by Leonard James Tivey, 1–12. Oxford: Martin Robertson.

TKİP Programı. 1998. 'Program'. 1998. http://www.tkip.org/index.php?id=46&no_cache=1.

Tonkin, Elisabeth, Maryon Mcdonal, and Malcolm Chapman. 1996. 'History and Ethnicity'. In *Ethnicity*, edited by John Hutchinson and Anthony D. Smith, 18–24. Oxford and New York: Oxford University Press.

Topal, Mustafa. 2003. *Ulusu Düşünmek*. 1st ed. Ankara: Özgür Üniversite Kitaplığı.

Treaty of Peace With the Turkey (Sévres) No. 11 (F.O.284) (29524). 1920. His Majesty's Stationary Office. http://treaties.fco.gov.uk/docs/pdf/1920/TS0011.pdf (Accessed 11 April 2014, at 11: 16).

Tuğul, Cihan. 2010. *Pasif Devrim: İslami Muhalefetin Düzenle Bütünleşmesi*. Translated by Ferit Burak Aydar. İstanbul: Koç Üniversitesi Yayınları.

Tunaya, Tarık Zafer. 1988. *Türkiye'de Siyasal Partiler; İkinci Meşrutiyet Dönemi*. İkinci. Cilt 2 vols. İstanbul: Hürriyet Vakfı Yayınları.

Turan, İlter. 1991. 'Siyasal İdeoloji Olarak İslam ve Milliyetçilik'. In *Çağdaş Türkiye'de İslam: Din, Siyaset, Edebiyat ve Laik Devlet*, edited by Richard Tapper, translated by Özden Arıkan, 39–69. İstanbul: Sarmal.

Turkish Statistical Institute. 2012. *General Election of Representatives Province and District Results 2011, 2007, 2002, 1999, 1995, 1991.* Ankara.

Turkish Statistical Institute. *General Election of Representatives Province and District Results 2002, 1999, 1995, 1991.* Ankara.

Türkiye Cumhuriyeti Cumhurbaşkanlığı. 2016. 'T.C. Cumhurbaşkanlışı : ABD'deki Türk STK'larla Bir Araya Geldiği Toplantıda Yaptıkları Konuşma'. Türkiye Cumhuriyeti Cumhurbaşkanlığı. 22 September 2016. https://www.tccb.gov.tr/konusmalar/353/52398/abddeki-turk-stklarla-bir-araya-geldigi-toplantida-yaptiklari-konusma.html.

Türkiye Kürdistan Demokrat Partisi Programı. 2014. The Partyis program and rules and regulations are available at; http://www.t-kdp.com/.

Türkiye Kürdistan Demokrat Partisi Tüzüğü. 2014. The Partyis program and rules and regulations are available at; http://www.t-kdp.com/.

Türkmen, Hamza. 2009. *Ulusçuluk Çıkmazı: Kürtler ve Çözüm Arayışı.* İstanbul: Ekin Yayınları.

Tutar, Cemal. 2011. 'Cemal Tutar'ın Savunması'. In *Hizbullah Ana Davasi Savunmalar,* 109–348. İstanbul: Dua Yayıncılık.

Ulusoy, Kıvanç. 2011. 'The European Impact on State–Religion Relations in Turkey: Political Islam, Alevis and Non-Muslim Minorities'. *Australian Journal of Political Science* 46 (3): 407–23.

Ülsever, Cüneyt. 2011. *Yeni-Osmanlıcılık ve Kürt Açılımı.* İstanbul: Kırmızıkedi.

United Nations' Universial Declaration of Human Rights. 1948. 60th Anniversary Special Edition.

Uslu, Emre. 2010. *Derin Devletin Tehdit Haritası : Dün Kürtler Bügün Cemaatler.* İstanbul: Karakutu.

Uslu, Emrullah. 2007. 'From Local Hezbollah to Global Terror: Militant Islam in Turkey'. *Middle East Policy* xıv (1): 124–41.

Vali, Abbas, ed. 2005. 'Kürtlerin Soykütükleri: Kürt Tarihi Yazımında Ulus ve Ulusal Kimliğin İnşaası'. In *Kürt Milliyetçiliğinin Kökenleri.* İstanbul: Avesta.

Van Bruinessen, Martin. 1983. 'Kurdish Tribes and the State of Iran: The Case of Simko's Revolt'. In *Tribe and State in Iran and Afganistan,* edited by Richard Tapper, 364–400. New York: Routledge.

Van Bruinessen, Martin. 1992. 'Kurdish Society, Ethnicity, Nationalism and Refugee Problems'. In *The Kurds: A Contemporary Overview,* edited by Philip G. Kreyenbroek and Sterl Stefan, 26–52. London: Routledge.

Van Bruinessen, Martin. 1996. 'Kurds, Turks and the Alevi Revival in Turkey'. In *Minorities in the Middle East: Power and the Politics of Difference,* 200:7–10. Middle East Report.

Van Bruinessen, Martin. 2000a. *Kürtlük, Türklük, Alevilik; Ethnic ve Dinsel Kimlik Mücadeleleri.* Translated by Hakan Yurdakul. İstanbul: İletişim Yayınları.

Van Bruinessen, Martin. 2000b. 'Religion in Kurdistan'. In *Mullas, Sufis and Heretics: The Role of Religion in Kurdish Society: Collected Articles,* 13–36. İstanbul: The Isis Press.

Van Bruinessen, Martin. 2000c. 'Popular Islam, Kurdish Nationalism and Rural Revolt: The Rebellion of Shaik Said in Turkey (1925)'. In *Mullas, Sufis and Heretics: The Role of Religion in Kurdish Society: Collected Articles*, 143–57. İstanbul: The Isis Press.

Van Bruinessen, Martin. 2000d. *Kurdish Ethno-Nationalism Versus Nation-Building States; Collected Articles*. İstanbul: The Isis Press.

Van Bruinessen, Martin. 2003. *Ağa, Şeyh, Devlet*. Translated by Banu Yalkut. İstanbul: İletişim.

Van Bruinessen, Martin. 2006. 'Kurdish Paths to Nation'. In *The Kurds: Nationalism and Politics*, edited by Faleh A. Jabar and Hosham Dawod, 21–48. London, San Francisco, CA and Beirut: Saqi.

Van Bruinessen, Martin. 2010. *Kurdistan Üzerine Yazılar*. Translated by Nevzat Kıraç, Bülent Peker, Leyla Keskiner, Halil Turansal, Selda Somuncuoglu, and Levent Kafadar. Yedi. İstanbul: İletisim.

Van Den Berghe, Pierre L. 2005. 'Ethnicities and Nations: Genealogy Indeed'. In *When Is the Nation? Towards an Understanding of Theories of Nationalism*, edited by Atsuko Ichijo and Uzelac Gordona, 113–18. London and New York: Routledge.

Van der Laan Bouma-Doff, Wenda. 2007. 'Confined Contact: Residential Segregation and Ethnic Bridges in the Netherlands'. *Urban Studies* 44 (5/6): 997–1017.

Vanli, Ismet Şerif. 1992. 'The Kurds in Syria and Lebanon'. In *The Kurds: A Contemporary Overview*, edited by Philip G. Kreyenbroek and Stefan Sperl, 143–70. London and New York: Routledge.

Van Wilgenburg, Wladimir. 2012. 'Post-Jihadism and Kurdish Hezbollah'. *Near East Quarterly*, 26 June. http://www.neareastquarterly.com/index.php/2012/06/26/post-jihadism-and-kurdish-hezbollah/?output=pdf.

Veer, Peter van der. 1999. 'The Moral State: Religion, Nation,and Empire in Victorian Britain and British India'. In *Nation and Religion: Perspectives on Europe and Asia*, edited by Peter van der Veer and Hartmut Lehman, 15–43. Princeton, NJ: Princeton University Press.

Vincent, Andrew. 1987. *Theories of the State*. Oxford and Cambridge: Blackwell.

Vorhoff, Karin. 1998. '"Let's Reclaim Our History and Culture!": Imagining Alevi Community in Contemporary Turkey'. *Die Welt Des Islams, New Series* 38 (2): 220–52.

Walker, Joshua W. 2013. 'International Dimension of the "Kurdish Question" in Turkey'. In *Understanding Turkey's Kurdish Question*, edited by Fevzi Bilgin and Ali Sarihan, 223–37. Lanham, MD, Boulder, CO, New York, Toronto and Plymouth: Lexington Books.

Waller, Micheal, and Andrew Linklater. 2003. 'Introduction Loyalty and the Post-National State'. In *Political Loyalty and the Nation-State*, edited by Micheal Waller and Andrew Linklater, 1–14. London and New York: Routledge.

Wall, Steven. 2007. 'Collective Rights and Individual Autonomy'. *Ethcis* 117 (2): 234–64.

Watt, Montgomery. 1970. 'Muhammed'. In *The Cambrdige History of Islam: The Central Islamic Lands from Pre-Islamic Times to the First World War*, edited by P. M Holt,

Ann K. Lambton, and Bernard Lewis, First, 1A:30–56. Cambridge: Cambridge University Press.

Watts, Nicole. 1999. 'Allies and Enemies: Pro-Kurdish Parties in Turkish Politics, 1990-94'. *International Journal of Middle East Studies* 31 (4): 631–56.

Weber, Max. 1978. *Economy and Society*. Edited by Guenther Roth and Claus Wittich. Berkeley, Los Angeles and London: University of California Press.

Weber, Max. 2004. 'The Nation'. In *Nationality and Nationalism/Volume 1*, edited by Athena S. Leoussi and Steven Grosby, 1:40–46.London and New York: I.B.Tauris.

Weller, Marc. 2009. 'Settling Self-Determination Conflicts: Recent Developments'. *The European Journal of International Law* 20 (1): 111–65.

Westrbeim, Kariane. 2010. 'Dağları Seçmek: Alternat'f Bir Kimlik Projesi Olarak PKK'. *Toplumsal Tarih Dergisi* (4) (Güz): 39–68.

Wheatley, Jonathan. 2010. 'The Case for Asymmetric Federalism in Georgia: A Missed Oppurtunity'. In *Asymmetric Autonomy and the Settlement of Ethnic Conflicts*, edited by Marc Weller and Kathrina Nobbs, 213–30. Philadelphia and Oxford: University of Pennsylvania Press.

White, Jenny B. 2002. *Islamist Mobilization in Turkey*. Seatle and London: University of Washington Press.

White, Paul J. 2003. 'The Debate on the Identity of "Alevi Kurds."' In *Turkey's Alevi Enigma; A Comprehensive Overview*, edited by Paul J. White and Joost Jongerden, 88:17–29. Leiden and Boston, MA: Brill.

White, Paul J. 2012. *İlkel İsyancılarmı? Devrimci Modernleştiriciler Mi? Türkiye'de Kürt Ulusal Hareketi*. Translated by Mustafa Topal. İstanbul: Vate.

Wiktorowicz, Quintan. 2006. 'Anatomy of the Salafi Movement'. *Studies in Conflict & Terrorism* 29 (3): 207–39.

Wimmer, Andreas, and Yuval Feinstein. 2010. 'The Rise of the Nation-State across the World, 1816 to 2001'. *American Sociological Review* 75 (5): 764–90.

Wong, Mabel. 2013. 'Reclaiming Identity: Rethinking Non-Territorial Autonomy'. *Journal on Ethnopolitics and Minority Issues in Europe* 12 (1): 56–75.

Woodhead, Linda. 2011. 'Five Concepts of Religion'. *International Review of Sociology: Revue Internationale de Sociologie* 21 (1): 121–43.

Xanthaki, Alexandra. 2005. 'The Right to Self-Determination: Meaning and Scope'. In *Minorities, Peoples and Self-Determination*, edited by Nazila Ghanea and Alexandra Xanthaki, 15–54. Leiden and Boston, MA: Martinus Nijhoff Publishers.

Yalçın-Mousseau, Demet. 2012. 'An Inquiry into the Linkage among Nationalizing Policies, Democratization, and Ethno-Nationalist Conflict: The Kurdish Case in Turkey'. *Nationalities Papers* 40 (1): 45–62.

Yavuz, M. Hakan. 2001. 'Five Stages of the Construction of Kurdish Nationalism in Turkey'. *Nationalism & Ethnic Politics*. 7 (3): 1–24.

Yavuz, M. Hakan.2003. *Islamic Political Identity in Turkey*. Oxford and New York: Oxford University Press.

Yavuz, M. Hakan. 2006. 'The Renaissance of Religious Consciousness in Turkey : Nur Study Circles'. In *Islam in Public*, edited by Nilüfer Göle and Ludwig Ammann, 129–61. İstanbul: İstanbul Bilgi University Press.

Yavuz, M. Hakan. 2011. *Erbakan'dan Erdoğan'a Laiklik, Demokrasi, Kürt Sorunu ve İslam*. Translated by Leman Adalı. İstanbul: Kitap yayınevi.

Yavuz, M. Hakan, and Nihat Ali Özcan. 2006. 'The Kurdish Question and Turkey's Justice and Development Party'. *Middle East Policy* XIII (1): 102–19.

Yayman, Huseyin. 2011. *Turkiye'nin Kürt Sorunu Hafizasi*. İstanbul: Dogan Kitap.

Yeğen, Mesut. 1996. 'The Turkish State Discourse and the Execution of Kurdish Identity'. In *Turkey Identity; Democracy, Politics*, edited by Sylvia Kedourie, 216–29. New York: Frank Cass.

Yeğen, Mesut. 2007a. 'Türkiye Solu ve Kürt Sorunu'. In *Modern Türkiye'de Siyasi Düşünce: Sol*, edited by Tanıl Bora and Murat Gültekingil, 1208–36. İstanbul: İletişim Yayınları.

Yeğen, Mesut. 2007b. 'Turkish Nationalism and the Kurdish Question'. *Ethnic and Racial Studies* 30 (1): 119–51.

Yeğen, Mesut. 2011. *Son Kürt İsyanı*. İstanbul: İletişim.

Yeğen, Mesut. 2013. 'Türkiye'de Kürt Sorunu'. In *Türkiye'de Milliyetçilik ve Politika: Politik İslam, Kemalizm ve Kürt Sorunu*, edited by Marlies Casier and Joost Jongerden, translated by Pınar Uygun, Batu Boran, Muhtesim Güvenç, and Metin Çulhaoğlu, 109–36. İstanbul: Vate.

Yeğen, Mesut. 2016. 'Armed Struggle to Peace Negotiations: Independent Kurdistan to Democratic Autonomy, or the PKK in Context'. *Middle East Critique* 25 (4): 365–83.

Yenişafak Newspaper. 2005. 'Kürt Sorunu Benim Sorunumdur'. 13 August 2005. http://yenisafak.com.tr/arsiv/2005/agustos/13/p01.html, (Accessed 4 March 2014).

Yildiz, Hasan. 1989. *Asiretten Ulusalliga Dogru Kurtler*. Stockholm: Firat-Dicle Yayinlari.

Yildiz, Hasan. 2006. *20. Yüzyılın Başlarında Kürt Siyaseti ve Modernizm*. 2nd ed. İstanbul: Doz.

Yıldız, Kerim. 2004. *The Kurds in Iraq: The Past, Present and Future*. London and Ann Arbor, MI: Pluto Press.

Yıldız, Kerim. 2005a. *The Kurds in Turkey: EU Accession and Human Rights*. London: Pluto Press.

Yıldız, Kerim. 2005b. *The Kurds in Syria: The Forgotten People*. London and Ann Arbor, MI: Pluto Press.

Yıldız, Kerim. 2012. 'Turkey's Kurdish Conflict: Pathways to Progress'. *Insight Turkey* 14 (4): 151–74.

Yilmaz, İhsan. 2013. 'Türkiye'de Yeni Anayasa Tartışmaları: Din Özgürlüğü ve İslama Ters Düşmeyen Laik Devlet Üzerine Bir Yorum Denemesi'. *Yeni Türkiye* 50: 684–93.

Yilmaz, Sait, and Osman Akagündüz. 2011. *Kürtler Neden Devlet Kuramaz?* İstanbul: Milenyum Yayınları.

Yinger, Milton J. 1985. 'Ethnicity'. *Annual Review of Sociology* 11: 151–80.

Yin, Robert K. 2002. *Case Study Research : Design and Methods*. Second. Thousand Oaks, CA, London and New Delhi: Applied Social Reserach Method Series 5, Sage Publications.

Yin, Robert K. 2011. *Qualitative Research from Start to Finish*. London and New York: The Guildford Press.

Yirmi Birinci Yuzyilda Özgürlük ve Sosyalizm Manifestosu. 2008. İstanbul: Gün Yayıncılık.

Yörük, Zafer F. 1995. 'Türk Kimliği'. In *Irkçılık ve Milliyetçilik*, edited by Collec, 60–79. İstanbul: Belge Yayınları.

Zelkina, Anna. 2000. *Sufi Response to the Russian Advance in the North Caucasus in Quest for God and Freedom*. London: C. Hurst and Co.

Ziadeh, Rodwan. 2009. *The Kurds in Syria Fueling Separatist Movements in the Region?* Special Report 220. United States institute of peace.

Zınar, Muhyiddin. 2011. 'Said-I Nursi ve Kürt Meselesi'. In *Vefatının 50. Yılında Uluslararası Bediüzaman Said Nursi Sempozyumu*, 133–69. İstanbul: Nûbihar.

Zubaida, Sami. 2006. 'Religion and Ethnicty as a Politicized Boundaries'. In *The Kurds: Nationalism and Politics*, edited by Faleh A. Jabar and Hosham Dawod, 93–102. London, San Francisco, CA andBeirut: Saqi.

Zürcher, Erik J. 2004. *Turkey : A Modern History*. 3rd ed. London and New York: I.B.Tauris.

Zürcher, Erik J. 2010. *The Young Turk Legacy and Nation Building: From the Ottoman Empire to Atatürk's Turkey*. London and New York: I.B.Tauris & Co Ltd.

Index

Note: In this index, page references followed by *n* indicate notes.

Aba, Vahit 182
Abdulkhadir, Sayyid 51, 53, 57, 58
Açikbaş, Orhan 164
Adiyaman, Mehmet Emin 89–90
Afrin 85, 210, 223, 224–5
Ağri rebellion 63
Ahl-e Haqq 47–8
Ahmet, 126 128–9
Ak, Aziz Mahmut 166, 167
Akar, Muhammed Dara 137
Akat Ata, Ayla 96
AKP. *See also* Erdogan, Recep Tayyip; Turkish state
    Afrin and KRG 224–5
    Alevis' mistrust of 131–3
    cultural rights 3, 4, 111, 115–19, 121, 122–3, 125, 200
    development of 113–15
    Dolmabahce Declaration 89–90, 193–4
    general elections (2015) 84, 85
    Kurdish support for 83, 205, 219
    refusal of Kurdish national status 88, 92
    repression of Kurds 88, 89, 92, 155, 194, 210, 222–3, 224–5
    Turkish nationalism 90, 114–15
Alabat, Mustafa 134
Alevis 46–7, 48, 121–2
    cultural rights 120–1, 130–6, 202–3, 219
    democratic autonomy 96–7, 101, 102, 194, 215–16, 219
    federalism 164
    Koçgiri and Dersim revolts 64–5
    Marxist-Leninist organizations 178
    mistrust of Sunnis 212, 244 n.58
        cultural rights only model 131–6, 202–3, 219
        democratic autonomy 98–100, 102, 194, 216, 244 n.58
    religion 129–30, 202–3
    Sheikh Said rebellion 61, 202–3

Ali 189
Altaç, Aydin 126
Amasya Protocol 58
Anderson, Benedict 52
ANLI, Firat 88–9, 239 n.24
Arcan, Semra 161
armed struggle
    DTP 83
    nation state advocates' views on 180–1, 249 n.17
    PKK 72, 73–4, 77, 78, 83, 84–5, 118 (*see also* People's Revolutionary War)
Armenians, Kurds and 58
Aslan, Burkay 157, 166–7
Aslan, Ruşen 181, 185
assimilation 60, 86–7, 179, 218, 237 n.4
    Alevis and Zazas 97–8, 102
    asymmetric federalism 15, 17
    Atatürk, Mustafa Kemal 58, 59
    cultural rights only model and 127, 189–90, 198, 199, 200–1
    democratic autonomy and 90–1, 97–8, 102, 106–7, 222
    federalism and 13, 161, 203–4, 220
    Kurdish feudal class 73
    nation state model and 181, 183, 192, 196, 209
    political parties' opposition to 66, 69
    post-Ottoman period 38
    tribalism protection against 50
    use of religion 152–8, 205, 206, 220
autonomous regions: Alevis and Zazas 97, 100–2
autonomy 10–13, 57, 58. *See also* self-determination, national; self-governance
    democratic (*see* democratic autonomy)
    identity 12
    Koçgiri rebellion 64

Ayna, Emine 87–8, 93–4, 95–6, 100–1, 103, 106
Ayyildirim, Azad 157, 158, 170
Azadî initiative 3, 4, 60–1, 175–6, 236 n.2

Baggasi, Isa 143
Baran 108
BDP 83–4, 88, 89, 91, 239 n.22
   Alevis' mistrust of 132, 133, 136–7
   Alevi supporters 97–100
   democratic autonomy 3, 4, 19, 25, 83–4, 214, 215
Bedirkhan family 51, 53, 57–8
Beş Parçacılar 69
Beşikçi, İsmail 177, 184, 210
Bey, Memduh Selim 53
Bozkurt, Kemal Deniz 124, 127, 136
Brochmann, Grete 193
Buchanan, Allen 209–10
Burkay, Kemal 149, 160, 161–2, 171
Burulday, Irfan 180–1

Çakan, Eşref 166
Caliphs, dismissal of 60
capitalist modernity 20, 21–3, 24, 25, 26, 27
   Kurdish 103
Catalans 210
Çelik, Hidir 97
Cemilpashazade family 51, 57–8
Cevdet, Abdullah 51, 53, 54
Çevik, Süleyman 160
Ceyhan, Ciwanroj 159, 173
CHP 66, 111, 112, 119, 242 nn.4–5
   cultural rights 3, 4, 121, 200, 203, 219
Çiçek, Rauf 156
Çiftyürek, Sinan 151, 167
citizenship, participant 19, 20, 24, 31, 193, 215
Cizre 238 n.11
Clark, Gordon L. 12
Clark, William Roberts 14–15, 16–17, 17–18
Coakley, John 211
collective rights 35
collectivism 23, 54, 91–2
communalism 21, 22, 23–4, 27, 29
confederations, tribal 49–50
congruent federalism 15, 16
conservatives: religion 111–13
constitution, Turkish (1961) 67

constitutional recognition, demands for 191–2
Coşkun, Vahap 238 n.12
coup, military (1960) 66–7, 112, 237 n.4
coup, military (1980) 69, 112, 237 n.4
coup d'état, attempted (2016) 114–15, 119
cultural rights 1, 3, 4, 10, 67, 68
   democratic autonomy 32
   individual 91, 92, 121, 172, 189, 200, 201, 235 n.3
cultural rights only model 34–6, 111–37, 197–203, 217–20
   rejection of 172–3, 189–90, 200–1, 214, 222, 224

Dabakoğlu, Cudi 158, 163, 167, 172
DAVA (magazine) 141, 168, 172
DBP 84–5, 89, 91
   democratic autonomy 3, 4, 19–20, 25, 84, 214, 215
   democratic confederalism 84
DDKO 68–9
DEHAP 82–3
democracy: AKP 114, 115–16
democratic autonomy 1–2, 3, 4, 9–10, 19–36, 191–7, 213–17. *See also specific groups, organizations, issues*
   demand for 71–109
   rejection of 136–7, 158, 170–2, 187–9, 219, 222, 224
democratic confederalism 20, 21, 23, 24–6, 29, 31, 75–6, 84, 95, 106, 194, 215
democratic modernity 20, 21–7, 75–6
democratic nation, concept of 28, 195, 214, 221–2
'Democratic Opening Process' 115, 116–17
democratic republic, concept of 27–8, 30, 31
democratic rights 78–9
demographic density: nation state solution 183–5, 188, 209, 210–11, 223
demographic dispersion of Kurds in Turkey
   cultural rights only model 127, 198–201, 218
   democratic autonomy model 93–6, 193, 215, 221
   federalism 206–7, 221
   nation state model 188–9, 211
DEP 80
Dersim (person) 182
Dersim (region) 65, 100, 202–3

DHF 175, 177–8
diplomacy: democratic autonomy 33
discriminatory redistribution 209
Dolmabahce Declaration 89, 118, 193–4, 239 n.27
Dorşin 105–6
DP 66, 111
DTK 25, 31
DTP 82–4

Eastern Meetings (*Doğu Mitingleri*) 54, 68
Eastern Reformation Plan 62
eco-industrialism 23, 26–7
ecology: democratic autonomy 33
economic resources, control of: federalism 165–8, 208, 221
economic system: democratic autonomy 33
education: Kurdish language 123–4
Ekrad 39–40
Elçi, Şerafettin 150
EMEP: democratic autonomy 3, 4
Eminoglu, Nevzat 169
Enes 155, 169
equality, demand for
  cultural rights only model 123, 124, 173
  federalism 160–2, 163, 173, 204, 206–7, 223–4
Erdogan, Recep Tayyip 85, 87–8, 89, 90, 118
  AKP 113, 114, 115
  Dolmabahce Declaration 118, 239 n.27
Eren, Mehmet Emin 168
Erol, Arif 86, 109
ethnic identity, Kurdish. *See* identity, Kurdish
ethnic tensions, resolution of: federalism 162–5, 206–8
ethnic territorial national status: federalism 158–60, 214–15
ethnicity: AKP 128
ethnicity *vs.* religion 125–6, 128, 129–36, 154, 201–3, 205–6, 218–19
ethno-national identity. *See* identity, Kurdish
ethno-symbolism: concept of nation 52–3

federalism 2, 9–10, 13–19
  administrative 15
  Belgium 16, 207–8
  Canada 16–17, 207
  ethnic 1, 3, 4, 9, 15–16, 75, 139–73, 185–6

Germany 1–2, 31
India 18, 207–8
Spain 19–20, 207–8
Switzerland 16
United Kingdom 18, 207–8
United States 16, 17
  analysis of model 203–8, 214–15, 220–2, 223–4
  DDKO 68–9
  proximity to nation state model 234 n.2
  rejection of 93–6, 100–1, 107, 186, 217, 241 n.80
  TKSP 69
  in practice 17–19
  in structure 14–17
Fidan, Hakan 116, 117
Firat, Adnan 179–80, 181–2, 190, 249 n.17
Firat, Seydi 90, 103, 106, 108
FP 112, 113

Galnoor, Itzhak 211
Gellner, Ernest 52
gender equality 29
general elections (2015) 84, 88, 119, 176
Geveri, Adem 176
Ghanem, As'ad 210–11
globalization, nation state and 108, 196
Gök, Aydan 154, 156–7
Gökhalp, Ziya 43
Golder, Mark 14–15, 16–17, 17–18
Golder, Sona Nadenichek 14–15, 16–17, 17–18
Güçlü, İbrahim 161, 163, 164, 166, 167, 170
Güçlü, Mirza 124–5, 130
Gül, Abdullah 113
Gülen, Fethullah 114–15, 117, 118–19
Gülün, Kudret 86, 107
Güneş Dil Teorisi 1, 60, 236 n.2
Gurani 42
Gürbüz, Adile 129–30

HADEP 81–2
Hak-Par 149–50
Halis 152
Halit, Cibranli 61
Hamidiye corps 61
Hasan 136–7
HDP 84–5, 88, 89, 91, 238 n.11, 245–246 nn.10–11

Alevi supporters 97–100
Azadî initiative and 176
democratic autonomy 3, 4, 19, 25, 171, 214, 215
general election (June 2015) 118
Oslo Talks 118
repression of 119
Helin 186
HEP 79–80
Hezbollah 142–8, 212, 245 nn.8–10, 246 n.11
history: Kurds and Kurdistan 39–42
'hogties' 146, 147
Houston, Christopher 154
Hroch, Miroslav 53, 54, 55
Hüda-Par 142–3, 148–9, 169, 172, 234 n.3, 245 n.10
human rights, cultural rights and 123–4

IBV 175, 177
identity, Kurdish 37–55
    cultural rights only advocates 218–20
    DDKO 68–9
    democratic autonomy and 85–92, 191–4, 213–17
    DEP 80, 81
    federalism 152–8, 159–60, 172, 197–208, 220–2
    HADEP 81, 82
    Hak-Par 149, 172
    HEP 79, 81
    Hezbollah 145, 148, 172
    nation state advocates 187, 189–90
    Turkish state denial of 38–9, 59–60, 180, 199, 209–10, 213, 221, 222
    Turkish state pressure on 76, 77, 80, 81, 224–5
    Zehra 142, 156, 172, 205
Ilim bookstore 143, 245 n.9
immunity, power of: autonomy 12
incongruent federalism 15, 16
independence 2, 3, 57–8, 162, 210–11, 212, 223–4, 234 n.2. *See also* nation state; Sheikh Said rebellion
    Azadî initiative 61, 175–6
    DDKO 68–9
    DHF 177–8
    IBV 177
    Kizilbayrak/TKİP 178
    KKH 177

KRG 168, 223, 225
PAK 176–7
PKK 75
T-KDP 68
TKSP 69
Xoybun 63
initiation, power of: autonomy 12
instumentalism: ethnicity 37
integration: Kurds in Turkey 124–5, 126–9, 198–9, 200, 201, 218, 222
İpek, Halim 159–60, 161, 163–4
Irak 182
Iraq
    ISIS attacks on Kurds 182, 186, 190, 223
    Kurdish economic development 167
    Kurdish independence referendum 168–9
    Turkish state intervention 210
Isik, Fehim 239 n.27
ISIS attacks on Kurds 182, 183, 186, 188, 190, 209, 223
Islam
    Kurdish 44–8
    Sunni Islam 44–5, 46, 47, 48
    Sunnis
        Alevis' mistrust of (*see* Alevis: mistrust of Sunnis)
        cultural rights 113, 129–30, 201, 202, 218–19
Islamists, Kurdish: federalism 152–8, 169–70
Ismail 159
Izady, Mehrdad R. 40, 42, 51

JITEM 76, 146
Jiyan 92

Kadep 150, 172
Kahraman, Vasif 167
Kalkan, Duran 106–7
Kanilga, Rahime 87
Karasu, Mustafa 101, 105
Karataş, Aydın 125, 133
Kardaş, Mehmet Emin 150, 172, 188
Kaypakkaya, İbrahim 177–8
KCK: democratic autonomy 3, 4, 19, 25
Kelman, Herber C. 209
Kemalism 67, 88, 153, 164, 242 n.5
KİP 69
Kızılbayrak/TKİP 175, 178

KKH (Kurdistan Communist Movement) 175, 177, 187
Kobani 182, 245–246 n.10
Koçgiri rebellion 54, 64–5, 202–3
KONDA 162–3
Konur, Kadir 238 n.11
Koyî, Hacî Qadrî 43
Koyuncu, Mahmut 179, 186, 187, 188, 189–90
KRG 168–9, 182, 223, 224–5
KTC 57–8
KUK 69, 72
Kurban, Mustafa 123–4, 127, 131–2, 135
Kurbanoğlu, Selim 91, 95, 104
Kurdish identity. *See* identity, Kurdish
Kurdish language 32, 41, 42–3, 49, 126, 200–1. *See also* Kurmanji; Zazaki
    AKP 88, 115–16, 117, 123
    cultural rights only model 123, 124
    democratic autonomy 96, 189, 195
    education 32, 123–4, 180, 181
    federalism 160
    HADEP 82
    Hüda-Par 148
    nation state model 181
    Nûbihar 245 n.6
    prohibition 62
    Sheikh Said rebellion 61
    SHP 120–1
    TKDP 67–8
Kurdishness. *See* identity, Kurdish
Kurdistan (term) 38, 40–1, 140, 151, 156, 158, 159, 190
Kuriş, Konca 147
Kurmanji 42, 46, 47, 175–6
Kurmanji-speaking Kurds: Sheikh Said rebellion 61
Kurt, Abdulrahman 130
Kuru 111–12
Kymlicka, Will 36

language. *See also* Kurdish language; Kurmanji; Sun Language Theory; Turkish language; Zazaki
    establishment of common 192
    federalism 16
Lausanne, Treaty of (1923) 58, 59, 80, 121
leftist movements. *See* socialist movements

Lenin, Vladimir 209
Levey, Geoffrey 35–6
Lijphart, Arend 15

Marxism-Leninism 209
    DHF 177–8
    PKK 72, 73, 74–5, 145–6
    TKİP 178
Med-Zehra: federalism 3, 4, 139–42, 205
Mem û Zîn (Xanî) 41, 43
Menzil bookstore 143, 245 n.9
MHP 90, 224
Middle East: oppression of Kurds 179, 182, 186
migration, internal. *See* demographic dispersion of Kurds in Turkey
military memorandum (1971) 69
Miller, David 209, 210, 211, 212
millet system: RP 113
minorities, Kurdish internal 96–103, 194, 210, 215–16, 222
modernism: concept of nation 52
modernity. *See* capitalist modernity; democratic modernity
moral and political society 21–2, 23–4, 26, 29
Murat 154, 169
Mustazaf-Der Movement 148

Nabikoğlu, Adnan 123, 127, 129
Naqshbandi tariqa 45, 61
nation, democratic, concept of 28, 195, 214, 221–2
nationalism, Kurdish
    Azadî initiative 60–1, 175–6
    DDKO 68–9
    demand for nation state 175–90, 214–15
    democratic autonomy and 85–92, 191, 213–14
    federalism 139–73
    IBV 177
    KKH 177
    Nurcus 245 n.3
    PAK 175, 176–7
    PKK 72–3, 74–5, 77, 213–14
    TİP 67
    TKDP 67–8
    Xoybun 62–3

nationalism, Turkish 87–8, 90, 239 n.18
   AKP and 114, 115–16, 118–19, 224, 225
   CHP 119
   Nurcus 140–1
   religion and 204–5
   RP and 113
nation state 1, 3, 4, 9, 27–8, 175–90, 195–7. *See also* territorial models
   analysis of model 208–12, 214–15, 222–4
   capitalism and the 22–3, 24
   emergence of the 235 n.2
   proximity of model to federalism 234 n.2
   rejection of model 93, 100–1, 103–9, 168–70, 196–7, 216–17, 221
national boundaries, decline in 107–9, 196–7
national identity, Kurdish, formation of 51–5
national status, ethnic territorial: federalism 158–60
National Turkish Students Association 143–4
nationalists on Kurdish ethnicity 39
Nikitin, Bazil 40
Nûbihar (magazine) 142, 156, 245 n.6
Nurcus 139–42, 245 nn.3–4
Nursi, Said-i 53, 139–40, 141, 144, 157, 169, 244 n.1, 245 nn.2–3

Obligatory Settlement Law 65, 236 n.3
Öcalan, Abdullah
   Alevis' mistrust of 134, 136
   democratic autonomy 19, 20, 21–4, 25–30, 31, 214
   Dolmabahce Declaration 89
   ethnic federalism, views on 241 n.80
   Oslo Talks 116, 117–18
   PKK 72, 74–5
   the state, views on 22–3, 24, 25, 27–8, 30, 75–6, 103–4, 108, 216
Önen, Fuat 183, 188
organizations, social: democratic autonomy 32
Oslo Talks (2009) 116–18
ÖSP 151, 172
Ottoman Empire
   Kurds and Kurdistan 41, 44, 49, 50–1, 53, 57–8, 162
   Sunnis and Alevis 98
   Turkification 60
Özçelik, Candaş 122–3
Özçelik, Mustafa 176, 182, 187–8
Özdemir, Necat 169
Özdemir, Suat 124
Özgürlük Yolu 69

PAK 175, 176–7
participant citizenship 19, 20, 24, 31, 193, 215
Paşa, İhsan Nuri 63
peace process 89–90, 244 n.51
Pehlewani 42
Peköz 172
People's Revolutionary War 117
personal law: autonomy 11
Péşeng 69
PKK 68, 70
   Alevis' mistrust of 134, 136, 137
   cooperation with PYD/Peshmerga 182
   creation of political parties and 78
   democratic autonomy 3, 4, 19, 71–7, 91, 213–14, 215, 217
   DEP and 80, 81
   DTP and 83
   ethnic awareness 51, 54
   HADEP and 82
   Hak-Par and 149
   HDP and 85
   HEP and 79, 80–1
   Hezbollah and 145–7, 148
   Kurds distancing from 217
   Oslo Talks 116–18
   peace process 89–90
pluralism
   AKP 115
   democratic autonomy 20, 26, 30, 83, 193–4, 214
   Dolmabahce Agreement 89, 118
   DTP 83
   ethnic federalism 16
   HDP 84
political models 1–4, 9–36. *See also specific political models*
political parties, Kurdish, creation of 78–85
politicization, Kurdish 68, 73, 199–200, 220
   identity 53–4, 70, 76–7, 80, 213–14

participatory democracy 23, 24
religion 114, 119
power sharing: autonomy 11, 13, 14, 207
Pratchett, Lawrence 12–13
primordialism 37, 39, 41–2, 49, 50, 51–2
PYD 71, 117, 118, 182, 250 n.43

Qadiriyya tariqa 45

rebellions, Sheikh-led 45–6. *See also* Said, Sheikh, Sheikh Said rebellion
Recep 153, 155–6
regions, autonomous 1–2, 31, 34
religion
   AKP 113–14, 116, 129–30, 205
   Alevis 130–6
   assimilation through, reaction against 152–8, 220
   CHP 130–6
   cultural rights only advocates 113, 129–30, 201, 202, 218–19
   DP 111–12
   DTP 83
   ethnicity *vs.* 125–6, 128, 129–36, 154, 201–3, 205–6, 218–19
   federalism 152–8, 158–9, 204–5, 220, 221
   HADEP 83
   influence of 111–13
   Kurds and 40, 44–8, 54–5
   PKK 74
   restrictions on 60–2
   Sunnis 129–30
research method 4–6
Resulalan, Osman 168, 172
Riza, Sayyid 65
Rizgari 69
Rojava 71, 117, 120, 188, 250 n.43
   Afrin 85, 210, 223, 224–5
RP 112–13, 114, 205

safety. *See* security
Şahan 142, 153
Şahin, Edibe 99, 102
Said, Sheikh 60–1
   Sheik Said rebellion 54, 60–2, 175, 202–3
Sako 90, 93
Salafism 144
Sari, Muslim 131, 132, 133–4
Sarigöl, Zeki 205

secessionism 77, 129, 207
secularism
   AKP 113–14, 116
   Alevis and CHP 119–20, 132, 242 n.5
   DP and 111, 112
   HDP 84
   Hesbollah and 143
   RP and 113, 114
   Turkish state 111–12, 139, 143, 152
security
   cultural rights only advocates 135
   democratic confederalism 26
   ditch digging 84–5, 172, 227, 238 nn.11–12
   nation state advocates 179–83, 186, 187–8, 190, 208–9, 223–4
self-defence: democratic autonomy 32
self-determination, national 68, 75, 223, 249 n.17
   democratic autonomy 30, 93
   federalism 151, 168
   nation state 1, 3, 175, 176, 177, 178, 183–4, 185, 187, 189, 190, 209–11, 212, 223
self-governance 10–11, 53, 113
   democratic autonomy 21, 31, 33, 34, 88, 91–3, 136, 171
   federalism 156, 157–8, 159, 163
   nation state model 176, 187
   Spain 17
Seljuk period 40
Serhat 238 n.11
SETA & POLLMARK 129
Sevinç, Arif 90
Shafi school of jurisprudence 44
Sharafname (Sharafkhan) 41
SHP 79, 120–1
socialist movements 67, 68–9, 209
   DEP 80
   DHF 175
   Hak-Par 149–50
   HDP 84
   HEP 79–80
   IBV 177
   Kızılbayrak/TKİP 175, 178
   ÖSP 151
   PKK 72–6, 214
Solgun, Cafer 99
Sorani 42
Sözen, Ziya 136

state. *See also* nation state
　definitions of 234 n.1/1, 235 n.2
　Kurds' distrust 85–91, 93, 185–6, 188, 189, 190, 219
　Öcalan's views 22–3, 24, 25, 27–8, 30, 75–6, 103–4, 108
statelessness
　democratic autonomy 107
　federalism 13–14, 16, 203, 222
　nation state model 179–80, 180–1, 182, 184, 185, 190, 209
Steen, Eveline Van Der 48
Steiner, Henri J. 11
Storey, David 211
Sukutu, Ishak 53
Sun Language Theory 1, 60, 236 n.2/2
supranational governance, nation state and 196
symmetric federalism 15, 17
Syria
　ISIS attacks on Kurds 182, 190, 223, 225
　Kurdish exiles 62–3
　Rojava (*see Rojava*)
　uprising 117–18

Tahir 152–3, 154–5, 158
Tan, Altan 88, 92, 94
Tan, Sami 102, 105, 107–8
tariqas 45, 112, 205
Tasali, Hamdullah 171
Taskin, Riza 122
TDRA 204
Tek, Mesut 158, 159, 170
Teker, Zubeyde 100
Tekoşin 69
Telo, Broyé Heski 63
territorial autonomy 11, 14, 33–4, 193, 205
territorial consciousness 41–2, 49, 211, 223
territorial models. *See also* federalism; nation state
　rejection of
　　cultural rights only model advocates 124, 125–37, 199–200, 201, 203, 218–19
　　democratic autonomy advocates 93–6, 100–1, 105, 108–9, 193, 196–7, 216–17
territorial rights 54
territory and nation: relationship 195, 211

TİP 67, 68
TKDP 67–8, 150, 237 n.4
T-KDP 68, 150–1, 172
TKSP 69
Treaty of Lausanne (1923) 58, 59
tribalism, Kurdish 40, 48–50, 54–5
Turan, İlter 204
Turgut, Vedat 143, 161
Turkey
　capitalist modernism 27
　as democratic republic 27–8
Turkification 59–60, 62, 229
Turkish History Thesis 38, 39, 60, 235–236 n.1
Turkish Islamic Synthesis 220
Turkish language: use by Kurds 126
Turkish state. *See also* AKP
　denial of Kurdish ethnicity 38–9, 59–60, 180, 199, 209–10, 213, 221, 222
　repression of Kurds 59–60, 62, 63, 65, 66, 67, 90, 222
　　nation state solution 179–82, 209–10
　　PKK and 70, 72, 76–7, 116, 119, 146, 147, 210, 213–14
　　political parties 78–9, 80–1, 82
Turkish–Kurdish relations, cultural rights and 122–5, 218
Turkism, Kurds and 53–4, 59–60, 140

UDG 69
underdevelopment: Kurdish region 165–8
UNESCO: cultural rights 35

Vahab 183
Vatan Party 224
Velioglu, Hüseyin 143–4, 147, 245 nn.8–9
village guards (*Köy Korcuları*) 74, 212

Wall, Steven 35
War of Independence 57–8, 59, 64
Weber, Max 234–235 n.1/1
West, the: impact on creation of Kurdish political parties 78
women: democratic autonomy 32, 33

Xanî, Ehmedê 41, 43, 50, 181
Xoybun 62–3

Yado, Kani 183, 184, 188–9
Yalçın, Lokman 90
Yazidi 47
YDG-H 137, 172, 238 n.11
Yekitiya Komelén Kurdistan 150
Yildirim, Izzettin 142, 147, 152, 245 n.4
Yildiz, Hasan 86, 94–5, 98–9, 101
YPG 71, 85, 117, 118, 210, 224, 225, 245–246 n.10
Yurtseven, Halis 101

Zazaki 42, 43, 46, 97–8, 175–6, 194

Zazas 128, 212
   democratic autonomy 96–8, 99, 100, 101, 102, 215–16
   federalism 164
   Sheikh Said rebellion 61
Zehra 147, 152, 156
   federalism 3, 4, 139–42, 205
Zehra Education & Cultural Foundation 142
Zelal 180
Zeynep 132–3
Zuhal 98, 99, 104–5

www.ingramcontent.com/pod-product-compliance
Lightning Source LLC
Chambersburg PA
CBHW070016010526
44117CB00011B/1597